CORPORATE GOVERNANCE IN CENTRAL EUROPE AND RUSSIA

VOLUME 1

Banks, Funds, and Foreign Investors

CORPORATE GOVERNANCE IN CENTRAL EUROPE AND RUSSIA

VOLUME 1

Banks, Funds, and Foreign Investors

Edited by
ROMAN FRYDMAN
CHERYL W. GRAY
ANDRZEJ RAPACZYNSKI

CEU
CENTRAL EUROPEAN UNIVERSITY PRESS
Budapest London New York

First published in 1996 by
Central European University Press
1051 Budapest,
Nádor utca 9,
Hungary

Distributed by
Oxford University Press, Walton Street, Oxford OX2 6DP
Oxford New York Athens Auckland Bangkok Bombay Toronto
Calcutta Cape Town Dar es Salaam Delhi Florence Hong Kong
Istanbul Karachi Kuala Lumpur Madras Madrid Melbourne
Mexico City Nairobi Paris Singapore Taipei Tokyo Toronto
and associated companies in Berlin Ibadan
Distributed in the United States
by Oxford University Press Inc., New York

British Library Cataloguing in Publication Data
A CIP catalogue record for this book is available from the British Library

ISBN: 978-1-85866-035-6

Library of Congress Cataloging in Publication Data
A CIP catalog record for this book is available from the Library of Congress

CONTENTS for Volumes 1 and 2

Volume 2: Insiders and the State

ACKNOWLEDGMENTS

We are grateful to the World Bank and the Central European University Foundation for their support of our joint research project on Corporate Governance in Central Europe and Russia. The project culminated in the Conference on Corporate Governance in Central Europe and Russia, on December 15-16, 1994, in Washington, D.C. The chapters in these volumes are updated, revised, and edited versions of papers originally presented at the conference.

The editors

CONTRIBUTORS to Volumes 1 and 2

Roman Frydman, Professor of Economics, Department of Economics, New York University, and Co-Director, Central European University Privatization Project.

Cheryl W. Gray, Principal Economist, Policy Research Department, World Bank.

Andrzej Rapaczynski, Professor of Law, Columbia University School of Law, and Co-Director, Central European University Privatization Project.

Herbert L. Baer, formerly Financial Economist, Policy Research Department, World Bank. Tragically, Herb Baer died on February 27, 1995, from injuries sustained in a bicycle accident.

Bernard Black, Professor of Law, Columbia University School of Law.

Joseph Blasi, Professor, School of Management and Labor Relations, Rutgers University, and Fellow, Institute for Advanced Study, Princeton.

John C. Coffee, Jr., Adolf A. Berle Professor of Law, Columbia University School of Law.

Peter Dittus, Special Assistant to the General Manager, Bank for International Settlements (BIS).

John S. Earle, Associate Professor of Economics, Central European University; Center for International Security and Arms Control (CISAC), Stanford University; and Deputy Director, Central European University Privatization Project.

Saul Estrin, Professor of Economics, London Business School.

Jonathan Hay, Director, Harvard Institute for International Development Legal Reform Project, Moscow.

Bruce Kogut, Professor of Management, Wharton School, and Director, Emerging Economies Program, University of Pennsylvania.

Reinier Kraakman, Professor of Law, Harvard Law School.

Roland Michelitsch, Regional Economist, Sub-Saharan Africa Department, International Finance Corporation.

Katharina Pistor, Research Associate, Harvard Institute for International Development; formerly, Senior Research Fellow, Central European University Privatization Project.

Jane E. Prokop, graduate student, Harvard University, and Research Associate, Central European University Privatization Project.

Stephen Prowse, Senior Economist and Policy Advisor, Federal Reserve Bank of Dallas.

Charles F. Sabel, Professor of Law and Social Science, Columbia University School of Law.

Andrei Shleifer, Professor of Economics, Department of Economics, Harvard University.

David Stark, Associate Professor of Sociology and International Business, Department of Sociology, and Johnson Graduate School of Management, Cornell University.

Joel Turkewitz, Deputy Director, Central European University Privatization Project and Assistant Professor of Law and Economics, Central European University.

Dmitry Vasiliev, Deputy Chairman, Russian Federal Securities Exchange Commission.

Dimitri Vittas, Advisor, Pensions and Insurance, Financial Sector Development Department, World Bank.

1

OVERVIEW of Volumes 1 and 2

ROMAN FRYDMAN, CHERYL W. GRAY, and
ANDRZEJ RAPACZYNSKI

Ownership reform was one of the earliest axioms of postcommunist transition. The fall of communism came at a time when belief in markets and private property was at its highest point since World War II. It is not surprising, therefore, that it was acknowledged by both Western observers and liberal East European reformers that the state was not capable of running most productive enterprises and should not attempt to do so in the future. The severing of the ownership link between the state and the firms quickly became one of the main planks of the reform program.

But the meaning of the much championed "privatization" was far from clear beyond its role in ending the politicization of economic governance. At the beginning, many reformers – most notably the Czechs, who also happened to be the most decisive, and later the Russians – consciously focused on this aspect of the process, disclaiming most efforts at further engineering the postprivatization ownership structure. Once the state was removed and the free market forces were allowed to operate, they believed, secondary markets could be trusted to lead to acceptable new arrangements.

It is safe to say that this optimistic view seriously underestimated the complexity of the problems presented by the postulate of privatization. To begin with, the very mechanics of state divestment turned out to be much more complicated than expected. Many countries, especially those that acted early like Poland and Hungary and so could not benefit from the experience of other economies in transition, attempted elaborate sales programs modeled on Western privatizations. They spent extensive time and resources selling a small portion of their state assets. Political resistance to privatization also turned out to be very strong and much more effective than many reformers had imagined. Privatization was inherently threatening to incumbent nomenklatura managers, who feared for their jobs and privileges. The employees of state enterprises were similarly hostile to the change, as many of them could expect layoffs to be among the first measures of postprivatization restructuring. Together, these insiders formed a formidable political coalition, which either blocked privatization altogether or extracted costly concessions. These took the form of various illegal or semilegal transfers (often referred to as "spontaneous privatization") or of an official system of preferences and giveaways for insiders, without which no privatization program could proceed. As a result, privatization led to a general strengthening of the managerial classes in nearly all the postcommunist countries, both by converting many of their previous inchoate entitlements into outright legal ownership and by reducing external accountability and control.[1]

Moreover, when some kind of privatization is finally accomplished, even the hoped for benefits of depoliticization cannot be said to follow automatically. After all, private firms also turn to the state for all kinds of rents that states the world over are unable to resist. Subsidies, tariff protection, legal monopolies, and redistributive regulation are rampant even where direct state ownership is rare. Indeed, there is no *a priori* reason to believe that private businesses are any less adept at attracting state largess than the notoriously inefficient state enterprises. What is necessary to achieve a measure of separation of the firm and state is a *modification of incentives* of the most important corporate actors – a modification that would make them look to benefits of enhanced economic efficiency for the maximization of profits, rather than to rents they could extract from the state.

Such a modification of incentives, most observers now believe, can only come as a result of a panoply of institutional changes, both economic and political. It is clearly necessary to reform the state and the political system to make those in authority more accountable for their actions and stronger in resisting pressures for inefficient redistribution. Basic legal guarantees of property and contract must be re-established. Product markets must be made competitive, so that firms falling behind are forced to restructure or cease operations. Standards of conduct must be instituted to provide for a measure of transparency into corporate affairs, and they must be enforced by an army of accountants, lawyers, rating agencies, regulators, and the press. Managerial labor markets must be perfected to make corporate executives mindful of how their performance is perceived. Credit and equity markets must be set up to evaluate corporate behavior and enforce financial discipline. And, finally, owners must be firmly established in every firm to ensure that profit maximization is an underlying goal. Where separation between

[1] For further discussion of this and other themes discussed in this overview, see Frydman and Rapaczynski (1994); Gray (1996).

ownership and management is necessary or desirable, these owners must be interested in and capable of monitoring managerial performance and intervening when necessary to eliminate managerial slack, foster entrepreneurial decision-making, and prevent the insiders from diverting corporate resources to their own ends.

While ownership change is certainly not all there is to enterprise restructuring, it is, nevertheless, the (not unquestioned) assumption of the studies in these volumes that it is an important component of microeconomic reform efforts in the postcommunist transition countries. From the point of view of this reform, the central objective of privatization is not merely the elimination of the state's direct nonregulatory authority over enterprises, but also a coupling of new ownership with effective governance mechanisms capable of aligning the objectives of management with those of corporate efficiency. In some cases, especially those of small and medium-size businesses, such an alignment may be most simply achieved through managerial ownership, which is likely to be the dominant form of ownership in any case. But in large companies, where separation of ownership and management is much more likely, not only would extensive managerial ownership imply an enormous (and perhaps politically intolerable) degree of wealth inequality, but also many of these firms badly need a new infusion of capital and expertise available only from outsiders. In these cases finding an appropriate kind of owner and instituting a system of governance in which the new owner can have effective influence over the firm are tasks of great importance. While it is possible that markets can re-engineer postprivatization ownership and governance structures to achieve this result, it is evident (as shown by some of the chapters in this book) that the design of the privatization program itself creates certain institutions and incentives that either enhance or retard the subsequent role of market forces. "Bad" designs may cause the loss of years or even decades of potential restructuring and the economic growth that could accompany it.

This book examines emerging forms of ownership and complementary monitoring institutions in the countries of Eastern Europe and the role they may be expected to play in the development of a new structure of corporate governance. For this purpose we brought together a number of experts on corporate governance in advanced economies with regional specialists. Not only did we believe that more systematic knowledge of ownership and governance issues would enlighten the studies of postcommunist transition, but we were also convinced that East European reform raised enough fundamental issues concerning the very nature of capitalism that an immersion in the subject by Western specialists could provide new theoretical insights of more general significance.

There were two distinct yet related clusters of issues we hoped would be examined in these studies. The first concerns the extent of institutional diversity that is compatible with a well working structure of corporate governance. We started from the idea that there exists in the world a certain portfolio (or perhaps a limited set of distinct portfolios) of institutions associated with successful "market" or "capitalist" economies – or, for that matter, all successful economies, since there are no clear examples of successful economies based on collective or state ownership. To what extent are these familiar institutions likely to be reproduced in Eastern Europe? The editors did not assume that institutions of a different kind would not develop in Eastern Europe or that those belonging to the "standard" portfolio would not take very distinct forms there, as indeed they do in any special environment of a local economic culture. (Banks in France might be quite different from banks in England or Germany, and they are likely to have special features in Eastern European countries.) But institutions belonging to the standard portfolio known from successful capitalist economies do bear some family resemblances across different countries and share some important characteristics. Moreover, given the fact that the standard portfolio has evolved historically in a large number of countries, there may be reasons to believe that entirely new institutions are less likely to be successful than mutations of the standard ones. This may be the main thrust of many East Europeans' decisive rejection of a search for some "third way" between socialism and capitalism.

The second cluster of issues concerns the problems of cross-cultural transplantation of economic institutions. Economic development is likely to be "path dependent," and thus the starting point of East European transition is apt to determine to some extent (how much being one of the questions to be examined here) the future viability of different institutions that may be taken as models for the region's development. Unfortunately, even if our first hypothesis – that successful economies are associated with a relatively limited portfolio of institutions – is true, the existing historical configuration of economic and political forces in Eastern Europe, together with a peculiar capital stock resulting from decades of resource misallocation, may make the development of such institutions particularly difficult or unlikely.

In any case the path dependence of economic development implies that successful corporate governance structures of Western Europe, North America, or East Asia cannot be mechanically transplanted to Eastern Europe. There are, moreover, two senses in which this is true. The obvious, oft-repeated sense is that cross-cultural transplantations are always risky and that one has to attend to the special historical, cultural, and institutional environments of the host countries. But there is also a less obvious (and more specific) sense of the proposition that cross-cultural borrowings in Eastern Europe must be scrutinized with care. The governance institutions of the region are facing *a very different task* than those in more advanced economies. Corporate governance institutions in the advanced economies function in an environment is which most changes are *marginal in nature* (i.e. involving gradual, incremental modifications), while Eastern European institutions, precisely because they function in an environment of *transition,* face a situation in which most reforms must be *global.*

The role of the new owners in this environment is different at the level of both individual firms and the whole portfolio. On the level of individual firms, the task is usually not simply making sure that the value of the firm is maximized within a given technological and organizational framework (so that production reaches an optimal level, costs are minimized, returns on investment are higher than other opportunities, etc.). Instead, the firm must often go through a rather complete reorientation of its activities. It might need to be drastically scaled down or liquidated. The organizational structure might have to be revamped and component parts spun off. Product lines might have to be completely changed. Labor relations and the supporting social structure might have to be transformed. Whole new departments (marketing, etc.) might have to be created. Accounting procedures might have to be modernized. On the level of the whole portfolio of an owner, the fact that nearly *all* the firms in its portfolio require drastic changes is also unusual in the Western environment. Thus, instead of being mostly a passive monitor of a large part of its portfolio, a new East European owner is likely to have to be active across the board, stretching to the maximum its scarce human capital.

Moreover, because the change is global also on the scale of the whole economy, the new corporate monitors in Eastern Europe must function in an external environment characterized by much greater unpredictability and much weaker external economic, legal, and cultural constraints on managers than those that buttress and thus lighten the monitors' governance task in the West.[2] Because relatively few aspects of their activities may be routinized

[2] Existing institutions inherited from the dysfunctional order of the old regime have a life of their own and exercise an important "pull" on most piecemeal measures. Until a sufficient critical mass of changes is introduced, so that a viable nucleus of a normally functioning economic system is established, attempts to make incremental changes may have unpredictable effects or even stunt rather than facilitate growth. For example, new bankruptcy procedures may give incentives to managers to bring down their state-owned firms, so that they (or their associates) may later purchase their assets outside normal privatization channels (Gray, Schlorke, and Szanyi 1995).

and many more must be entrepreneurial in nature, many institutional owners in particular might find these requirements very difficult to accommodate. Finally, the new institutions must also operate in a peculiar political environment. The role of the state in Eastern Europe is, and will probably continue to be in the near future, pervasive, and the bigger the monitor the more likely it is to have to deal with the state. Given the massiveness of the required restructuring and the uncertain chances of many firms to survive at all, it is always tempting for the new owners, as for the old managerial nomenklatura, to orient their activities toward rent seeking rather than economic efficiency. This temptation might pervert the "normal" functioning of many monitoring institutions transplanted from more stable conditions into the environment of transition.

All this suggests that if one wants to examine the prospects of some known forms of governance institutions in the context of Eastern Europe, it is not enough to point to the success or failure of their operation under Western (or East Asian) conditions. Nor is it enough to be aware that foreign institutions may not be easily transplanted into a new environment. What is needed above all is a *careful matching of various institutions with different types of monitoring required under the conditions of postcommunist transition.* The fact that, for example, bank monitoring works in Germany or that corporate cross-ownership leads to an exploitation of many interfirm synergies in Japan does not mean that, *even if they could be successfully transplanted to Eastern Europe,* such a transplantation would be appropriate, given the tasks faced by corporate monitors in the transition environment.

Certain East European institutions may rely on rather routine forms of monitoring well adapted to firms with a pattern of gradual changes, and their actions, even in distress situations, may follow relatively conventional ways of fixing things. But these forms and actions may not work in more unpredictable environments. Other types of monitors may be more "entrepreneurial" and have special skills initiating and monitoring an organizational restructuring process in which various subsidiaries are spun off, assets are stripped, and cash flows are redirected. Some institutions (such as holding companies) may be better at monitoring particular branches of industry, and others may be better at funding and monitoring startup business and more risky projects. Still others (such as foreign trade investors) may be able to provide technological support and access to relevant markets or facilitate financial restructuring. Which types of skills can be most effectively deployed in the East European environment is a vital question for the region's economies.

Finally, intermediary governance institutions (whether banks, funds, or other enterprises) need oversight and monitoring themselves to prevent self-dealing and encourage responsible fiduciary behavior. The thorny question of "who monitors the monitors," so difficult even in advanced economies, is exacerbated by the weakness of general oversight capabilities (whether laws, institutions, information, or norms of conduct) in transition settings. Certain configurations of institutions might be better at promoting the development of responsible fiduciary behavior among intermediaries than others.[3]

Volume 1

The studies in the first volume focus on the creation of new institutions, mostly in the financial sector, which many have expected to become the backbone of the new corporate governance system in Eastern Europe. Some of these financial institutions, such as private pension funds, were entirely unknown to the region before the fall of communism, and some, such as the new privatization investment funds in the Czech Republic or Russia, have special features that make them in many respects unique. Others, mostly banks, did exist in name before the change of regime, but they functioned according to completely different rules and in completely different roles from those of their Western equivalents.

The last few years have witnessed a lively debate among corporate governance experts and policymakers about the relative advantages and disadvantages of the so-called Anglo-American and German or Japanese governance systems.[4] The Anglo-American system is said to rely on liquid capital markets, with their ease of shareholder exit and lively takeover activity, as the most important disciplining factor in controlling managerial incompetence, slack, or outright abuse. The German and Japanese systems, by contrast, are said to rely more on stable relations between firms and their owners, especially large banks, which own significant amounts of equity or monitor corporate performance on behalf of their client shareholders. Whatever the accuracy of these boilerplate descriptions (and they have not gone unquestioned), the debate has created its offshoots among East European specialists, with a number of them arguing that the region should follow the German

[3] For example, limits on the percentage of enterprise shares that can be owned by individual funds may promote cross-monitoring among funds (see Coffee in this volume), and rules giving banks fiduciary responsibilities to other creditors or owners of firms in financial distress may constrain their self-dealing in bankruptcy or workout processes (see Baer and Gray in this volume).

[4] For example, see Edwards and Fischer (1994) and Aoki and Sheard (1994).

model. Among the reasons cited for this option, aside from Germany's geographical proximity, is that the creation of liquid capital markets is a slow process for which the mismanaged enterprises of the region can hardly afford to wait. At the same time, the existing banking system is in need of rapid restructuring; among the most attractive forms of such restructuring, it has been argued, is the familiar debt-for-equity swap, which could make banks into major shareholders of most East European firms. With an upgrading of the banks' ability to monitor corporate performance being also an indispensable element of their own restructuring as lending institutions, bank restructuring could be combined with the creation of a new governance system for the nonfinancial sector. Even if banks could not become good monitors overnight, they may still be the best hope given the institutional vacuum of Eastern Europe.

The studies by Dittus and Prowse and by Baer and Gray look in more detail at the state of East European banking systems and the role they could play in the future corporate governance system in the region. Dittus and Prowse take on directly the viability of German and Japanese examples and argue that the existing banks in Eastern Europe are not likely to be successful in playing the role assigned to them by the proponents of these models, at least not in the short-to-medium run. Their research shows that East European banks not only lack the skills necessary for managing large equity portfolios, but are also not particularly interested in developing such capacity. Their disinclination is not hard to understand: given the quality of their organizational and human capital, building their ability to act as real lenders is a large enough job for the foreseeable future, to say nothing of the dangers that large debt-for-equity swaps could pose to their own solvency. These arguments rest in part on the particular approach taken in Central Europe where (in contrast to Russia) governments decided early on to build the postcommunist banking system largely on the basis of existing state banks. This has required extensive government intervention and major resource transfers to recapitalize existing banks and has limited the entry of new domestic and foreign banks that might have been more capable and more interested in acting like their German or Japanese counterparts.

While Dittus and Prowse examine the role of banks as potential equity holders, Baer and Gray analyze the prospects of their becoming meaningful corporate monitors in their capacity as lenders. They focus on the impact of three factors – the information base, the policy environment for banks (including various recapitalization schemes), and the law and practice of debt collection – on banks' incentives and compare the experiences of Poland and Hungary. They argue that the choice of recapitalization scheme makes a difference and that banks in Poland (where recapitalization was both smaller and accompanied by much stronger directives for market-oriented reforms than in Hungary) do play an increasingly important role in prompting the restructuring of nonperforming borrower enterprises. They note, however, that "creditors in both countries are still quite passive when it comes to initiating and overseeing the *liquidation* of nonperforming borrowers," and that the modest gains achieved so far could be reversed by failure to privatize state banks and discipline poorly performing managers. Inflation, combined with lack of competition, has allowed banks in the region to benefit from high spreads on deposits – when this source of profits disappears, the banks will have much less leeway for mistakes.

While the future role of banks in Eastern Europe depends on the chances of successfully restructuring existing institutions, the problems in the functioning of the so-called privatization investment funds involve the creation of entirely new financial institutions. Indeed, the East European privatization investment fund may so far be the region's most original corporate governance innovation.

The privatization investment funds were established as intermediaries in mass privatization programs in which unprecedented amounts of assets have been transferred (mostly without payment) from the state to the citizens. As part of these programs, individuals received special privatization vouchers, which could be used to purchase shares of privatized enterprises. To avoid excessive fragmentation of ownership (which would have led to a governance vacuum), governments allowed the creation of special intermediaries, which would compete for the vouchers received by the citizens (offering their own shares in exchange) and invest them on the citizens' behalf. It was envisaged that the new intermediaries would function both as mutual funds providing the option of diversification and special investment expertise for their shareholders, and as active shareholders holding significant stakes in the companies in their portfolio, sitting on boards of directors, monitoring corporate performance, and fostering the restructuring process.[5]

Two countries – the former Czechoslovakia and Russia – were in the forefront of mass privatization, and hundreds of new privatization investment funds were created in each country. The study by Coffee analyzes their role in corporate governance in the Czech Republic, while that by Frydman, Pistor, and Rapaczynski examines their performance in Russia. Together, the

[5] For early proposals of mass privatization plans with the use of financial intermediaries, see Blanchard and Layard (1990); Lipton and Sachs (1990); and Frydman and Rapaczynski (1990a). A revised version of the last paper was published in Polish as Frydman and Rapaczynski (1990b).

studies show how similar institutions can differ in their actual functioning in different environments.

The Czech privatization experiment has been by far the boldest of all countries in transition. Coffee describes the speed with which privatization occurred and the market forces it liberated. Although they are still inexperienced and are often said to lack a clear strategy, the new funds sit on boards of directors of most Czech companies, influencing and sometimes firing management and often pushing for serious restructuring. A number of factors, however, including weak regulation and an authorization for (perhaps even reliance on) state banks to become active in establishing new privatization investment funds, led to an extreme concentration of new privatized holdings among a small number of mostly bank-managed funds. To make matters worse, the banks, which were partially privatized in the same wave in which the funds under their control were the prime actors, used the opportunity to create a web of cross-holdings, effectively insulating themselves from outside influence other than that of the state (which remains their largest shareholder). As a result, Coffee demonstrates, many new funds face serious incentive problems, since they are controlled by banks that do not own equity in either the funds or the companies in their portfolios. Thus, they may use their managerial control of the funds to strengthen their lending position with the companies in the funds' portfolios, rather than maximize the value of the funds' equity holdings. To prevent future conflicts of interests, Coffee proposes a mandatory bank divestment of the privatization investment funds and an end to bank cross-holdings and interlocking directorships. He is also not sanguine about the future of the German model of corporate control, as it developed in the Czech Republic, and advocates separation between equity investment and lending activity.

While the future of the privatization investment funds in the Czech Republic is somewhat clouded by their relation to the partially privatized banks, the activities of Russian privatization intermediaries, argue Frydman, Pistor, and Rapaczynski, can be understood only against the background of the thorough domination of Russian companies by their management and (to a lesser extent) employees, which the Russian privatization program made into the primary owners of their enterprises. This move may have been politically necessary to make privatization a reality, but the price is also considerable. Frydman, Pistor, and Rapaczynski, who conducted an extensive empirical study of the Russian privatization investment funds, show that many of these funds may very well be eager to foster the more radical restructuring sorely needed by most Russian firms but are effectively blocked by a solid wall of insider resistance. Moreover, the prospects of lessening the insider domination, at least in the near future, appear less bright than the architects and observers of the Russian program expected, since, as the authors argue, the workers' interest in preserving their employment may make them supportive of the oft-reported management efforts to prevent their employees from selling shares to outsiders.

Since Russian funds are often huge and capital markets are still underdeveloped, many funds may be effectively locked into their holdings. They either remain essentially passive, management-dominated shareholders or try to find some ways of working with the management to exert limited influence. But some funds seem to have responded to the insider domination of Russian companies by trying to preserve their option of "exit" and engaging in surprisingly large amounts of trading. They may create a nucleus of active secondary stock markets and, should the grip of the insiders relax somewhat in the future, move Russia toward a more Anglo-American model of corporate governance.

The emerging private pension funds are the last type of financial institution whose potential role as owner of East European corporations is considered in this volume. The state pension systems everywhere in Eastern Europe are still entirely unfunded, pay-as-you-go schemes, and the level of future benefits (expenditures) and contributions (taxes) threatens to bankrupt the states and stifle the region's economies. Partly in response to this, many proposals have been suggested to combine privatization with a reform of state pension systems. Some of the shares of privatized enterprises would be put in special pension accounts held, or at least managed, by private funds.[6] Very little has been done to realize these proposals so far, although some countries are still reserving some assets for this purpose.

In the meantime, the Czech Republic and Hungary have passed legislation promoting the creation of voluntary private pension funds, and in Poland similar funds have been formed without special legislation. The chapter by Vittas and Michelitsch describes this legislation and examines the prospects of shareholder monitoring by the emerging pension funds. They believe that a number of obstacles must be overcome before private pension funds can play a significant role as active shareholders. They point out that pension plans have become important financial intermediaries in only a handful of OECD countries, in which the state pension systems are rather modest. Given the bloated state of the public pension systems in Eastern Europe, it is unlikely that additional savings will be channeled into private pension plans, even though the Czech and Hungarian governments provide rather generous

[6] A central tenet of all proposals is that these new funds should form the core of a new private pension system, rather than simply funding existing state systems, as has been tried, for example, in Hungary.

subsidies and tax incentives for such purposes. Furthermore, even if such savings were to occur, pension plans are usually restricted in their activism by legislation designed to protect the security of the beneficiaries' investment, as well as by the high cost of shareholder activism. The experience of the more advanced economies suggests, say the authors, that pension funds are more likely to exercise "voice" in corporate affairs if they act through collective bodies monitoring on their behalf.

Although the inflows of foreign capital to Eastern Europe have been relatively modest compared to other developing areas, attracting foreign investment has been an important motivation behind reforms in Eastern Europe. This has been especially true in those countries, like Hungary, which did not choose the route of mass privatization and preferred instead to rely on an extensive sales program to find new owners for their privatized firms. The reformers in those countries often looked to foreign investment as a major source not only of capital, but also of corporate governance expertise. The chapter by Kogut looks at foreign investment from this point of view. He interprets corporate governance rather broadly, going beyond the traditional issues of monitoring and aligning the incentives of managers and owners. Kogut argues that the most important contribution of foreign investment in this area extends beyond the firms in which foreign owners are directly involved by encouraging experimentation in the whole environment with which the foreign-owned firms come into contact, thus resulting in a diffusion of better production and monitoring practices. Since search for better practices is often costly and complex, their import from abroad via foreign direct investment may substantially lower the cost of institutional innovation in transition economies. In particular, Kogut points to the role of foreign direct investment in creating new firms, in increasing competition in product markets, and in providing organizational solutions that serve as templates to be imitated by domestic firms. Thus, a foreign firm may bring new technology and organization to local suppliers, whose products it needs to upgrade for its purposes, or it may facilitate access to new markets for local products with a competitive advantage. The presence of a foreign-owned competitor may also bring new pressure on domestic companies to improve their performance.

But foreign investment is not always an unmixed blessing. Foreign firms may also acquire a domestic company in order to restrict competition for its products in the world markets. Their entry may also destabilize existing networks of interfirm relations, which constitute an important part of many firms' intangible capital, thus eliminating otherwise viable enterprises in a period of transition.

Volume 2

The second volume deals with the less "planned" aspects of postcommunist transition, focusing instead on the more spontaneous development of existing institutions and the "second best" designed solutions. The volume opens with a discussion of employee ownership, which appeared quite attractive to many people brought up on socialist ideology but was firmly opposed by a number of liberal reformers eager to move as quickly as possible to the more standard capitalist forms of corporate property. The authors, Earle and Estrin, argue that a normative evaluation of the possible effects of employee ownership cannot be made in the abstract. Rather, it depends on the characteristics of the firm, the market conditions under which it operates, and the relative weights attached to the various objectives of economic policy. They acknowledge that the attractions of employee ownership may be limited relative to an "idealized form of external ownership" based on a well-functioning legal system and competitive capital markets, but they believe that, in the reality of Eastern Europe, it may be superior to many options under discussion and to the status quo (i.e. continued state ownership). They suggest that moving toward employee ownership may be particularly appropriate when the existing insiders are able to block alternative privatization paths. Such a change can at least lead to a clarification of property rights and a lessening of agency problems endemic to state-owned firms.

As to the type of firms best suited for employee ownership, Earle and Estrin argue that it might be particularly appropriate for loss-making enterprises, because outside owners of declining firms are unlikely to take into account the externalities for workers and their communities of plant closures or massive layoffs. But when the social costs of restructuring are less pressing, even in those cases in which privatization to outsiders is not a viable option, it may be preferable to transfer a large part of an enterprise to managers rather than employees, since managers are more likely to be effective in restructuring.

Managerial ownership is the subject of the next two chapters by Shleifer and Vasiliev and by Blasi and Shleifer. They both use Russia as their case study and attempt to predict the course of further development. In the more theoretical study, Shleifer and Vasiliev examine the pros and cons of managerial ownership and come to the conclusion that managerial shareholding in the range of 5 to 10 percent is optimal from the point of view of incentives, and that higher levels of managerial ownership lead to managerial entrenchment that may be very costly to shareholders. They also argue that managerial entrenchment is likely to be more detrimental to Russian companies than in the West. Unlike their Western counterparts, who had to prove their competence before their ascension to their present positions, Russian managers are mostly survivors from the old regime and were selected with little regard for their ability to lead their firms through the difficult process of transition restructuring. Moreover, Shleifer and Vasiliev point out that the official levels of managerial ownership in Russia, which were intentionally made quite large to secure political support for the privatization process, probably still underestimate the level of managerial entrenchment, since managers very often also control the votes of their employee shareholders. Nevertheless, the authors are rather optimistic about the prospects of a future opening up of Russian enterprises to outside ownership. They cite a number of examples in which outsiders were successful in gaining control of corporate boards or ousting incumbent managers, and they argue that the dire capital needs of most Russian firms are likely to force insiders to cede a portion of their equity in exchange for an infusion of new funds.

Additional evidence for some of these claims is provided by the empirical study of Blasi and Shleifer, which reports on a series of interviews with managers of Russian corporations. They detect a growth in significance of outside blockholders, but although their figures are somewhat more encouraging than those reported by Frydman, Pistor, and Rapaczynski, they also document the persisting phenomenon of managerial dominance of corporate boards and decisions. In particular, managers seem to have ignored a number of presidential decrees mandating enhanced board representation for outside shareholders and found numerous ways of disregarding outsiders who managed to acquire board seats in their companies. The authors advocate a number of measures to strengthen outside ownership but also stress that too much emphasis may have been put on the dangers of insider control. They point in particular to many radical changes that insider-picked board members have forced on such Western companies as General Motors.

The chapters by Stark and by Sabel and Prokop pose the most direct challenge to the assumptions underlying many studies in the present collection. Although their arguments are very different, they all hold that much of the corporate governance scholarship is either out of date or inapplicable to the special East European conditions.

According to Stark, the description of the change taking place in Eastern Europe as "transition" is inappropriate, since it assumes that the end point of the process is already known – the successful institutional pattern of Western Europe and North America. Instead, Stark argues that the process should be understood as "transformation" or "rearrangements, permutations, and reconfigurations of existing organizational forms." In particular, Stark believes that the conventional distinction between private and state property is not applicable to postcommunist economies and that the East European evolution is toward a system that blurs the boundaries between private and public ownership. Using Hungary, where an extremely complex web of cross-ownership has developed since the late 1980s, as his empirical base, Stark analyzes the resulting "recombinant" property and describes it as a form of "organizational hedging, or portfolio management, in which actors are responding to extraordinary uncertainty in the organizational environment by diversifying their assets, redefining and recombining resources." State ownership is combined with elements of private property and inter-enterprise links that, unlike the standard Western institutions that assume the basic continuation of the capitalist system, promise the new Hungarian firms a chance of survival in the face of various unforeseen developments.

Stark acknowledges that the emergence of recombinant property might impede Schumpeterian "creative destruction" in Hungary. But he also argues that the "risk-sharing networks" it creates might save some struggling but capable firms and enhance their adaptability to massive changes in post-socialist economies. Under some circumstances – for example the massive state bailout of Hungarian companies through the "debt consolidation" of 1994 – the new institutions will be induced to highly inefficient behavior, such as shedding their liabilities onto the state and preserving assets in endlessly complicated webs of corporate forms. But the answer to such behavior, Stark concludes, lies not in "the right mix of public and private," but in "the right mix of adaptability and accountability."

The standard learning in corporate governance is attacked by Sabel and Prokop from a different angle: they believe that the traditional institution of corporate property is becoming largely irrelevant in all economic systems, and not just in Eastern Europe. Sabel and Prokop argue that modern technological and organizational developments demand constant cooperation among a number of independent producers and among different parties within the same firm, and a correspondingly continuous renegotiation of their mutual relations. Indeed, in a world in which "standard" mass-produced goods are replaced by custom-designed products resulting from inseparable efforts of many diverse parties, firm boundaries become as open-ended as the division of returns from production, and the traditional concept of the firm may become obsolete together with the traditional concept of property. Corporate monitoring, according to Sabel and Prokop, is no longer a function of owners entitled to "residual returns" on investment, but that of parties that learn from each other even as they police their mutual arrangements.

The new production modes know no boundaries, Sabel and Prokop argue, and they are as applicable in Russia as in the most advanced countries of

Europe, Asia, and North America. Consequently, they argue that the countries in transition should not be expected to reproduce earlier organizational forms and governance mechanisms, but to move directly to the new system. They see signs of precisely such developments in Russia, where large firms are reaching complex accommodations with their labor to share the costs and benefits of transitional changes. Instead of following the traditional pattern of price competition, these firms adapt their organization to the "discursive" ISO standards that allow them to enter directly into partnerships with similarly organized businesses around the world.

Our studies conclude with two chapters devoted to the role of the state in the postcommunist world: the chapter by Pistor and Turkewitz deals with the activities of the state as an owner, while Black, Kraakman, and Hay focus on the regulatory role of the state and the most appropriate model of corporate laws for the period of transition.

Pistor and Turkewitz begin by emphasizing the significance of continued state ownership in Eastern Europe. Even in those countries, such as Russia or the Czech Republic, where privatization is said to have made the greatest strides, the state remains the single largest owner of corporate property. This is not just a function of the size of the fully state-owned sector, but also of the rather novel phenomenon of the state's ubiquitous and pervasive presence as a minority owner of nominally private enterprises. Thus, privatization is in practice not an end point of state property, but a transition to a different point on a "state–nonstate ownership continuum."

Given this evidence, Pistor and Turkewitz focus their analysis on the way in which the state manages its extensive holdings and the effect of state ownership on the activities of other parties, including other state organs. They argue that East European states generally lack coherent strategies for managing their assets, usually delegating the job to specialized and largely unsupervised agencies. This creates a classic moral hazard situation. Public officials are unlike "good" owners in that their objectives may not be identical with the maximization of the value of the firm; instead, officials may, in their capacity as owners, legitimately pursue other goals that may be seen as in the "public interest," such as preserving employment or protecting domestic production. But this means that the objective function of officials-as-owners is quite vague, and in the absence of a clear set of rules concerning the appropriate way of balancing competing social objectives, monitoring both of and by state bureaucracies is a nearly impossible task. Indeed, the same officials are usually charged with managing the state portfolio and with defining the set of objectives they are to pursue, thus effectively controlling the criteria according to which their own activities should be evaluated.

Pistor and Turkewitz further argue that extensive state ownership, by allowing a direct and largely unsupervised form of control, retards the development of the much needed transparent regulatory apparatus characteristic of democratic societies. By the same token, state ownership also adversely affects the incentives of nonstate owners, since state presence among owners provides a form of taxpayer-funded insurance against politically unacceptable outcomes. Given the inherent nature of these problems, the authors end by cautioning that they are not likely to be solved by a mere rationalization of the state's management of its assets. Instead, the state should gradually shift from ownership to regulation as the primary tool for the achievement of its economic objectives.

Finally, the question of what kind of regulation is the most appropriate under the conditions of postcommunist transition is the subject of the chapter by Black, Kraakman, and Hay. Using the preparation of new corporate law for Russia as their example, they argue that legislative schemes for the postcommunist countries should start from the assumption that the state itself is very weak and that the chances of satisfactory enforcement of complex regulatory schemes are rather slim. Consequently, they propose a system of maximally self-enforcing and largely procedural rules, usually relying on the interests of various private parties to make them work. Thus, for example, instead of a complicated system of substantive fiduciary duties designed to protect minority shareholders, the authors advocate a mandatory system of cumulative voting, extensive disclosure requirements, and supermajority provisions designed to cure most common types of conflicts of interests. These proposals present a radical departure from the company legislation now in force in most transition economies, which tends to provide few procedural safeguards for minority shareholders and gives substantial leeway to majority owners to tailor voting rights, board membership, and disclosure rules to suit their interests.

The studies in these volumes shed new light on the range and viability of the new governance institutions that are emerging in the transition settings of Eastern Europe. The portfolio of experiments and new institutions is already rich, and although they share many characteristics with institutions in advanced economies, these studies clearly show that each institution is unique. This is perhaps not surprising as the entire environment and experience of transition is itself unique in history.

Such uniqueness does not obviate, however, the commonality of the impact of basic incentives, the most important perhaps being the moral hazard engendered by selective state intervention and support. Although some of the "new" institutions in the first volume may hold more promise than some of the "old" ones in the second, none of the institutions looked at in these volumes (with the possible exception of certain foreign investors) is yet a "success" at the complex task of governance, either of individual firms or of an investment portfolio. Further fundamental change is necessary and desirable if these countries are to develop well-functioning capitalist economies. Yet none of the owners addressed in these volumes – banks, investment funds, pension funds, foreign investors, or inside managers and employees – will evolve into effective governance institutions (or, alternatively, change into "better" ownership forms) unless they are forced to function subject to market forces without the promise of state bailouts if they fail. Economic reforms that promote macroeconomic discipline, hard budget constraints, and increasing competition will enhance the process of "creative destruction" through which more effective institutions will emerge. However, the very process of emergence creates powerful new lobbies that will pressure the fragile political process for selective intervention. The tension between the continuing need for change and the onset of political sclerosis as new interim institutions (banks, funds, or inside owners) gain political power is at the core of reform in all East European economies. Although progress to date is significant, the process of transition is clearly not yet over, and its ultimate outcome is still an open question.

References

Aoki, Patrick, and Paul Sheard. 1994. "*The Japanese Main Bank System: Its Relevance for Developing and Transforming Economies.*" New York: Oxford University Press.

Blanchard, Olivier, and Richard Layard. 1990. "Economic Change in Poland." Working Paper, Center for Research into Communist Economies, London.

Edwards, Jeremy, and Klaus Fischer. 1994. *Banks, Finance and Investment in Germany.* Cambridge, Eng.: Cambridge University Press.

Frydman, Roman, and Andrzej Rapaczynski. 1990a. "Privatization in Poland: A New Proposal." Mimeographed.

——. 1990b. "Sprywatyzowac Prywatyzacje: Nowa Propozycja Przemian Wlasnosciowych w Polsce" (On Privatizing Privatization: A New Proposal of Ownership Transformation in Poland). *Res publica* (September).

——. 1994. *Privatization in Eastern Europe: Is the State Withering Away?* Budapest: Central European University Press.

Gray, Cheryl W. 1996. "In Search of Owners: Lessons of Experience with Privatization and Corporate Governance in Transition Economies." *World Bank Research Observer*, Washington, D.C., forthcoming.

Gray, Cheryl W., Sabine Schlorke, and Miklos Szanyi. 1995. "Hungary's Bankruptcy Experience, 1992–93." World Bank Policy Research Working Paper 1510, Washington, D.C. (September).

Lipton David, and Jeffrey Sachs. 1990. "Creating a Market Economy in Eastern Europe: The Case of Poland." Brookings Papers on Economic Activity, no. 1: 75-147. The Brookings Institution, Washington, D.C.

2

CORPORATE CONTROL IN CENTRAL EUROPE AND RUSSIA
Should Banks Own Shares?

PETER DITTUS and STEPHEN PROWSE

The views expressed in this paper are our own and not necessarily those of the Bank for International Settlements or of the Federal Reserve Bank of Dallas. We owe a great debt of gratitude to staff at the Czech, Hungarian, and Polish National Banks for very useful discussions and for support in setting up meetings, and to managers of commercial banks for their willingness to take the time and discuss with us their banks' strategy. Herbert Baer, Stijn Claessens, Cheryl Gray, Mirsolav Hrncir, and Ian Mladek provided valuable comments or ideas. We are grateful to participants at a BIS seminar for their suggestions on an earlier draft of this chapter.

Introduction

Five years after the start of economic reforms in Central and Eastern Europe, the issue of corporate governance remains largely unresolved. While privatization, foreign direct investment, increasingly competitive markets, and the introduction of hard budget constraints have enforced some discipline on managers and encouraged rationalization and downsizing in firms, there is undeniably a great need for a strong mechanism of corporate governance in these countries that can effectively replace managers where appropriate and actively restructure firms. Some observers have argued that banks should fill the vacuum by swapping debt for equity, or purchasing equity outright, and taking an active role in the restructuring and governance of nonfinancial enterprises. They base their recommendation on the experience of countries like Japan and Germany where banks have played an important role in corporate governance.[1] Do these countries provide an appropriate role

[1] See, for example, Hoshi, Kashyap, and Loveman (1994). Others advocating a primary role for banks in the governance of firms include van Wijnbergen (1992), Corbett and Mayer (1991), Scharfstein (1992), and Sarcinelli (1992).

model? Should banks in Central Europe and Russia own shares and help govern nonfinancial firms? These are the questions we attempt to answer in this paper. We do so by analyzing the corporate governance systems in different Western countries and attempting to derive lessons for the countries in Central Europe, recognizing the existing conditions in these transition countries of their capital markets and banking systems.

Doubtless, banks are already playing a major role in corporate governance in Central Europe and Russia and will continue to do so. The reason is that they hold the lion's share of enterprise debt, most of it being of short maturity. The ability to refuse to roll over credit gives banks a potentially powerful control instrument over enterprises. A chapter in this volume by Baer and Gray deals with this aspect of corporate control by banks. Our focus is narrower. We ask whether banks can and should play a role in corporate governance based on ownership rights.

We conclude that a corporate governance system based primarily on ownership and governance by banks is not appropriate *at this stage* for Central Europe and Russia. *This is not to say that such a system may not eventually be appropriate.* But, for this, banks must be free from state interference and subject to strong competition from market forces and adequate supervision. Beliefs that the state will continue to bail out banks in difficulties must be credibly dispelled. Clearly, some progress has been made on all these fronts in the last few years. Nonetheless, we are convinced that much more needs to be done before an active role for banks in governance based on ownership can be envisaged. Interviews with bank managers in the region have reinforced our view. There may, however, be benefits from allowing a limited role for some banks to own equity and restructure firms that have defaulted on loans to the bank. This would enable them to obtain experience in the ownership and governance of firms that may bear fruit later when the banking system is in a position to play a more active role in this area.

The arguments we advance to make our case against a major role for banks in the ownership and control of nonfinancial firms might be understood as suggesting that existing banks in some countries should also not lend in current circumstances. This question has been subject to heated debate before but is not addressed here. We feel that in all the countries under review the decision has been taken to build a functioning banking system on the basis of existing banks. The question now is not what to do with the existing banks, but how to develop them into efficient intermediaries as quickly as possible. This chapter points out that tight restrictions on the ownership of nonfinancial firms should form part of the strategy to develop an efficient financial industry.

The next section analyzes corporate governance systems in the West. We compare the market-based system in the United States to the more bank-based systems in Japan and Germany. No attempt is made to evaluate which system is the best. The focus is on the conditions necessary for different models of corporate governance to flourish. We then analyze the current conditions existing in Central and Eastern Europe. We concentrate on the degree of liquidity of corporate securities markets, the restructuring requirements of firms, and conditions in the banking sector including the degree of state influence, the bad debt burden, competition, supervision, and the incentives banks face about their asset portfolio.

Finally, we draw the threads of the two previous sections together and compare the conditions necessary for successful operation of the various governance models in the West with the existing conditions in the transition countries. Implications are drawn for the appropriate role of banks in the ownership and governance of firms.

Banks in Western Corporate Governance

As a field of research, comparative corporate governance is in its infancy. The major industrialized countries in the West appear to present us with dramatically different institutional arrangements for corporate governance. Yet we lack a consensus as to why these different arrangements came about, what the advantages and disadvantages are, and whether one system is clearly better at the resolution of agency problems between the various stakeholders of the firm. This poses a problem for scholars attempting to derive lessons from the West for the countries in Central Europe and Russia undergoing the transition from socialism. In putting forward recommendations for these countries on the role of banks in corporate governance, this chapter will consequently be somewhat circumspect. It will try to identify common points of agreement among researchers on Western models of corporate governance and derive implications for the countries in transition.

We start with a description of the corporate governance mechanisms in the United States, Japan and Germany. Particular attention is paid to the role of banks and their ownership of firms in each country. Then we describe the main costs and benefits of having banks play a primary role in the governance mechanism through the ownership of firms. While not drawing any conclusions about the relative superiority of one Western model over another, we identify the underlying conditions of capital markets, the restructuring requirements of firms, and the bank supervision, governance, and competition that appear necessary for the successful operation of each system. By comparing these requirements with the existing conditions in

Central Europe and Russia, we draw implications for the feasibility of the different Western models in the transition countries.

We begin with the role of banks in the corporate governance mechanism in the United States, Japan and Germany, with a particular focus on three important characteristics in each country: the structure of corporate ownership, bank-enterprise relations, and the market for corporate control.

Structure of Ownership

Differences in the ownership of firms across countries are illustrated to some degree by simple inspection of the aggregate statistics on the ownership of listed companies in Table 2.1, which reveals the far heavier weight of banks in Japan compared with the United States. Germany appears to lie somewhere between Japan and the United States in bank ownership of corporate equity. In Germany, however, banks have wide powers to exercise the voting rights owned by individuals but held in trust.[2]

These aggregate figures, however, reveal nothing about the concentration of ownership or who the large shareholders are in a typical firm, facts that are important in understanding corporate control. Table 2.2 gives some data on ownership concentration in a sample of large, listed U.S., Japanese and

Table 2.1. Ownership of Common Stock, 1990
(percentage of outstanding shares owned)

	United States	Japan	Germany
All corporations	44.5	72.9	64.0
Financial institutions	30.4	48.0	22.0
Banks	0	18.9	10.0
Insurance companies	4.6	19.6	
Pension funds	20.1	9.5	12.0
Other	5.7		
Nonfinancial corporations	14.1	24.9	42.0
Individuals	50.2	22.4	17.0
Foreign	5.4	4.0	14.0
Government	0	0.7	5.0

Sources: U.S. Federal Reserve Flow of Funds, Japanese Flow of Funds, Deutsche Bundesbank Monthly Report.

[2] The law on proxy voting has been tightened over the years, but it still appears to confer a wide power on banks to vote stock as they wish. Purrucker (1983) has estimated that 95% of private shareholders do not make use of their rights to instruct the bank on voting matters, leaving the bank with substantial discretionary voting power.

Table 2.2. Summary Statistics of Ownership Concentration of Large Nonfinancial Corporations
(percentage of outstanding shares owned by the five largest shareholders)

	United States	Japan	Germany
Mean	25.4	33.1	41.5
Median	20.9	29.7	37.0
Standard deviation	16.0	13.8	14.5
Minimum	1.3	10.9	15.0
Maximum	87.1	85.0	89.6
Mean firm size[a] (millions of $, 1980)	3,505	1,835	3,483
Mean firm size[b] (millions of $, 1980)	1,287	811	1,497

Sources: For the United States and Japan, Prowse (1992); for Germany, Prowse (1993). Size data converted to $, using 1980 average exchange rates and deflated by U.S. consumer prices.
Samples: United States: 457 nonfinancial corporations in 1980; Japan: 143 mining and manufacturing corporations in 1984; Germany: 41 nonfinancial corporations in 1990.

[a] Measured by total assets.
[b] Measured by market value of equity.

German nonfinancial firms. The table highlights a number of differences: first, ownership concentration varies quite widely across countries. In the United States the largest five shareholders hold on average about 25 percent of the outstanding shares of the firm. Ownership concentration is significantly higher in Japan, but is by far the highest in German companies, where the holdings of the largest five shareholders average over 40 percent. In addition, voting power in German firms may be more concentrated than even these data suggest. As mentioned above, banks in Germany have traditionally been given a wide latitude to vote the shares they hold in trust for smaller shareholders. Proxy votes exercised by the banks on behalf of beneficial shareholders are very important in the large German corporations and concentrate voting rights in the banks.[3] This may be particularly important in those few widely held companies in Germany where small shareholders typically deposit their shares with the banks.[4] Finally, many large German

[3] For example, of the 100 largest joint stock companies (AGs) in Germany in 1978, banks had a combined voting power (from their direct holdings and proxies) of greater than 25% in 41 of them. In the 56 AGs in which banks had a combined voting power of greater than 5%, their average share of the vote was almost 57%. In the remaining 44 AGs, there existed a dominant nonbank shareholder owning greater than 25%, but even among these firms, banks often held large combined voting stakes.

[4] Even those companies that are widely held in terms of beneficial ownership may have their voting rights concentrated in the hands of a few banks. For example, Pfeiffer (1989) reports that throughout most of the 1980s, the big three universal banks controlled over half the voting rights in BASF, a widely held company.

firms exhibit a pyramid holding company structure, where ownership is concentrated in successive layers of holding companies, many of which are ultimately controlled by either a wealthy family or a bank (see Prowse (1994)). This structure serves to increase the control of banks over firms through their equity ownership.

One major reason for the differences in the ownership of enterprises by banks is differences in the legal and regulatory environment in the three countries. Banks in the United States are prohibited from owning any stock on their own account, while bank holding companies cannot own more than 5 percent of the firm, and their holdings must be passive. Japanese commercial banks are not prohibited from owning corporate stock, although they are subject to antimonopoly regulations that until 1987 limited a single bank's holdings of a single firm's shares to 10 percent (the limit has since been lowered to 5 percent). Banks in Germany can hold whatever share of equity they like in any nonfinancial firm, limited only by a number of prudential rules which do not appear to be particularly binding.

Bank–Enterprise Relationships

There are likely similar differences between countries in the ownership concentration of debt claims on firms, although the available data are much more sparse. The greater reliance on securities markets than on intermediated markets for debt finance in the United States (illustrated in Table 2.3) may be taken as a rough indicator that fragmentation of debt claims is higher there than in Japan or Germany. A second indicator may be differences in the regulatory limits on banks' exposures to individual customers – these limits are generally less binding in Germany and Japan than in the United States. For example, in the United States, banks are limited to lending 15 percent of their capital to an individual borrower, whereas in Japan and Germany the limits are 30 percent and 50 percent respectively (see Borio (1990)).There are also legal and regulatory differences in the degree to which investors are permitted to

Table 2.3. Composition of Companies' Credit Market Debt, 1985
(percentage)

	United States	Japan	Germany
Intermediated debt	45	91	94
From banks	36	n.a.	88
Securities	55	9	6

Sources: Borio (1990) and national data.

Note: Credit market debt excludes trade debt. Intermediated debt refers to loans from financial intermediaries. Securities includes commercial paper and other short-term bills and long-term bonds.

Table 2.4. Gross Funding of Nonfinancial Corporations, 1970-85
(percentage of total gross financing)

	Japan	Germany
Retentions	52	76
External finance	48	24
Intermediated debt	41	21
Securities	7	3

Sources: OECD Financial Statistics, Part III, and national data.

Note: Total gross financing excludes trade credit and some overseas financing. Intermediated debt refers to loans from financial institutions. Securities includes public equity and short- and long-term bills and bonds.

take debt and equity stakes in the same firm. The legal doctrine of equitable subordination discourages all creditors in the United States from taking an equity position in the borrower, since the creditors are potentially liable to subordination should they be perceived to exert control over the firm.

Differences in the strength of bank–firm relationships are consequently significant. Bank–enterprise relations in Japan have traditionally been very strong. Not only have banks typically held equity in firms, they have also been an extremely important source of financing. From 1970 to 1985, for example, Japanese firms relied on loans from financial institutions for more than 40 percent of their total financing needs (Table 2.4). This may have given the main bank of a Japanese firm effective control over the firm's access to working capital and thus a much enhanced power to influence the firm's activities. In Germany the story is somewhat different. German firms have never relied heavily on banks to finance their investment needs, because they have obtained most of their finance from internal funds.[5] From 1970 to 1985, for example, German firms raised only about 20 percent of total funds from financial institutions (primarily banks). What governance power the banks have does not appear to stem from any control over the firm's access to funds.[6] In the United States, banks do not own equity and are not an important source of funds to

[5] This is partly a function of the differing institutional arrangements for pension provision in Germany. About two-thirds of the funds earmarked for the payment of private pensions is retained by the company as an unfunded loability. Only the remainder is invested outside the company via private pension funds. The funds retained by the company are used for general corporate purposes. The result is that there is less capital available for the capital market and less demand for outside financing than in Anglo-Saxon countries where the bulk of private pensions are channeled through private pension funds (see Edwards anf Fischer (1994)). The Japanese private pension system is relatively small compared with the public pension system and is funneled largely through the banking system via trust banks.

[6] It is true that, as universal banks, German banks typically underwrite equity and bond offerings by the firm, giving them more influence in this sense than Japanese banks, which are precluded from acting as investment banks. However, the low demand by German firms for external finance means that this power may not amount to much.

the typical large firm. Bank–firm relationships in the United States are typically "at arm's length."

The strength of bank–firm ties in Japan is reflected in the frequency with which creditors are simultaneously equity holders of firms. For example, Prowse (1990) reports that in over 40 percent of a sample of large Japanese manufacturing firms the largest debtholder was also the largest shareholder; on average the largest debtholder held almost one quarter of the firm's outstanding debt and over 5 percent of the firm's outstanding equity, while the largest five debtholders of the firm held over half of the firm's debt and almost 20 percent of its equity. In contrast, Clyde (1989) finds in a sample of U.S. Fortune 500 companies that in only a few cases do any of the largest five shareholders hold any of the firm's debt and that in these few cases the debtholdings of the largest shareholders are minuscule.

Market for Corporate Control

Another dramatic difference between the United States and Germany or Japan is the frequency of mergers and acquisitions. The market for corporate control is much less active in Japan and Germany. Data on the volume of completed domestic merger and acquisition transactions for the second half of the 1980s are displayed in Table 2.5, which reveals large differences between countries. Part of the reason for the greater merger activity in the United States is, of course, the larger number of companies listed on the U.S. stock market. However, even normalizing the dollar value of mergers and acquisitions by stock market capitalization fails to alter the impression that the merger market is much more active in the United States – 15 to 20 times more so according to Table 2.5.[7]

Table 2.5. Average Annual Volume of Completed Domestic Mergers and Corporate Transactions with Disclosed Values, 1985-89

	United States	Japan	Germany
Volume (in billions of $)	1,070	61.3	4.2
As a percentage of total market capitalization	41.1	3.1	2.3

Sources: For the United States and Germany, Securities Data Corporation, Mergers and Corporate Transactions database; for Japan, Yamaichi Securities Corporation, as reported in Beiter (1991).

Note: Dollar values calculated at current exchange rates for each of the five years covered. Market capitalization figures are for 1987, converted to dollars at prevailing exchange rates.

[7] Other empirical evidence supports the claim that mergers and acquisitions in Japan are far lower than in the United States. Kaplan (1993) found that just over 2% of his sample of large Japanese firms were taken over or merged between 1980 and 1989 in contrast to over 22% of his sample of large U.S. firms.

The differences across countries in the frequency of hostile takeovers are even more striking.[8] Since World War II, for example, there have been only four successful hostile takeovers in Germany (see Franks and Mayer (1993)).They appear to be almost as rare in Japan. Kester (1991) claims that the use of takeovers for replacing inefficient management in large Japanese firms is very infrequent. Conversely, in the United States almost 10 percent of the Fortune 500 companies in 1980 have since been acquired in a transaction that was hostile or started off as hostile.

The Role of Banks

In the United States, the banks' primary part in corporate governance is through their role as lenders. Even here the equitable subordination fear may make banks reluctant to play a big role in the governance of the firm. They typically own no equity in the firm, are infrequently represented on the board, and maintain only arm's-length relationships with their borrowers. Their main governance tool appears to be covenants they insert in the loan contract and the maturity they set for the loan.

This does not mean however that banks do not exert control over firms in the United States when the law allows them to do so. For example, in firms that file for bankruptcy or restructure their debt privately, bank lenders and other financial institutions with debt outstanding to the firm frequently receive significant blocks of voting stock, appoint their representatives to the board of directors, and insert restrictive covenants in the companies' restructured lending agreements to give them more say in the firm's investment and financing policies (see Gilson (1990)).[9] U.S. firms that undergo financial distress thus appear to take on some of the characteristics that the typical Japanese and German firms exhibit – notably, high ownership concentration, large equity and debt stakes held by banks, and bank representation on the board of directors.

In Japan the corporate control framework is related to the *keiretsu* form of corporate organization, where a group of firms based in different industries are centered around a bank. The nonfinancial firms in the group tend to have product market links among them and take small equity stakes in each other. They all tend to have strong but not exclusive borrowing links with the banks and other financial institutions in the *keiretsu*, which also take large equity stakes in the nonfinancial firms. While individual banks will take

[8] Hostile takeovers are thought to be motivated by corporate control considerations to a greater extent than friendly mergers.

[9] U.S. law allows banks a significantly more active role in the governance of the firm once it defaults on loans owed to the bank.

stakes of less than 10 percent in firms, collectively banks will own about 20 percent of the firm, and banks and life insurance companies together may own around 35–40 percent. Ownership concentration is relatively high, as is the concentration of debt claims. Collectively, banks are the most important large shareholders of firms and until recently have also been their only major source of external finance. Consequently, they have had a potentially very powerful position as active monitors of management either through the board or more informally through the Presidents' Club meetings, and by controlling the firm's access to external funds. Banks monitor firms continually; they have regular and substantive discussions with management on policy and actively intervene in the case of financial distress. The market for corporate control among large firms is inactive. Hostile takeovers and other transactions between firms about corporate control changes are rare. This does not mean that management turnover in response to poor performance is infrequent, merely that it occurs by other means, namely, pressure from banks.

In Germany there appears to be more reliance on nonbank direct shareholder monitoring than in Japan. Ownership concentration is high among large firms, high enough to give the large shareholders strong incentives to monitor management.[10] Banks generally take small stakes directly in firms (with some important exceptions such as Daimler-Benz in which Deutsche Bank has a 25 percent stake) but monitor and exert control through proxy votes, a pyramid structure of holding companies, and representation on the supervisory board (often in the chairman position). Banks appear to have the potential to engage in monitoring and influencing management particularly in the diffusely held firms where their control of voting rights may be important. They seem to have much less control (compared with Japanese banks) over firms through their control of external sources of finance, since German firms rely more on internally generated funds. Hostile takeovers are almost nonexistent. The success of the German corporate control mechanism appears, in brief, to stand on the ability of large shareholders, often banks, to monitor management.

The academic literature suggests a number of potential advantages, from a corporate governance perspective, of a system that allows large equity and debtholders of the firm to be the same agents, that encourages the concentrated holding of debt and equity claims, and that restricts firms' sources of external finance to one investor (see, for example, Stiglitz (1985)).The legal and regulatory environment of the German and Japanese economies has

[10] This, of course, assumes that the monitors are themselves value maximizers, which may not be the case. The issue of "who monitors the monitor?" is addressed in the following section.

encouraged this concentration of firms' claims in banks to a much greater extent than that of the United States. It has also given the banks – in Japan particularly – a potentially effective monitoring role by allowing them to control much of the firm's external financing. *A priori* then, one might expect that the German and Japanese model would encourage a more efficient form of corporate governance than that in the United States.

Recent research provides some empirical evidence on this issue. Prowse (1990) finds that the tendency for financial institutions to take large debt and equity positions in the same firm may mean that the agency problems of debt finance are lower for firms in Japan than in the United States, where institutional investors are prohibited from being large debt and equity holders in the same firm. Leverage ratios are higher in Japanese firms than U.S. firms partly because of their lower agency costs of debt. Hoshi *et al.* (1990a) find that Japanese firms that are members of *keiretsu* experience fewer liquidity effects on investment than those firms that are not members. *Keiretsu* members typically have strong ties to a main bank, which along with other group firms takes a significant equity position in the firm and holds a large fraction of the firm's outstanding debt. They conclude that membership in a group and close ties to a group main bank are important in mitigating the information problems that are typically associated with external finance and governance. Lichtenburg and Pushner (1993) provide evidence that suggests that financial institutions are the major monitors of firm behavior in Japan. Japanese firms with high financial institution ownership show higher levels of productivity and profitability than other Japanese firms.[11]

There is less empirical evidence available on Germany. Cable (1985) until recently was the only one to comprehensively analyze German firm performance and its relation to the tightness of its bank ties. He showed that banks do play an important corporate control function: profitability among the large German firms was positively related to the proportion of equity voting rights controlled by the three big universal banks and by bank representation on the board of directors.[12] He concluded that banks did use their control of

[11] They also analyze *how* financial institutions exert their control over firms in which they have large stakes. They distinguish between two methods of monitoring: continuous direct monitoring of the firm versus significant intervention in the firm's business only after the firm has encountered financial difficulties. They find that high financial institution ownership reduces both the severity and the frequency of lapses from efficiency and profitability. This would suggest that, in contrast to the conventional wisdom on how Japanese financial institutions behave toward the firms which they own, financial institutions conduct *both* types of intervention. The conventional wisdom has been that banks use their monitoring and disciplining role only in times of financial distress. See Sheard (1989).

[12] The three big universal banks are Deutsche Bank, Dresdner Bank, and Commerzbank.

voting rights and their presence on the board to monitor and influence management toward profit maximization. Elston (1993), in a study modeled on that of Hoshi, Kashyap, and Scharfstein (1990a), finds evidence that firms with tighter bank ties in Germany exhibit investment functions that are less sensitive to liquidity constraints than firms with weaker ties, suggesting that bank ties are important in mitigating the information and agency problems associated with external finance and governance.[13]

Overall, the general consensus of the existing empirical literature is that strong bank–firm relationships may significantly reduce agency and information costs and improve efficiency. However, there are clearly some potential disadvantages of allowing banks to own equity and to take a primary role in the governance of nonfinancial firms. One potential disadvantage is the conflicts of interest such arrangements may generate within banks. Saunders (1994) identifies a number of concerns regarding such conflicts of interest. The most important is that the bank may have incentives to make either subsidized or unsound loans to enterprises in which it has an equity stake. Such practices might ultimately threaten the safety of the bank itself.[14]

[13] Edwards and Fischer (1994) take issue with much of the conventional wisdom on the role of banks in the corporate governance system in Germany. They present a variety of evidence suggesting banks may not have the degree of influence as lenders, shareholders, voters of proxies, or representatives on the board as has been widely thought. They find that bank control of voting rights is only weakly related to the number of bank representatives on the supervisory board, a result somewhat at odds with the belief that banks use their control of voting rights to further their control over management (though not completely inconsistent if banks use their votes to elect members to the supervisory board who are sympathetic to bank interests even though they are not themselves bankers – a distinct possibility in Germany where there has been a tradition of criticism of the banks for exerting undue influence over firms, and where there may be a strong incentive for banks to conceal their influence). They also find that bank representation on the supervisory board does not mean that the firm borrows more from banks, again something that might be expected if banks used their board membership to reduce the costs of providing external finance to the firm. As Edwards and Fischer admit, the evidence provided both for and against the importance of banks in the corporate control function of German firms is incomplete. Probably the most that can be said about the issue is that, while it is likely that banks in Germany probably play some role in the corporate control of firms, it is unclear that they play the primary role. The structure of corporate ownership in Germany presented earlier suggests that nonfinancial firms and individuals that are large shareholders may play an equally important role as banks. Indeed, Edwards and Fischer's results may be a product of the fact that banks play an important corporate governance role *only in those firms that are widely held and that do not enjoy the benefits of large shareholder monitoring.* The Monopolkommission's (1978) findings that banks' voting power from direct holdings and from proxies is greatest in those firms that are widely held is consistent with this view.

[14] Other potential conflicts of interest include (1) the bank's restricting the supply of credit to an enterprise that competes with an enterprise in which the bank has an equity stake (an "affiliate"), (2) the bank's passing on privileged information about a borrower to competing affiliates, and (3) the bank's using its lending powers to tie customers in to the products of affiliated enterprises.

Another potential disadvantage is that allowing banks to invest in equity as well as debt might lead to an increase in the risk of bank failure. By their nature equity investments contain more risk than loans. Allowing banks to take equity stakes in firms could, therefore, increase the riskiness of the banking system and the potential cost to the deposit insurance system. Of course, it is not clear whether expanding the permissible asset class for bank investments will result in an overall increase or decrease in bank risk. Allowing banks to invest in equity could conceivably *lower* overall bank risk by allowing the bank more avenues for diversification and opportunities to hedge their loan risk more effectively. Although this issue has not been addressed directly by researchers, it has been addressed by empirical investigations into the possible effect on overall bank risk of the introduction of universal banking in the United States (see Saunders and Walter (1994)). The bulk of the research on this issue suggests that there are potential *risk reduction gains* from allowing commercial banks to expand into universal banking activities. However, these empirical results are hard to translate into implications for banks in the transition countries with their drastically different conditions and environment.[15]

A final possible disadvantage in allowing banks to own equity in firms stems from the power a large equity holding confers on a bank to influence the firm to take out loans from the bank (or purchase other bank services) at premium prices. The bank may be able to extract rents from the firm by virtue of its large equity stake in it. Here the equity stake held by the bank may frustrate the ability of the firm to take advantage of a competitive loan market. This problem may be all the more important in banking systems where there is not much competition.

Empirical evidence about the importance of these potential disadvantages of allowing banks to own equity in firms is scarce. The Gessler Commission (1979), in its study of universal banking arrangements in Germany, concluded that potential conflicts of interest in universal banking probably were only responsible for minor restraints of competition that could be remedied by marginal changes in the law. It appears that most of the potential disadvantages mentioned above can be substantially mitigated by a combination of a high degree of competition in the banking and financial

[15] This is partly because the introduction of universal banking includes a wide expansion of bank powers – into insurance and corporate securities underwriting – in addition to the holding (and trading) of corporate equity securities. Thus, the results cited here probably do not have much to say on the narrower issue of the effect on bank risk of the holding of equity securities. Perhaps more importantly for the focus of this chapter, banks in the United States are completely different entities from their namesakes in the transition countries in terms of their sophistication, the reputations they have at stake, and the supervisory and competitive environment.

sector and a sophisticated and intensive prudential supervision and regulation of banks. Absent such an environment, of course, these arguments are likely to take on a much greater importance. In particular, they are likely to be far more relevant for the transition countries.

Requirements for Efficient Operation

In analyzing the relevant lessons for Eastern Europe and Russia, a clear understanding of the conditions necessary for the successful operation of each system observed in the West is needed. What are the requirements of the different systems in the West in terms of liquid capital markets, the severity of the information asymmetries between insiders and outsiders, the independence and governance of the banking system, the degree of competition within the banking system, and the type of monitoring and restructuring that firms require? After answering these questions, we can then compare the requirements of each system with the existing conditions in Eastern Europe and Russia and draw some implications for the operation of each system under these conditions.

Capital Market Liquidity

The Anglo-Saxon system of corporate governance relies crucially on liquid securities markets that can transmit new information rapidly and efficiently and come close to being efficient markets in the sense that there is a large amount of publicly available information about the financial and operating characteristics of firms, which is incorporated into prices. Without such conditions, hostile takeovers become virtually impossible. In contrast, the German or Japanese system of large shareholder monitoring by banks and others does not rely on liquid corporate securities markets and may even be hindered by their presence.

The Anglo-Saxon capital market liquidity system requires a large amount of publicly available information about firms so that the information asymmetries between insiders and outsiders are not severe. If they were, outside investors would never risk their money by buying corporate securities, and a corporate securities market would consequently be very illiquid. It is not a coincidence that corporate disclosure requirements in the United States are much more comprehensive and demanding than those in Japan and Germany (see Prowse (1994)). Capital market liquidity not only requires that large amounts of information be available to outside investors, but also that there be sufficient expertise among outsiders (investment banks, ratings agencies, buyout firms, and takeover specialists) to analyze, interpret, and understand the financial and operating information disclosed by firms, so as to evaluate whether a firm is being badly run or not. In the German and Japanese systems, this expertise is also required but need be concentrated only among the large shareholders who, as insiders, have access to the appropriate information and do most of the monitoring. There is thus likely to be a lower requirement for such expertise overall in the Japanese or German system than in the Anglo-Saxon system.

Some authors claim that the role of the large, active shareholder in Germany and Japan is buttressed by, or may even require the existence of, illiquid securities markets. One reason is that illiquid equity markets preclude the possibility of large equity blockholders simply selling their stakes in firms in which they become dissatisfied ("exit"), thereby increasing the incentives for large shareholders to monitor and influence management ("voice") (see Coffee (1991)). Another reason may be that in undeveloped capital markets, firms often have only one source of external capital – bank loans. This reliance solely on banks for external finance may strengthen banks' corporate governance role by giving them control over the cash raised by the firm to finance activities (see Scharfstein (1992) and Prowse (1994)).

There is some evidence – particularly from Japan – that the existence of illiquid securities markets contributes importantly to the power of large shareholders to monitor the firm and, indeed, that they may be a necessary condition for the large shareholder system to operate efficiently. For example, in Japan corporate securities markets until the early 1980s were very illiquid. In addition, banks have traditionally been important providers of external finance to firms through their role as lenders. As capital markets have been deregulated in Japan and firms have had access to a wide variety of sources of finance apart from bank loans, their reliance on bank loans has fallen sharply. If the banks' role as corporate monitors depended crucially on their role as providers of external finance to firms, we might expect that their effectiveness as monitors may have declined recently. Some evidence suggests that this is indeed the case. Hoshi, Kashyap, and Scharfstein (1990b, 1993) provide evidence of agency problems among Japanese firms, the source of which appear to be the increasing accessibility to nonbank finance. They find that despite the advantages for Japanese firms from tight bank relationships, including fewer information problems and liquidity restraints, many Japanese firms were actively *reducing* the strength of their bank ties in the 1980s as deregulation led to many nonbank opportunities for external finance. They analyze the firms that have increased their use of the public debt markets and reduced their reliance on bank loans. They find that more profitable and successful firms, as well as less successful firms in which managers have significant share ownership, have been the most aggressive in reducing their reliance on banks.[16] Their findings indicate that corporate control in Japan may have ceased to operate as effectively as it had done over the period when the legal and regulatory environment precluded firms from tapping nonbank sources of external finance.

In Germany the story is somewhat different. The German financial system has typically been characterized by illiquid and shallow securities markets. This may have induced large shareholders to exert voice rather than exit. However, as mentioned earlier, despite the absence of many alternatives to bank loans, German firms have never relied heavily on banks to finance their investment needs. What governance power the banks have does not appear to stem from any control over the firms' access to funds.

In sum, while deep and liquid corporate securities markets are clearly a necessary condition for the operation of the Anglo-Saxon system of corporate governance, there is some evidence that they may be a hindrance to the operation of the Japanese model. This is clearly of importance to East European countries, which currently have underdeveloped capital markets and are considering whether to devote resources to making them more liquid.

Governance

The German/Japanese system requires that the institutions that are the primary monitors perform their monitoring function properly. How is this ensured? Who monitors the monitor? In most German and Japanese banks, there appears to be no large shareholder to perform such monitoring of the monitor. Banks in Germany and Japan are widely held (see Prowse (1994)), suggesting that this may be an important issue in both countries. Diamond (1984) has demonstrated that, under certain conditions, banks can alleviate problems of monitoring the performance of enterprises and financial institutions. By investing in a large number of firms, banks smooth their earnings and are able to offer investors fixed return debt (deposit) contracts. By issuing debt, managers of banks are provided with incentives to maximize

[16] They interpret these findings as follows: first, because intermediated finance involves a significant amount of monitoring by the bank, it has costs that successful firms with good investment opportunities would prefer not to bear. Thus, when the opportunity to tap public debt markets arises, these firms react in a profit maximizing way by tapping these cheaper forms of finance. However, managers of *all* firms have incentives to tap such finance, because they will then be subject to less scrutiny and monitoring from stakeholders and will have more opportunity to shirk. Thus, firms in which managers are entrenched may also be expected to reduce their reliance on banks and finance themselves through the public markets. In this case their response is not the profit maximizing one, but the one that maximizes the managers' preferences. Hoshi *et al.*'s evidence points to some degree of management entrenchment in Japanese firms.

the performance of the firm. However, there are a number of real world complications that may cloud the applicability of Diamond's result to the German and Japanese banks. The most important is the existence of deposit insurance, which removes depositors' incentives to penalize the bank, through higher interest rates, if the bank does not monitor efficiently.

The monitoring function may also be performed in part by the banking supervision authorities. Japan and Germany have fairly intensive prudential supervision and regulation with which to monitor and control banks. Admittedly, the primary focus is to protect the government from failure of the bank rather than the maximization of bank equity value, which is what would ensure optimal monitoring behavior by the bank. However, adequate supervision would presumably mitigate one of the conflict of interest problems that Saunders (1994) identifies – namely, that banks would not easily be able to make unsound or subsidized loans to affiliates in financial distress.

Ultimately, whether or not the "who monitors the monitor?" issue is a problem for Germany and Japan is a matter of empirical evidence, of which we have little. However, it is clear that the German and Japanese models work more efficiently the greater the incentives are for the banks to perform efficient monitoring of the firms they lend to and own. Regardless of how well banks monitor in Germany and Japan, this issue clearly acquires great significance for the countries of Eastern Europe, where the banks are still state owned, suffer from incentive problems, and are subject to fairly weak prudential supervision and regulation by the banking authorities.

Competition

Given the potential for conflicts of interest in a system that allows banks to own equity in firms, it follows that the greater degree of competition in the banking system, the less this potential is likely to be a reality. Many of the conflicts of interest to which a bank might be susceptible would be mitigated to the extent that competitive market conditions imposed external discipline – through the loss of reputation – on the bank. Competitive conditions in the banking system would, for example, make it impossible for a bank to insist upon product market tie ins. Similarly, it would make it impossible for a bank to threaten to disrupt credit flows to the competitor of an affiliate. And the incentive to pass on private information to affiliates about their competitors who borrow from the bank would be mitigated by the threatened loss of reputation.

One reason these problems have not been serious in Japan and Germany may be because their banking systems are reasonably competitive (see Corbett and Mayer (1991)). There are many banks and concentration levels tend to be low. For example, in 1986 the 13 largest city banks in Japan held just under 50 percent of all banking assets, and the six largest banks in Germany accounted for less than 10 percent of all banking assets. However, this issue is clearly of importance for Eastern Europe, where the concentration of the banking system is much higher.

Enterprise Restructuring

The most effective system of corporate governance for any particular firm is likely to depend on its line of business, its stage in the life cycle, and the technological and market conditions it faces. For example, old established firms in basic industries that suffer from overcapacity and need to downsize by selling off assets, cutting capacity, laying off workers, and cutting wages may be subject to agency and information problems that are quite different from those of young firms in expanding industries that need to invest large amounts of capital in research and development to stay competitive.

How are corporate control arrangements suited to different problems of adjustment and restructuring? First, there is evidence that hostile takeovers are a particularly effective mechanism of achieving the painful restructuring required of a firm in an industry with large overcapacity problems. Morck, Shleifer, and Vishny (1989) found that U.S. firms suffering from such problems were more likely to undergo a corporate control change through a hostile takeover than through internally precipitated removal of management by the board of directors. This may be because hostile takeovers entail the intervention of an outsider who has no previous relationship with the managers and employees of the firm and who thus has more freedom to enact the painful measures necessary to maximize equity value (see Shleifer and Summers (1988)). Conversely, firms that are governed by a large institutional shareholder (bank or other) may plausibly not be as responsive to overcapacity conditions by virtue of the long-term relationships that they have built up with other stakeholders (such as management and workers).[17] Mizsei (1994) claims that the reliance on the impersonal takeover mechanism has meant that firms in the United States in industries characterized by overcapacity have restructured and downsized themselves much more quickly than firms facing similar requirements in Japan and Europe.

Second, there is evidence that the corporate governance arrangements we observe in risky startup firms may be a response to their particular needs. They typically need an active investor who brings not only capital, but also an expertise in the marketing, accounting and financial aspects of the firm.

[17] As Shleifer and Summers point out, these long-term relationships may be of some significant value in many firms in market economies.

Sahlman (1990) and Fenn, Liang, and Prowse (1995) describe the corporate governance arrangements of venture capital firms in the United States as being dramatically different from those of large firms. Venture capital firms typically have an active investor (the venture capitalist) who takes a majority equity stake in the firm, sits on the board, finds other sources of capital for the firm if necessary, and provides marketing, financial, and technical expertise to the firm. This large shareholder role seems particularly suited to mitigating the problems facing risky startup firms where the original management team may have plenty of technical expertise but little or no business expertise.

Third, Franks and Mayer (1992) speculate that there are certain lines of business that are likely to benefit more from the Japanese or German style of corporate governance and others that benefit from the U.S. style. They suggest that the U.S. system is best suited to situations in which corporate activities include subjective assessments of future prospects, while evaluation of the quality of employees and managers is of little relevance, on the assumption that the market for corporate control is really a market for corporate strategy with managers competing for the right to implement their preferred strategies. They assert that this function is quite different from the one performed by the German or Japanese system, which relies on banks to be active investors. The primary role that the main bank or *Hausbank* plays in corporate governance, along with other interested stakeholders (such as suppliers and customers), ensures that the influential parties have a lot of information about the quality of management and employees. Thus, the German or Japanese system is particularly well suited to evaluating managerial performance in industries where there are standard operating procedures and known skills that can be evaluated.

Franks and Mayer associate the former type of activities where the U.S. system is preferred with more speculative risky industries such as biotechnology and pharmaceuticals. The German or Japanese system may be superior in lines of business associated with standard methods of production, such as basic manufacturing, where there are known skills that can be transferred from one firm to another. It may be no accident that the comparative performance of different countries in different industries appears to be related to the advantages of alternative corporate governance systems.[18]

What implications does this have for Central Europe and Russia? Ultimately, it depends upon the view one takes of the nature of the restructuring activity facing firms in these countries. The restructuring requirements

[18] Which way the causality runs is, of course, unclear: the German system may have evolved as a response to its comparative strength in manufacturing, not the converse.

of firms in Eastern Europe and Russia are likely to be quite diverse, with a large number of firms requiring fairly radical downsizing or even liquidation, but also a significant number requiring expansion and investment in new methods of production and new lines of business. In almost all cases there will be a need for the injection of expertise in marketing, accounting, and financial operations. In relatively few cases will there be firms that have already invested in the most up-to-date operating procedures and require little or no radical restructuring.

Corporate Control in Central Europe and Russia

The United States, Japan and Germany present us with three different models of the governance role of banks. These models have unique requirements in terms of the conditions under which they can operate efficiently. These conditions comprise the degree of liquidity in the capital markets, the governance and supervision of banks, the degree of competition within the banking system and the particular restructuring needs of firms. These conditions are now examined for the countries of Central Europe and Russia.

Business Skills, Capital Market Liquidity, and Firm Restructuring

Perhaps the most serious legacy of central planning is the acute lack of business skills and expertise throughout all firms, including banks. Among nonfinancial firms there is an urgent need for marketing, accounting, and financial skills. Many managers need to acquire these skills or be replaced. Among banks there is a need for loan evaluation skills, which require accounting and other financial expertise. Under central planning these skills were not needed. The rudimentary banking system was part of the budget; its role was to distribute funds according to the plan and to monitor consistency of expenditures with the plan. The monobank and the sector-specific specialized banks were active in keeping accounts and extending working capital credit in accordance with plan targets. In short, banking was equivalent to bookkeeping by a monopolist.[19] It is not surprising that banking skills like evaluating creditworthiness, pricing risk, processing loans, and offering customer-oriented products to attract funds did not develop in such circumstances.

Firms in the transition countries suffer acute information asymmetries

[19] Sometimes enterprises did not have their own accounting section and relied mostly on the account-keeping services of banks.

between insiders and outsiders, in particular because the system transformation radically altered the economic environment in which enterprises were operating. Changes in relative prices, the collapse of the Council of Mutual Economic Aid (CMEA) export markets, sudden import competition, reduced subsidies, and the sudden sharp increase in real interest rates made a large number of existing enterprises unprofitable, while others found their profit situation improved. These changes debased the value of accumulated information on enterprises, held by banks and others. In addition the lack of reliable enterprise accounting and the absence of auditing reduced the amount of information on companies outsiders could gather. Uncertainty surrounding ownership and the legal framework has made the situation more difficult still. To illustrate, in cases where independent auditors from the West were called in to evaluate the value of a firm to set a sale price, their estimates often differed by several hundred percent.

Severe information asymmetries and the lack of expertise in the transition economies in evaluating information about firms have meant that securities markets have been slow to develop. Stock markets (with the exception of the Czech and Slovak Republics) are small, consisting of perhaps the largest 20 to 30 firms in the country. Corporate bond markets are almost nonexistent. Further, the institutional and regulatory infrastructure that can provide for the growth of corporate securities markets is currently lacking. Bond rating agencies, investment advisory firms, and securities regulatory bodies are in the early stages of development if they exist at all. This suggests that it will be a long time before corporate securities markets in the transition countries approach the breadth and liquidity of even the Japanese and German markets, let alone those of the Anglo-Saxon countries.

The restructuring requirements of firms in Eastern Europe and Russia are diverse. Many firms will have to undergo radical downsizing and even liquidation. Others must be relieved of their debt burden and restructured. In almost all cases there is an urgent need for a complete reorientation of the management of the business, in many cases requiring the replacement of management. As Phelps *et al.* (1993) point out, the need to replace old management with new is hard to underestimate in the transition countries, in which the old managers have the skills appropriate for success in a command economy but in many cases completely inappropriate for success in a market economy. In other firms, new funds will be necessary to invest in new technologies and new lines of business. Finally and perhaps most importantly, there will almost always be the need for additional expertise in marketing, accounting, and finance.[20] Obviously all these elements are

[20] The Czech economy provides a vivid example of this point. Arguably, the Czechs have

linked. Firms that are well managed will have better access to external finance and will more quickly attain the necessary business skills. In practice, however, marketing and financial skills may often be better imported through foreign trade partners or investors.

In sum, there appears to be a premium in the transition economies on a corporate governance system that can effectively fire unsuitable managers and attract the active investor who contributes to the firm's financial and accounting expertise.

Banking Sector

Nonperforming Loans

The appearance of a large portfolio of nonperforming loans was to be expected once the reform of Eastern European economics was under way.[21] As a result of market-oriented reform and the shocks stemming from the collapse of CMEA export markets, a large number of existing enterprises became unprofitable. Not surprisingly, a substantial debt overhang developed: many firms could cover operating costs but were not able to service their debt. Banks were saddled with many nonperforming loans and often found themselves with negative net worth.

Estimates for nonperforming loans at the end of 1992 are shown in Figure 2.1.[22] It suggests that about a third of loans were nonperforming, although variations between banks are considerable and average figures have to be interpreted with caution. Many banks were weighed down with many nonperforming loans. The undesirable incentive effects resulting from a low net worth of banks are well known: in many cases they lead to opportunistic behavior by bank managers and owners. Banks have an incentive to "gamble for resurrection" by making risky loans or engaging in activities that benefit the management and owners at the expense of depositors or, where these are insured, taxpayers.

The disincentive effects of a large debt overhang on firms are also well

advanced the furthest in addressing problems of governance and access to external finance by enterprises. Yet, some success stories notwithstanding, a large number of firms still languish, suffering from an acute lack of marketing and financial skills.

[21] This and the following paragraphs draw on Dittus (1994a).

[22] Nonperforming loans in banks' portfolios are not easily identified because of inadequate accounting standards, the only partial availability of portfolio reviews, and tax rules that discourage provisioning. Moreover, once many enterprises are illiquid or insolvent, they "contaminate" the economic environment if they are allowed to remain in operation because bankruptcy rules are either weak or not enforced. As they do not pay suppliers, these in turn cannot pay their suppliers, and as payment arrears spread. so does the difficulty of distinguishing good from bad enterprises.

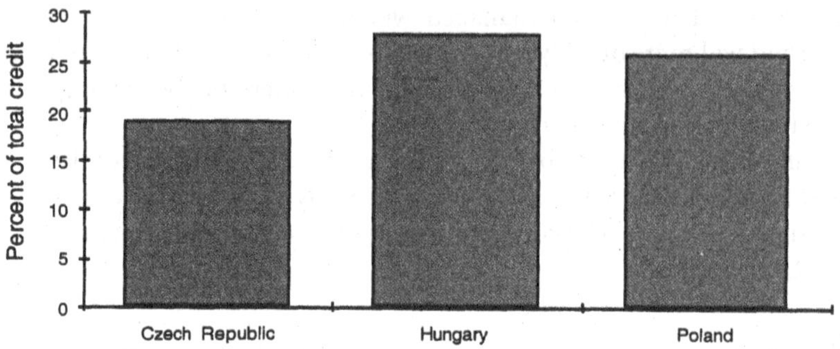

Fig. 2.1 Nonperforming loans, 1992

known. Enterprises are preoccupied by the debt burden instead of focused on survival in the new market environment.[23] The aim of financial restructuring is to eliminate the disincentives stemming from past lending. Bygones should be treated as bygones and should not influence current and future lending decisions.

Countries have addressed problem loans and the resulting weak capital bases in various ways and have sometimes changed their approach over time.[24] Broadly speaking, two approaches can be distinguished. The Central European countries have recapitalized their *existing banks* to such a degree that by mid-1994 the portfolio problem of most banks was under control (Dittus (1994a)). In the Czech Republic in 1991, most of the nonperforming loans were carved out of the commercial banks; this, together with an additional injection of fresh capital, brought the capital-to-asset ratio of the major banks to 4.5 percent. In Hungary, after several rounds of recapitalization, the capital-to-asset ratio of banks was brought to 4 percent by mid-1994. Through the issue of subordinated debt, a further increase to 8 percent was planned by the end of 1994. In Poland in 1993, the nine commercial banks that took over the former monobank's assets in 1989 were recapitalized to more than 8 percent.[25]

In contrast, in Russia the problem of nonperforming loans has been

[23] In addition, a debt overhang makes it very difficult to borrow new funds, even for clearly profitable projects. Another risk is that borrowers may not behave in a prudent manner as long as they expect a bailout in the future (moral hazard).

[24] This chapter does not summarize or discuss the respective merits and drawbacks of the different proposals that have been advanced on how to deal with problem loans; there are numerous suggestions in the literature. Early papers were by Hinds (1990) and Brainard (1991). Convenient summaries do exist, for example, in Schmieding and Buch (1993). Nor does the chapter describe in detail the measures countries have taken to tackle the problem of nonperforming loans; these are analyzed in Dittus (1994b).

[25] However, the situation of some other banks, in particular in the cooperative sector, remains precarious.

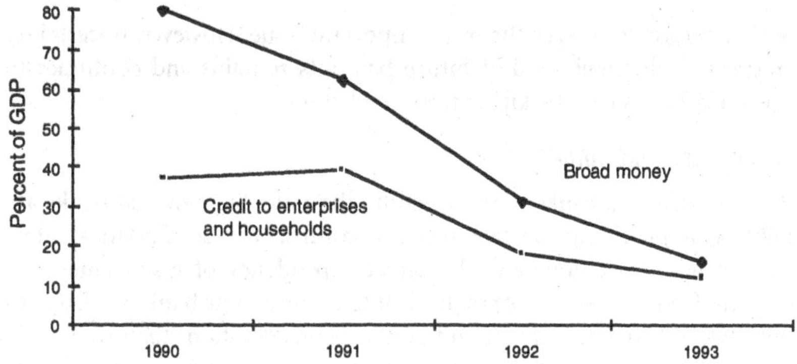

Fig. 2.2 Financial disintermediation in Russia

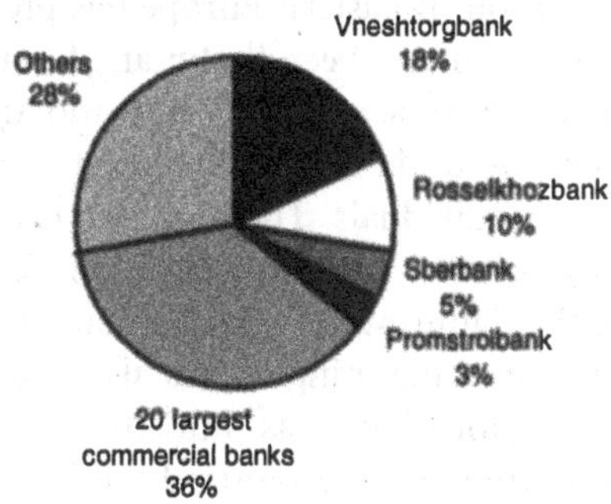

Fig. 2.3 Distribution of bank assets in Russia, 1993

reduced through hyperinflation (Claessens and Pohl (1994)). The broad money supply contracted from 80 percent of gross domestic product (GDP) in 1990 to 16 percent in 1993, and credit to the enterprise and household sector shrunk to a mere 12 percent of GDP (Figure 2.2). Even if problem loans as a share of total loans were large, their size in relation to GDP would be modest. Moreover, the contraction of the overall balance sheet of the banking system was accompanied by a large change in its structure. The share in total assets of the formerly dominating specialized banks has declined to about a third. For example, Sberbank, which continues to hold most of the country's savings, now accounts for only 5 percent of the total.[26] Two-thirds of total banking assets are held by the approximately 2,000 newly created banks, of which about 20 to 30 are relatively large (Figure 2.3). In sum, both in Central Europe and in Russia past problem loans have been provided for

[26] Of the old state banks, only Vneshtorgbank (which holds most of the foreign exchange) and Rosselkhozbank (which channels subsidized credit to agriculture) remain of some importance.

and are, therefore, no longer the most important issue. However, uncertainty with respect to the likelihood of future bail-outs remains and continues to provide many banks with bad incentives (see below).

State Ownership and Influence

Before the reforms all banks were owned by the state. State-owned banks are generally bad at providing effective corporate control because of political interference in lending decisions and the direct dependency of management on government. Even in the absence of direct interference, state banks are likely to give more weight to employment and political considerations than to narrow financial returns. For banks to play an effective role in corporate control, therefore, their links to government need to be severed through privatization.

Generally, bank privatization in Eastern Europe has proceeded at a slower pace than hoped for. One reason has been that many foreign banks consider the retail markets in Eastern Europe still very risky and are content to focus on a few profitable niches – trade finance, credit to joint ventures, and services for high net worth individuals. They can do this easily through the opening of a branch or subsidiary without taking a stake in the large state banks, thereby avoiding the daunting task of overhauling the bureaucracies that have evolved under central planning. It has also taken much longer to restructure the banking sector than was initially anticipated. Although governments in Central Europe have recognized the importance of putting the banking sector on a sound footing, in some cases the difficulties of doing so were at first significantly underestimated. In particular, correctly valuing bank portfolios has proved extremely difficult, and many more banks than initially anticipated appeared to have negative net worth. In other cases, it has proved difficult to implement the necessary measures. The result has been that financial sector reform has lagged, with the exception perhaps of the Czech Republic where balance sheets were cleaned early in the process.

Privatization has proceeded fastest in the Czech Republic. In the first wave of mass privatization in 1993, majority stakes in all state banks (with the exception of the Consolidation Bank) were distributed to the public. In Poland, three state banks have been privatized through direct sale, and more are awaiting privatization. At several others political influence has been reduced by insulating the management from ministries through a supervisory board. The laggard in privatization has been Hungary which privatized the first state bank in 1994. The other main banks are still directly owned by the government. In Russia, the old state banks have not been privatized. However, a large number of regional branches of these banks, often on an oblast level, have established themselves as independent commercial banks (so-called "spin-offs"), contributing to the rapid growth of the total number of banks.

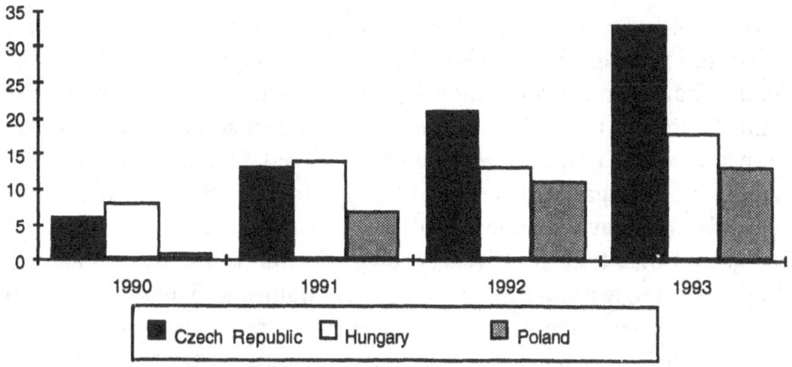

Fig. 2.4 Number of banks with foreign participation

Competition

Competition in the banking sector has increased markedly in most countries. In Russia, market entry has been extremely rapid: the total number of banks has risen within a couple of years from a handful of state banks to about 2,400 banks. Most of these are small, and many are owned by one or a few enterprises, which use them mainly as cheap sources of credit.[27] Nonetheless, about 20 to 30 banks appear to have developed into well-managed commercial banks. Within a few years these banks have come to dominate the commercial banking market, while the role of the old state banks, which are not involved in the distribution of directed credit, has shrunk (see Figure 2.3). Market entry has been rapid in the Czech Republic and also, though to a lesser degree, in Hungary. The number of banks with foreign participation (including joint ventures, subsidiaries, and branches) has increased substantially in these countries (Figure 2.4). The new banks have contributed to heightened competition. In contrast, the issuance of new banking licenses in Poland has been very restrictive.[28]

Despite the entry of new banks, the "old" banks, whether privatized or not, continue to dominate the lending and deposit business. In the Czech Republic and Poland, the old banks hold more than 80 percent of loans and deposits and in Hungary about two-thirds. Only in Russia do new banks dominate the scene, accounting for two-thirds of the banking system's assets.

[27] Many of these enterprise-owned banks appear to be plagued by bad loans. Reportedly, fraudulent and even criminal behavior has been quite common.

[28] After more than 50 new banks, mostly small and undercapitalized, had sprung up in the wake of reforms and presented the authorities with difficulties of supervision, the Polish authorities all but stopped issuing licenses.

Another element of competitive pressure, particularly in the Czech Republic and Hungary,[29] has been the access of enterprises to direct lending by foreign banks and of households to foreign currency instruments. The amounts borrowed by enterprises directly from abroad have risen substantially in the recent past and were likely to exceed $1 billion in the Czech Republic and Hungary by year-end 1994. On the deposit side, foreign currency deposits have become available to households. They have used their newly gained freedom to diversify their portfolios by increasing their holdings of foreign exchange accounts with domestic banks. As a result, banks have to offer interest rates on domestic currency deposits that, after allowing for devaluation expectations, are competitive with those offered on foreign exchange accounts.

Overall, competition in all countries has increased substantially. In Russia, the seeds of a competitive banking market are apparent as a small number of new banks make up a large part of total lending; however, many of the 2,400 banks have a captive market in the enterprises that own them. In the Czech Republic, competitive forces in banking are quite strong, due both to the rapid entry of new banks and the access of many companies to foreign loans. Such access also plays a role in Hungary. In particular, joint ventures between domestic and foreign companies have access to foreign finance, and competition to lend to these enterprises is fierce among the smaller private banks. In contrast, the market for loans to large companies is dominated by a few banks and is much less competitive, partly because many of these companies need restructuring and lending to them at present is not attractive. There is even less competition in Poland. New private banks have not played a major role, and until recently, entry by foreign banks has remained limited. The market remains dominated by the major state banks. Despite heightened competition in these countries, it would appear unwise to rely solely on competitive forces as a disciplinary mechanism to ensure that banks use their control powers over enterprises in a profit-maximizing way.

Supervision

In all countries, a regulatory framework has been put in place that is modeled closely on rules in Western countries. For example, a capital-to-asset ratio of 8 percent or more is now required, and new accounting, loan classification schemes, and mandatory provisioning have been introduced.[30] While bank

[29] Until recently, enterprises in Poland found it difficult to tap foreign sources of capital owing to the arrears on foreign debt. After a settlement was reached with commercial creditors in 1994, direct foreign lending and investment have tended to increase.

[30] An overview of bank regulation and supervision is in Group of Banking Supervisors from Central and Eastern European Countries (1992). See also Dittus (1994, section 3).

regulations have been tightened and to a large degree brought into line with international practice, implementing them has not been easy. This is partly due to the difficulties of establishing reporting systems for banks and partly to the lack of experience of the supervisory agencies. All countries have established such agencies, either in the form of departments of the central bank (Czech Republic, Poland and Russia) or of a separate government body (Hungary). Initially, as was to be expected, the new supervisory bodies experienced difficulties, partly because of the inexperience of staff and the absence of established procedures for off-site and on-site inspection. These difficulties have been recognized, however, and have begun to be addressed in all countries, often with the help of foreign technical assistance.

Despite substantial progress, two fundamental problems remain. The first is that despite some foreign assistance, there is still an acute lack of human capital and developed information systems that the supervisory authorities can draw on to perform their function. The second is the credibility of bank supervision. If banks do not or cannot comply with the new regulations, perhaps because the gap between the initial situation and the newly required standards is too wide, bank supervisors may be faced with a difficult choice between regulatory forbearance and the closure of banks. Given the banks' initial situation, many of the new rules could not be complied with immediately. To some extent the countries in question have attempted to deal with these circumstances through transitional provisions that phase in the new regulations over time. In some cases, however, even transitional provisions cannot be complied with.

Under these circumstances it is difficult to enforce high regulatory standards. Strict application of the law might require the closure of a large segment of the banking industry or of major banks. Mergers with other banks may provide a partial solution but can work only if potential partners have a strong capital base, which in most cases appears unlikely. The threat to close large banks is not credible because of the large costs associated with it. If the regulatory rules are such that banks can comply at reasonable cost to themselves and the economy, then the imposition of such rules can be expected to lead to changed bank behavior and efforts to comply. The government and the legislature are then in a position to induce changed behavior through better regulations and tighter supervision.[31] This is not the case when banks can argue that compliance with the regulations would be prohibitively costly or simply impossible. The government can then be expected to show regulatory forbearance if many banks or a large bank do not comply with the rules, and the banks know this.

[31] In game-theory parlance, they are able to occupy a Stackelberg leadership position.

Table 2.6. Elements of the Legal and Regulatory Environment

Item	Czech Republic	Hungary	Poland
Rules for share ownership	Ownership of shares is restricted to a maximum of 10% of own capital and 25% of capital and reserves. Limit does not apply to debt–equity swaps, where shareholdings have to be reduced to the legal limit within 2 years.	Ownership of shares is restricted to a total of 60% of own capital and that of one enterprise (direct and indirect) to 15% of capital for universal banks and 40% for investment banks. Limits do not apply to separately recorded and handled shareholdings arising from debt–equity swaps for a maximum period of 18 months.	Ownership of purchased shares is restricted to 25% of bank capital but the president of the National Bank of Poland can raise this limit to 50%.
Exposure rules	As proportion of capital: individual customers, max. 25%; entities with special relationships (e.g. more than 10% of shares owned by bank), max. 20%; banks in Czech/Slovak Republic or in OECD area, 80%; 10 largest debtors, max. 230% (to be attained by end-1995, with transitional provisions).	As a proportion of capital: individual customers, max. 25%; total of large loans, max. 600%. Restrictions on insider lending.	As proportion of capital: individual customers, (including guarantees) max. 15% and any one loan agreement max. 10%. President of the National Bank can relax these rules by allowing banks to count long-term loans toward capital and can increase the limit to 50%.
Bank representation on board of directors	No limitations	No limitations	No limitations

In practice, governments have opted for a mixed strategy to overcome the lack of credibility of the new regulatory regimes. To some extent they have showed regulatory leniency and have extended the period for complying with the new regulations. At the same time, they have helped banks meet the standards in question through measures to improve banks' balance sheets. They have also shown a willingness to merge and even close smaller banks.

There is little doubt that supervision has become increasingly tight. But it is also clear that there is still much room for improvement and that bank supervision is not yet effective in insuring that regulations are respected. Currently, the supervisory capacity in all countries under review is not at the level required to provide effective monitoring and supervision for banks.

Legal and Regulatory Framework

In Central Europe and Russia the current legal and regulatory framework does not restrict bank involvement in corporate control to the extent found in the United States. Banks are allowed to hold shares in nonfinancial companies and to exercise control rights. However, prudential regulations apply, which are more restrictive than, for example, those in Germany (Table 2.6). In the Central European countries, ownership of shares is restricted to a certain percentage of a bank's own capital (10 percent in the Czech Republic, 25 percent in Poland and 60 percent in Hungary). In the Czech Republic and Hungary in cases where shares are acquired through a debt for equity swap, these rules are relaxed for a limited time (see Table 2.6). Current regulations are probably not now a binding constraint on bank equity holdings in nonfinancial firms.[32] However, they do clearly limit a large-scale expansion of such activity.

Incentives for Sound Investments

This section examines the investment policies of banks. First we argue that bank behavior has changed substantially since the inception of reform and that the days of large-scale, indiscriminate lending to old customers are over. Second, we analyze how strong the current incentives are for banks to make sound investments. Third, we look at banks' strategy about share ownership. This analysis is largely based on interviews with bank managers in Hungary and Poland, but ancillary information on intentions and behavior in the Czech Republic and Russia is used, too.

In the past, bank lending was entirely passive and basically the accounting reflection of the plan. When a two-tier banking system was established, the new commercial banks maintained close links with their former clients, partly

[32] This is despite the fact that probably the lion's share of bank equity holdings in Poland and Hungary is in related financial companies rather than nonfinancial firms.

Table 2.7. Indicators of Behavioral Change

	1991	1992	1993
	Net lending to enterprises (percentage of GDP)		
Czech Republic	6.4	2.9	5.5
Hungary	1.6	−2.5	1.6
Poland	8.0	1.1	3.3
	Interest rate spread (Q4)		
Czech Republic	5.9	6.7	7.2
Hungary	4.0	11.2	8.8
Poland	14.2	15.5	20.7

out of inertia and partly because of the lock-in effect created by large loans that many enterprises were no longer able to service. Initially, banks often rolled over loans or capitalized interest to avoid revealing their own insolvency.

Since 1991, however, bank behavior appears to have changed. An illustration of these changes is provided in Table 2.7. Net lending by banks to enterprises declined dramatically in 1992 and even turned negative in Hungary. At the same time, the spread between lending and borrowing rates widened. Tighter lending policies and the increased spread are probably best understood as banks' reaction to the visible emergence of a large portfolio of bad loans, combined with a tightening of accounting standards, regulation, and supervision. While other interpretations of developments in 1992 are also possible, the explanation that banks altered their behavior as a reaction to changed circumstances seems to be the most convincing one.[33] The National Bank of Hungary has come to this conclusion (Bod, 1993), as has Hrncír (1994) in the case of the Czech Republic. For Poland, the Organization for Economic Cooperation and Development (OECD) (1995) notes that automatic extension of credit to troubled firms – which dominated in 1990-91 – has clearly come to an end.

It would be premature, however, to conclude from this evidence that the incentive problems of banks have disappeared. A sound capital base is a necessary but not sufficient condition to ensure that banks have incentives to make good investments. The expectations of bank managers are critical. If they believe that poor performance will trigger a government bailout in the future with little or no consequences for themselves, then their incentive to take difficult decisions on existing borrowers and to carefully screen potential borrowers is not strong. If they cannot expect such government support, then the incentive for good performance is much stronger.

[33] The evidence is analyzed in detail in Dittus (1994a, 1994b).

For outsiders it is difficult to understand well the incentives banks are facing. Personal relationships and tacit understandings between bankers and government agencies are difficult to evaluate. Nonetheless, three indicators can be helpful in evaluating the chances of future bailouts. The first one is the degree of government influence and control over banks. The more control the government has, the higher is its responsibility for the banks' policies and the more it is likely to support banks that are experiencing difficulties as a result of decisions that were influenced, directly or indirectly, by the government. A second indication is provided by government behavior in the past. Governments that have bailed out banks without implementing tough measures are likely to be expected by bank managers to do so again in the future. A third indication may be the degree of industry concentration. Often governments have allowed smaller banks to fail but have extended safety nets under the larger ones (too-big-to-fail).

On all three counts the Russian banking system appears to be the least likely to get government support. Government influence in the new banks is almost nonexistent. Banks also have not been bailed out in the past as there was no need to do so. Both debts and assets in the Russian economy were wiped out by hyperinflation in the past few years. The share and influence of the formerly large and powerful state banks have dwindled as a consequence. Finally, the degree of industry concentration is low. The failure of one of the larger private banks would not be contagious and, therefore, the government could afford to let it fail.

In the Czech Republic majority stakes of all banks have been privatized (except for the Consolidation Bank, the "loan hospital"); the remaining share is held by the National Property Fund that provides an insulating layer between banks and the government. State influence is minimal. Government behavior suggests that the likelihood of future bailouts is small. The recapitalization of the banking system was done early and was clearly linked to past loans. Banks that got into difficulties later were either closed or taken over by other institutions, and management paid for their mistakes by losing their positions. Since the inception of reforms, the banking industry has become less concentrated with the largest bank holding less than a third of total assets. Two or three banks may be (implicitly) covered by a too-big-to-fail insurance, but it is clear that existing management would be fired should such intervention be required.

Although three banks have been privatized in Poland, the major banks remain state owned. They are shielded to some degree from government interference through independent supervisory boards and so far the owner of the banks – the Ministry of Finance – has acted to protect bank management from the requests of other ministries. The banks have been recapitalized as part of a tough restructuring program, including major behavioral and organization changes. Finally, industry concentration is low. However, the regional specialization means that the failure of one of the major banks would probably be solved through mergers and takeover (as has already happened).

The threat of no further bailouts is probably least credible in Hungary. The government continues to own the major banks directly and has in the past exerted its influence through management reshuffles. Government support policies likewise suggest a certain likelihood of future bailouts should difficulties arise. The government has injected new capital into the banks in several rounds over the past few years, each one coming shortly after the previous one. Bank management was not changed in any of the rounds. The major banks remain too large for the government to consider letting them fail.

In sum, in all countries the incentive to make good investments has improved. Differences between countries are pronounced, however. Powerful market incentives seem to be at work at the private larger banks in Russia[34] and in the Czech Republic. Incentives for making good investments are still strong in Poland. Market incentives are probably weakest in Hungary.

Attitude toward Share Ownership and Corporate Control

We now discuss how banks are using the leeway they have and to what extent they want, from a purely commercial point of view, to acquire shares and to exercise active shareholder control. Although opinions vary widely depending on the individual bank's history, market position, and ownership structure, three themes come out clearly from our interviews with bank managers and officials.

1. *New private banks in Central Europe and Russia do not want to own companies and to take part in corporate governance through ownership.* Four main reasons are given for this. First, private banks consider that an active shareholder role is extremely costly in human capital and management time, while the payoff is low compared with the core business of relationship banking. Several banks made it quite explicit that, with a staff of a few hundred people and the given skill profile, they could not take an active role in restructuring and supervising a company in more than a few cases. Second, they want to avoid the "moral obligation" to extend financing to a company they own in part, and they perceive a strong conflict of interest

[34] To the degree that supervision is weak and legal enforcement lacking, these market incentives may, of course, in some cases lead to illegal behavior.

between ownership and independent credit appraisal. Most consider that a very strong Chinese wall would be necessary, so strong that the investment banking part might as well be constituted as a separate legal unit. Third, these banks do not see much synergy between the lending business and corporate control through partial ownership. Several were quite explicit, saying that commercial and investment banking require completely different skills, and they would not want to use their loan officers for restructuring activities. Fourth, these dynamic new banks think that their lending and account relationship with customers give them enough information and leverage over companies already. They do not feel that ownership would give them much in addition.

The only exception these banks are willing to make – and this is equally true for the better Russian banks – concerns small share holdings of up to about 5 percent in order to cement a business relationship with a client enterprise, provided the enterprise requests the bank to take such a stake. Indeed, in several cases companies have approached the banks and asked them to take up a small stake. In general, the position of these banks can be summarized as a strong determination to focus on the core business of relationship banking and not to be distracted by other activities.

2. *The large, and partly state-owned, banks see a role for themselves in restructuring and corporate control only to the degree that it is necessary to recover their loans.* Both in Hungary and Poland, the recapitalization programs force banks to take a more active role in the restructuring of insolvent clients. Thus, banks have little choice. However, even these banks do not usually actively seek equity stakes. Their first experiences with workout units has taught them how skill-intensive and demanding an active role is, and the general conclusion seems to be to avoid being dragged too deeply into active shareholder roles.

The behavior of banks under the financial restructuring law in Poland provides perhaps the best illustration of these points. This law obliges recapitalized banks to come to agreements with their defaulting debtors. They have three options: they can swap debt for equity, write down and reschedule loans in a Chapter 11-type procedure, which does not include the courts, or sell nonperforming loans at a discount on the secondary market. Banks resorted to debt-for-equity swaps in about 30 percent of all cases (see Baer and Gray in this volume). For example, the Polish Development Bank engaged in two swaps and has equity investments in about 15 other enterprises. Its workout department, which handles equity investments, has a staff of eight and often draws on foreign consultants to leverage its resources. Despite its limited involvement and staff, this bank is one of the most active large banks in equity investment and restructuring activity. This only serves to highlight the general reluctance of banks to get actively engaged in corporate control. Clearly, the financial restructuring law has forced many banks to acquire expertise in this area and to build up expert staff. The law may thus have contributed to overcoming the reluctance of commercial banks to shoulder the set-up costs for equity ownership and to exercise corresponding control rights.

Nonetheless, the recently introduced strategy of the Polish Development Bank (PDB) toward equity investments clearly indicates that the reluctance to enter this line of business remains high. PDB intends to limit equity holdings to less than 20 percent; it prefers investments where a strong partner takes care of corporate control, because it believes that its capacity to engage in corporate governance and restructuring is limited to only three or four firms;[35] it wants to be able to exit the investment after three years (a requirement that highlights the importance of liquid securities markets); and, finally, it will exit investments in any case after five years. Management feels that equity ownership and corporate control on a larger scale are distinct from commercial banking and best pursued by separate units. Indeed, PDB is setting up separate investment funds and has established a joint venture with Kleinwort Benson to manage one of the soon-to-be established national investment funds. It is also worth noting that equity ownership of Polish banks is already close to the legal limit, although most of this is in the form of equity stakes in other financial institutions.

There appear to be two major exceptions to the general rule of banks' reluctance to own equity. First, in some cases the bank realizes that enterprise management is consciously driving down the value of the firm to pick up the pieces at low prices. Then banks are sometimes prepared to buy stakes in these companies to replace management. Second, in some enterprises banks perceive a clear underexploited upside potential. In this case several of the larger banks are prepared to buy minority stakes of up to 20 percent, *provided there is a good and active shareholder* (e.g. a foreign investor) who can provide effective governance.

3. *Debt-for-equity swaps are not popular with banks.* In Poland, as mentioned above, swaps have occurred in only about 30 percent of all cases. In Hungary, debt–equity swaps appear even less popular. Debt-for-equity swaps are often avoided because of the implied loss of collateral. Banks are reluctant to "swap bad debt for bad equity." This may be particularly the case in Poland where bank loans – whether secured or not – are senior to all other types of loans. In addition, in the case of unlisted companies, Polish prudential regulations require that a zero value is assigned to such stakes in the balance sheet, forcing banks to fully provision against the swapped loan.

[35] However, their capacity to search for attractive investment opportunities is much higher.

This section has analyzed the existing conditions in Central Europe and Russia. A number of these conditions are important to the issue of the most appropriate form of corporate governance. In brief, they are:

1. very illiquid corporate securities markets, with little prospect that they will develop quickly;
2. diverse restructuring requirements of enterprises, with an emphasis on the need for accounting, marketing, and financial expertise;
3. continued state influence in some countries over large parts of the system;
4. relatively weak competitive forces in banking;
5. the need for improved supervision of the banking system;
6. continued expectations in some countries among bank managers that the government will subsidize losses from bad investments;
7. lack of bank expertise in the restructuring of firms (but in some countries like Poland, banks have been forced to attain such expertise).

Should Banks Be in Corporate Governance?

The impracticality of relying on liquid securities markets and takeovers as a means of governance in Eastern Europe and Russia leaves a primary role to large shareholder monitoring. The combination of severe information asymmetries between insiders and outsiders and a lack of expertise in evaluating any information that is publicly available means that securities markets in Eastern Europe and Russia are likely to remain undeveloped for quite some time. This essentially rules out any role for the U.S. model of corporate governance, which relies to a substantial extent on anonymous securities markets and the threat of takeover as a method of management discipline – Tirole (1991) and Phelps *et al.* (1993) reach a similar conclusion; however, note that Mizsei (1994a) argues the opposite point. Indeed, there may be some danger in trying to create more liquid securities markets while relying primarily on an active shareholder to monitor firms. First, a higher degree of liquidity may lessen the incentives of investors to monitor their investments rather than sell them. Second, as the example of Japan illustrates, if banks are chosen to play a primary role as active investors in firms, their ability to do so may be hampered by not being able to control firms' access to external finance. The question we address here is whether banks are the appropriate institutions for this role.

The Case against Participation

Our snapshot of existing conditions in Eastern Europe shows that banks suffer from a severe lack of expertise and human capital in evaluating and monitoring firms. At first glance, this would appear to provide a clear case against a large bank role in restructuring and corporate governance. But this lack of expertise characterizes not just banks, but all domestic institutions in Eastern Europe and Russia. Thus, any arguments against banks based *solely* on their limited capacity are not particularly strong.

However, there are reasons to suspect that state-owned banks might have less expertise compared with other possible domestic candidates for the role of active investor. Many of the current management and staff at the banks were hired and trained under central planning. The emphasis was on bookkeeping, not on commercial banking and certainly not on the skills required to manage a portfolio of large equity stakes in firms. Thus, management and staff are unlikely to be able to quickly develop the entrepreneurial and business skills necessary to play a major role in corporate governance. Indeed, some observers have gone so far as to talk about the "negative human capital" embodied in the state-owned banks, suggesting that their breakup or scaling down would be beneficial. In countries like Poland and Hungary where the state banks still comprise the vast majority of the banking sector, this may be a much more powerful argument against banks' playing a primary role in corporate control than it is in Russia where private banks are far more predominant.

In addition, banks have other functions that are just as important, if not more important, than corporate control. In the transition economies, banks provide the only payment services available; they are almost the only providers of financial instruments; and they are the predominant sources of external finance for enterprises. The financial services they provide may be poor, but currently, they are the only game in town. Ensuring continued provision of these services and overall confidence in the financial system is clearly essential. Banks are also at the interface between the central bank and the economy through their large presence in the money markets. Given the limited experience of bank management, it will almost certainly be stretching their capacity to conduct normal commercial banking activities if the ownership and control of firms are an additional responsibility for them. In other words, banks may simply not have the capacity to play an important role in the ownership and control of firms given their limited ability even to conduct more traditional commercial banking operations.[36]

Even if banks had the managerial capacity to be important players in the governance of firms, their incentives may be such that they fall prey to conflicts of interest in conducting their activities. Bank credit to enterprises in Central Europe (though not in Russia) is highly concentrated among a few mostly state-owned banks that have yet to be fully weaned off bailouts from

[36] See Scott (1992) for an argument along these lines.

the state and that are inadequately supervised. Such a situation would appear to be very susceptible to banks' abusing or misusing any powers of ownership and control over firms that they might have.

First, given that most large banks are still state owned, they could be put under pressure by the government to subsidize loans to firms whose bankruptcy would create political problems. This, of course, is true whether or not the banks own and control firms. However, the situation is worsened if banks do have this power, since large stakes held by banks might preclude the ownership by a nonpoliticized agent that may have genuine interests to maximize the value of the firm.

Second, the relationship between banks and the government is further complicated by the fact that in some countries the expectation persists that the government will bail out banks that get into trouble by making unsound loans. Giving banks an ownership role in enterprises under conditions in which bank management is not held responsible for their investment decisions would mean that firms are unlikely to be monitored efficiently.

Third, the current state of supervisory capacity in the transition countries means that even without the perverse incentives introduced by state ownership and expectations of future bailouts, there is little safeguard against banks making unwise or imprudent loans. Giving banks the opportunity to make equity investments, which by their very nature are more risky than debt investments, could be a recipe for disaster when bank supervision is weak.

Finally, the concentrated nature of the banking system means that the discipline imposed by market competition is weak in some market segments, notably in that of large loans to nonprime borrowers. In addition, the opportunities for banks to extract rents from firms in which they have large equity stakes are enhanced by a lack of competition.

In sum, even if banks had the ability to govern without impeding their ability to conduct traditional commercial banking activities, several arguments suggest that they might not use their control powers constructively. State ownership, the persistence of expectations of future bailouts, weak bank supervision, and a lack of competition, all mean that banks' incentives to use corporate control powers to maximize firm value are not strong. At worst, the incentives created by these conditions might lead not only to a failure to restructure firms properly, but to the re-emergence of bad asset problems in the future.

The description of the restructuring needs of Eastern Europe and Russia suggests that banks may not be the most suitable institutions to play the primary role of active investor in the firm. First, as part of their inherited relationships with the large industrial firms, the banks may have established links with current management or other stakeholders that make it harder for them to engage in radical downsizing and restructuring than other active investors with no such links.[37] Second, banks are unlikely to be able to supply the expertise in financial management, accounting, marketing, and inventory control that enterprises desperately need and that a successful active investor would be expected to provide. Once again, arguments against banks versus any other domestic active investor based solely on the ability to supply such expertise are not strong, since there is no competing domestic candidate for active investor that has these skills in any abundance;[38] what it does point to is the desirability (as far as is politically possible) of a large element in corporate governance of capital like foreign venture capital.

The Case for Participation

One argument for giving the current state banks a role in corporate governance stems from two political realities. The first is that it may not be politically feasible to supplant the state banks with completely new institutions, as proposed by a number of Western economists.[39] Given that these institutions will continue to exist and given that they have a large presence in the banking and financial sectors of many transition countries (Russia excepted), they are likely to play some role in the corporate control of large firms. The second reality is that the state banks in some transition countries have already been playing an important role for a number of years in the restructuring of large firms. Primarily motivated by their need to do something about the bad loans on their books, some state banks have swapped debt for equity in a few of these firms and have made attempts at restructuring them.[40] This has occurred to differing degrees in different countries and probably not to the extent anticipated a few years ago, *but nevertheless, it has occurred and with some degree of success.* Indeed, some state banks (for example, PDB in Poland) have arguably the greatest expertise in the country in the restructuring of large enterprises.

[37] Shleifer and Summers (1988) point out that long-term relationships between financiers, managers, and other stakeholders in the Western firm may be of considerable valuable. In the context of a firm in one of the transition economies, these long-term relationships may be a carryover from the days of central bank management of the central plan and thus be of considerable negative value to the extent that they lead bankers to continue lending money to their friends in the state firms regardless of the economic prospects of the firm.

[38] Although, as argued earlier, it may well be the case that the managers of the state banks have substantially less such expertise than other domestic candidates.

[39] See Phelps *et al.* (1993). Of course, in Russia this has been largely achieved as an unintended side effect of the hyperinflation.

[40] The relatively small number of bankruptcies in these countries (Hungary excepted) is not a good indicator of banks' involvement in corporate restructuring. Bankruptcy proceedings in all countries are very slow. Banks have attempted to deal with defaults by threatening to shut down firms' access to trade finance to force restructuring. And at times they have taken equity stakes in companies in default to them to exert direct influence on management.

Thus, any policy on the development of corporate control should recognize the state banks' current and likely continued role in this area.

Related to the above point is the question of who could be an active investor if it is not to be the state banks? Private and foreign banks – which might appear to be the better agents to accomplish ownership and governance tasks because they are not burdened by bad debts or do not have any state involvement – do not appear to be doing so but are content with sticking to basic corporate lending to the best credits. There are a limited number of other candidates that could be viable and important players in a governance role in all but the long term. For example, pension funds or insurance companies will not be large enough to be important players in the financial markets or in corporate governance for some time to come. The only serious alternative to banks, in the medium term at least, appear to be investment funds. A detailed analysis of investment funds in the Czech Republic can be found in Coffee (volume 2 of this book), Shafik (1994), and Claessens (1994). How effective these bank-managed funds will be from a corporate governance perspective remains to be seen.[41]

While banks in the Czech Republic appear to have chosen not to become too involved in corporate governance and restructuring, at least through the Investment Privatization Fund (IPF), it is noteworthy that other private investment companies have chosen the corporate governance road. And judging from first, preliminary evidence, it seems is if concentrated ownership were indeed perceived by the market to be a sign of better prospects: large, strategic ownership by domestic or foreign investors has had a strongly positive influence on share prices (Claessens, 1994). Investment funds based

[41] Two features stand out. First, the largest bank-affiliated funds created broad portfolios, comprising between 200 and 500 companies. Hence, they deliberately refrained from gaining effective control in a smaller number of companies. This is in marked contrast to some of the larger and successful private investment funds and the ones established by foreign banks, which deliberately went for controlling stakes in companies, sometimes in violation of the (apparently not too strongly enforced) rules. Why did domestic banks forgo this opportunity? A number of explanations can be advanced. Perhaps the most convincing is that bank-affiliated funds try to obtain small stakes in a large number of firms in the hopes of attracting banking business through those relationships. Second, banks apparently do not enforce strict fire-walls between themselves and their investment funds. In some cases bank management or employees have been used to fill the supervisory board positions the banks' IPFs are entitled to. In others there is a regular exchange of information between the bank and its IPF. The close cooperation between banks and their IPFs has not, however, led to improved corporate governance, as some had hoped. On the contrary, providing effective corporate governance and being actively involved in restructuring is seen by banks as high-cost activities with little return – given their generally low stakes in the companies. Instead, they are using their information to actively trade securities. It would appear that bank involvement in company ownership has done more to promote the trading of securities than to improve corporate governance directly.

on the Czech model may, therefore, be a viable alternative to banks as primary agents of corporate governance.

Banks may be best placed to mitigate the severe information problems between managers and any potential owners. This still seems to apply in Central Europe even though much of the banks' interaction with borrowers was under a completely different regime. This comparative advantage in gathering information about enterprises stems from their ongoing relationship with the firm as a creditor and payment settler. To the degree that enterprises require new loans or the rollover of existing ones, banks can and do request privileged access to internal information about the firm. They are also, in the case of large customers, likely to know the enterprise managers and their capacities fairly well. Banks' monitoring capabilities are strengthened by the fact that they require enterprises to hold their deposit accounts with the main lending bank. In Russia, regulations remain effective that forbid enterprises to open more than one current account, giving banks a full view of the cash flow of their customers.

Are Banks Ready to Play a Major Role?

We have argued that for some time to come effective corporate governance in Central Europe and Russia will need to come from large, active shareholders. Even if securities markets developed rather rapidly, it would take years before a reliance on them and the takeovers associated with them as a means of governance could be envisaged. The question of whether banks, in their present condition, are the right institutions to play this role has been the focus of this chapter. The strongest argument for banks appears to be the lack of obvious alternatives and the (limited) experience they have gained over the last few years. These arguments, however, appear to be outweighed by the potential disadvantages. The banking system has other tasks to fulfill that are clearly more along the lines of traditional commercial banking and arguably more important than that of the governance of firms. At present, many banks are struggling to master their more traditional businesses. In addition, the environment for banks needs to be substantially improved before a larger role in governance becomes a recommended option. Incentive problems have not been resolved and supervision is still weak.

Some comparisons with the current situation in the transition countries and the situation in Japan in the immediate post-World War II period may be instructive; as pointed out by some observers advocating the adoption of Japan-like bank–firm ties for the transition countries, there are many similarities between the two situations (see Hoshi, Kashyap, and Loveman (1994)). In 1946, Japan was faced with a transition from extreme centralization and government intervention in the economy to a market economy.

Postwar Japan had a severely limited productive capacity, a very high rate of inflation, and extremely close ties between large banks and government administrators. The banking system was highly concentrated and burdened with an immense amount of bad debts as a result of previous government directed and unmonitored lending. Despite these problems, the Japanese were able to install a system of corporate governance of enterprises led by the banks that coincided with a rapid recovery from the immediate postwar chaos and 40 years of subsequent rapid economic growth.

The conditions in Japan in 1946 mirror those currently in the transition countries. However, there are two crucial differences. The first is that, although market-based lending had been suspended in Japan for a number of years before and during the war, there was an inherited institutional and human capital base in the banking system embodying knowledge of how to evaluate investments and the soundness of loans. In contrast, market-based lending and the evaluation of investment proposals in the transition countries have been suspended for over 40 years, and there currently is *no* inherited expertise whatsoever in these areas in their banking systems.

Perhaps more important, however, is the fact that the Japanese adopted a conscious policy of restructuring and placing the banking system on a sound financial footing *before* the restructuring of nonfinancial firms. Indeed, banks cleaned up their balance sheets relatively quickly in Japan, and by early 1948 they could be considered to be relatively sound and largely free of perverse incentives (see Hoshi (1994)). They had never, of course, been under the ownership of the state. The banks were well placed to take an active role in the restructuring of the industrial sector without succumbing to the dangers entailed in doing so while still burdened by substantial bad debts or undue state influence. In contrast, although the importance of putting the financial sector on a sound footing was recognized early in Central Europe, it has taken a long time to make substantial progress in this area. Although much has been achieved in the last few years, much remains to be done.

Indeed, perhaps a more relevant comparison to make is with the sad experiences in a number of countries with emerging financial markets – such as Argentina, Chile, Venezuela, and Mexico.[42] In these countries the existence of close bank-enterprise relationships (often including the holding of equity stakes in enterprises by banks) led to well-publicized asset problems

[42] We refer here to the banking system problems in Chile and Argentina in the early 1980s and in Venezuela in 1994. The problems in Mexico over the last year have been much less extensive than in the previously mentioned countries, being largely confined to one or two banks that have made large insider loans to affiliated companies.

and even bank failures.[43] A major reason for these problems was a legal and supervisory structure in these countries that was unable to enforce "good" behavior on the banking system. This may be the more relevant comparison because it is quite clear that the legal and supervisory structure in the transition countries is much closer to that in countries like Argentina and Chile than it is to the current situation in Japan or Germany, or arguably, even to the situation in Japan in 1946.

Implications for Regulation

Our analysis suggests that for now banks should not be allowed to take large equity stakes and play a primary role in nonfinancial companies. Banks are still subject to perverse incentives arising from weak competition and supervision and the weak credibility of government pledges that there will be no further bank bailouts. In addition, most banks appear not to have the managerial capacity or the requisite business skills to take on the governance role that many firms in the transition countries require. Once banks are free from their current problems, a system of corporate governance based primarily on banks might be appropriate in the medium term, particularly since well-developed and liquid capital markets are unlikely to play a major governance role in these countries for the foreseeable future. However, if banks are to play such a role, they would benefit from opportunities to experiment with limited equity participations and governance roles now, to build up the experience necessary to play a more important role in the future.

While banks should not become large shareholders in firms, there is a case for adopting a more lenient stance toward their equity participation and governance role in firms that have defaulted on loans to them. Not only would banks be allowed to gain some experience in owning firms, but also they already know more about those firms than other potential primary shareholders. Such opportunities should be strictly controlled as to how long the bank is allowed to own equity obtained through a swap of debt and, perhaps, taking into account the strength of the bank itself.

The implications for regulation are: first that banks should be restricted in the amount of equity they own. The current prudential limits in Central European countries seem appropriate. But second, banks should be given limited opportunities to swap bad debt into equity and become active in governance. The current waiver period in the Czech Republic and Hungary of 18 to 24 months for equity acquired through swaps of debt appears to

[43] In some cases, the nature of the bank–enterprise relationship was enterprises taking large equity stakes in banks, which in turn made large loans to the enterprise or enterprise affiliates.

accord well with this principle. In addition, there may be a case for enabling the authorities to bar extremely weak banks from making use of this waiver.

Conclusions

Our review of corporate governance arrangements in the West suggests that, for a system based on bank ownership and control of firms to be successful, the banking system must be free of perverse incentives and state interference and subject to adequate supervision by the banking authorities and competition from market forces. Admirable progress over the past few years notwithstanding, these conditions do not currently exist in the countries of Central Europe and Russia. Therefore, a corporate governance system based on bank ownership is not appropriate. That is not to say that such a system would not eventually be appropriate for these countries, but before that can happen more effort is needed to create a competitive, private, and well-supervised banking system. This effort is needed in any case, regardless of any possible participation of banks in corporate governance.

The changes in the banking system that are necessary before any large-scale bank involvement in the ownership and governance of firms are simple to enunciate but much less easy to implement. First, existing relationships between the state and banks must be severed. Privatization is the strongest guarantee that bank investment decisions will not be subject to state influence. However, bank privatization in most countries has been slow, because in part of the difficulties of fully understanding the poor condition of the financial sector. It also reflects the many institutional and political obstacles to bank reform. In addition, the initial decision in some countries to focus first on the "real economy" may have played a role. With the benefit of hindsight, that decision now appears somewhat unfortunate, though understandable in the circumstances of the early reform years.

Another important step is the dispelling of the belief – that still exists in some countries – that poor lending and investments will eventually be underwritten by the government with little consequences for managers. Here, some countries have clearly made more progress than others. Political factors have weighed heavily in some cases. But this issue must be resolved before banks can be entrusted to make investment decisions or even rational traditional loans.

Strong competition in the banking system is another necessary condition. The foundation of new private banks and the entry of foreign banks should, therefore, be encouraged. Some countries, like Poland, have been taking the opposite tack in refusing to issue new licenses.

Effective bank supervision is essential for the soundness of the banking system in general and for the success of any corporate governance system based on bank ownership and control in particular. An effective prudential and regulatory framework requires a substantial investment in setting up institutions, accounting systems, and information networks; hiring and training qualified personnel; and ensuring the system is immune from political intervention. Given the size of this task, this will inevitably be a long process. However, if the establishment of a privatized and competitive banking system is viewed as critical to the development of a successful financial system and corporate governance system, then these countries must give priority to establishing a sound prudential and regulatory framework. Foreign assistance will be crucial to the development of such a system.

While a governance system based on bank ownership and control of firms is not yet feasible, banks should be allowed to gradually gain experience through limited equity ownership, in particular by swaps of bad debt for equity. The current regulations seem conducive to such experimentation, while being sufficiently tight to prevent the emergence of large-scale conflicts of interest.

References

Beiter, J. 1991. "The Japanese Market for Corporate Control." Saloman Center Occasional Paper no. 10. New York University.

Bod, Peter. 1993. "Monetary Policy and Exchange Rate Policy in Hungary during the Years of Transition." Paper prepared for the Conference on Monetary and Exchange Rate Policies in Small, Open Economies, April, Vienna.

Borio, Claudio. 1990. "Leverage and Financing of Non-Financial Companies: An International Perspective." Bank for International Settlements Economic Paper No.27.

Brainard, L.J. 1991. "Strategies for Economic Transformation in Central and Eastern Europe: Role of Financial Market Reform." In *Transformation of Planned Economies: Property Rights Reform and Macroeconomic Stability*, edited by H. Blommestein and M. Marrese. pp. 95–108. Paris: OECD.

Cable, J. 1985. "Capital Market Information and Industrial Performance: The Role of West German Banks." *Economic Journal* 95.

Claessens, Stijn. 1994. "Corporate Governance and Equity Prices: Evidence from The Czech and Slovak Republics." World Bank (October). Mimeographed.

Claessens, Stijn, and Gerhard Pohl. 1994. "Banks, Capital Markets, and Corporate Governance." World Bank Policy Research Working Paper No. 1326.

Clyde, P. 1989. The Institutional Investor and the Theory of the Firm, unpublished manuscript, UCLA, Los Angeles, Calif.

Coffee, John S., Jr. 1991. "Liquidity versus Control: The Institutional Investor as Corporate Monitor." *Columbia Law Review* 91, no. 6: 1277–1368.

Corbett, J., and C. Mayer. 1991. "Financial Reform in Eastern Europe: Progress with the Wrong Model." *Oxford Review of Economic Policy* 4: 57–75.

Diamond, Douglas W. 1984. "Financial Intermediation and Delegated Monitoring." *Review of Economic Studies* 51: 393–414.

Dittus, Peter. 1994a. "Bank Reform and Behaviour in Central Europe." *Journal of Comparative Economics* 19: 335–61.

—— 1994b. "Corporate Governance in Central Europe: The Role of Banks." Bank for International Settlements Economic Paper No.42.

Edwards, Jeremy, and Klaus Fischer. 1994. *Banks, Finance and Investment in Germany.* Cambridge: Cambridge University Press.

Elston, J.A. 1993. Firm Ownership Structure and Investment: Theory and Evidence from German Panel Data, unpublished manuscript.

Fenn, G., N. Liang, and S. D. Prowse. 1995. "The Economics of the Private Equity Market." Board of Governors of the Federal Reserve System Staff Study, forthcoming.

Franks, J., and C. Mayer. 1992. Corporate Control: A Synthesis of the International Evidence, London Business School, London, England, unpublished working paper.

—— 1993. "German Capital Markets, Corporate Control and the Obstacles to Hostile Takeovers: Lessons from 3 Case Studies." London Business School Working Paper.

Gessler Commission. 1979. "Grundsatzfragen der Kreditwirtschaft." *Shcriftenreihe des Bundesministeriums der Finanzen* 28.

Gilson, Stuart C. 1990. "Bankruptcy, Boards, Banks and Blockholders: Evidence on Changes in Corporate Ownership and Control When Firms Default." *Journal of Financial Economics* 27, no. 1: 355–88.

Group of Banking Supervisors from Central and Eastern European Countries. 1992. "Report on Banking Supervision in Central and Eastern European Countries." Basle.

Hinds, M. 1990. "Issues in the Introduction of Market Forces in Eastern European Socialist Economies." World Bank, Washington, D.C. Mimeographed.

Hoshi, Takeo. 1994. "Evolution of the Main Bank System in Japan." Center for Japanese Economic Studies Working Paper 93–4, Macquarie University, Sydney.

Hoshi, Takeo, Anil Kashyap, and G. Loveman. 1994. "Lessons from the Japanese Main Bank System for Financial System Reform in Poland." Economic Development Institute Working Paper 94–18.

Hoshi, Takeo, Anil Kashyap, and David Scharfstein. 1990a. "Bank Monitoring and Investment: Evidence from the Changing Structure of Japanese Corporate Banking Relationships." In *Asymmetric Information, Corporate Finance, and Investment,* edited by R. Glenn Hubbard. Chicago: Chicago University Press.

——. 1990b. "The Role of Banks in Reducing the Costs of Financial Distress in Japan." *Journal of Financial Economics* 27, no. 1: 67–88.

——1993. The Choice between Public and Private Debt: An Analysis of Post-Deregulation Corporate Financing in Japan, University of Chicago, unpublished manuscript.

Hrncír, M. 1994. "Reform of the Banking Sector in The Czech Republic." In *The Development and Reform of Financial Systems in Central and Eastern Europe,* edited by J.P. Bonin and Istvan P. Szekely. Brookfield, Vermont, U.S.: E. Elgar.

Kaplan, Steven N. 1993. "Top Executive Rewards and Firm Performance. A Comparison of Japan and The U.S." University of Chicago Working Paper (1994. *Journal of Political Economy* 102: 510–46).

Kester, W. Carl. 1991. *Japanese Takeovers: The Global Quest for Corporate Control.* Boston, Mass.: Harvard Business School Press.

Lichtenburg, F., and G. Pushner. 1993. "Ownership Structure and Corporate Performance in Japan." National Bureau of Economic Research Working Paper no. 4092.

Mizsei, K. 1994. "Financial Intermediaries and Corporate Governance: Prospects and Pitfalls." Institute for East–West Studies, New York. Mimeographed.

Monopolkommission. 1978. "Hauptgutachen II: Fortschreitende Konzentration bei Grossunternehmen."

Morck, Randall, Andrei Shleifer, and Robert Vishny. 1989. "Alternative Mechanisms of Corporate Control." *American Economic Review* 79: 842–52.

Organization for Economic Cooperation and Development (OECD). 1995. "Country Survey of Poland." Paris.

Pfeiffer, H. 1989. "BASF und die Deutsche Bank – Eine Fallstudie zum Bankeneinfluss in der Wirtschaft." *WSI-Mitteilungen* 42: 9–16.

Phelps, E.S., Roman Frydman, Andrzej Rapaczynski, and Andrei Shleifer. 1993. "Needed Mechanisms of Corporate Governance and Finance in Eastern Europe." World Bank Discussion Paper No. 1.

Prowse, Stephen D. 1990. "Institutional Investment Patterns and Corporate Financial Behavior in The United States and Japan." *Journal of Financial Economics* 27, no.1: 43–66.

——— 1992. "The Structure of Corporate Ownership in Japan." *Journal of Finance* 47, no. 3: 1121–40.

——— 1993. The Structure of Corporate Ownership in Germany, Federal Reserve Bank of Dallas, unpublished working paper.

——— 1994. "Corporate Governance in an International Perspective: A Survey of Corporate Control Mechanisms among Large Firms in The United States, United Kingdom, Japan and Germany." Bank for International Settlements Economic Paper 41, Basle (July).

Purrucker, M. 1983. *Bank in der Kartellrechtlichen Fusionskontrolle.* Berlin.

Sahlman, W. 1990. "The Structure and Governance of Venture Capital Organizations." *Journal of Financial Economics* 27: 473–524.

Sarcinelli, M. 1992. "Eastern Europe and the Financial Sector: Where Are They Going?" *Banco Nacionale del Lavoro Quarterly Review* 183: 462–92.

Saunders, A. 1994. "The Separation of Banking and Commerce." *Journal of Banking and Finance.*

Saunders, A., and I. Walter. 1994. *Universal Banking in The United States: What Could We Gain? What Could We Lose?* New York: Oxford University Press.

Scharfstein, David. 1992. "Japanese Corporate Finance and Governance: Implications for the Privatisation of Eastern European Enterprises." Massachusetts Institute of Technology. Mimeographed.

Schmieding, H., and C. Buch. 1993. "Better Banks for Eastern Europe." Kieler Diskussionsbeitrage No. 192.

Scott, D. 1992. "Revising Financial Sector Policy in Transitional Socialist Economies: Will Universal Banks Prove Viable?" World Bank Policy Research Working Paper No. 1034.

Shafik, Nemat. 1994. "Marking a Market: Mass Privatization in the Czech and Slovak Republics." World Bank Policy Research Working Paper No. 1231.

Sheard, Paul. 1989. "The Main Bank System and Corporate Monitoring and Control in Japan." *Journal of Economic Behavior and Organization* 11: 399–422.

Shleifer, Andrei, and L. Summers. 1988. "Breach of Trust in Hostile Takeovers." In *Corporate Takeovers: Causes and Consequences,* edited by A.J. Auerbach. Chicago, Ill.: University of Chicago Press.

Stiglitz, Joseph E. 1985. "Credit Markets and the Control of Capital." *Journal of Money, Credit and Banking* 17, no. 2: 133–52.

Tirole, J. 1991. "Privatisation in Eastern Europe: Incentives and the Economics of Transition." National Bureau of Economic Research Macroeconomics Annual, pp. 221–59.

Van Wijnbergen, Sweder. 1992. "On the Role of Banks in Enterprise Reform: The Polish Example." Center for Economic Policy Research (CEPR) Discussion Paper 898.

3

DEBT AS A CONTROL DEVICE IN TRANSITIONAL ECONOMIES

The Experiences of Hungary and Poland

HERBERT L. BAER and CHERYL W. GRAY

Thanks are extended to Bernard Black, John Bonin, Gerard Caprio, Constantijn Claessens, Millard Long, Roman Frydman, Olivier Godron, Stephen Prowse, Andrei Rapaczynski, Roberto Rocha, and Ilham Zurayk, who offered helpful comments on earlier drafts. The findings, interpretations, and conclusions expressed in this chapter are entirely those of the authors and should not be attributed in any manner to the World Bank, to its affiliated organizations, or to members of its Board of Executive Directors or the countries they represent.

Introduction

The most fundamental economic challenge in the transition from socialism to capitalism is creating incentive structures and institutions that promote enterprise change and restructuring. Creating these incentives is the motivation for most of the reforms that are discussed in transition debates about privatization, demonopolization, trade reform, or financial sector reform. All these reforms revolve around one central theme: imposing market-based constraints on enterprise managers through competition or direct corporate governance. Most research on corporate governance and privatization has focused on the role of owners, either on the problems inherent in the separation of ownership and management (most Western literature) or on the need for true owners who represent the interests of capital (most literature on transition economies). Yet debt is also an important control device, as is increasingly recognized in Western corporate finance literature.

This chapter explores the role of debt as a control device in transition economies. It focuses on Hungary and Poland, two of the countries that are farthest along in implementing reform. The chapter first asks how creditors exert control over firms in advanced market economies and how such control interacts with that exerted by equity holders. It then asks whether creditors in Central European countries play similar roles, what roles they should play, and what could give them the capacity and incentives to play these roles. Although this chapter concentrates on Hungary and Poland, the legacy and the resulting shortcomings are similar in many transition economies. Yet Hungary and Poland illustrate only two of many approaches. As discussed in the concluding section of this chapter, other transitional economies – such as Russia, Estonia, and the Czech Republic – provide different approaches that should be explored in future comparative work.

A Framework for Analysis

Debt as a Monitor in Market Economies

Investments in capitalist firms can take two forms: equity and debt. From the perspective of the investor, an important difference between these two is risk. Equity theoretically shares fully in both the successes and the failures of the firm, while debt receives a fixed return and thus shares much less if at all in the upside or the downside.[1] These roles for equity and debt hold, however, only in situations with full information and no agency costs; that is, where both owners and creditors know the actual financial condition of the firm and where managers work fully in the interests of these financiers. Corporate governance – monitoring and control – is necessary to gain access to available information, make informed investment decisions, and motivate agents to act in the interests of principals. While holders of both equity and debt must monitor to protect their financial investments, the goals, incentives, and capacities that underlie such monitoring differ. Furthermore, the tools at hand to effect monitoring vary, as only equity involves ownership, that is, the legal right to make management changes. Debt is thus an important, albeit different, control instrument from equity.

As with equity holders,[2] creditors can monitor either actively or passively

[1] The main risk to debt in stable market economies – the risk of default (uncompensated by collateral) – can be compensated through higher interest margins, which translate into some limited sharing of both downside and upside risks. A second risk to debt, particularly in less stable transition economies, is unanticipated inflation. In environments with high or erratic inflation, equity may be less risky than debt.

[2] Much of the Western corporate governance literature has contrasted U.S. and German or U.S. and Japanese modes of governance by equity holders. The U.S. system is a model of

(Holmström 1992; Holmström and Tirole 1993, as cited in Berglöf 1994). The active mode includes hands-on evaluation of a firm's operations and investment decisions. The passive mode depends on collateral for security, and to the extent there is analysis behind a lending decision, it is primarily about the value of the security interest rather than the operations of the firm. In practice even fully secured lending in advanced market economies generally includes some degree of active monitoring on the part of the creditor given the significant transaction costs in foreclosing on collateral.

Regardless of the form or intensity of oversight, debt plays a different – and in some ways complementary – monitoring role to equity. Corporate finance literature generally views equity investors as less risk averse and thus control by equity holders as appropriate for "normal" (profitable) times, in particular for times when entrepreneurial risk-taking is needed. Owners need to monitor to prevent managerial largess, asset-stripping, or misuse or wastage of retained earnings or free cash flow. Monitoring by equity holders has its inherent weakness. It may lead to overly risky investments at the expense of debt holders, to the extent that equity can appropriate all upside gain but shares in any downside loss. However, owners are unlikely to prematurely liquidate firms with long-term potential viability.

Unlike owners, creditors are expected to be more risk averse because they do not share in upside gains. For this reason, creditor monitoring is generally considered to be more appropriate when tight controls on spending and investment are needed, particularly in times of financial distress (Aghion and Bolton 1992; Hoshi, Kashyap, and Sharfstein 1990).[3] Foreclosure and bankruptcy laws tend to shift control to creditors in such times. Because of creditors' tendency to risk aversion and shortsightedness, creditor control carries the danger of premature liquidation of potentially viable debtor firms (the mirror image of the danger of overly risky investments under owner control).

Within categories of debt, short-term creditors have more control levers at their disposal and thus tend to exert the strongest control. First, because short-term credit is refinanced more often, it provides more opportunities

passive governance, including primarily entry and exit of investors and disciplining primarily through the indicator of stock price. German and Japanese systems are models of active governance or "relational" investing with monitoring by membership on boards, shareholder voting, and other hands-on means. In the United States, however, the passive mode can revert to active governance through corporate takeovers, as the purchase of blocks of shares gives new owners the power to change firm policy and management. The mere threat of takeover acts as a powerful control device.

[3] Financial distress can result from intentional actions of agents as well as from impersonal market forces. Just as owners must monitor to prevent asset-stripping by managers, so debtors must monitor to prevent asset-stripping by owners.

for creditors to review investment decisions, adjust interest rates to account for risk, or refuse to roll over or grant additional loans altogether. Second, because short-term credit is often secured (if at all) by short-term assets (such as inventories or accounts receivable), foreclosure on these assets is relatively easy. Thus a creditor can easily impose a credible threat of foreclosure (perhaps leading to liquidation of the borrower) if the debt is not repaid. Long-term credit is less flexible because of the typically thinner market for long-term assets and the creditor's less frequent involvement in rollover decisions; thus long-term creditors tend to be weaker, less credible monitors. This partly explains why short-term and long-term credits are often held by different parties, the former by the better and more aggressive monitor (Berglöf and von Thadden 1994).

Even within the category of short-term (or long-term) debt, the monitoring challenge is greater for new credit than for rollovers of existing credit. New credit puts an additional debt service burden on the debtor firm and is therefore riskier than a rollover. Yet as a source of financing, new credit has certain advantages to new equity from a control perspective because it can encourage optimal effort from managers who are also owners or otherwise share in gains through profit-sharing compensation.

Legal and Institutional Requirements for Effective Monitoring

Equity and debt monitoring use different mechanisms and are therefore appropriate in different institutional settings. The requirements for good corporate governance by equity holders have been extensively analyzed. Passive monitoring primarily through entry and exit (as is typical in the United States) cannot take place unless equity markets are sufficiently deep and unless law and supporting institutions require extensive disclosure to shareholders and provide adequate protection for the interests of minority shareholders. Active monitoring by owners (as in Germany and Japan) depends less on the equity market and underlying institutions, but it still requires supportive corporate laws and adequate disclosure.

The legal and institutional requirements for effective debt monitoring have not been as thoroughly analyzed but are no less important. Passive monitoring by creditors (by collateral contracts) requires efficient property markets. Such markets in turn require clear legal definition and enforcement of property rights (both existing and contingent), low-cost information (generally by property and collateral registries), and asset markets of sufficient size and depth. Active monitoring by creditors relies less on underlying property markets, but it does require sufficient flexibility in debt contracts to allow such monitoring, adequate availability of information from reliable accounting and sufficient disclosure requirements, and workable frameworks for reorganization and liquidation.

Because of these institutional requirements, the degree of active monitoring by owners and creditors may be correlated in particular settings. Economies with hands-on owners are more likely to have hands-on creditors. More active monitoring – whether by debt or equity – grows out of other characteristics of the financial and legal systems in a country and reinforces them. For example, active monitoring is generally correlated with stronger banks but weaker capital markets and less onerous public disclosure rules for firms.[4]

The effectiveness of debt or equity monitoring also depends on the capacities and incentives of the monitors. In the case of equity the capacities and incentives of institutional investors (such as pension funds, mutual funds, or universal banks) are likely to be critical. In the case of debt one must consider the incentives and capacities of bank, trade, and government creditors, as well as other individuals or institutions that may hold publicly traded debt.

In sum, debt and equity play somewhat different, complementary roles. The appropriate balance between debt and equity (i.e. the firm's capital structure) depends, among other factors, on the balance between these various monitoring needs and institutional characteristics.[5] Greater debt might be warranted if (1) the legal framework for debt collection is strong; (2) the returns to additional managerial effort are high; (3) there is relatively little downside risk (and therefore interest margins can be modest); (4) there is large risk of misuse of free cash flow by managers (because of agency problems due to the separation of ownership and management); and (5) the control powers of equity are weak because of dispersed shareholding, poorly defined shareholder rights, or owners without monitoring competence. In contrast, greater reliance on retained earnings and closely held equity stakes may be warranted if the legal framework for debt collection (i.e. collateral, foreclosure, and bankruptcy laws and procedures) or the monitoring competence of creditors is weak, or if there is large downside risk causing investors with lower risk aversion to be desirable.[6]

[4] For one attempt to formulate various characteristics of "bank-oriented" vs. "market-oriented" financial systems, see Berglöf (1994).

[5] There are of course many factors other than monitoring needs that influence the capital structure of firms. For a summary of the literature, see Harris and Raviv (1991) and Myers (1989) and for developing countries, Glen and Pinto (1994).

[6] These conclusions about capital structure and monitoring needs are drawn largely from recent theoretical work in corporate finance. In addition, there is a small but growing body of empirical work on the role of debt as a control instrument and on the practice of bankruptcy and financial reorganization in advanced market economies. This work, focused mostly on

The Need for Creditor Monitoring in Transitional Economies

The framework presented above illustrates the magnitude of the challenge of developing effective corporate governance in the transition economies of Eastern Europe. Several preliminary lessons stand out about the need for monitoring by owners and creditors. First, given the high degree of economic uncertainty (including inflation) and the "noisiness" of the environment, financing through retained earnings and tightly held[7] equity investments is likely to be particularly important (McKinnon 1991), and ratios of debt to total assets can be expected to be low under market forces. Debt finance fits uncomfortably in such an environment, and creditors are likely to demand large premiums to compensate for the large downside risks inherent in transition, the difficulties of monitoring, and the high costs of debt collection (as discussed later). Furthermore, because the existence of debt can make equity holders more willing to take risks, rational creditors will be more hesitant to lend to highly leveraged firms.[8]

Second, even if equity (including retained earnings) serves as the largest source of financing,[9] the complementary control and monitoring roles played by creditors are still needed, particularly given the urgent need for change and restructuring in many firms. For potentially good firms, debt finance can provide incentives for greater effort from owners and managers,

U.S. experience, attempts to analyze the impact of large increases in leverage on firm performance, the costs of various reorganization routes, the conditions under which reorganization can or cannot successfully occur, and the effects of bankruptcy on the debtor firm. For example, on reorganization routes Gilson, John, and Lang (1990) found that in the United States firms with few debtors and no publicly held debt have an easier time restructuring out of bankruptcy. Another study by Gilson (1989) found that bankruptcy and out-of-court debt workouts led to large changes in management and ownership. Hotchkiss (1992) studied 197 companies that successfully completed a Chapter 11 procedure and found significant evidence that the process was biased toward a continuation of firms that should be liquidated. While creditors clearly have the capacity and incentives to assert strong control over firms in financial distress in the United States, the literature on U.S. bankruptcy indicates that this control is somewhat weakened due to the pro-debtor provisions embodied in Chapter 11. There is also a significant body of literature on the control roles of Japanese main banks and German universal banks (see Sheard (1994), Aoki (1994), and Baums (1994)). It generally supports the more theoretical treatment summarized above. However, there is virtually no in-depth analytical, empirical work that assesses the influence that creditors have over debtors through informal debt workouts or bankruptcy processes in those countries.

[7] Equity needs to be tightly held to avoid the agency problems inherent in dispersed shareholding, particularly if monitoring by debt holders is weak.

[8] This lesson has an important corollary: transitional economies that develop the proper incentives and institutions to support equity financing *and* monitoring by owners are likely to prosper compared with those that do not. Privatization policies play a significant role here.

[9] Retained earnings are the largest source of financing in advanced market economies, but debt levels are still higher than in transition economies (Mayer 1990).

allowing them to reap most upside gains. For nonviable firms, creditor monitoring (including refusal of credit when appropriate) is needed to spur exit and to prevent further wastage of resources. For firms with an uncertain future, creditor monitoring is needed to put a brake on overly risky behavior. In all cases creditor monitoring is important to the extent equity monitoring remains weak, because the state is the owner, new owners (especially insiders) are unwilling to cede control to outside equity investors, or capital markets and/or shareholder rights and disclosure rules are underdeveloped.

Third, creditors should always monitor their investments. Owners and managers can strip assets at the expense of creditors, just as managers can do so at the expense of owners. The principal-agent problems inherent in the separation of ownership and management are no less relevant to the conflicts of interest between a firm and its creditors.

Creditor Control in Hungary and Poland

While many economic *policies* can be changed overnight, it takes time to develop the complex *institutions* needed for a market economy to function properly. This is especially true in the financial system, which in market economies operates through a web of complex, interlinked rules and institutions. The economies of Eastern Europe are now completing their first half-decade of full-fledged transition, although Hungary and Poland began the process in the 1980s. The rules and institutions needed for debt to play a strong and independent monitoring role did not exist in the socialist period and must be created from scratch. After a brief look at the structure of enterprise debt, the rest of this section discusses this difficult process of institutional change.

Selected financial data for enterprises in Hungary and Poland for 1992 are shown in Table 3.1. Three characteristics stand out. First, Polish and Hungarian enterprises, while carrying a significant amount of debt, still tend to have rather moderate ratios of debt to total assets and low ratios of bank debt to total assets.[10] Because 1992 was an early year in the transition process, much of the debt on enterprise books at that time was carried over from socialism (or was a rollover of debt incurred during socialism) and thus reflected nonmarket financing processes. New flows of voluntary debt finance have continued to be scarce. Macroeconomic constraints in both countries have led to major credit tightening, and the total real value of

[10] These averages, of course, mask differences among individual firms. Bank debt appears to be concentrated in a small number of firms in Poland, whereas it is more evenly spaced among a larger number of firms in Hungary (Gomulka 1993; Bonin and Schaffer 1994).

Table 3.1. Debt Burdens of Hungarian and Polish Firms, 1992
(in percentages)

	Hungary		Poland	OECD
	57,000 firms	603 firms (loss makers)	200 firms	(range)
Total debt[a]/total assets	34	43	41	42–69
Percent of debt owed to:				
Banks		45	24	
Government		27	16	
Suppliers		21	36	
Others[b]		7	24	
Total percent		100	100	
Percent of debt that is:				
Short-term (< 1 year)	82	80	86	50–82
Long-term	18	20	14	12–50

Source: Polish data are from a survey of approximately 200 firms conducted by a team led by Dr. Marek Belka and financed by a World Bank research project on Enterprise Reform in Eastern Europe. The Hungarian data are from a survey of tax returns carried out by the Hungarian Ministry of Finance. The OECD data are from Rajan and Zingales (1993).

[a] Total debt includes short-term payables to suppliers and government as well as long-term bank debt.

[b] From other data gathered in the Polish survey, it appears that most of the debts included in "other" in Poland should be allocated to the three earlier categories, primarily suppliers.

outstanding bank credit to enterprises has declined since 1991 in both countries (Figure 3.1).

Second, debt carried on the books of enterprises is not owed exclusively or even primarily to banks. Trade partners and government (i.e. tax, customs, and social insurance agencies) are also significant creditors, albeit often involuntarily. A major category of debt in advanced market economies that has not yet developed on a large scale in the transitional economies is the corporate bond market.

Finally, enterprise debt – even that owed to banks – is overwhelmingly short term with maturity periods of less than one year. While to some extent this is an accident of history, short-term debt may well persist under market forces because of the need of lenders in this environment to monitor their borrowers through regular review as loans are rolled over.

In sum, enterprises carry substantial amounts of primarily short-term debt to various types of creditors. Does this debt play a significant role as a market-based constraint on managerial behavior? There are three crucial

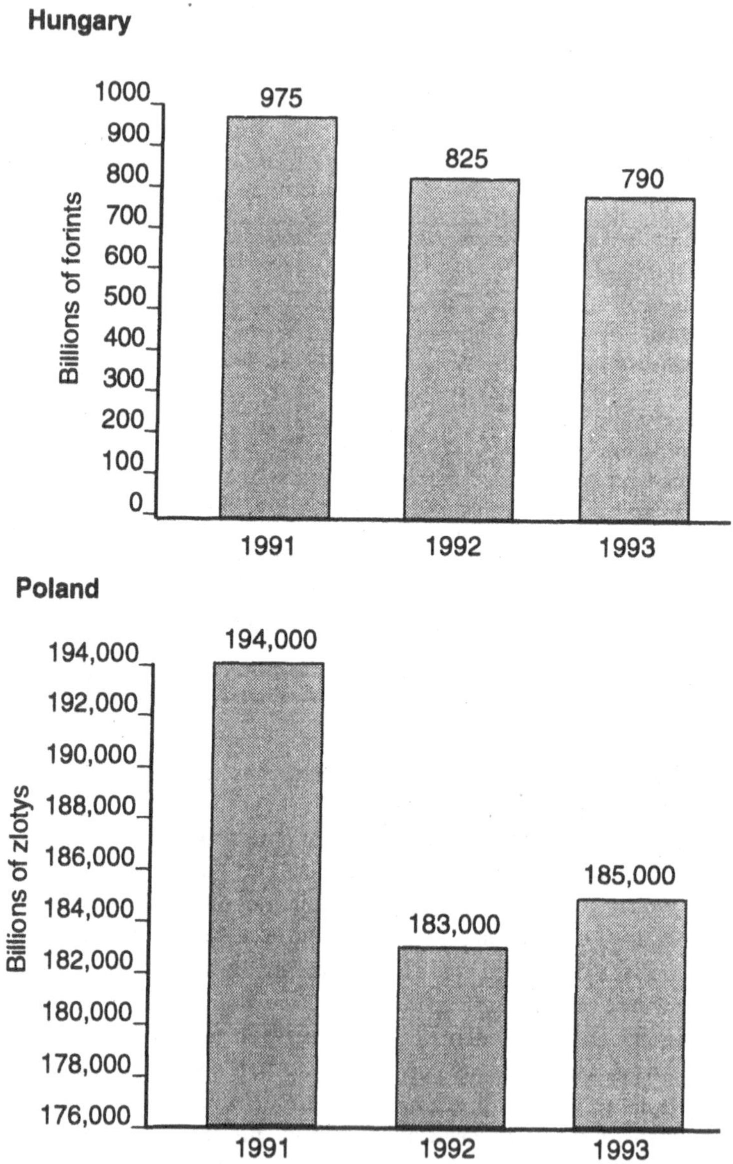

Fig. 3.1 Real bank credit to enterprises and households (1991 prices)

underpinnings to creditor monitoring and control in market economies: (1) adequate information, (2) market-oriented creditor incentives, and (3) an appropriate legal framework. To what extent are they now developing, and what lessons can be learned from progress to date?

The Problem of Information

If debt is to serve as an instrument to influence firm behavior, the first critical requirement is information. While this fact may seem obvious, the constraints imposed by the lack of information in transitional economies must not be underestimated. Viable lending requires that the lender have access to information on the borrower and the capacity to act on that information. Likewise, viable intermediation requires that depositors and bank supervisors have access to information on bank portfolios. In Hungary and Poland, as in other transitional economies, information asymmetries – in firms and banks – are frequently severe.

In the case of enterprises, financial and cost accounting systems were poorly developed before transition. As a result, asset values are not well inventoried, and changes in asset holdings may be poorly documented in many firms. In those instances where accurate information systems did exist before transition, dramatic changes in the structure of input prices, demand, competition, and distribution channels have reduced the value of this information. High tax rates and weak tax enforcement have created strong incentives in both Hungary and Poland for profitable enterprises to mask their performance, further reducing the value of information. Reputation, the basis for much lending in advanced market economies, is of limited value in transitional settings. Private entrepreneurs must build a reputation for integrity from scratch, while the managers of state-owned enterprise with a reputation for integrity may see their reputation devalued. From an information viewpoint, every post-transition firm is to some extent a new firm, even if it has been operating for 50 years.

In addition to shortfalls in accounting systems and the information "chaos" that results from rapid changes in the external environment, information problems are exacerbated in transitional economies by institutional weakness. This is true within banks themselves. Many bank employees are not trained in techniques of market analysis and loan appraisal and thus have difficulty in analyzing and using information from potential borrowers. This is also true for the financial sector generally. Even when lending between bank and borrower is viable in theory, the cost and viability of bank intermediation may be threatened by insufficient outside controls on bank management. Monitoring by bank supervisors and depositors is needed to counteract fraud, moral hazard, and inefficiency among bank owners and employees – public or private.[11] Bank supervisors may lack not only the technical ability but also the political will to carry out tough supervision.[12] Furthermore, the watchdog professions – including accounting, law, securities, and credit rating services – are still in their infancy, which makes it difficult for outside investors to monitor firms or intermediaries and to prevent fraud or misuse of their investment.

When information asymmetries are significant, adverse selection may make it costly if not impossible for outsiders to fund the growth of a firm with either debt or equity (see Diamond (1991), for example). Enterprises will be forced to rely almost exclusively on retained earnings and injections of capital by insiders (see Myers and Majluf (1984)). The most profitable enterprises will grow the most rapidly. If lending occurs, it will typically be based on collateral rather than cash flow. Indeed, these patterns describe the transition economies today.

The Problem of Creditor Incentives

The second essential requirement for debt to serve a control function is appropriate market-based incentives for creditors. Before turning to banks, let us look briefly at the incentives of the other creditors listed in Table 3.1. In Hungary and Poland the principal creditors aside from banks are government and trade creditors. The government creditors include the tax office, the social security service, and the customs office. Debt to these agencies became a substantial portion of the debt on the books of problem firms in Hungary and Poland in the early 1990s. While some of this debt simply reflects payment lags built into law, much of it reflects overdue arrears. These authorities were not known for active law enforcement and collection of arrears; in contrast, their legacy was one of pervasive bargaining and redistribution from profitable and loss-making firms (Kornai and Matits 1984; Vodopivec 1994; Schaffer 1989). These habits are not easy to change overnight, although there is some evidence (in part from the authors'

[11] The problems of the savings and loan industry in the United States vividly illustrate the problems that can arise under private as well as public ownership if supervision is weak and deposit insurance insulates depositors from the incentive to monitor the banks entrusted with their money. Problems also plague the private banking sectors of many transitional economies. One expert has suggested that 90 percent of the private banks in Poland are corrupt or insolvent and should be shut down. Many of Russia's private banks are similar.

[12] Some transition countries have had more aggressive banking supervision that others. Most notable is Estonia, which has forced depositors of insolvent institutions to bear losses. Hungary's banking supervision is thought to have been particularly weak during the transition process.

discussions with bankruptcy trustees and liquidators) that budget pressures have made government creditors more vigilant in both countries. However, tax and social security arrears clearly are a major source of financing for firms in financial distress (Belka *et al.* 1994; Bonin and Schaffer 1994). With regard to voluntary credit, governments are poorly positioned either to evaluate and monitor firms or to extend large amounts of credit to them. The latter is especially true in Poland and Hungary, where both governments have been under severe budgetary pressures.

As with government debt, a significant portion (although clearly not all) of the debt to trade creditors consists of overdue receivables. Many of these receivables arose in 1991 and 1992, when the enterprise sector in both countries was subject to serious demand and liquidity shocks. These shocks resulted in a stock of inter-enterprise credits that itself undercut discipline due to the fear of domino bankruptcies if any one party attempted to collect debts. As with government credit, however, there is evidence that trade creditors are slowly becoming more active in preventing the emergence of new overdue receivables by requiring payment before goods are shipped to problem firms (Belka *et al.* 1994).

The rest of this discussion on creditor incentives focuses on bank creditors. As noted earlier, credit from banks represents less than half the total liabilities of troubled firms in both Poland and Hungary. Yet banks arguably play the pivotal role among creditors in maintaining borrower discipline. Apart from self-financing and temporary involuntary financing from government, trading partners, and employees through arrears, banks are the only source of financing available to most Hungarian and Polish firms.

By 1992 many of the state-owned commercial banks in Hungary and Poland were insolvent when evaluated using internationally accepted accounting principles. These insolvencies were the result of several factors, including bad loans inherited from the socialist "monobank," transition-induced defaults on existing loans, and defaults on new credits extended after the onset of relative price reform. While part of the problem was inherited from the breakup of socialism, much of it arose from postsocialist lending, particularly lending during the 1990-91 period.[13] Not only was this period particularly difficult economically, with the breakup of the CMEA trading regime and deep domestic recessions in both countries, but the initial postsocialist incentive structure did not encourage banks to expend time or resources cleaning up loan problems and exercising control over their borrowers. While many state-owned enterprises found themselves subject to hard budget constraints, the same could not be said of the state-owned

[13] Ábel (1994) provides supportive data for Budapest Bank.

commercial banks. Government decisions to guarantee the deposits of state-owned banks (explicitly or implicitly) exempted the troubled banks from depositor discipline. In practice, state-owned banks in both countries were also exempt from international risk-based capital requirements.[14] Further confusing the situation was the perception that both economies were "under-banked." There were too few branches, too few skilled lenders, and too few resources devoted to providing payments services. While unprofitable enterprises in the manufacturing sector were laying off employees and cutting back production, unprofitable banks were hiring employees and expanding.

Hungary and Poland both responded to the problems in the banking system by reinvigorating existing banks via recapitalization. A one-time recapitalization early in the transition process is arguably necessary (but not sufficient) to establish viable institutions, given the undercapitalized state of most commercial banks when initially separated from the monobank. Undercapitalized banks cannot operate for long without government support and may face perverse incentives to continue distress lending and engage in ever riskier behavior to avoid bankruptcy. But, growing experience from around the world is showing that recapitalization is itself a risky undertaking, particularly if undertaken repeatedly. In the absence of other changes in policies and bank management, recapitalization of insolvent banks may actually make matters worse by skewing incentives even further away from efficient bank restructuring. Bank managers may begin to believe that future losses will also be offset by the government. This will encourage fraud and moral hazard and further undercut the incentives of banks to expend time and energy pursuing delinquent borrowers.

The concurrent adoption of other policies may partially offset the adverse consequences of recapitalization by strengthening the market-based incentives facing managers. For instance, when bank recapitalization is conducted in preparation for privatization, competent bank managers may exert additional effort to enhance their postprivatization employment prospects. Alternatively, it might be possible to develop incentive systems that motivate managers in banks that continue to be state owned. The importance of implicit and explicit incentives cannot be overemphasized. Managers' efforts to maintain their reputations might be sufficient to head off outright fraud. However, if laws and norms on fiduciary responsibility

[14] In Poland published financial numbers were in violation of the international risk-based capital guidelines until the March 1993 recapitalization. In Hungary accounting rules before December 1991 did not require banks to recognize and make provision against their bad loans. Even after the adoption of the new banking law and implementing regulations in late 1991 and early 1992, anecdotal evidence suggests that banks often continued to roll over loans to large state-owned firms rather than recognize them as problems.

are weak and information on banks' financial status is scant, as it is in all transitional economies, reputation alone may not be enough to lead managers to develop appropriate credit policies, to force turnarounds in delinquent borrowers, or to resist political pressure to extend new credits to ailing state-owned enterprises and politically connected new borrowers. Theoretically, one could design incentive systems to press managers toward fundamental reform.[15] However, the state as owner would have to set up, monitor, and enforce such systems, and most state agencies suffer from similar incentive problems.

While recapitalization is not the only option open to transitional economies (as discussed further in the last section of the paper), it was the option chosen by Hungary and Poland. Experience in these two countries illustrates the importance of carefully chosen incentives and appropriate accompanying policies in mitigating the moral hazard inherent in such recapitalization.

Hungary's Banking Reforms

Hungary's bank reform until mid-1994 paid relatively little attention to the dangers of potentially negative incentives from recapitalization. Hungarian banks were effectively recapitalized four times during that period – in 1991, 1992, 1993, and 1994. In the 1991 programs, the government issued guarantees for Ft 21 billion (about $280 million) of doubtful loans, equal to one-half of the doubtful loans that had been transferred to the commercial banks when they were created from the monobank in 1987. In the second program, the 1992 Loan Consolidation Scheme, the government purchased Ft 120 billion of the state-owned commercial banks' problem loans for approximately Ft 98 billion (about $1.2 billion) in state bonds.[16] Of the Ft 120 billion in debt, Ft 41 billion was transferred to a new institution, the Hungarian Investment and Development Rt. (HID), while the remainder

[15] There are two general approaches to the incentive problems in this situation. The first is to mandate the desired behavior (as opposed to outcomes) through directives or management contracts. Managers who failed to meet their goals are fired. Managers who met or exceeded their goals are rewarded. The second approach is to give managers a claim whose value is tied to the performance of the bank. Possible forms include contracts in which the government rewards performance (for instance, performance-based pay) and instruments in which performance is rewarded by the market (for instance, warrants to purchase shares of the bank at privatization). Properly constructed, these claims give managers incentives to identify and undertake actions to increase the bank's value. The two approaches are not mutually exclusive. Management mandates may be necessary to preclude strategies that are clearly against the best interests of the bank, while performance-based claims may be necessary to encourage managers to choose the most effective of a number of courses of action.

[16] The numerical figures on the 1992, 1993, and 1994 programs are taken from World Bank data and Bonin and Schaffer (1994).

stayed with the banks, which were to act as collection agents for the Finance Ministry. HID was envisioned as a collection/workout agency with a mandate to restructure debtor enterprises where possible.

In late 1993 the government implemented a Bank Recapitalization and Loan Consolidation Program, pursuant to which it issued state bonds worth Ft 171 billion (almost $2 billion) to eight problem banks. Of this, Ft 114 billion was a direct capital infusion, ostensibly to bring banks' capital asset ratios (CAR) up to 0%, and Ft 57 billion was government purchases from the banks of the loans of 14 large ailing Hungarian enterprises (plus a large number of smaller agricultural cooperatives) that had been explicitly targeted for rescue. Subsequently, in May 1994, another Ft 19 billion (about $200 million) was injected into five of the eight banks to raise their CARs to 4%. Finally, the government injected another Ft 16 billion into these banks in December 1994 to bring their CARs to 8 percent.

Over four years more than $3.4 billion – equivalent to about 9 percent of 1993 gross domestic product (GDP) – was injected into Hungarian state banks. Yet little else was done to create strong and appropriate incentives for bank restructuring. No independent, in-depth portfolio or operations reviews were completed by the government before the recapitalizations. Performance-oriented management contracts were not implemented, and bank managers were not given strong and clear incentives to undertake actions that would increase the value of the banks they managed.[17] The government did not formulate a clear plan for state bank privatization, although two banks (the foreign trade bank and Budapest Bank) undertook privatization programs on their own initiative.[18] Most observers agree that banking supervision has been weak.

Poland's Banking Reforms

The government of Poland, after a rocky start, appears to have made more significant efforts than Hungary in the four years to mid-1994 to deal with the perverse incentives faced by the managers of state-owned banks. Like Hungary, it opted to recapitalize its commercial state banks, but unlike Hungary, it

[17] The 1993 recapitalization was designed to create incentives for bank-led enterprise restructuring, because it required the banks to enter into workout procedures with certain problem debtors. However, as discussed later, the government buyout option in the plan led some banks to consider the government – rather than the problem debtor – as the main negotiating partner. Although the conciliation process is ongoing, it has not imposed strong market-based incentives on banks.

[18] The foreign trade bank (OTP) was privatized in January 1995. Budapest Bank has not yet finalized privatization. It should be noted that the new government that took office in mid-1994 appears to be intent on moving forward with positive reforms in these areas, undertaking in-depth audits of the banks and working on a program of bank privatization.

carried out only one recapitalization (of zl. 11 trillion or $650 million). Furthermore, this recapitalization was embedded in a much larger program designed to change incentives and promote privatization in commercial banks. The program was made credible by the strong and consistent leadership of the Polish Ministry of Finance from 1990 through early 1994.

Changes in incentives began in 1992 and culminated in the adoption of the Enterprise and Bank Restructuring Program (EBRP) in February 1993. The government sought to affect management behavior directly and indirectly – directly by mandating certain actions and indirectly by creating incentives to maximize the value of the banks. Direct controls began in the spring of 1992, when the Ministry of Finance actively discouraged banks from making loans to problem debtors. An outright prohibition on such lending was enacted into law with the passage of the EBRP. The policy of prohibiting new lending to nonperforming borrowers had several positive features. It required the government to deal with strategic enterprises in a more transparent fashion by placing greater reliance on allocation of subsidies through the budget rather than through the treasury-owned commercial banks. It also created incentives for borrowers to make operational changes to survive. With new credit cut off, working capital could only be generated by reducing costs, collecting past due receivables, or selling assets. The EBRP also required banks to set up workout departments and resolve those loans that had been classified nonperforming at year-end 1991. This again strengthened the banks' hand in negotiations with problem borrowers. In addition, the treasury-owned commercial banks were required to undergo repeated portfolio evaluations by outside auditors. This forced the creation of management information systems and provided the government with a mechanism for verifying banks' compliance with restrictions on lending to problem borrowers.

These direct mandates were accompanied by other less direct changes in incentives. In 1992 bank employees were given the right to purchase up to 20 percent of their banks' shares upon privatization at half-price. This strengthened the incentives of competent managers at solvent banks to adopt prudent policies, with respect to the workout of the existing loan portfolio and to the creation of new loans. Furthermore, the recapitalization was accompanied by a clear plan for privatization of the nine treasury-owned commercial banks. As of mid-1995, three commercial banks had been privatized.[19]

[19] Bank Wielkopolski in Wroclaw was privatized in 1993; Bank Slaski in Katowice, in early 1994; BPH in Krakow, in January 1995. To encourage privatization of the commercial banks, donor countries contributed $500 million to the Polish Bank Privatization Fund. As banks are privatized, the funds are released to the Polish government to cover interest payments on the recapitalization bonds. Only banks privatized before March 1996 qualify.

Discussions of the bank recapitalization plan began in 1992, were put into law in February 1993, and were implemented in September 1993. From the outset, the government sought to determine the amount of capital to be injected based on the value of loans that were nonperforming at year-end 1991. This was designed to avoid penalizing those banks that had already taken aggressive action to deal with their problems and to maintain incentives for managers to oversee other loans in the banks' portfolios.

While Poland's banking policy made greater efforts to deal with incentive problems than did Hungary's, it has been far from perfect. First, large segments of the financial system initially escaped coverage, including the housing bank, cooperative banks, private banks, and the problem-plagued agricultural bank. Second, Poland's program assumes that bank management is competent and will respond to incentives. There are no explicit criteria governing the dismissal of management for poor performance, and there has been little turnover in senior management. Third, while bank policies focus extensively on how to work out bad debts, there are few directives aimed at correcting deficient lending procedures. This leaves open the possibility that a bank can create a large quantity of new bad loans before preventive action is taken. These shortcomings are of more than academic interest; at least two treasury-owned commercial banks continued to deteriorate in 1994.

Banking Performance

Are these differences in policy affecting the way banks behave in general, and how they deal with nonperforming borrowers in particular? While the jury is still out, available data and anecdotal evidence suggest that they could be. Tables 3.2 and 3.3 show basic data on the banks that have been the primary focus of reform efforts in the two countries.[20] The differences in the banks' overall capital position in the two countries are striking. Risk-based capital ratios for Poland's seven treasury-owned banks in mid-1994 ranged from a low of 9 percent to a high of 45 percent.[21] Excluding the 1993 capital injection, they ranged from a low of –10 percent to a high of 28 percent, with three of the banks above 6 percent. Excluding the effects of recapitalization, the equity of the treasury-owned commercial banks remained steady between December 1991 and December 1993, with five of the banks posting significant improvements. In contrast, before the year-end 1993 recapitalization, equity levels at Hungary's three largest banks

[20] In both cases these banks account for approximately 30 percent of total banking system assets in their respective countries. However, the agricultural loan portfolio, often a source of problem loans, is included in the Hungarian sample but excluded in the Polish sample.

[21] In comparison, the range among U.S. banks is 10 to 18 percent.

Table 3.2. Financial Data for Seven Polish State-Owned Commercial Banks

	1991		1992		1993	
	Billions of zlotys	% of total assets	Billions of zlotys	% of total assets	Billions of zlotys	% of total assets
Total assets	80,620		119,699		170,874	
Credit to non-governmental sector[a]	44,434	56	52,846	44	60,934	35
Bad loans[b]	14,038	19	17,906	16	19,382	12
Equity & other capital	3,452	4.3	4,040	3.4	15,086	8.8
Minus recapitalization	3,452	4.3	4,040	3.4	3,798	2.2
Risk adj. capital ratio[c]		2.7		3.9		23.6
Profits after tax	690	0.85	2,621	2.18	7,915	4.63
Real values (1991=100)[c]						
Total assets	100		109		118	
Loans to nongovt.sector	100		87		76	

[a] Excludes central investment loans (which are government guaranteed).
[b] For six banks only (data on seventh bank not available).
[c] Deflated using GDP deflator.

Table 3.3. Financial Data for Six Hungarian State-Owned Banks

	1991		1992		1993	
	Billion forint	% of gross assets	Billion forint	% of gross assets	Billion forint	% of gross assets
Total gross assets	751		805		781	
Credit to nongovt. sector	565	75.3	544	67.6	519	66.4
Loans transferred as part of 1992 LCS					98	
Write-offs and provisions	21	2.8	60	7.4	158	20.2
Equity (before 1993 recap.)	62	8.3	27	3.4	-62	-7.9
Profits after tax			-21	-2.6	-125	-16
Real values (1991=100)[a]						
Total gross assets	100		92		75	
Credit to nongovt. sector	100		82		66	
Credit to nongovt. sector including LCS	100		82		79	

[a] Deflated using GDP deflator

Table 3.4 Interest Rates in Poland and Hungary

Poland	Minimum loan rate	Treasury bill rate	CD rate
January 1992	45.5	43.5	42.7
January 1993	45.0	41.3	39.8
January 1994	40.6	34.9	32.9
May 1994	39.3	32.0	32.4

Hungary	Average rate on new loans	Minimum reported rate on new loans	Average treasury bill rate	Interbank rate	CD rate
January 1992	36.8	21	31.3	35.9	31.5
January 1993	29.8	19	15.1	17.0	17.3
January 1994	26.3	20	23.4	22.6	17.8
March 1994	26.7	20	23.5	23.9	17.6

were all negative and were strongly negative in two of the three.[22] Even after the enormous 1993 recapitalization, equity remained negative for five of the eight banks in the program (Bonin and Schaffer 1994).

The stronger equity position of banks in Poland is unlikely to result from differences in GDP performance or in the competitive environment in the two countries. The shock to GDP was similar in both countries from 1990-93. Furthermore, banks in both Poland and Hungary have not operated in competitive environments as markets have been fragmented and new entry in banking – particularly by foreign banks – has been controlled (or prohibited). One potential indicator of competition is the spread between interest rates on demand and time deposits, treasury bills, and loans. Interest spreads in the two countries in late 1994 are shown in Table 3.4. The data suggest more competition on the deposit side and perhaps less competition on the lending side in Poland than in Hungary.[23] However, although spreads are

[22] Although no exact figures exist, because of the absence of detailed audits, estimates of negative bank equity range up to –25% for one of the largest state banks.

[23] Rates on demand deposits are very low in both countries – currently 5% in Poland and 3% in Hungary. In Poland rates on time deposits are much higher and are above the rates on treasury bills, indicating significant competition in raising funds at the margin. But in Hungary rates on time deposits are almost 6 percentage points below the treasury bill rate, and over 6 percentage points below the interbank rate. This suggests that the market for time deposits in Hungary is less competitive than in Poland.

It is more difficult to assess the degree of competition on the lending side of the balance sheet. As of March 1994, spreads between lending rates and treasury bill rates in Poland were much larger than analogous spreads in Hungary. While this could point to a more competitive banking environment in Hungary, it could also point to hidden fees that increase effective lending rates, greater restrictions on access to lending at those rates, and nonprofit-maximizing

somewhat higher, Poland's rate structure may better reflect a market-based approach to risk pricing in this high-risk environment.

Although differences in competitive environments may not be of major importance, it is difficult to make judgments on relative incentives and performance based on aggregate capital ratios alone. The differences could result from other factors that are not directly comparable. First, they could result from differences in initial positions. Hyperinflation may have eroded a greater portion of the inherited bad loan portfolio in Poland, or the initial allocation of loans to these Polish banks may have been of higher quality than in Hungary. Second, they could result from differences in accounting and provisioning policies. The timing of the rapid deterioration in capital in Hungarian banks has been attributed to the adoption in 1991 of banking and bankruptcy laws that forced a rapid provisioning of existing problem loans (i.e. a recognition of problems that already existed) in 1992 and 1993 (Bonin and Schaffer 1994). In contrast, as far back as mid-1990 the Polish authorities commissioned diagnostic bank audits based on international accounting standards (even though regulatory capital requirements continued to be calculated using Polish accounting standards), and it is these audited figures that are shown in Table 3.2. Thus, the Polish year-to-year figures are directly comparable to each other, while the Hungarian figures reflect changes in provisioning policies as well as the underlying quality of the loan portfolio.

However, the differences in reported equity of Polish and Hungarian banks cannot be ignored. To the extent that the decline in Hungarian bank equity from 1991 to 1993 reflected continued deterioration in the quality of the loan portfolio rather than merely a recognition of historical losses (due to changes in accounting practices), the differences suggest that Hungary's commercial banks did not stabilize as quickly as Poland's. Furthermore, the timing of the decline, which reflected the desire and ability of Hungarian banks to avoid recognizing losses when they initially occurred, suggests weak incentives[24] and lax supervision. In particular, the banks may have had strong incentives to avoid forcing borrowers into bankruptcy or liquidation, since they would then be forced to provision fully against the bad loans. This

behavior by Hungarian banks. The extremely small spread in Hungary between the riskless rate (on treasury bills) and the rate on much riskier assets (smaller even than in the United States) seems infeasible in a competitive market and is difficult to understand without further information. Data on minimum loan rates suggest that some short-term loans in Hungary are being priced *below* rates on treasury bills and interbank placements of comparable maturity. Moreover, in Hungary the spread between loan rates and these reference rates has been highly variable, sometimes reaching extraordinarily high levels and at other times falling to unreasonably low levels.

[24] Some Polish bank managers may have desired to hide their losses but repeated external audits made this more difficult.

may partly explain why one-half of Hungary's largest loss makers in 1992 had still not entered bankruptcy or liquidation by early 1994. Also, some have suggested that banks may have overstated their problems to gain a larger bailout (Bonin and Schaffer 1994). While this could be true, it is unlikely to account for a large share of the capital deterioration. Any of these explanations raises questions about the efficacy of Hungarian policies on banking reform during that period. The opaqueness of the Hungarian situation, caused by the absence of in-depth external bank audits, makes it difficult to draw firm conclusions and is an indication of policy weakness.

The Legal Framework for Debt Collection

The third critical requirement for creditor monitoring and control in a market economy is an appropriate legal framework and effective procedures for debt collection. Without an effective system of debt collection, debtors lose repayment discipline, the flow of credit is constrained, and creditors may be forced to turn to the state to cover losses. Both Hungary and Poland are still in the early stages of developing market-oriented debt collection mechanisms, although they have made some initial progress and are further down this path than other reforming socialist economies. However, there is still a long way to go. It is still difficult for creditors to collect unpaid debts in Hungary or Poland, and until this changes, credit cannot flow freely and efficiently. In addition to problems in some of the laws, the debt collection system is subject to tremendous institutional deficiencies, which are typical in transition and will take time to resolve. For example, the courts are understaffed and their personnel underpaid; judges are often not familiar with bankruptcy principles; bailiffs are not always well trained or accountable; and the receiver profession is still in its infancy (particularly in Poland).

The legal framework for debt collection can be divided into three parts: collateral/secured lending, the workout process, and bankruptcy/liquidation.

Collateral

In Hungary and Poland, the laws regarding collateral date from the prewar period and fail to provide an adequate foundation for a strong financial system or an efficient market economy. The problems are many. First, the definition of property that can be used as collateral is narrow, particularly in Poland. Real property can be the subject of a mortgage, but liens on movable property are in theory limited by the legal requirement that they be possessory, that is, the property subject to the lien be physically in the possession of the lender. In fact lenders appear to be able to circumvent this requirement in practice (for example, by retaining title in the hands of the lender while transferring physical possession to the borrower), but not without some risk.

Second, the registration of liens, needed to inform third parties and thus to establish priority, is inadequate. Mortgages on real property do not present a major legal problem, as they can be registered in the land records. The problem with the registration of liens is about movable property. There is no way to register liens on movables in either country. Thus it is common to have several liens secured by the same property. To increase their security in such a situation, banks take liens on far more property than the value of the loan. When everyone secures everything, nothing is secured.

The third major problem in both countries is the priorities of liens. Pursuant to the Polish Code of Civil Procedure, secured creditors come far down in priority, below procedural costs, payments to employees, taxes, and rents on government-owned property. Furthermore, under other provisions of Polish law, the government has an automatic lien over all property of any party in arrears to the government (for taxes, social security payments, or customs duties). This lien need not be written or formalized to have priority. Since most problem debtors have large arrears to the government, this automatic lien severely impinges on the security provided by any other liens. Furthermore, under current Polish law not the first but the *last* lien taken on a piece of movable property has priority, if that lien was taken by the creditor in good faith (i.e. not knowing that other liens existed). This rule contrasts with the "first-in-time-first-in-right" rule typical in market economies. Finally, nonbank-secured creditors are at an extreme disadvantage under current Polish law, because all bank loans, whether or not secured, have priority over other creditors, even if the latter are secured.

Although formerly quite reasonable, Hungary's priority scheme has also become problematic (but not so confused as that of Poland). Under a new law adopted in September 1994,[25] Hungarian secured creditors were demoted in priority to come *after* liens to the government. As the latter can be very high for problem firms, this change severely undercuts the value of collateral in Hungary.

Fourth, the process of execution of liens is fraught with problems in both countries, whether the lien arises from a collateral property right or from a court decision that a debt is overdue. Creditors must go to court (or arbitration) to get a decision that the loan is indeed due, which gives them "executory title" to the debtor's property. This can take months. In Poland banks have the right to issue their own executory title,[26] but they still must go to

[25] Law No. 53 on Debt Recovery through a Court Process.

[26] Changes in Polish law allowing bank lenders to avoid courts in gaining executory title (a prerequisite to foreclosure) have expedited the seizure of collateral. The behavior of other creditors suggests that this procedural shortcut is valuable; privately owned Polish banks, for

court to have it stamped and thus "perfect" the title (which gives them the right to order the bailiff to attach the property). All creditors must pay the bailiff a large fee up front – reportedly 10 percent of the loan amount in Poland – to begin the actual collection process. Yet once the bailiff receives the money, he seems to have little incentive to move speedily, and thus creditors can wait years for anything to happen. It is not surprising that bailiffs (who apparently constitute a powerful and tight-knit group) have a negative image.

Finally, even if a creditor does succeed in gaining execution on a lien, the market for many assets is thin, and it is often not easy to sell the collateral and collect on the loan.[27] Even in the case of real property, which one might expect would be easy to sell, much of the property is encumbered by other liens (including tenants' rights) that lower the value and marketability of the property. For residential property, for example, it is virtually impossible to evict tenants and sell mortgaged property unencumbered by tenants' liens.

The difficulty in acquiring, registering, and foreclosing on collateral rights has meant that certain kinds of lending are not profitable for lenders. For instance, commercial bank loans collateralized by residential real estate are relatively rare because the current legal system makes foreclosure difficult and costly. Working capital loans and longer term lending for investment are hindered by the overlapping claims and unclear rights and priorities attached to movable collateral.

Given these many problems, how easy is it to reform collateral laws and procedures to make collateral finance feasible and attractive in transforming economies? Poland is the first test case, as it has moved faster than any other transforming economy to strengthen its collateral system. A modern collateral law has been drafted and debated over the past three years, and a close-to-final draft is ready for consideration by Parliament. This draft reforms the priority rules to eliminate the automatic priority given to government claims, to put secured creditors at the top (albeit after costs of collection), and to remove the preference currently given to banks above other creditors (regardless of who is secured). It also provides for a central registry for all liens on movable property, and specifies that the first lien to be registered has first priority. Finally, it simplifies somewhat the execution procedure.

example, lobbied extensively to have this power, initially reserved for state-owned banks, extended to them. In addition, nonbank creditors now hire banks to conduct foreclosures for them to obtain faster execution.

27 Shleifer and Vishny (1992) point out the importance of liquid asset markets and high liquidation values in making collateral effective as a liquidation threat and hence making collateral-based finance attractive.

Debt Workouts

A second critical component of the legal framework for debt collection is the procedure for workouts and formal reorganizations,[28] through which a problem debtor tries to negotiate a reduction in immediate debt service requirements to keep the firm alive. In return for the reduction in debt service, creditors may insist upon partial payments or upon fundamental changes in the size or functioning of the firm to increase their chances of future repayment of the remaining debt. As public policy, these procedures are to promote reorganization of firms whose going-concern value (post-reorganization) exceeds their liquidation value. Such firms, for example, may have assets (such as specialized machinery or unique trademarks) with little value in alternative settings.

Poland and Hungary have taken far-reaching steps since 1991 to adopt market-based workout processes. Poland has two procedures for debt workout – one judicial and the other extrajudicial. Judicial debt workouts occur under the law on "Arrangement Proceedings," which provides a means for restructuring a firm's debts, thereby allowing it to continue in operation. This law dates from 1934 (although significant amendments were made in 1990), and its main disadvantage is its extreme inflexibility.[29] To overcome the deficiencies in the Arrangement Proceedings law, Poland adopted a new procedure in February 1993 for working out bad loans – the bank conciliation agreement.[30] This new procedure shifts power from the courts and the borrower to the banks. Banks are empowered to negotiate a workout agreement on behalf of all creditors, providing they receive approval of creditors

[28] The major difference between a workout and formal reorganization is the identity of the parties bound by the agreement. A workout is essentially a renegotiation of one or more debt contracts, carried out pursuant to contract law. It binds only the parties to the relevant contracts. If a firm has only a few important creditors, workouts can be attempted quite easily by negotiating solely with those creditors (and ignoring or buying out the claims of other smaller creditors). However, if a firm has many large and important creditors or if much of its debt is in the form of bonds owned by the public at large, the transaction costs of dealing with each one individually can be prohibitive (Gilson 1990).

[29] For example, workouts under this law exclude secured creditors and government creditors (such as tax and social security offices), and thus in most cases the proceeding covers only trade creditors (since banks typically secure their loans). Furthermore, all relevant creditors must be treated identically under the law. The concessions given to different creditors cannot be tailored to their specific needs. In addition, the procedure only provides for financial terms in the resulting agreement. Broader restructuring provisions, such as changes in employment, investment, or management, are not envisioned. Finally, only parties attending the proceedings are allowed to vote on the proposed agreement. It may be difficult for a debtor with many creditors to assemble the required majority in one place for the vote.

[30] For an in-depth description, see Kawalec, Sikora, and Rymaszewski (1994) and van Wijnbergen (1993). For a preliminary analysis of results, see Kawalec *et al.* (1994), Belka (1994), and (in Polish) Chmielewski *et al.* (1994).

Table 3.5. Outcome of Poland's Enterprise and Bank Restructuring Program (the status, as of 30 April 30 1994, of nonperforming borrowers that owed money to seven Polish treasury-owned commercial banks on 31 December 1991)

	1991 balances (percentage)	Number of firms
Signed conciliation agreement	50	202
Partially serviced debt	25	98
Resumed scheduled debt service[a]	19	102
Repaid debt	13	211
Entered bankruptcy	10	121
Debt sold or posted for sale	5	89
Entered Article 19 liquidation	3	50

[a] Paid past due interest and scheduled repayments of principal. This category includes nominally short-term loans that are rolled over.

representing over 50 percent of the value of outstanding debt. The conciliation process is being used extensively (Table 3.5), even by banks that were not required to do so under the EBRP. Moreover, the seven treasury-owned commercial banks are initiating conciliation negotiations with borrowers even when the law does not require action.

Borrowers and certain creditors acquire several potential advantages if they opt for restructuring under bank-led conciliation rather than judicial conciliation. First, the process is likely to be somewhat quicker and less cumbersome, because the courts are not involved except to hear an appeal against an agreement. Second, priority rules change. The state treasury loses its superpriority. Only the social security office and secured creditors retain priority. Third, the ability of a minority of creditors to block agreements is limited. Fourth, responsibility for monitoring the restructuring program is explicitly delegated to the lead bank. If the lead bank does not terminate the agreement when the restructuring plan is violated, it becomes liable for any additional losses incurred by the other creditors. Fifth, the range of potential outcomes is broader under conciliation. For example, banks may exchange debt for equity. Finally, if the conciliation agreement is declared void, any concessions by the treasury or the social security agency are unwound. This gives the borrower and the lead bank strong incentives to develop a reasonable plan.

Hungary is significantly ahead of Poland in developing its judicial workout system, although in practice creditors may still derive relatively little benefit from the law and procedure (due primarily to information and incentive problems discussed above). In 1991 the Hungarian Parliament adopted a tough new bankruptcy/liquidation law that took effect on 1 January 1992. It

Table 3.6. Hungarian Bankruptcy and Liquidation Processes
(1 January 1992 through 31 December 1993)

	Bankruptcy	Liquidation
Filings	5,156	17,133
State-owned enterprises	429	1,820
Cooperatives	965	2,768
Business entities	3,762	12,545
Limited liability companies	2,959	8,927
No. of employees (approx. %)		
Over 300	6	—
51-300	24	—
50 or fewer	70	—
Closed (as of 31 Dec. 1993)	4,627 (90)[a]	[a]
With ageement	1,250 (27)	
Reversion to liquidation	1,377 (30)	
Administration completion	2,000 (43)	
Pending (no./percentage)	529 (10)	

Source: Ministry of Finance data
[a] As a percentage of filings.
[a] Over 10,000 liquidation cases were completed by the courts in 1992 and 1993, but these included cases filed in earlier years under the previous law. Furthermore, over three-quarters of those completed cases were administrative completions, i.e. cases withdrawn or rejected on administrative grounds rather than completed on the merits. Only a small number of the 17,133 cases filed since 1 January 1992 have been completed to date. The law officially gives liquidators two years to finish a liquidation, and that deadline is only now being reached in a significant number of cases.

required managers of firms with any arrears of 90 days or more to file for reorganization (called "bankruptcy" in the Hungarian case) or liquidation. On its face, the 1991 law looks similar to the reorganization provisions of bankruptcy laws in advanced market economies, particularly Chapter 11 of the U.S. Bankruptcy Code. Managers of bankrupt firms retain their jobs after filing and have the first opportunity to present a reorganization plan. Creditors then vote on the plan and have the opportunity to present alternative plans. If an agreement cannot be reached, the procedure reverts to liquidation. From the first filing until the final agreement is reached, the courts have little involvement; the main actors are the parties themselves and the trustee (selected by the creditors from a list of licensed trustees/liquidators). The law was amended (effective September 1993) to remove the automatic trigger and change several other significant features.[31]

[31] The 1993 amendments also (1) removed the requirement that a debtor file for bankruptcy if 90 days in arrears, making it optional; (2) reduced the required majority for approval of a reorganization agreement from 100% to two-thirds (in value) and a half (in number) of

The 1991 law led to a wave of filings for reorganization and liquidation (see table 3.6). Over 22,000 cases were filed in the two-year period from January 1992 through 1993, including over 5,000 bankruptcy cases and over 17,000 liquidation cases. Resolution of the bankruptcy cases has typically been quite speedy, with more than 90 percent completed during that period. Liquidation cases take much longer, and most cases filed during 1992-93 are still pending.

In addition to the judicial bankruptcy process, the Hungarians adopted a nonjudicial workout procedure (the "loan consolidation" process) concurrent with the year-end 1993 recapitalization in an attempt to force banks to resolve problem loans expeditiously. The number of reorganization filings under the bankruptcy law declined dramatically in 1994, in part due to the changes in the law and possibly to the adoption of this process. While in theory something like the Polish scheme, in fact the loan consolidation process is very different. The process is more akin to a general workout under contract law, in that any agreement binds only those parties that negotiate it – primarily the major banks, with government creditors agreeing to go along on a pro rata basis. In the first round, the so-called "simplified process," in which 55 firms picked by the government (on unclear, seemingly political grounds) and representatives of line ministries were invited to participate in the negotiations, and the State Property Agency (SPA) was given the right to purchase the bad debts of firms from banks if no agreement could be reached in the case. Although SPA's resources to buy debt were limited in the first round, the buy back option and the line ministry involvement gave an impression of softness that appears to have reinforced some of the negative incentives discussed earlier and undermined the discipline of the banks and the enterprises to reach agreement and take difficult steps toward enterprise restructuring. Unlike the Polish conciliation process, the 1994 Hungarian nonjudicial procedure does not appear to have strengthened the capacity of debt to serve as a control instrument. To the extent it undermined the developing bankruptcy process, it may have been a setback.

Liquidation

In addition to being an important means for closing ailing firms, liquidation

mature claims plus a quarter (in number) of not yet mature claims; (3) allowed the debtor a 90-day moratorium on debt service payments, previously automatic, only if the same majority agrees; (4) raised compensation levels for liquidators; (5) required the appointment of a trustee in bankruptcy, optional before; and (6) allowed debtors to resort to bankruptcy every two years (measured from filing date), previously in the 1991 law only every three years (measured from the date of agreement).

is the final link in the debt collection chain. Creditors' control rights over firms in financial distress derive ultimately from their power to force the closure of the firm. Yet in many transition economies the laws governing liquidation give little power to creditors (particularly nongovernmental ones).

In Poland, the liquidation of financially distressed firms may occur under the Bankruptcy Law (*upadlosc*) or under Article 19 of the Law on State Enterprises (see Tables 3.7 and 3.8).[32] The Bankruptcy Law is modeled on prewar European statutes and provides only for liquidation.[33] Creditors or the debtor may file for bankruptcy, a liquidator is appointed, and the law provides standard rules for winding up the estate and satisfying claims in order of priority (as discussed earlier). The law as now designed has several major deficiencies. First, the priority list discourages any active involvement by nongovernment creditors in the bankruptcy process, because it makes it virtually impossible for banks and other creditors to recover anything.[34] Creditors often express the view that "the government always comes first." In fact, if the government and procedural costs do not consume the entire estate, it is likely that employees' claims will. A second deficiency is that the law provides few means for a receiver or judge-commissioner to void fraudulent transactions made by managers or owners at the expense of creditors before the bankruptcy filing.[35] Fraudulent transactions are thought to be common, and the legal system must find a way to identify and punish them if the bankruptcy process (or indeed any debt collection process) is to be credible.

[32] Liquidation privatization, under Article 37 of the Privatization Law, is limited to healthy firms and is not considered here.

[33] However, it is possible for the firm to continue operating under the supervision of the liquidator while in liquidation.

[34] Although secured creditors can be satisfied first (as in Western bankruptcy law), the priorities among secured creditors are subject to the same priorities outlined in the earlier discussion on collateral; collection fees, taxes, and social security arrears automatically precede bank creditors, which in turn precede nonbank creditors. Once claims secured by collateral are satisfied, the remainder of the assets (and any excess of proceeds from the sale of secured property over the value of secured claims) becomes the bankruptcy estate. This estate is used to satisfy creditor claims in the priority specified in the bankruptcy law. According to this latter bankruptcy specific priority, bank and trade creditors come after (1) the costs of the proceedings (which include all amounts due to the court, the receiver, and employees for wages, severance payments, etc.), (2) taxes, and (3) social security contributions.

[35] The law provides that only *gifts* made within six months before filing can be voided. It does not extend to sales or other types of contracts (even if they contain an element of gift through underpricing). Under the Civil Code transactions made before filing may be voided, but such a process is extremely difficult to implement because it requires proof of *intent* to defraud.

Table 3.7. Judicial Bankruptcy and Conciliation Procedures in Poland, 1990–92

	1990	1991	1992	Total
State-owned enterprises	8	62	212	282
Communal enterprises	0	0	23	23
Cooperatives	68	100	152	320
Private enterprises	87	386	552	1,025
Other	0	8	1	9
Total	163	556	940	1,659

Source: Polish Central Planning Office (CUP). This office did not collect data on bankruptcies after 1992.

Table 3.8. "Exit" Process for Polish State-Owned Enterprises (cumulative through 31 March 1994)

Bankruptcies (pending or completed)	602
Liquidations (Art. 19, State-Owned Enterprise Law)	1,125
Completed	203
Converted to bankruptcy	258
Taken over by Rural Property Agency	51
Pending	613

Source: Ministry of Ownership Transformation.

Article 19 is a legacy of the socialist legal system. Under Article 19, creditors may initiate the liquidation of a state-owned borrower by petitioning the governmental entity charged with exercising ownership control. Liquidation is managed by a trustee charged with selling off the assets in whole or part. Only companies that are still solvent are eligible for this procedure. However, interviews suggest that many of the companies in liquidation prove to be insolvent and ultimately end up in the bankruptcy courts. Lenders may be choosing the Article 19 liquidation because the costs of realizing collateral are lower and because it affords an opportunity to neutralize the superpriority of state claims.

Liquidation procedures in Hungary are contained in the same law as the reorganization (or bankruptcy) process discussed earlier. As in Poland, the process is a fairly standard one, at least on paper. Creditors or the debtor can petition for liquidation, a liquidator is appointed, a list of assets is drawn up, and the assets are then supposedly sold to satisfy claims in the order of priority. While the Hungarian law does not have the same confused and counterproductive priority rules found in the Polish case (although of all collateral interests only mortgages on real property appear to have priority over unsecured claims), the incentives in the process (particularly the compensation formula for liquidators) appear to lead many liquidators to keep firms in operation for as long as possible and to act more as restructurers and privatizers than as agents of creditors (Gray, Schlorke, and Szanyi 1995). Furthermore, the Hungarian process is thought to be compromised by fraud, both on the part of managers (who may remove valuable assets before filing for liquidation) and on the part of liquidators (who can find many ways to profit from their near monopoly control over the process). In Hungary, the problem is not so much the legal framework as it exists on paper as the difficulty of administering it properly in an atmosphere with poor information, little accountability, and confused incentives.

Is Debt Emerging as a Control Device?

The three areas discussed above – information, creditor incentives, and the legal framework for debt collection – are all important in determining the power of creditors to monitor and exert control over managerial decision-making. Poland and Hungary have faced similar challenges in all three areas. In the legal area, both have made significant progress in developing workout processes, but they have further to go in streamlining liquidation processes and developing workable systems of collateral. Liquidation and collateral laws appear to be somewhat less developed in Poland than in Hungary, although in the latter area Poland may soon take a big step forward with the passage of a new collateral law. In the area of creditor incentives, Poland's policies to date appear to have imposed stronger market-oriented incentives on its commercial banks. Polish treasury-owned commercial banks have stabilized their overall performance, strengthened their capacity to exert pressure on nonperforming borrowers, and improved their ability to allocate new credit. While data for Hungary are far less complete, numerical and anecdotal evidence indicates a less promising picture, due to the moral hazard caused by successive recapitalizations and the absence of mitigating policies to strengthen bank incentives. In both countries banks have been protected not only by segmented markets and entry restrictions, but also (at least in Hungary) by the position of the banks as "monopsonist" buyers of the treasury bills issued to finance government budget deficits.

It appears that debt is slowly emerging as a control device, although further development and strengthening of information, incentives, and legal frameworks are needed if it is to play the important monitoring role (alongside equity) outlined in the first section of the chapter. Some empirical support for its slow but steady emergence is presented below.

Dealing with Nonperforming Borrowers

Data from both countries indicate that banks are sensitive to nonperformance by their borrowers. From early 1993 through 1994, the seven Polish treasury-owned commercial banks made *no* new loans to nonperforming firms (internal World Bank data). Furthermore, by the end of 1994, 13 percent of the loans of those banks that were classified as nonperforming on 31 December 1991 had been repaid in full, another 19 percent had become current on principal and interest, and another 25 percent had been partially serviced (Table 3.5). Thus, borrowers accounting for a total of 57 percent of loans that were classified as nonperforming on 31 December 1991 had made partial or full payments to the banks by end-1994. Although data for Hungary are less complete, some evidence suggests that Hungarian banks, while perhaps continuing to roll over bad debts and capitalize unpaid interest for some nonperforming borrowers, are not offering new money on a large scale to problem firms (Bonin and Schaffer 1994).

Restructuring Unprofitable Firms

There are also signs that Polish banks are growing in their ability to take an active role in workout situations and that the restructuring process is being governed, at least in part, by rational economic considerations. In general, Polish banks seem to have approached the conciliation process in a strategic fashion. For example, banks sometimes chose to purchase additional debt to qualify for bank-led conciliation. In other cases where bank loans were secured with valuable collateral, banks waited until unsecured creditors wrote down their debt under a court arrangement proceeding and then initiated bank-led conciliation or a contract renegotiation under the civil code. A number of banks indicated that when they distrusted management, they sought a debt for equity swap so that they would have the option of replacing managers (although this was by no means the only motivation for debt for equity swaps).

Furthermore, initial results indicate a clear correlation between the outcome of the process and the economic prospects of the debtor firm. Data indicate that two-thirds of the firms that have successfully reached conciliation agreements with banks have positive operating profits (before interest payments). Another 21 percent are close to the breakeven point and are likely to post operating profits as the Polish economy strengthens. In contrast, the less profitable of the nonperforming borrowers are more likely to be liquidated.[36] Potential profitability may be necessary but does not appear to be

[36] In a sample of problem debtors of two of the seven treasury-owned Polish commercial banks, all firms being liquidated through bankruptcy procedures registered negative operating

sufficient to convince the bankers. Workout directors in Polish banks look for a borrower's demonstrated ability to make at least partial payments on its debt before agreeing to a restructuring plan. Indeed, 50 percent of the borrowers signing conciliation agreements have made some payments since 31 December 1991 (internal World Bank data).

In Hungary, there also appears to be a significant push of unprofitable firms into restructuring. Of the 603 largest loss-making firms in the country, almost one-half have been the subject of a bankruptcy or liquidation filing. (Why the other firms in that group are not yet subjects of similar filings is an interesting unresolved question.) Initial results from ongoing World Bank research on Hungarian bankruptcy (Gray, Schlorke, and Szanyi 1995) give mixed results as to the effect of the process on enterprise restructuring. Financial restructuring appears quite limited in many cases. In the sample of 63 finalized bankruptcy agreements studied, the majority envision only short extensions in the maturity of outstanding debt, often combined with some write-off of debt principal and/or partial repayment of principal or accrued interest. Only six of the 63 cases provide for debt for equity swaps, and only three have any provisions for new financing (two from bank creditors and one from suppliers). But, many of the plans do envision some rationalization of the operations of the debtor firm or at least to have been accompanied by such rationalization. A full 37 of the 63 agreements included some reduction in employment in the debtor firm, and 19 included provisions for either asset sales or sales of part of the firm. However, only four provided explicitly for a change in top management of the debtor firm, and only two for a change in board membership. Along with these substantive results, the survey found that managers and owners were always active and were often the *de facto* controlling party in the cases, while banks were sometimes active, sometimes passive, but never in control. These preliminary findings suggest that creditors were quite weak in 1992–93 and that the process may indeed have been used by managers for their own ends – for example, as a means of "spontaneous privatization."

Liquidating Unviable Firms

Although workouts are becoming common, creditors in both countries are still passive when it comes to initiating and overseeing the *liquidation* of nonperforming borrowers. In Hungary banks have initiated only a handful

profits in 1992. Firms being liquidated under Article 19 of the Law on State Enterprises were somewhat more profitable than firms being liquidated under the bankruptcy law. In a few instances, firms being liquidated under Article 19 improved their operations enough to convince their banks to enter into conciliation agreements.

Table 3.9. Who Filed Liquidation Cases in Hungary, 1992–93?

Entities filing petitions	Percentage
Bank creditors	1.5
Government creditors (tax, social security, customs)	13.0
Other trade creditors, liquidators, conversions from bankruptcy	67.5
Firms themselves	18.0
Total	100.0

of the many liquidation cases filed since 1992 (Table 3.9), and they are reported to behave passively in many of the cases that are filed by others. In Poland banks typically allow other creditors to initiate judicial liquidation proceedings. Once proceedings are initiated, banks typically spend little time overseeing the liquidation. This passivity is partly explained by incentives problems (as discussed above), particularly in Hungary. However, it may also have some economic logic given the low returns that banks can expect to receive from liquidations under present laws. In Poland the low returns are a consequence of high court fees and the near impossibility of banks' recovering anything given the priority rules described earlier. In Hungary creditors also appear to doubt their ability to recover any funds under liquidation, not only because of priority problems but also because of opportunities both managers and liquidators have to divert assets and sales receipts. This lack of control may mean that firms are not liquidated until everything of value has been transferred from the firm. Interviews suggest that this is clearly an issue with small privately owned firms in both Hungary and Poland. Whether this is the case with larger firms remains an open question.

Allocating New Credit

Evidence on aggregate lending may provide subtle evidence that market-oriented incentives may be stronger for banks in Poland than in Hungary. While commercial banks in both countries have downsized their loan portfolios and substituted government securities for loans, Poland's commercial banks have done both more aggressively than Hungary's (Figure 3.2). Poland's more aggressive action is surprising, given the banks' higher capital ratios and the country's faster economic growth, and may be evidence of stronger market-oriented incentives than in Hungary.

Of the new loans that were made during this period, there is evidence of improvement in the allocation of new credit by certain Polish banks. At least some of Poland's treasury-owned commercial banks have succeeded in implementing effective credit policies. At five of the nine commercial banks created in 1989, default rates on loans not already in default in 1991 have

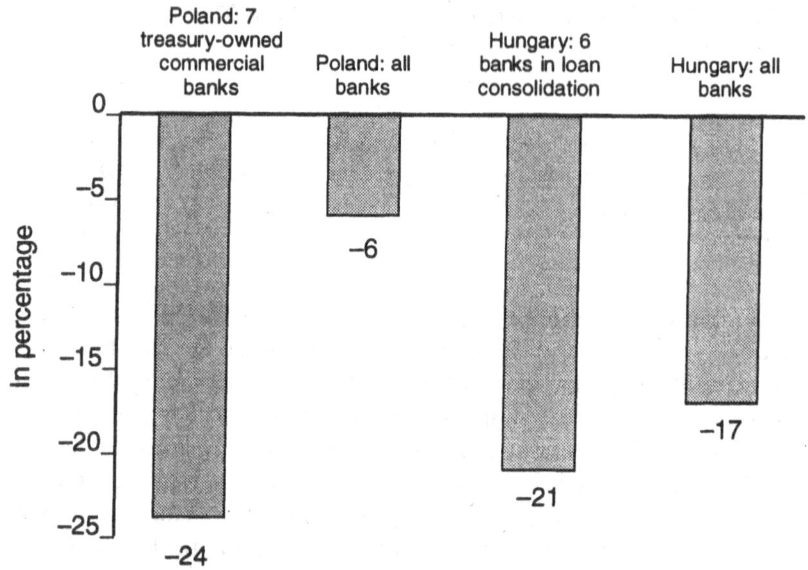

Fig. 3.2 Change in real lending, 1991–93

been relatively reasonable (less than 20 percent). Data from the other four indicate higher default rates on post-1991 loans, and it is not clear whether the credit allocation process is improving in those cases.

Table 3.10 presents data on the borrowing patterns of a sample of 151 Polish firms, classified according to the percentage growth in their bank credit. Interestingly, the two extreme categories – firms that repaid all bank debt and firms that increased their debt by over 100 percent – were dominated by profitable firms. Of the firms that did not fully repay their debt (probably because they did not generate as high a level of retained earnings), Table 3.10 indicates that the allocation by Polish banks of new credit in 1993 was positively correlated with the profitability of the borrower. Regression results using this data[37] also indicate that, controlling for

[37] Numerous regressions were run on the Polish survey data to test the influence of various factors on the allocation of bank credit. One of two dependent variables was used: the change in bank debt of the firm from end-1992 to end-1993 divided by the total assets of the firm (chBD/TA) or the percentage change in bank debt of the firm from end-1992 to end-1993 (%chBD). Among the independent variables included in the various regressions were the firm's profitability, i.e. return on assets in 1993 (PR93/TA); the share of fixed assets in total assets in 1993 (FA/TA); the ownership status of the firm (dummy variables NP for new private firm, PRI for privatized firm); the ratio of bank debt to total assets in 1992 (BD/TA92); and the overall size of the firm (TA93). Firms that totally repaid their debt in 1993 were omitted from the sample for purposes of the regressions, in the belief that such repayment may have

Table 3.10 Changes in Bank Credit in 1993 in a Sample of 151 Polish Firms

Change in indebtedness	Fully repaid bank debt	Decreased bank debt (by less than 100%)	No change in bank debt	Increased bank debt (by less than 100%)	Increased bank debt (by more than 100%)
Number of firms	17	49	12	50	23
Average profit as a share of total assets	0.8%	–10.8%	–6.6%	–4.7%	0.2%
Average bank debt as a share of total assets (1992)	2.3%	12.5%	16.0%	10.4%	5.9%
Average bank debt as a share of total assets (1993)	0%	9.4%	15.4%	12.8%	19.2%
Total flow of credit to/from this group (billion zlotys)	-3.4	-245	0	450	644

Source: World Bank Survey

profitability, banks preferred to lend to new private firms (as opposed to state-owned or privatized firms).

The only detailed lending data available for Hungary do not cover 1993 and are therefore not directly comparable to the Polish results reported above. (Even in Poland, 1991 and 1992 data may well show different patterns than 1993 data.) Statistics on changes in bank credit in 1992 for a sample of 3,273 Hungarian firms compiled by Bonin and Schaffer (1994) indicate that the 5 percent of firms with the lowest profitability increased their total indebtedness in 1992 significantly more than the total sample of firms, although this was primarily due to the capitalization of unpaid interest rather than to any extension of new credit. There are no Hungarian data that indicate a correlation between bank lending and firm profitability as in the 1993 Polish figures.

Changing Ownership

Finally, information, incentives, and laws appear to be interacting in both countries to stimulate some degree of ownership change, albeit in different ways and perhaps for different reasons. In Poland the ownership change arises in part through the bank-led conciliation process. Seven treasury-owned commercial banks interviewed by the authors had negotiated 44 conciliation agreements that included debt for equity swaps, and one of the banks had completed additional debt for equity swaps outside of the conciliation process. However, these banks are still state owned, and this ownership change will not constitute true privatization until the banks are privatized. In contrast to Poland, the most substantial changes in ownership in Hungary have arisen not from debt for equity swaps (which to date appear to have been rare, as noted above), but rather from the sizable reallocation of assets (i.e. asset privatization) that appears to be occurring as a result of the many bankruptcy and liquidation cases now reaching fruition.[38]

indicated a lack of demand for credit altogether (and the regressions were intended to test the influence of various factors on the *supply* of credit, assuming demand existed). Although the wide scatter of the data and the generally low *R*-squares of the regressions indicate that many other factors influence patterns of bank debt, profitability, private ownership, share of fixed assets, and level of indebtedness in 1992 all have some explanatory power (and all have positive signs). Because profitability and private ownership are correlated, the explanatory power of the former drops if the latter is included in the regression. Two of the resulting equations (*t*-statistics in parentheses) are:

$$\underset{}{chBD/TA} = -0.016 + \underset{(1.88)}{0.059\,PR93/TA} + \underset{(0.89)}{0.041\,FA/TA} + \underset{(2.39)}{0.159\,BD/TA92} + \underset{(0.12)}{0.00\,TA}$$

$$chBD/TA = -0.029 + \underset{(1.00)}{0.033\,PR93/TA} + \underset{(1.02)}{0.047\,FA/TA} + \underset{(2.14)}{0.045\,NP} + \underset{(1.58)}{0.036\,PRI} + \underset{(1.51)}{0.106\,BD/TA92} + \underset{(0.70)}{0.00\,TA}$$

[38] While such reallocation is a normal result of workout and liquidation processes in any country, it may be exacerbated in transforming economies because of information asymme-

Prospects for the Future

The foregoing analysis suggests that Poland has been more successful in developing an appropriate policy framework for transforming its state-owned banks into effective financial intermediaries. But, Hungary has made more progress in developing debt collection mechanisms that will address the economy's longer-run needs. *However, the situation is not static.* The progress achieved in Poland with bank incentives can be easily undercut if not reversed by a failure to privatize the banks, to strengthen the laws for debt collection, or to dislodge poorly performing managers.[39] Furthermore, Hungary's failures in the area of incentives can be reversed with the adoption of a program of in-depth external portfolio audits, clear and credible policies on privatization, safeguards to limit lending to problem borrowers, and an end to no-fault recapitalizations. This is no time for complacency in either setting. Greater competition and falling inflation are likely to remove an important source of profits for both banking systems – high spreads on demand deposits (and in Hungary, time deposits). These spreads have helped banks compensate for their lending mistakes. As these spreads are reduced through competition, the ability to cross-subsidize their lending operations will disappear. Thus, banks in both countries must also concentrate on improving their credit allocation skills.

Beyond Poland and Hungary: Other Approaches to Reform

There has been widespread debate about the best approach to strengthen the role of debt as a control device in transitional economies. Although most observers agree on the need to reform accounting and disclosure standards and to take other steps to improve the flow of information, there is intense debate in the other two areas of reform discussed in this chapter. Regarding the legal framework, for example, various approaches to reforms in

tries and insiders' desires to expropriate valuable assets from firms at the expense of creditors or owners. For example, managers may deliberately delay payments in order to qualify for bankruptcy or liquidation procedures and then purchase assets sold through liquidation at low prices. Alternatively, managers may transfer valuable assets to private firms and then send the remaining "shell" companies into liquidation. In any case, extensive privatization of assets is likely to result.

[39] Unfortunately, recent proposals to consolidate four of the state-owned commercial banks into a single entity may only entrench some poorly performing managers and slow the development of competitive forces.

bankruptcy and debt collection have been put forward,[40] and countries have moved in many different ways and at different speeds to promote strong debt collection procedures.[41] This discussion has mirrored the widespread dissatisfaction with bankruptcy processes in the West (see Bradley and Rosenzweig (1992)), and at the same time has reflected the political and economic tensions associated with rapid change and restructuring in the transition setting.

Most of the controversy to date has surrounded the question of how to reform creditor (particularly bank) incentives. Although this chapter has focused on the differences between the Hungarian and Polish programs, both countries have followed a broadly similar approach. This approach can be questioned on at least three fundamental levels: the desirability of relying on government-funded recapitalization to make insolvent banks solvent; the desirability of attempting to make the successors of the old monobanks the cornerstone of a new market-oriented financial system; and the desirability of relying on banks to play a significant role in corporate governance and the allocation of financial flows.

Early in the transition process, Poland and Hungary implicitly committed to protect depositors in state-owned banks by injecting new capital into those banks. Alternatively, insolvent banks could have been recapitalized by restructuring the banks' liabilities instead, by writing down deposits and by converting some of the deposits to equity (thereby forcing depositors to share in the loss). In contrast to recapitalization through government injection of new capital, this latter approach causes the bank to shrink as losses on the asset side are reflected in writedowns on the liability side.[42]

Two concerns typically push governments to inject new capital rather than restructure liabilities: fear of a political backlash from depositors and fear of a systemwide financial crisis.[43] Recent research casts doubt on the conventional wisdom that forcing depositors to bear loss inevitably risks serious macroeconomic disruption. A recent study identified five cases where governments dealt with significant insolvency problems by restructuring

[40] For examples of different approaches and views, see Aghion, Hart, and Moore (1992), Mizsei (1993), Bonin and Schaffer (1994), and Gray (1995). Still others see the development of secondary debt markets and extensive set-off rights as a way to avoid reliance on formal debt collection procedures.

[41] The Czech Republic, for example, deliberately delayed the implementation of its bankruptcy regime, in stark contrast to Hungary's aggressive approach.

[42] A combination of some writedown and some injection of new capital is another possibility.

[43] Proponents frequently offer a third argument, the preservation of informational capital. However, this can also be accomplished by restructuring liabilities to bring them into line with decreased asset values.

bank liabilities.[44] In no case did a significant decline in economic activity result. Indeed, in several cases an economic turnaround began within a month of the restructuring of liabilities. Although the restructuring of liabilities may not have *promoted* macroeconomic growth, these findings indicate that the deleterious effects of liability restructuring were not severe enough to derail recovery.

On a more fundamental level, other observers have questioned whether reform of existing banking institutions is an efficient use of resources, given the huge weight of the socialist legacy. As an alternative they have suggested "creative destruction" – downsizing existing banks while new ones grow – with the view that new banks would not carry the burdens of the past and would thus be more likely to internalize the appropriate incentives (Phelps *et al.* 1993; Pohl and Claessens 1994). Proponents of this view argue that existing state banks should be quickly downsized, their capital being brought to adequate levels by removing assets (or shrinking them through hyperinflation as in Russia) rather than increasing capital. This view assumes that the corporate governance mechanisms of new private intermediaries will be more effective in avoiding fraud and moral hazard than those of the post-socialist successors of the monobanks.

If the newly chartered banks are clearly outside the safety net, this approach may be useful in creating new, effective financial intermediaries. However, one cannot assume that new banks will behave better than old ones if the fundamental underpinnings – information, incentives, and laws – are not changed. In the early stages of transition, information problems make it difficult for depositors (or anyone else) to identify private bank owners who are engaged in fraud. For reasons that we do not fully understand, countries that liberalize domestic chartering policies almost always fail to follow up with reforms mandating adequate disclosure and creating a well functioning

[44] Baer and Klingebiel (1995). The cases studied are the United States (March 1933), Japan (1946), Malaysia (1986), Argentina (1989), and Estonia (1992). Estonia's 1992 experience with liability restructuring is informative. In December 1992 the government closed one problem bank and merged two others together. Liabilities were written down in all three cases, with depositors in the closed bank incurring losses and depositors in the other two banks incurring a risk of future loss if problem debts could not be recovered. This program led to no systemic financial crisis. Indeed, in early 1993 Estonia became the first of the former Soviet Union (FSU) economies to post an increase in industrial production, and by the third quarter of 1993 growth in the industrial sector was accompanied by growth in GDP. The liability restructuring, rather than impeding the growth of credit to the private sector, seems to have reversed a year long decline in real credit to the private sector. The Estonian experience suggests that the governments of Eastern Europe could perhaps have restructured their banking systems with considerably less fiscal burden and fewer incentive problems without sacrificing growth. Political pressures of course play a major role in the choice of strategy. Depositors were fully protected in the more recent failure of the second largest Estonian bank.

supervisory system. Ex post legal sanctions are unlikely to be an effective deterrent, given shortfalls in institutional capacity and precedent in the legal system. In this environment, new banking licenses may initially be nothing more than a license to steal.[45]

Neither Hungary nor Poland has fully opened its doors to unhindered foreign investment in the banking sector. Foreign banks can bring capital, skills, reputation, and supervisory practices – assets that can improve the chances that creative destruction or more traditional banking reforms can succeed.

Finally, others have questioned the role of banks and credit more generally, suggesting that equity funds should be the primary mechanisms for channeling finance in transition economies. As discussed earlier, however, theory and evidence reinforce the view that equity and debt each has an important and complementary role to play in monitoring and exerting control over enterprise managers. While debt need not, and probably cannot lead in corporate governance and finance in these economies soon, the experiences of the early reformers – Hungary, Poland, and Estonia among them – provide clues to what must be done to make debt a meaningful control device that can contribute to the enormous task of enterprise restructuring.

[45] For an interesting discussion of these issues, see Akerlof and Romer (1994). The track record of Poland's domestically owned private banks, which are in much worse shape than its state-owned commercial banks, does not give much comfort.

References

Ábel, István. 1994. "A Gradual Approach to Banking Reform: The Hungarian Bad Loans Problem." Paper presented at International Conference on Bad Enterprise Debts in Central and Eastern Europe, 6–8 June, Budapest, Hungary.

Aghion, Philippe, and Patrick Bolton. 1992. "An 'Incomplete Contract' Approach to Bankruptcy and the Financial Structure of the Firm." *Review of Economic Studies* 59: 473–94.

Aghion, Philippe, Oliver Hart, and John Moore. 1992. "The Economics of Bankruptcy Reform." *Journal of Law, Economics and Organization* 8: 523–46.

Akerlof, George A., and David M. Romer. 1994. "Looting: The Economic Underworld of Bankruptcy for Profit." Brookings Papers on Economic Activity. The Brookings Institution: Washington, D.C.

Aoki, Masahiko. 1994. "Monitoring Characteristics of the Main Bank System: An Analytical and Developmental View." Economic Development Institute EDI Working Paper No. 94–5, The World Bank, Washington, D.C.

Baer, Herbert L., and Daniela Klingebiel. 1995. "Systemic Risk When Depositors Bear Losses: Five Case Studies." In *Research in Financial Services*, forthcoming.

Baums, Theodor. 1994. "The German Banking System and Its Impacts on Corporate

Finance and Governance." Economic Development Institute EDI Working Paper No. 94–13, The World Bank, Washington, D.C.

Belka, Marek. 1994. "Financial Restructuring of Banks and Enterprises: The Polish Solution." Paper presented at International Conference on Bad Enterprise Debts in Central and Eastern Europe, 6–8 June, Budapest, Hungary.

Belka, Marek, Mark Schaffer, Saul Estrin, and Inderjit Singh. 1994. "Evidence from a Survey of State-Owned, Privatized, and Emerging Private Firms." Paper presented at Workshop on Enterprise Adjustment in Eastern Europe, 22–23 September, The World Bank, Washington, D.C..

Berglöf, Erik. 1994. "Corporate Governance in Transition Economies: The Theory and Its Policy Implications." Paper written for World Bank project, The Roles of Banks in Corporate Governance in Transition Economies, The World Bank, Washington, D.C.

Berglöf, Erik, and Ernst-Ludwig von Thadden. 1994. "Short-Term vs. Long-Term Interests: Capital Structures with Multiple Investors." *Quarterly Journal of Economics* 109 (November).

Bonin, John, and Mark Schaffer. 1994. "Banks, Firms, Bad Debts, and Bankruptcy in Hungary 1991–94." Paper presented at Workshop on Enterprise Adjustment in Eastern Europe, 22–3 September, The World Bank, Washington, D.C.

Bradley, Michael, and Michael Rosenzweig. 1992. "The Untenable Case for Chapter 11." *Yale Law Journal* 101: 1043–1089.

Chmielewski, Mariusz *et al.* 1989. "Restrukturyzacja Finansowa Przedsiebiorstw I Banków." Report on the Polish program of enterprise and bank restructuring, Gdansk Institute, Poland.

Diamond, Douglas W. 1991. "Debt Maturity Structure and Liquidity Risk." *Quarterly Journal of Economics* (August): 709–37.

Gilson, Stuart. 1989. "Management Turnover and Financial Distress." *Journal of Financial Economics* 25: 241–62.

Gilson, Stuart. 1990. "Bankruptcy, Boards, Banks, and Blockholders: Evidence on Changes in Corporate Ownership and Control When Firms Default." *Journal of Financial Economics* 27: 355–87, North-Holland.

Gilson, Stuart, Kose John, and Larry Lang. 1990. "Troubled Debt Restructuring: An Empirical Study of Private Reorganization of Firms in Default." *Journal of Financial Economics* 27: 315–53.

Glen, Jack, and Brian Pinto. 1994. "Debt or Equity? How Firms in Developing Countries Choose." International Finance Corporation Discussion Paper No. 22, The World Bank, Washington, D.C.

Gomulka, Stanislaw. 1993. "The Financial Situation of Polish Enterprises 1992-93 and Its Impact on Monetary and Fiscal Policies." Studies and Analyses 6, CASE Research Foundation, Warsaw.

Gray, Cheryl W. 1995. "Some Common Misconceptions about Bankruptcy and Conciliation in Hungary and Poland." Washington, D.C., World Bank, unpublished, March.

Gray, Cheryl W., Sabine Schlorke, and Miklos Szanyi. 1995. "Hungary's Bankruptcy Experience, 1992–1993," World Bank Policy Research Working Paper 1510 (September).

Harris, Milton, and Artur Raviv. 1991. "The Theory of Capital Structure." *The Journal of Finance* 46, no. 1 (March).

Holmström, Bengt. 1992. "Financing Investment in Eastern Europe: A Theoretical Perspective." Yale University. Mimeographed.

Holmström, Bengt, and Jean Tirole. 1993. "Financial Intermediation and the Real Sector." Centre for Economic Policy Research. Mimeographed.

Hoshi, Takeo, Anil Kashyap, and David Scharfstein. 1990. "The Role of Banks in Reducing the Costs of Financial Distress in Japan." *Journal of Financial Economics* 27.

Hotchkiss, E. 1992. "The Post-Bankruptcy Performance of Firms Emerging from Chapter 11," unpublished manuscript, New York University.

Kawalec, Stefan, Slawomir Sikora, and Piotr Rymaszewski. 1994. "Polish Program of Bank and Enterprise Restructuring: Design and Implementation, 1991–1994." Paper presented at Central and Eastern European Privatisation Network's Workshop on Linking Bank Rehabilitation with Enterprise Restructuring and Privatisation, 24–5 June, Budapest, Hungary.

Kornai, Janos, and Agnes Matits. 1984. "Softness of the Budget Constraint – An Analysis Relying on Data of Firms." *Acta Oeconomica* 32: 3-4.

Mayer, Colin. 1990. "Financial Systems, Corporate Finance, and Economic Development." In *Asymmetric Information, Corporate Finance, and Investment*, edited by Glenn Hubbard. Chicago, Ill.: University of Chicago Press.

McKinnon, Ronald. 1991. "Financial Control in the Transition from Classical Socialism to a Market Economy." *Journal of Economic Perspectives* 54: 107–22.

Mizsei, Kálmán. 1993. *Bankruptcy and the Post-Communist Economies of East Central Europe.* New York: Institute for EastWest Studies.

Myers, Stewart C. 1989. "Still Searching for Optimal Capital Structure." *Are the Distinctions between Debt and Equity Disappearing?* Proceedings of a conference held in October. Conference Series no. 33, sponsored by Federal Reserve Bank of Boston.

Myers, Stewart C., and Nicholas S. Majluf. 1984. "Corporate Financing and Investment Decisions When Firms Have Information That Investors Do Not Have." *Journal of Financial Economics* (13 June): 187–221.

Phelps, E.S., Roman Frydman, Andrzej Rapaczynski, and Andrei Shleifer. 1993. "Needed Mechanisms of Corporate Governance and Finance in Eastern Europe." World Bank Discussion Paper No. 1.

Pohl, Gerhard, and Stijn Claessens. 1994. "Banks, Capital Markets, and Corporate Governance. Lessons from Russia for Eastern Europe." World Bank Policy Research Working Paper No. 1326 (July).

Rajan, Raghuram, and Luigi Zingales. 1993. "Is There an Optimal Capital Structure? Evidence from International Data," unpublished manuscript, August.

Schaffer, Mark E. 1989. "Redistribution of Profit, Financial Flows, and Economic Reform in Polish Industry: Evidence from the Lista 500," unpublished manuscript, February.

Sheard, Paul. 1994. "Main Banks and the Governance of Financial Distress." Economic Development Institute EDI Working Paper No. 94–7, The World Bank, Washington, D.C.

Shleifer, Andrew, and Robert Vishny. 1992. "Liquidation Values and Debt Capacity: A Market Equilibrium Approach." *Journal of Finance* 47: 1343–66.

van Wijnbergen, Sweder. 1993. "On the Role of Banks in Enterprise Restructuring: The Polish Example," unpublished manuscript.

Vodopivec, Milan. 1994. "Appropriability of Returns in the Yugoslav Firm." *Eastern Economic Journal* 20:3 (summer).

4

INSTITUTIONAL INVESTORS IN TRANSITIONAL ECONOMIES

Lessons from the Czech Experience

JOHN C. COFFEE, JR.

Professor Coffee would like to acknowledge the valuable assistance received from a variety of persons whose knowledge and experience with the Czech context vastly exceeds his own. A partial list would include: Dusan Triska, Jan Mladek, Joel Turkewitz, Stijn Claessens, and various commentators at the World Bank.

Introduction

This chapter has a dual aim. On one level, it attempts to provide a detailed explanation of the Czech experience with voucher privatization, because, put simply, that experience has been the success story of Eastern European mass privatization. But this chapter also has a second objective. For those interested in corporate governance, Czech voucher privatization represents a natural experiment in ownership structure – one in which special monitors and a uniquely concentrated shareholder ownership structure were intentionally created to ensure the accountability of managers at the newly privatized companies. What happens under such an ownership structure? Will large financial intermediaries created specifically to monitor managements function as planned? Or, are the incentives to monitor weaker and more problematic? Are there also perverse incentives that can lead such institutions to pursue ulterior ends unrelated to, or conflicting with, the interests of shareholders?

Answers to these questions (if definitive answers were possible) would transcend the Eastern European context. For example, in the United States, the capacity and incentive of institutional investors to monitor managements have been the subject of a continuing academic debate. On one side of this debate, a group of critics argue that institutional investors, if deregulated and liberated from existing restrictive federal regulations, would become active monitors and thus end (or at least reduce) the separation of ownership and control (see Roe 1991; Black 1990; Grundfest 1990). On the other side, another group are skeptical that institutional investors have adequate incentives to monitor, both because of principal/agent problems and a general preference for liquidity that leads them to limit their ownership stakes (see Coffee 1991; Rock 1991). Thus, although they agree that much federal regulation is burdensome, they believe deregulation may produce only marginal differences.

Against the backdrop of this debate, the Czech experience is particularly interesting because the trade-off between liquidity and control in economies with developed securities markets simply does not exist within the Czech system. The Czech equity markets are extremely "thin," lacking both liquidity and transparency. As a result, large shareholders are effectively locked in and may not choose between "exit" and "voice." In fact the Czech market may be among the most concentrated in the world, and thus the separation of ownership and control is minimized. Accordingly, the Czech market presents a unique natural experiment: to what degree will newly created institutional investors engage in costly monitoring when they are denied the opportunity to engage in other distractions (such as noise trading)?

In truth the Czech experience with privatization is still too brief to permit any quantitative assessments. But preliminary data and qualitative evidence do lead to one conclusion. Institutional and legal details are critical. Concentrated ownership, by itself, may not lead to active monitoring because the economic incentives to monitor may be weak or overshadowed by more powerful incentives. In this light, the Czech experience suggests that the incentives of outwardly similar institutions to engage in monitoring can vary greatly, depending in large part on their own institutional affiliations and sponsorships.

At first glance, the Czech institutional context seems roughly to resemble that of Germany, where a small number of "universal" banks have long played a significant role in corporate governance.[1] But there is an important difference: the major Czech financial institutions that founded the majority of the investment privatization funds (or IPFs), on which this chapter will

[1] For the traditional view of German banks as active monitors, see Cable (1985); Gorton and Schmid (1994). But for a revisionist view that doubts the extent of such monitoring, see Edwards and Fisher (1994) (discussed later in the chapter).

focus, do not themselves hold, directly or indirectly, significant equity stakes in the newly privatized companies. Although they may possess *de facto* control over the IPFs that they have sponsored, their relationship with their IPFs is that of an agent, rather than an owner; they receive a management fee but do not share in equity appreciation. In turn this means that they may have control over, but not ownership of, the portfolios that their IPFs hold in the newly privatized Czech companies. Control without ownership can create perverse incentives, particularly when Czech financial institutions have a direct creditor relationship with the newly privatized companies. Either because of such a creditor relationship or the desire for it, there is the prospect of a conflict of interests. Both these factors – control without ownership and a potentially overshadowing creditor relationship – can undercut the incentive to be an active monitor, even when the structure of share ownership is uniquely concentrated.

In overview the contemporary Czech pattern of corporate governance is probably best described as a hybrid of the German system of corporate governance (i.e. heavily bank centered with thin equity markets) and the U.S. and U.K. systems (i.e. institutional investors holding substantial equity stakes in companies traded in deep and active equity markets). The key financial intermediaries in the Czech system are specially designed investment privatization funds, which resemble a U.S. or U.K. closed-end mutual fund, but these IPFs are often affiliated with banks or other financial institutions (as under the German approach) and their shares trade in a market that has little liquidity. Many observers have predicted that Czech corporate governance will evolve in the direction of the German banking model. But the likely future evolution of Czech governance may depend in substantial part on Czech regulatory policy, which seems today uncertain as to whether Czech financial institutions should be able to integrate their creditor and equity operations to achieve monitoring synergies.[2] The likely costs and benefits of a German policy of consolidating equity and credit operations in one mega-monitor need to be contrasted with those of the alternative American approach of requiring strict fire walls between banks and their equity-trading affiliates. The final section of this chapter will focus on these trade-offs, which are important for all transitional economies.

However, for most of Eastern Europe, the leading current issue in privatization is not how the Czech system will evolve, but how it can be emulated. Alone among the several Central European nations that began at the same starting point with the collapse of the Communist bloc in 1989, the Czech

[2] The leading example of this tendency is the Ministry of Finance's position that "fire walls" should be maintained between the parent bank and the IPF. See discussion later in the chapter.

Republic has created functioning capital markets and a truly privatized corporate structure. In this respect, voucher privatization has been an unqualified success. With the completion of the second privatization wave at the end of 1994, the postprivatization landscape of the Czech economy can be sketched in at least its broader outlines, as follows:

1. Over 80 percent of adult Czech citizens are now shareholders in the 1,849 companies that were privatized (in whole or in part).[3]
2. Although estimates vary, between 65 percent and 90 percent of all assets in the Czech economy are now privately owned (up from a mere 4.5 percent in 1990).[4]
3. The Czech economy has the lowest rate of inflation in Central Europe (currently, 10 percent) coupled with an unbelievably low rate of unemployment (currently 3.5 percent).[5]
4. The market capitalization of the Czech stock markets is estimated at around $12 billion, and a small debt market has also begun (hesitantly) to develop (Crawford 1994). Although the Czech stock market suffered a severe 35 percent decline between April and October 1994, it continues to attract Western institutional interest.[6]
5. The Czech economy has also attracted $2.7 billion in direct foreign investment since 1990 (see Crawford 1994).
6. The Czech Republic's sovereign rating of BBB+ in international credit markets is also the highest in Central Europe (see Rehak 1994).
7. Politically, the Czech Republic has a stable, free-market oriented government, which (despite one serious political scandal)[7] has been able to survive the process of privatization without seriously trimming its sails.

By any standard, these criteria define success.

Meanwhile, the progress toward privatization in other East European countries has been hesitant and halting, one step forward followed by one

[3] For detailed recent reviews, see "Czechs turn out to buy into industry privatization," *Los Angeles Times*, 26 November 1994, D–1; "Czech sell-off round ends," *Wall Street Journal*, 28 November 1994, A–14; Rocks (1994).

[4] For the estimate that 65% of "economic activity" has now been transferred to the private sector, see "Czechs complete privatization plan," *San Francisco Chronicle*, 26 November 1994. For the 90% estimate, see Jaros and Sanders (1994).

[5] For these estimates, see Rehak (1994); Cox (1994).

[6] See, e.g. "A Surge of funds to Eastern Europe," *Financial Post*, 29 November 1994, 26. But see also Fleming (1994) (noting retail mutual funds' reluctance to invest in uncertain markets.)

[7] The arrest late in 1994 of Jaroslav Lizner, head of the Coupon Privatization Center, while in possession of an alleged $300,000 cash bribe, has proven to be the major political scandal of the privatization process. The facts still appear to be in dispute, but prosecutors allege that he was bribed to intervene in a privatization dispute over the sale of a controlling block of the shares in a dairy (see Rocks 1994).

step backward. Although Poland began at the same starting point, it has only recently adopted privatization legislation;[8] the Slovakian effort remains mired in political controversy; and the Ukrainian, Bulgarian, and Hungarian efforts are well behind the Czech pace. Only Russia has moved with comparable speed, but Russian privatization (although relying on basically similar methods of voucher privatization) has produced insider-dominated firms in which management controls on average 70 percent of the shares in the privatized firm. As of the end of 1993, outsiders held on average only 21.5 percent (and a median of 20 percent) in privatized firms in Russia (see Frydman, Pistor, and Rapaczynski in this volume; Blasi and Shleifer in volume 2).

In sharp contrast, Czech privatization granted few concessions to insiders and, at the end of the first wave of privatization, the average employee stake across all privatized firms in the program was only 4.4 percent.[9] In short, the Czech experiment appears not only to have worked, but to have succeeded without the compromises that (in Russia and elsewhere) undercut the original goal of a rapid transition to a market economy. At least potentially, Czech corporations are today fully subject to capital market discipline, whereas elsewhere privatization remains stalled or (as in Russia) has ushered in a long transitional period of managerial domination.

The Czech success thus raises two very different types of questions: first, for planners and politicians seeking to design a privatization program, the Czech program – in particular, its emphasis on open access and free entry and its reliance on private agents, rather than governmentally created investment vehicles – provides a feasible model that has worked and a logical one to emulate. These practitioners of privatization will sensibly focus on the steps taken by the Czech government to implement voucher privatization. Their chief concern will be how easily can the Czech model be copied. Second, for academics and others interested in corporate governance, the more interesting question is: how will the Czech system evolve? Should it be redesigned in any material respect to secure better monitoring and capital market discipline? In particular in the concentrated Czech market, how will the IPFs perform? This chapter addresses both sets of questions and examines the mechanics of the Czech privatization process in some detail to inform those principally interested in the first set.

Nonetheless, a bottom-line assessment of the Czech experience is not yet possible. One can fairly conclude that the techniques and decisions most

[8] Polish Prime Minister Pawlak signed legislation clearing the Polish privatization process to begin after several years of delay in late October 1994. See *Christian Science Monitor*, 24 October 1994.

[9] See Earle and Estrin in vol. 2 of this book. They also report that in only seven companies (out of 988 projects approved for privatization) did the employee ownership stake exceed 30%.

identified with Czech privatization – namely, (1) the use of vouchers to effect a rapid disposition of state-owned property, (2) the free entry permitted to privately formed Investment Privatization Funds, and (3) the use of such IPFs as a corporate governance solution to the problem of dispersed share ownership – have worked well to end state control of the economy and to facilitate the rapid creation of secondary markets. But, the Czech achievement is qualified by the facts that (1) its securities markets possess neither transparency nor liquidity, (2) a curious and potentially collusive system of cross-ownership has arisen among the major banks, and (3) the state continues to hold a potentially decisive "swing" block of stock in the largest corporations and blocks. Most importantly, the efficacy of the IPFs, themselves, remains unproven. Although the IPFs have shown that they can be powerful intermediaries when they want to be, their incentives to monitor vary greatly and depend on their widely varying individual circumstances. Some close observers view the major Czech banks that control the largest IPFs to be a restraining force, one holding back the pace of restructurings (see, e.g. Rocks 1994; "Czechs turn out to buy into industry").

As a model for future privatization programs, the Czech experience also illustrates the inevitable limitations of planning and the likelihood of spontaneous developments having no clear precedents or parallels in other systems. Two examples will illustrate. First, despite the clear intentions of those planning Czech privatization, one unexpected development was the appearance of a concentrated system of cross-ownership under which the leading Czech financial institutions (i.e. banks and insurance companies) indirectly hold substantial and potentially controlling blocks in each other. When these reciprocally held stakes are added to the substantial residual interests indirectly retained by a quasi-governmental agency, the National Property Fund (NPF), the resulting structure seemingly insulates the management of each major financial institution from any effective challenge to its control. In turn through the investment company subsidiaries that each of these financial institutions has established to manage IPFs, these institutions, at least in conjunction with the NPF, hold blocks of stock in the aggregate sufficient to control all but the largest of the newly privatized firms. Thus, at a minimum, the state retains a substantial potential voice in corporate governance, even if the current administration (whose free market preferences are beyond dispute) declines to exercise that voice.

The second major unplanned development involved the IPFs, themselves. Although their appearance was intended and encouraged, the manner in which they evolved and competed for dominance surprised Czech regulators and shocked the Czech Parliament into enacting hastily drafted restrictions on their activity. The most spontaneous element in the Czech privatization process was the appearance of IPFs that were not controlled by banks or other financial institutions. Basically, Czech IPFs can be loosely classified as either "bank affiliated" or "independent" (that is, neither founded nor managed by a substantial Czech commercial or savings bank). Many predicted that the larger bank-affiliated IPFs would dominate the post-privatization economy, both because their bank relationship gave them a marketing advantage (as Czech citizens were more likely to trust their local bank than strangers) and because banks could realize economies of scope and scale from their joint roles as creditors and equity shareholders in the privatized companies. Yet, at least to date, Czech privatization has been more influenced by the independent IPFs – new entrants who, without ties to the existing Czech financial establishment, have successfully competed like classic entrepreneurs against larger entities with greater resources. Without the best known of these rugged individualists (Harvard Capital and Consulting (HC&C)),[10] it is doubtful that voucher privatization would have won public acceptance or that IPFs would today occupy the dominant position they now hold as the key financial intermediaries in the structure of Czech corporate governance. Not only did HC&C perfect the marketing techniques that caused an initially apathetic Czech public to accept IPFs and to identify its own interests with voucher privatization, but HC&C and similar independent IPFs seem to have outperformed the "bank" funds in designing and bidding for portfolios. Although the initially slow and bureaucratic performance of the largest bank funds may yet improve (and some smaller banks have established funds that have been aggressively entrepreneurial), there are reasons to believe that bank and independent funds will behave in characteristically different ways. This hypothesis flows from the fundamental fact that these two classes of IPFs face very different incentive structures: the independent IPFs have no other relationship with their portfolio companies and can succeed only as fund managers, while the bank funds may often have a greater (or, at least, offsetting) interest in maximizing bank-lending opportunities for their parent.

Both these developments – the aggressive behavior of the independent funds and the cross-ownership phenomenon – force us to focus on a new level of corporate governance at which the interests of principal and agent can diverge: IPF governance. For several reasons, market forces appear inadequate to control agency costs at the IPF level. One indication is that most

[10] For a review of the controversies surrounding HC&C and its founder, Victor Kozeny, see King (1993). It should be emphasized that HC&C has no connection with Harvard University (other than for the fact that Mr. Kozeny is an alumnus). Although Mr. Kozeny was forced to flee the Czech Republic in 1994 under the threat of an indictment, HC&C remains an active and seemingly successful manager of both IPFs and other (so-called "cash") funds.

IPFs trade at substantial discounts from the apparent net asset value of their portfolios (sometimes up to 80 percent). Such a closed-end fund discount is a well-known phenomenon in mutual funds, but in theory it should attract bidders to acquire these funds and oust at least the worst performing fund managers. The problem with this simple scenario for market discipline is that (1) legal restraints preclude one IPF from purchasing shares in another, and (2) shareholders in IPFs often lack voting rights and thus cannot oust the incumbent IPF management. With the "second wave" of voucher privatization in 1994, entrepreneurs founding IPFs began to use the unit trust format in preference to joint stock companies as the preferred organizational form for IPFs. Because unit trusts lack voting rights, they thus insulate their investment company sponsors from the threat of hostile takeovers or a shareholder decision to vote their directors off the IPF's board. Interestingly, this transition occurred just as the size of the closed-end discounts on most IPFs was becoming visible to the market. Analogous techniques to frustrate fund shareholders are also available to IPFs organized as joint stock companies – for example, long-term noncancelable management contracts. The net result is that the oldest question in governance – Who will guard the guardians? – now arises at least as much at the IPF level in the Czech Republic as at the corporate level.

These introductory comments should not be misinterpreted. On balance, IPFs seem an ingenious adaption to the special problems encountered by privatizing economies and vastly preferable to state-created funds. Still, their use carries risks that policy planners need to address. The intent of this chapter is not to reach a final dispositive assessment of the IPFs (or of the agencies regulating them), but to highlight the public policy issues associated with their creation and use. Moreover, any generalized assessment of IPFs would obscure the remarkable diversity that today exists among the IPFs. In style, philosophy, and priorities, they are different, and at each stage – in marketing their shares, investing their voucher points, and monitoring companies – these differences in approach have translated into differences in performance.

An Overview of Voucher Privatization

Voucher privatization was the concluding stage in the overall program of Czech privatization. First, it was preceded by a restitution program, which was adopted in 1990 and vigorously pursued during 1990 and 1991. The principal impact of restitution was on housing, retail trade, and agriculture. Then, a second stage – known as "small-scale privatization" – was inaugurated in 1991 and was primarily implemented through public auctions that lasted into late 1993. Neither technique attempted to privatize large companies, but rather typically separated discrete assets from a state enterprise.

Large-scale privatization was the final stage, and focused on the state owned assets in industry, agriculture, and trade. When the Velvet Revolution in 1989 brought the collapse of the Communist government, productive enterprises in Czechoslovakia were almost entirely state owned. Of the gross national product, 86 percent was produced in the state sector, 10 percent in the cooperative sector, and only 4 percent in the private sector (Mladek 1994). Given the relatively small domestic savings of the Czech citizenry, standard privatization techniques – sales, stock flotations, or auctions – would have predictably resulted in transferring most state property to foreign owners (possibly at bargain prices as well). In addition such a process would have been slow and extended, both because foreign purchasers would want to conduct a "due diligence" investigation of the assets to be purchased and because political controversies would inevitably result over to whom and at what prices the country's national assets were to be sold.

Rationale

Given these realities, voucher privatization had three obvious advantages: (1) it could be effected very quickly, because there was no need to negotiate the terms of a gratuitous transfer; (2) it distributed assets broadly and democratically to the entire citizenry (rather than to the small percentage of the population with financial resources); and (3) it averted the political controversies inherent in selling a majority interest to foreign interests in prized national industries (which the Czechs generically refer to as "the national silver"). In contrast, if the citizens later resold these same assets to foreign interests, that was another matter, without the same political overtones. Realistically, a fourth reason may also explain why voucher privatization was politically popular: for those managing the to-be-privatized enterprises, voucher privatization was not perceived as a threat to their position or control because it was expected to result in a very dispersed (and thus weak) class of stockholders. In contrast, private sales would bring in "true" owners, who could control the incumbent managers.

In retrospect the conclusion now seems inescapable that the Czech privatization program succeeded (albeit imperfectly) in realizing the first three goals, but sorely disappointed those who supported it for the fourth reason. Although there was considerable delay, some favoritism, and occasional controversy, other techniques would probably have exacerbated these problems to a considerably greater degree. But incumbent managers who expected to exploit voucher privatization were quickly surprised and frustrated by the success of the IPFs in asserting control.

Initially, voucher privatization was intended to be the exclusive mechanism for privatization. The architects of large-scale privatization rejected arguments that vouchers should be used as only one of several interchangeable techniques for restructuring enterprises. Their view was that privatization should precede restructuring in order that the "true" owners could decide on the form that restructuring should take (e.g. sales to foreign investors, managerial buyouts, strategic partners, employee stock purchases, etc.) (see Kotrba 1994). Other techniques would preempt that choice, they believed, before the new private owners of the firm appeared on the scene. Alone, voucher privatization was neutral and left all other options open. Given this philosophy, it was originally contemplated that 97 percent of the shares of all privatized companies would be distributed under the voucher program and 3 percent would be conveyed to the Restitution Investment Fund.

In reality this goal of exclusivity for voucher privatization was quickly compromised. The one major limitation of voucher privatization is that it does not bring new capital into the business. For some enterprises, the need for new capital required that they either be sold to another (usually foreign) firm or that a strategic partner (usually Western) be attracted that could be a source of future capital investments. At the outset of Czech privatization, such buyers and investors were in notably short supply. Partly for this reason, the National Property Fund (NPF) was assigned the custodial role of acting as interim caretaker for firms (and blocks of stock) that were ultimately to be marketed to such buyers.

The degree to which departures were made from the original concept of 97 percent reliance on voucher privatization appears to have depended on the size of the firm, with larger firms being more successful in arranging to park a controlling block of their stock in the NPF. Looking at the average percentage of stock included in the first wave of voucher privatization, one finds that voucher privatization was the method used to distribute 81 percent of the shares. However, if one looks more closely at the relative value of the stock included in the first wave, this percentage of stock value privatization through vouchers falls to 63.5 percent.[11] The difference points up the political compromise: larger firms were more successful in limiting voucher

[11] Mladek (1994), p.4. This is in effect a weighted average figure. In the second wave, the corresponding figure was 69.6% for companies that were not included in the first wave. Letter to the author from Jan Mladek dated 7 July 1994.

privatization to a minority of their shares in the first wave (with most of the balance of their shares remaining in the NPF).[12]

In turn this disparity highlights the significance of the NPF. Founded in August 1991, it was intended to play a passive role as the midwife of the privatization process. Once a privatization project was approved by the Ministry of Privatization, the project was to be handed over to the NPF for implementation. The NPF would form the joint stock company, register the shares in its name, and act as the new company's sole owner pending the sale or distribution of its shares. However, delay increased the period it acted as the *de facto* sole owner.

Potentially, the NPF could have functioned as the Treuhand did in Germany, playing the role of a policymaker, auctioneer, and amateur investment banker. Clearly, it has not attempted such a role. Rather, it largely persisted in playing a self-consciously passive role in order to leave discretion in the true owners. When the NPF became controversial (as it did in 1994), it was for its tendency to delay and avoid decisions, not for bureaucratic empire building. Tomas Jezek, the chairman of the NPF until June 1994 and one of the most philosophically committed architects of Czech privatization (and a former minister of privatization), strongly resisted the bureaucratic temptation to expand the power and authority of the NPF. Still, for those nations seeking to copy the Czech experience, the NPF was a problematic and potentially dangerous institution, which could have seriously sidetracked Czech privatization if its leaders had been more bureaucratically inclined. Even today, after the completion of privatization, the NPF continues to hold a potentially pivotal role in many major Czech corporations.

Timing and Procedure

Serious planning for voucher privatization began in 1991. Under the Large-Scale Privatization Law adopted on 1 February 1991, managements of approximately 70 percent of (then) Czechoslovakia's 4,800 state-owned enterprises were required to prepare specific plans for converting their enterprises to private ownership.[13] These plans, known as privatization projects, were submitted to the enterprise's supervising governmental ministry

[12] The argument of these firms was that they needed a large foreign corporation or investor that could make substantial investments in them in order to finance restructurings, or in other cases, to make the firm technologically competitive. This need was clear enough, but such investors were in limited supply and in most cases never materialized during the course of privatization.

[13] This chapter will refer to the Act on the Consolidation of Transfer of State Owned Property to Other Persons, Act no. 92/1991 Coll. of 26 February 1991 as the "Large-Scale Privatization Law." See also Mann (1993).

(usually the Ministry of Industry and Trade) for initial approval, and then to the Ministry of Privatization for final approval. The process was slow, cumbersome, and created the principal bottleneck in the privatization process.

Management's basic plan for the enterprise had to be submitted by 30 November 1991. However, others could submit competing proposals (including proposals to buy some specific unit or division), and competing proposals were given an extended deadline to 20 January 1992. Final decisions by the Ministry of Privatization were to be made by 30 April 1992 for those units to be included in the first wave. Some 23,478 projects (relating to 4,450 state-owned companies) were submitted. Nearly half were received from prospective buyers, but 21 percent were submitted by managements (Kotrba 1994, 8). One survey has found that the proposals submitted by management succeeded in over 62 percent of the cases, while other competitors succeeded in only 17.3 percent of the cases.[14] Nonetheless, from the outset of privatization, the attempt to ensure active competition seems to have been a primary focus of those overseeing the privatization process. On average, each firm in the first wave was the subject of four privatization proposals(Mladek 1994, 10). Against this backdrop, it may become more understandable why many managements preferred the voucher privatization option to direct sales to third party buyers, which buyers could have immediately removed them from office.

Much of the delay at this stage stemmed from two related factors. Managements tended to propose splitting enterprises into two or more units, each to be separately privatized (Kotrba 1994, 17). Possibly, this tendency was the product of internal tensions within the firm over who should run the privatized enterprise (which conflict a decision to split the enterprise effectively compromised), or possibly, it stemmed from a desire (in a Czech phrase) to "pick the raisins" – that is, to separate quality from junk. In response the Ministry of Privatization seems to have been strongly committed to inducing competition at the privatization plan stage, but at the cost of slowing down the process. Thus, the first goal of voucher privatization – speed in implementation – was significantly compromised. Voucher privatization was scheduled to occur in two waves, in theory based on the relative readiness of firms for privatization. Many of the more complex projects (such as those in energy, health services, and agriculture) and some of the largest enterprises (including public utilities and at least one major

[14] Kotrba (1994), 15. However, Kotrba's study finds that in cases of head-to-head competition (where management and buyers sought the same assets) buyers were more successful than the incumbent management. Most management proposals did not contemplate significant equity participation by management.

bank) were postponed until the second wave. For the first wave in 1992, some 2,285 large firms were originally selected for large-scale privatization (in both the Czech and Slovak Republics), but the number to be privatized through vouchers was gradually whittled down to 1,491 (with the balance being privatized chiefly through cash sales and auctions). There were 861 firms in the second wave (including minority stakes in firms partially privatized in the first wave).

Voucher System

As adopted in 1991, the voucher system entitled each Czechoslovak adult (i.e., a citizen over the age of 18) to buy a booklet of 1,000 voucher points for a cost of CSK 1,035 (or roughly $34.50), which cost at the end of 1991 approximated 25 percent of the average monthly wage. At the time of the second wave in 1993, the price for a voucher book of 1,000 points was modestly raised to CSK 1,050 (or $35), but by then this amounted to less than 18 percent of the average monthly wage. Voucher points could be used exclusively in a given privatization wave and not for other purposes (for example, voucher books could not even be used to purchase other shares in the same privatized company in a public auction by the government). Secondary trading in voucher points was forbidden (although this was not strictly enforced). However, because all voucher books were registered on a nationwide computerized system, it was possible to check ownership and minimize the opportunity for fraud.

Initially, interest in acquiring voucher books was slow to develop, and the original December deadline for voucher registration had to be extended. As of November 1991, public polls showed that only 25 percent of the adult population was interested in participating in the voucher scheme. Harvard Capital and Consulting (HC&C) began its advertising campaign in November 1991,[15] and public interest quickly increased. By the end of January 1992, the percentage of the adult Czech population that planned to participate had risen to 55 percent. Ultimately 75 percent of the adult population participated (77 percent in the Czech Republic), and over eight million citizens registered to be eligible to buy voucher books (Mladek 1994, 12). This level of participation nearly doubled the government's predictions, which anticipated the sale of only four to five million booklets.

What explained the sudden surge of interest? The answer is twofold: first, massive advertising by the IPFs did convince the citizens that value could be

[15] Interview with Dusan Triska, December 1994. Dr. Triska, the former vice minister for finance, was the Czech official in charge of (and most responsible for the design of) voucher privatization.

obtained at low cost. Second and more importantly, HC&C made its famous (and vague) promise that it would redeem shares in its IPFs beginning in one year at a price equal to 10 times the cost of a voucher booklet (CSK 10,350 or $345). Originally, Harvard's nontransferable option could be exercised at any time after the first anniversary of the transfer of voucher points by an investor to it.[16] Almost overnight, this tactic monetized the gains and established a short-term profit that motivated citizens to go through the tedious process of registering for vouchers by establishing their citizenship. Other funds followed Harvard's lead and outdid it. For example, KIS a.s. (a major insurance company's fund) offered CSK 15,000 for a voucher book, and SIS a.s. (the fund established by Ceska Sporitelna, the principal Czech savings bank) offered CSK 11,000 (see Jaros and Sanders 1994). PIAS, the investment company for Investicni Banka, gave investors the option between a CSK 15,000 collateralized loan or a guaranteed buyback at CSK 11,000 (Jaros and Sanders 1994).

First Wave: Rise of the Investment Privatization Funds

The architects of the Czech voucher privatization program – most notably, Dusan Triska – were aware that broad distribution of shares to some substantial percentage of the Czech public would produce an atomized ownership structure. Because this, in turn, implied that collective action among small shareholders would be infeasible, they envisioned from the outset of their planning the formation of intermediary financial institutions modeled loosely after Western mutual funds.[17] Much the same idea was also present in the contemporaneous Polish privatization plan, but the Czech scheme had one critical difference: the state would play no role in creating or staffing these funds, other than in establishing certain minimal ground rules for their creation and operation. Their scheme contemplated a Darwinian competition among funds to attract the voucher points of citizens. Citizens were, however, free to reject the overtures of the funds and invest their voucher points themselves in the stocks of privatized companies (in fact, 28 percent of all voucher points were retained by individuals).

Substantive regulation of the IPFs has been minimal. The rules under which IPFs were to be created were first specified in a federal government

[16] HC&C later reinterpreted the timing on its pledge, so that it became operative on the first anniversary of the later date on which the NPF transferred the shares in the privatized companies to the IPFs and other private parties.

[17] Dusan Triska reports that the idea of investment privatization funds can be traced back to a special Government Memorandum dated 6 April 1990 (see Pauly and Triska 1993).

decree of 5 September 1991.[18] Initially, it specified only three basic requirements:

1. The IPF must have minimum capital of CSK 100,000 (this was later raised to CSK 1,000,000 or $33,300);
2. The members of its supervisory board and its offices had to have certain professional qualifications (which were not spelled out with any specificity and never enforced as a practical matter) and a reputation for civic integrity.
3. The IPF had to contract with a bank to act as its depository.

In addition the founder/managers of IPFs were required to obtain a license from the Ministry of Finance, but all sources agree that the licensing procedure quickly became perfunctory and, for the remainder of the first wave, applications that satisfied the basic requirements seem not to have been rejected. The actual appearance of IPFs followed swiftly on the heels of the 5 September 1991 decree outlining voucher privatization. Shortly thereafter, on 1 October 1991, the Ministry of Finance issued regulations requiring all IPFs that wished to participate in the first wave to be established by the end of 1991. This three month deadline effectively discouraged some prospective fund managers, who as a result deferred their participation until the second wave.

The initial challenge for the Ministry of Finance was to alert and inform the public about opportunities for profit in voucher privatization. Toward this end, the ministry began its own advertising campaign in October 1991 to alert the public and inform them about the procedures necessary to register and obtain voucher booklets. Response was, at best, sluggish, but, once HC&C began advertising in November, the Ministry of Finance quickly recognized and accepted that the private IPFs could outperform it at this activity and suspended its own campaign.

HC&C's marketing success prompted, however, a legislative reaction. Its promise to buy back its shares at a tenfold price raised fears of a Ponzi type financial pyramid, whose failure could discredit voucher privatization. In January 1992, temporary regulations were adopted requiring portfolio diversification.[19] IPFs were required to diversify their assets so that they did not invest more than 10 percent of their capital in any one security and were restricted from owning more than 20 percent of the nominal value of

[18] Federal Government Decree No. 383/1991 Coll. This decree was less than three months before the deadline for fund registration on 31 December 1991.

[19] These rules were eventually codified as amendments to Decree No. 383: amendments No. 67/1992 Coll. and 69/1992 Coll.

securities issued by the same issuer.[20] Unquestionably, these rules reflected a concern on the part of Czech regulators that there might be a "run on the funds." However, the 20 percent limitation was only crudely related to any diversification goal (because 20 percent of a single issuer might amount to only 1 percent of a large IPF's assets) and reflects an independent debate among Czech policymakers over whether to encourage IPFs to become active owners.

The Czech Parliament was not satisfied with dealing with the problem simply through administrative regulations.[21] Alarmed by the prospect that HC&C would dominate the economy, many legislators demanded a special session of Parliament, which was convened in January, 1992. Although the Ministry of Finance opposed additional legislation, the Parliament insisted but settled largely for codifying the already adopted temporary regulations. Some of the political motivation for this statute appears to have come from concerns about insider trading and the sale of confidential information, and not simply from concerns about fund liquidity or the risk of a run on the funds.

In any event, the 28 April 1992 Law on Investment Companies and Investment Funds came too late to affect the first wave, but it did make several important changes applicable to the second wave in 1994. First, and most importantly, it authorized the unit trust format (whereas all IPFs in the first wave were formed as joint stock associations). Second, the statute contained a number of housekeeping rules designed to minimize the risk of fraud and embezzlement. For example, the statute provided that the property of an IPF could be managed only by itself or by an investment company; personal control of funds by founders was no longer permitted. By November, 1992, each IPF was required to appoint a bank as its depository and to deposit all securities and funds with it. By the same date, IPFs were required to appoint managing and supervisory boards. Other rules barred the issuance of bonds by IPFs (thus restricting the degree of leverage they could achieve and again reducing the prospect of a run on the funds). Finally, limitations were placed on the permissible compensation that IPFs could pay their investment companies under new management contracts (the ceiling was set at 2 percent of the average value of IPF property or 20 percent of the profits).[22]

[20] This provision was finally codified in §24(3) of the Investment Companies and Investment Funds Act 1992.

[21] In an interview, Dusan Triska described the Czech Parliament as having been in a "panic" during this stage over its fear that HC&C and other entrepreneurs would create a "bubble" and a resulting crash that would discredit Czech privatization.

[22] See §27 of the Investment Companies and Investment Funds Act 1992 (discussed later in the chapter).

Given the limited regulatory hurdles and a basically permissive attitude on the part of the Ministry of Finance, it is not surprising that a superabundance of IPFs were quickly formed and began to compete for investors' voucher points. Over 420 IPFs participated in the first wave of privatization, of which 260 were based on the Czech side of the Federal Republic and the balance on the Slovak side. Their collective marketing success is evidenced by a simple statistic: IPFs obtained 71.8 percent of all available voucher points in the first wave (Mladek 1994, 21). After an initially apathetic reception, public interest in the voucher program picked up markedly in January, 1992, and the registration process had to be extended through the end of February; 8.54 million citizens (out of an estimated 11 million eligible citizens) bought and registered voucher books. Of these 5.8 million (or 68 percent) chose to invest their entire voucher booklet with one or more IPFs, while another 4 percent split their investment, contributing some voucher points to an IPF, but also retaining some points for individual investment.

Despite this ease of entry, success still went to the powerful and well funded. Those funds with superior marketing and advertising capacities dominated the field and obtained slightly over 60 percent of all voucher points deposited with IPFs.[23] Bank-affiliated IPFs had three significant advantages in this process. First, banks had a natural and national retail network through their branches by which to reach the public across the country. Second, banks could lend funds to their investment company subsidiaries to cover marketing, advertising, and startup costs. Third, banks had at least relatively enviable reputations for integrity and competence and were subject to close governmental regulation. If they had not stolen their depositors' funds, voucher holders could logically reason that they would not embezzle the IPF's funds or securities. Lacking these inherent advantages, new entrants (such as HC&C) faced a marketing challenge: how to convince the public that they were safe and better. They responded with promises of a guaranteed return. HC&C was, however, the one private IPF to develop an elaborate retail marketing structure. It hired thousands of part-time agents to canvass voucher holders, even as they waited in line to purchase voucher booklets at the post office or to register their booklets at local centers. Other IPFs used school children to solicit voucher holders. Once Harvard began to succeed with its offer to redeem its share at 10 times their cost (i.e. CSK 1,035), other funds made similar guarantees. Some funds offered cash bonuses of CSK 2,000 to 3,000 for voucher booklet investments (see Brom and Orenstein 1993).

[23] Roland Egerer estimates that the 10 largest bank-sponsored funds held 61% of all points acquired by all IPFs (or about 43% of all voucher points) (Egerer 1994).

On the marketing level, HC&C succeeded largely in urban areas (most notably, Prague), while bank affiliated funds did better in rural areas. The IPF that attracted the largest number of voucher points in the first wave was founded by Ceska Sporitelna, the Czech Savings Bank. Based on its broad retail network, it won over 11 percent of the voucher points in the first wave; yet, it informed us that it received less than 10 percent of its total from residents of Prague. Essentially, banks won the trust of the rural population, which knew and presumably trusted them as local institutions, while the more sophisticated urban population preferred the financial guarantees of HC&C and others.

Most investment companies created only one fund for the first wave, but some of the more sophisticated companies tried to develop a diversified family of funds that resembled the marketing strategy of a typical U.S. mutual fund sponsor (e.g. Fidelity, Vanguard, or Dreyfus). For example, HC&C created eight funds, one emphasizing growth, another dividends, while a third was a "country" fund focused on Slovak-based companies. Prvni Investicni, a.s. (PIAS), the investment company of Investcini Bank, similarly established eleven funds. This strategy may have also had an ulterior purpose because at the time (although not today) an investment company could control up to 40 percent of the stock in a company (even though an individual IPF faced a 20 percent ceiling). In other words, by founding two funds, an investment company could control up to a 40 percent stake in an individual company.

The regulatory attitude of the Ministry of Finance during the critical first wave combined a largely laissez-faire attitude toward substantive regulation with close administrative oversight for fraud, insolvency, or embezzlement. According to Dr. Triska, the Ministry of Finance developed software that enabled it to monitor the voucher points held by each IPF and, later, its securities portfolio. When HC&C and others raised anxieties about a possible run on the funds, because of their financial guarantees, the ministry required all IPFs during the spring of 1992 to disclose to it the total number of promised cash payments each had made in return for voucher points, the total number of points each had thus acquired, and the total financial obligation that resulted (see Mejstrik 1994). The implication behind this informational request was that if the state determined that an IPF had not maintained a sufficient degree of liquidity in relation to its guarantee to shareholders, its license could be revoked. Much like a nuclear bomb, however, this threat of license revocation proved an unwieldy regulatory weapon. If license suspension was even threatened in a specific case, the likely result would have been to produce a run on the fund so threatened. Revoking a license might well produce insolvency (given the absence of liquidity on the Prague Stock Exchange), and the government might well bear much of the criticism for the consequences (which could induce a run on the funds as well). In any event, the sanction seems not to have been employed. From a distance, one might well ask why Czech regulators permitted HC&C and others to make seemingly dangerous guarantees, which later proved disastrous in the Russian context. Promises of tenfold returns in a single year bring to mind the classic Ponzi schemes, which have historically failed sooner or later. Several reasons probably explain the tolerance of Czech regulators. First, it must be remembered that voucher points were sold for an arbitrarily low price of CSK 1,000 (or about $35). Ultimately, the book value of the 1,849 companies privatized in the two privatization waves has been estimated at $12.3 billion (see Rocks 1994). Given that roughly six million Czech citizens each purchased 1,000 voucher points for slightly less than $35 each, their aggregate investment was thus in the neighborhood of $210 million. As a result, they collectively acquired $12.3 billion in property at an aggregate price of $210 million, yielding them a profit of roughly $12.1 billion. Viewed differently, the book value of the property that the average Czech citizen acquired was thus $2,000 (i.e. $12.3 billion divided by 6 million). In offering to pay ten times the citizen's voucher purchase price of $35, HC&C was thus offering $350 for $2,000. Rather than an illusory promise that could not be fulfilled, the greater danger may have been that Czech citizens would have accepted this offer and sold too cheaply (at least if one accepts the book value estimate).

Second, ideological considerations probably played an equal or larger role in shaping the Czech government's response to HC&C. Both Vaclav Klaus, then minister of finance, and Dusan Triska, then the vice minister and principal architect of voucher privatization, believed strongly in open access, free competition, and limited regulation. In particular they preferred *ex post* regulation in response to demonstrated problems to *ex ante* regulation through potentially overboard prophylactic rules. Thus, the Ministry of Finance had objected to legislative codification of the 20 percent ceiling on an IPF's stake in a single company.

A third and more political reason for the government's tolerance was simply that the government needed HC&C and the banks at least as much as they needed the government's tacit acquiescence. Alone, the Czech government had not been able to stir up citizen interest in its privatization program. HC&C and its imitators were the major factor in its sudden popularity; without them, it is questionable that a program critical to the government would have succeeded (at least in urban areas). In short the relationship was symbiotic – each needed the other.

In any event, HC&C and the others making guarantees won their gamble, and it has been estimated that only 7–15 percent of voucher investors chose to redeem their IPF shares for cash (see Brom and Orenstein 1993, 26). Although the market price of HC&C's principal IPF has fallen slightly below its guaranteed redemption offer of CSK 10,350, its net asset value per voucher book is estimated to be around CSK 40,000 (see Jaros and Sanders 1994, 7). Thus, HC&C might well benefit handsomely if investors in its IPFs demanded redemption from it, because HC&C would in effect be buying a right to CSK 40,000 per share for CSK 10,350 per share. Having so repurchased much of its IPF shares, HC&C could then liquidate the IPF and sell or distribute its securities to its shareholders (including itself). In such a context, the logical scenario would be for HC&C to encourage redemptions (at least if it had confidence in its ability to realize the estimated net asset value of its IPFs on the Prague Stock Exchange). In any event, by alone refusing to list its IPF's shares on the Prague Stock Exchange, HC&C is believed to be protecting itself against any significant market decline in its IPF share price.[24]

In retrospect the concern that the funds would be unable to honor their financial commitments appears to have rested to some degree on a misconception. The IPFs themselves were not authorized to repurchase their shares, and thus the guarantee came from their parent investment company. Those associated with banks had adequate financial resources to meet their commitments, and the others (such as HC&C) carefully maintained substantial cash reserves. Still, redemptions have occurred, and in consequence, some investment companies have become the largest holders in their own IPFs, thus further complicating the problem of fund accountability.

Bidding Procedures

The rule by which voucher points were converted into shares in privatized companies were (like much else in the Czech privatization process) highly complicated, slow, and controversial. Initially, there was a "zero round" at the beginning of both the first and second waves during which investors chose whether to invest their voucher books with one or more IPFs. As noted earlier, 72 percent of voucher points were invested with IPFs in the first wave and 64 percent in the second wave.

Thereafter, investments in actual companies were made through a complicated auction procedure, which used multiple rounds of bidding with prices being adjusted on an *ad hoc* basis from round to round in an attempt to

[24] Investors in the IPFs established by HC&C can trade their shares on the RM/S system, but in the auction system, it is easier for HC&C to stabilize the price of its funds.

equalize supply and demand. An informal "price commission" based in the Ministry of Finance oversaw this process and, as discussed below, administered the process chiefly with a view to avoiding the politically unacceptable result of permitting the demand for shares to exceed the supply so as to cause citizens to forfeit voucher points.

Initially, all shares were assigned a nominal value of CSK 1,000. Large companies simply issued more shares to reflect their greater book value. Of course, book value does not necessarily equate with market value, and thus some companies appeared to be bargains at CSK 1,000 per share, while other looked overpriced. As a result, in the first round of actual bidding, the demand for some stocks might exceed the available supply of shares, while other stocks might receive insufficient bids at the offered price of CSK 1,000. When demand exceeded supply by 25 percent or more, no sales would be affected in the first round, and prices would be raised in the second round.[25] When, however, supply exceeded demand, all bids would be accepted, and the remaining shares would be offered at a reduced price in the next bidding round. In effect the auction process was one-sided, with the state protecting its interests when a privatized company was oversubscribed, but denying any similar protection to investors when a company was undersubscribed.

Such a structure obviously creates an incentive to wait for later rounds to hunt for bargain stocks. In time Czech authorities acknowledged that the first round was in reality a phantom round in which few companies would be sold (only 15 companies out of the 861 in the second wave were sold in the first round – once the rules were better understood), while the later rounds were the "rounds of truth." But there was a risk in waiting. Voucher points can be wasted. If an IPF (or an individual shareholder) is unable to invest all its points by the end of the final bidding round, they simply expire, and in effect a forfeiture results. This could happen either because all underpriced companies in which the investor was interested were sold during intermediate rounds (five rounds were authorized) or a particular stock might still be oversubscribed in the final round when all buyers would be prorated. Clearly, there were traps for the unwary in this process – and also a political problem for the Czech authorities, as it was widely believed that if a significant percentage of voucher points expired unused, there would be political discontent. For this reason, a conscious effort was made to ensure that, in each bidding round, voucher points would be expended more rapidly than shares were acquired. From the regulator's perspective, an excess supply

[25] When demand exceeded supply by less than 25%, the bids of the IPFs would be cut back by an amount sufficient to achieve equilibrium. In short, individual shareholders received a priority in these circumstances (see Shafik 1993).

Table 4.1: Czech and Slovak First Privatization Wave Bidding Rounds (in percentage)

	Round 1	Round 2	Round 3	Round 4	Round 5
Shares	70.13	44.14	33.30	20.92	7.25
Voucher points	65.14	25.00	13.29	7.29	1.18
IPF-held voucher points	62.02	20.57	8.97	4.70	0.33
Individually held voucher points	73.10	36.28	24.11	13.70	3.35

of shares at the end of the bidding process posed little problem, because excess shares could simply be disposed of in the second wave the following year. But forfeited voucher points would predictably result in investor dissatisfaction and charges of favoritism. Table 4.1 shows the shares and voucher points remaining after each of the five bidding rounds in the first wave and how the Czech regulators succeeded in exhausting voucher points before shares. In addition, it also reveals the greater sophistication of the IPFs versus individual shareholders.

As the table shows, only 1.18 percent of all voucher points remained unused at the end of the final round, and most of these (by a ten to one margin) were held by individuals rather than IPFs. The greater tendency for individuals to retain voucher points is partly explained by the fact that many individuals simply died, moved, disappeared, or declined after some point to participate. But, it is also revealing that an estimated 2,000 citizens participated in every bidding round but still emerged with their voucher points unutilized and thus wasted.[26] The bidding process was clearly too complicated for some to follow.

Nonetheless, the basic strategy worked: the supply of shares was manipulated to exceed the demand for them, in order to avoid investor forfeitures and resulting dissatisfaction. As a result, some 7.25 percent of the offered shares were returned to the NPF at the end of the first wave.

In the second wave, the process went through six rounds of bidding, concluding in late November, 1994, but ultimately over 99 percent of the voucher points were applied (see BBC Summary of World Broadcasts 1994). Bidding in the second wave, of course, involved much less pricing uncertainty because many companies had already been partially privatized in the first wave and thus had an established (if volatile) market price. Although only roughly 54 percent of the shares remaining at the start of the sixth

[26] Interview with Dusan Triska.

round were sold in that round (BBC Summary of World Broadcasts 1994), the Czech government ended the process without proceeding to an additional round, because its political goal of exhausting the investors' supply of voucher points had been satisfied.

In both waves, individual shareholders invested their voucher points more slowly than the IPFs and ultimately suffered a higher rate of forfeiture. As Table 4.1 showed, in the first wave, IPFs ultimately expended all but 0.33 percent of their voucher points, while individuals failed to invest (and thus forfeited) 3.35 percent (for a weighted average between them of 1.18 percent). In the second wave, the disparity between them decreased (as both groups improved their performance) with IPFs failing to invest only 0.15 percent of their voucher points and individual shareholders forfeiting 1.2 percent.

IPFs reacted very differently to the incentives created by these bidding rules. One highly entrepreneurial "private" fund (YSE) deliberately withheld the majority of its voucher points until the final two rounds of the five round bidding process because at these stages shares originally valued at CSK 1,000 had been drastically reduced in price. Of course, the risk in this tactic was that it would be unable to fully invest its voucher points and they would expire. Risky as this strategy was, YSE's gamble seemingly paid off., and it is generally credited with having achieved the highest net asset value per voucher book.[27] Other funds were less successful at this tactic, and one major IPF was reportedly left with some 20 percent of its voucher points unused and worthless at the end of the first wave.[28] In contrast, both in the first and second wave, some of the largest bank-affiliated funds heavily invested their voucher points in the earliest rounds, thereby forgoing the opportunity to shop for discounted bargains later. This approach may have reflected risk aversion or, as discussed below, a desire to obtain a position in certain companies at any price for noninvestment-related reasons.

Portfolio Selection

Privately sponsored funds and bank-affiliated funds diverged even more diametrically in their portfolio selection policies. As others have noted, "the largest bank-affiliated funds created broad portfolios, comprised of 200 to

[27] See Jaros and Sanders (1994), 6. Others, however, claim that YSE acquired only low value companies in the final bidding round (joint stocks) and, as a result, changed its policy in the second wave so as to invest more at the intermediate stage.

[28] I here rely on an interview with Dusan Triska, who maintained the Ministry of Finance's records during this time.

500 companies."[29] In marked contrast, HC&C deliberately and carefully assembled a portfolio of some 51 companies. Creditanstalt and Zivnostenska (two investment companies that were each associated with foreign financial institutions) also assembled relatively consolidated portfolios in the first wave.[30] Those IPFs that assembled consolidated portfolios were consciously seeking to approach the 20 percent ceiling ownership permitted by law to assure representation and clout on their portfolio companies' boards.

But why did the bank-affiliated funds seek a much larger portfolio of 200 to 500 companies? Several explanations are possible. Ceska Sporitelna, the Czech Savings Bank, explained to us that most persons who deposited voucher points with its IPF were also depositors with the savings bank and were rural, relatively unsophisticated persons who could not afford to hold a high-risk, undiversified portfolio of securities. Thus, it claimed, it diversified broadly to reduce risk. Although this portfolio diversification explanation might explain a policy of holding a portfolio of 100 odd companies, it cannot adequately explain Ceska Sporitelna's decision to hold a 500 stock portfolio. Efficient diversification requires far less. Possibly, Ceska Sporitelna, as the sponsor of the IPF that had assembled the greatest number of voucher points at the end of the "zero round" of the first wave, feared that it would not be able to invest all the voucher points it had acquired and so bid for virtually every company reflexively. A number of interviewees expressed the view that Ceska Sporitelna's investment company had behaved reflexively and unthinkingly ("They haven't got a clue" was one characteristic phrase). But the same allegation of incompetence could not be made with respect to Investicni and Komercni, whose investment companies also assembled portfolios with five times the number of companies in HC&C's portfolio, but based on a similar level of voucher points to that held by HC&C.

Close observers in Prague of the bidding policies of the different IPFs saw a different purpose underlying the broad diversification strategy of the bank-affiliated IPFs; namely, a desire to obtain banking business by securing at least a toehold stake in the broadest possible number of companies. As a study by Wood Company Securities observed: "The strategy in many of these

[29] Jaros and Sanders (1994), 5. SPAS, Ceska Sporitelna's investment company, told us that they held a portfolio of 500 companies at the end of the first wave. Prvni Investicni held a 240 company portfolio and Komercni Bank's investment company held a portfolio of 265 companies (p. 7).

[30] Both Zivnostenska and Creditanstalt seem best classified as private IPFs. Although they are banks, they are foreign-controlled banks. A majority stake in the former was sold just before the first wave to a German bank and the International Finance Corporation, while Creditanstalt is owned by an Austrian bank. Zivno Fund, owned by the former, held a portfolio of 50 companies, while Creditanstalt assembled a portfolio of 76 firms (Jaros and Sanders (1994), 7).

cases, it seems, was for the bank funds to leverage stakes in companies into seats on their managing boards and later into banking business for the fund's sponsoring bank" (Jaros and Sanders 1994, 5). To achieve a seat on the managing board, an IPF might need a 10 percent stake, but not the 20 percent maximum stake that the privatization law permitted. A 20 percent stake would be useful if the IPF were intent on pursuing an active restructuring policy, but it was not otherwise essential. If the IPF was used to advance its banking parent's interests, then broad diversification makes sense (at least for the parent). Yet, such a conclusion raises the disquieting possibility that the German corporate governance model of bank participation in corporate governance carries with it more serious conflicts of interest than proponents of the German model have recognized or addressed.

Of course, from the bank's perspective, it might be argued that approaching the legally permissible 20 percent ceiling was undesirable because it would cost their IPFs liquidity in a thin market. Nonetheless, this same consideration would apply equally to private IPFs, and the contrast between the bank-affiliated IPFs and the privately sponsored IPFs seems striking in this regard. Portfolio concentration was pursued to a considerably greater extent by the private IPFs. In turn, this positioned these IPFs to be more aggressive monitors, while observers have generally reported the bank-controlled funds to be somewhat less active (see Rocks 1994; "Czechs turn out to buy into industry").

Although most private funds have not pursued to the same extent HC&C's strategy of holding a highly concentrated portfolio, many of the private funds have tended to focus on particular industries (i.e. glass, engineering, beer, etc.) or regional areas. This deviation from full diversification was in part a matter of marketing necessity, because these funds could stress their special competence and managerial background in these fields (which strategy may have partially compensated for their lack of instant name recognition or reputation for integrity in comparison to the better-known bank funds). As a result, these private funds may have acquired some monitoring advantages through economies of scope (at the cost of some diversification). For example, having board representation on several firms in the same industry, a nondiversified fund might be better positioned to compare performance among managements, to see industry trends, and to understand technological developments than a bank fund overseeing a portfolio of several hundred companies. At the same time, however, such cross-ownership raises antitrust issues that will be discussed later.

Second Wave

The second wave of privatization, which was completed in late 1994, was significantly smaller in scale than the first wave. Some 861 companies were included in the second wave (as opposed to 1,491 in the first wave, of which 988 were Czech companies), but 185 of these 861 were companies that had been partially privatized in the first wave. Both waves followed the same procedures and elicited roughly the same responses from investors. Approximately 6.15 million Czech citizens (74 percent of the eligible Czech population) purchased voucher booklets in the second wave (down slightly from 77 percent in the first wave) (Jaros and Sanders 1994, 4). Some 353 IPFs competed to attract voucher points in the second wave, and again they convinced the bulk of the population to invest with them (64 percent of all voucher points were invested with IPFs in the second wave as opposed to 72 percent in the first wave).[31] The largest funds again dominated, but the level of concentration declined. The 15 largest funds obtained approximately 2.5 billion points out of a total 6.15 billion points in the second wave (Jaros and Sanders 1994, 4) (or 40.65 percent – slightly below the 42.8 percent level that the largest 13 investment companies obtained in the first wave) (Mladek 1994).

The decline in the percentage of individuals electing to invest through IPFs may be attributable to several factors. Local observers in Prague emphasized that local newspapers had given considerable publicity to individual shareholders in the first wave who had not invested with IPFs but who had rather invested in individual companies whose stock price had skyrocketed (such as CEZ, the energy public utility whose stock price increased by four to five times).[32] The press attention given to these "instant millionaires" may have dissuaded some from investing with IPFs in the second wave. Another related possibility stems from the fact that stock exchange trading had begun in IPFs before the "zero round" of the second wave, and the amount of the closed-end discount on the IPFs had become painfully clear (up to 80 percent from net asset value in the case of some funds). The desire to avoid incurring such a discount could have influenced sophisticated Czech investors as well. Nonetheless, the consensus view at the beginning of the second wave was that at least some of the IPFs were professionally managed and had shrewdly invested in the first wave.

[31] Jaros and Sanders (1994), 4. The figure 353 comes from Table 2, which was supplied to me by Dusan Triska.

[32] To give one illustration: fifty shares of Opatovic Electrical Works could have been purchased for one voucher book in the first wave and later traded for CSK 500,000 at one point in 1994 – a 500% increase in little over a year.

The marketing of IPFs changed significantly with the second wave, and correspondingly, some IPFs that had dominated the first wave performed very poorly in the second. In particular Ceska Sporitelna's IPF, which had finished in first place with 950 million voucher points (or 11.1 percent) in the first wave, collected only 124 million points in the second wave and fell to ninth place. The new leader was the IPF established by Agrobanka, a mid-sized Czech bank (but with a national retail network), which had had only marginal success in attracting voucher points in the first wave. Nonetheless, under new and aggressive management in the second wave, it collected an estimated 320 million voucher points (or 5.2 percent). Agrobanka's marketing success rested on two distinct factors: (1) Agrobanka marketed an open-end unit trust, and (2) it offered immediate cash payments for voucher books invested with its IPF. Agrobanka structured its cash payment as a CSK 2,000 loan from itself to any investor who invested his voucher booklet with Agrobanka's IPF. The loan was collateralized by a portion of the shares acquired with the voucher booklet. In the typical case, if the voucher points were ultimately converted into 20 IPF shares, Agrobanka would receive two shares (or 10 percent) in return for its loan. By using this loan format, Agrobanka deliberately stole a march on its competitors, because the loan could be (and was) made weeks before the zero round began. Thus, Agrobanka could advance a portion of the loan proceeds on an effectively unsecured basis, retaining the balance until the borrower had registered for, received, and could invest his voucher booklet with Agrobanka's IPF. One consequence of this approach should be underscored: by lending in return for voucher points, Agrobanka became the largest investor in its own IPF. In the typical case, it would acquire 10 percent of the shares eventually issued on each voucher book in return for its loan. Other investment companies quickly copied Agrobanka's new technique, but they could not overtake its head start.

Viewed from a distance, the success of Agrobanka seems largely idiosyncratic, the result of its ability to steal a march on its competitors. A clearer pattern emerges, however, if we look at the performance of the major Czech banks relative to the largest "independent" funds. No other major Czech bank finished in the top five. Finishing in sixth place was HC&C, which also marketed a broad family of funds and also had other of its IPFs finish in 27th, 36th, 41st, 51st, and 66th positions, respectively. In contrast the highest ranking fund sponsored by PIAS, the investment company of Investicni Banka, finished in 32nd position, and other funds followed in 34th, 40th, 67th, and 102nd positions, respectively. Ceska Sporitelna marketed only one fund, which finished in seventh position (directly behind HC&C in sixth position), and Komercni Banka sponsored the eighth largest fund (but no others in the top 100). On this basis, out of the 100 largest funds, HC&C attracted over 265 million voucher points, more than double what either Ceska Sporitelna or Komercni collected by themselves. Moreover, despite the fact that Investicni Banka marketed multiple funds, its five leading funds obtained in the aggregate roughly one-third of the total voucher points that HC&C received.

Nor was HC&C alone in this respect. YSE's three largest funds finished in 14th, 16th, and 87th position, respectively, and in the aggregate collected more points than either Ceska Sporitelna or Komercni Banka. PPF, another prominent independent fund, sponsored IPFs that emerged in 13th and 25th positions and thus in the aggregate almost tied both Ceska Sporitelna and Komercni Banka. Several large insurance companies also did very well (in particular, Expandia and KIS, which finished in 2nd and 5th positions, respectively), but they did so without the same built-in networks that retail banks possess.

In short, by the second round, when the Czech citizenry had presumably grown more sophisticated about IPFs and voucher privatization in general, the public turned away from the largest banks (except for Agrobanka, which had developed a unique cash-on-the-barrel marketing strategy) and toward independent funds (at least in the aggregate).

As Table 4.2 shows, another major development in the second wave was the appearance of open-end and closed-end unit trusts. Of the 353 IPFs participating in the second wave, an estimated 195 were joint stock associations (of which 160 had participated in the first wave). These 195 joint stock IPFs received approximately 1.57 billion voucher points in the second wave;

Table 4.2. Czech and Slovak Second Privatization Wave Funds
(in millions of voucher points)

	Joint stock companies	Open-end unit trusts	Closed-end unit trusts	Total unit trusts	Total all funds
100 or more	3	2	3	5	8
50 to 100	7	4	6	10	17
10 to 50	20	8	18	26	46
5 to 10	22	4	17	21	43
1 to 5	48	10	23	33	81
0.5 to 1	27	4	8	12	39
0.1 to 0.5	39	3	15	18	57
Less than 0.1	29	3	30	33	62
Total	195	38	120	158	353

another 120 IPFs were closed-end unit trusts (these received 1.48 billion voucher points in the second wave), and finally, 38 were open-end unit trusts (these received 867 million voucher points in the second wave) (Jaros and Sanders 1994, 13). Thus, although Agrobanka succeeded with an open-end fund, the majority of investors still opted for closed-end funds, but unit trusts (both open-end and closed-end) received more voucher points than did joint stock associations (2.35 billion points to 1.57 billion). Table 4.2 summarizes this data and also provides a breakdown of the relative size of IPFs in the second wave.

To understand Table 4.2, it helps to recall that each investor received 1,000 points, and thus 100,000 investors held 100 million voucher points. Hence, the eight funds with over 100 million points each represent at least 100,000 investors (more if some investors split their points among funds or retained some of their points to hold on an individual basis). Of these eight giant funds, Ceska Sporitelna finished seventh and Komercni finished eighth, with the balance being accounted for by independent funds and insurance companies (and, of course, Agrobanka in first place).

What explains these trends? In both the United Kingdom and the United States, open-end funds have dominated closed-end funds by a wide margin. The same has not happened in the Czech Republic. Two reasons may explain why. First, Czech law requires a delay of between one to three years from the date of investment before an IPF can agree to redeem shares for the net asset value of their proportionate interest in the fund. That is, an open-end fund may specify a future date (between one and three years away) on which it will redeem its shares at their net asset value, but as a marketing matter that date may seem in the distant future for most investors. Those investment companies electing to offer open-end funds have generally chosen a date between two and three years away. Given the illiquidity in the Czech stock market, there is considerable reason to doubt that any IPF could liquidate a significant portion of its portfolio at or near its existing net asset value. Second, open-ended funds have primarily been organized as unit trusts without voting rights, and some investors may resist this loss of voting rights.

The popularity of the unit trust format among investment companies is much easier to understand. Fund managers defend its use by claiming that it is a cheaper, more efficient vehicle, largely because the unit trust is not a joint stock company. Thus, no annual meeting of shareholders is required, and neither a managing nor supervisory board need be appointed. These cost savings may be real, but they do not truly explain the popularity of the unit trust. In reality, because the unit trust is essentially a contractual device rather than a legal entity, no new legal entity is created, and hence no voting rights arise. Rather, the unit trust's "shareholders" are really just joint owners of an account with the investment company. The absence of voting rights is important chiefly because of the substantial discounts at which closed-end funds trade. For example, if an IPF with a net asset value of CSK 10,000 trades at CSK 4,000, then the prospect arises that a different management team could buy its shares (possibly by paying a small premium), acquire control, and then liquidate the IPF to realize its net asset value. In short, this scenario is that of a hostile takeover. However, if the buyers lack voting rights (as they would in a unit trust), this whole scenario fails.

In truth the use of the unit trust is not the only defensive technique that allows an incumbent management to frustrate a hostile takeover. Those IPFs that were formed as joint stock companies have typically signed long-term contracts with their investment company (often for 10 years or longer) that prevent any termination of the advisory relationship, except with mutual consent. Finally, as a result of buybacks, collateralized loans, and other guarantees, investment companies (or their banking parents) have become major shareholders in many of the largest IPFs.

Share Ownership Structure and Share Prices

Although IPFs obtained 71.8 percent of all voucher points distributed, this figure does not closely correlate with the considerably lower percentage that they hold in the typical privatized company. There were several reasons for this divergence: first, some shares were retained by the state, and other blocks of shares were sold directly to strategic investors. Second, IPFs tended to opt for quality, investing their voucher points in higher priced companies. As a result, the share distribution of the 1,491 Czech and Slovak firms included in the two privatization waves ultimately broke down as shown in Table 4.3 among five investor classes (see Claessens 1994,3, Table 1).

This data may understate the level of ownership concentration among the larger public firms in which IPFs tended to concentrate their investments. While Table 4.3 shows that all IPFs as a group own on average a 39.39 percent of the typical privatized company, the largest 10 IPF shareholders own an almost equivalent level (38.36 percent). Apparently then, IPFs do not typically hold small positions. As a result of the bidding process, the percentage of stock held by individuals rose to 36.53 percent (as opposed to 28 percent of voucher points), but this seems a statistical artifact of the preference of individuals to invest in smaller companies at cheaper prices. In some cases, families or residents of one town concentrated their investments in a smaller company to gain leverage.

Although a mean ownership level of 39.4 percent for all IPFs and 38.4 percent for the largest 10 IPF stockholders suggests that IPFs could exercise

Table 4.3. Czech and Slovak Share Distribution in the Two Privatization Waves (based on 1,491 firms, in percentage)

Investor class	Mean	Standard deviation	Minimum	Maximum
State	8.37	15.38	0.00	84.00
Individuals	36.53	21.62	1.56	96.82
IPFs	39.39	22.22	0.00	90.89
Domestic investors	3.25	12.51	0.00	84.00
Foreign investors	1.34	8.00	0.00	80.00
Not sold	11.12	N.A.	1.14	92.83
Total	100.00			
Investment funds as a class				
Top 1	13.42	6.26	6.00	32.44
Top 1 and 2	22.20	10.86	0.00	49.97
Top 10	38.36	21.32	0.00	86.52

de facto control over the typical Czech company (if they acted cooperatively to elect their own directors), it is far from clear that IPFs do cooperate in this fashion or that board composition correlates closely with share ownership. Surveying 1,491 privatized Czech and Slovak firms, Claessens investigated the premise (suggested by others) that effective control can be defined as the ownership of stock equal to, or greater than, 50 percent of that held by all other strategic investors (Claessens 1994, 4). On this basis, 10 percent ownership might carry effective control if, for example, all other strategic investors owned no more than an additional 10 percent. Applying this standard to his sample of 1,491 Czech and Slovak firms, he concludes that, under this definition of control, some 273 firms would be effectively controlled by a single IPF, whereas two IPFs would be able to control 793 firms, and three IPFs could control 1,013 firms (Claessens 1994, 4). As he recognizes, this finding seems to show the problematic character of its premise. The problem is that a large shareholder can be resisted by a coalition of smaller ones; thus, a 20 percent shareholder can be effectively resisted by four other shareholders, each holding 5 percent. Alternatively, each of these five significant shareholders might demand and obtain at least one seat on the board, with the result that the largest shareholder's voting power is diluted at the board level.

Claessens also investigated the relationship between shareholder concentration and stock prices. Examining equity price data for a sample of Czech and Slovak firms, Claessens initially finds that "higher [share] concentration tends to have a positive effect on prices. . . ." (Claessens 1994, 11). But, on closer examination, he finds that "high strategic ownership . . . is more important than ownership concentration . . . in terms of its effect on prices" (p. 11). Indeed, "high absolute strategic ownership has a positive effect on prices, but effective control, particularly by investment funds, does not have a positive influence on prices – actually a negative influence" (p. 11). In short the presence of an absolute majority shareholder seems to raise stock prices, but concentrated ownership among IPFs does not (and may have some negative impact).

What can explain this disparity? In the case of the majority shareholder, the market may expect that it will seek to buy the remaining shares or has the capital and incentive to make the firm profitable. In contrast, no such presumption apparently attaches to a consortium of IPFs. Perhaps the market perceives IPFs as ineffectual, but a negative price impact (in comparison with that applicable to even a dispersed shareholder structure) raises again the prospect that the market perceives the possession of *de facto* control by bank-affiliated IPFs to be a negative signal. The most plausible (if speculative) explanation for this market reaction is the conflict of interests issue: the market may fear exploitation of minority shareholders by bank-affiliated IPFs, who are more interested in maximizing their position as creditors.

Market Environment

A 1994 survey by Wood Company Securities finds that first wave IPFs now trade within three distinct price ranges. Smaller IPFs, and others viewed as risky, trade at apparent discounts to net asset value of between 70 percent to 80 percent. IPFs with a weak portfolio but with the backing of a large financial institution trade at apparent discounts between 55 percent and 70 percent. Strong IPFs with quality portfolios and competent managements trade at discounts between 25 percent and 45 percent (Jaros and Sanders 1994, 9). IPF trading prices have risen and fallen with the broader stock market, which rose steeply in early 1994 and crashed dramatically between April and October 1994. The severity of these discounts may be to some extent illusory, because they depend on the reported prices on the Prague Stock Exchange (PSE) for the underlying securities in the IPFs' portfolios. Many of these stocks trade infrequently. Although some 1,000 stocks are traded on the PSE, only about 30 stocks appear to be actively traded (see Crawford 1994). Particularly with the severe 35 percent decline in stock prices during mid-1994, the inevitable use of out-of-date prices for rarely traded stocks may overstate the amount of this discount.

Because the amount of discount differs among IPFs, this variation suggests that the market does discriminate among them. Still, as a measure of relative IPF performance, these discounts may again be misleading. Investors may believe, it has been suggested, that some of the bank-affiliated IPFs are "too big to fail." That is, they expect the government would step in to protect the largest IPFs from insolvency. In contrast smaller funds may be subject to an excessive discount if they hold investments that infrequently trade.

As a generalization, Czech IPFs do not seem to engage in the active portfolio management that one observes in the case of U.S. or British mutual funds. The leading reason for their inactivity as traders is the lack of liquidity. Even if they could sell stocks they wished to dump, the IPFs report that they doubt that they could find and purchase replacement equity investments in any substantial quantities. The market, they fear, is frozen. That trading that does occur chiefly takes place in an off-market environment totally devoid of transparency. The prices at which transactions occur off the Prague Stock Exchange (and off a smaller computerized over-the-counter system, known as the RM/S system) are simply not reported. Most observers that we interviewed estimated that over 90 percent of share trading in Czech stocks occurs off the exchange in this fashion. Although the IPFs are not permitted in principle, even in off-exchange transactions, to buy or sell stocks at prices better than the last transaction price on the Prague Stock Exchange (see Investment Companies and Investment Funds Act 1992, §17(3)), compliance with this rule cannot be monitored.

In general most trading among IPFs seems to be directed at consolidating the portfolios of each IPF – "swap" transactions, as they were described to us. Since the end of the first wave, many IPFs appear to have conceded the basic wisdom of HC&C's strategy of seeking concentrated holdings sufficient to entitle the IPF to board representation and are seeking to develop larger stakes through off-exchange swaps. Small stakes in other stocks are likely to be swapped for positions in companies where the IPF is already a substantial holder.

The absence of liquidity may deter some fund managers from selling even stocks they consider to be overpriced. Their fear is that they could not reinvest the proceeds of a sale (in particular because no bond or money market has yet developed that provides an alternative to equity investments). This does not mean, however, that there are no active traders in the Czech market. The CEO of A-Invest, the investment company for Agrobanka, told us that 90 percent of his firm's profits came from trading activities, while 90 percent of its costs came from corporate governance activities. His point was that "trading in the dark," at least on a small scale by professionals, can be highly profitable for investment companies, even if it is infeasible (as he also conceded) to implement a broad portfolio reallocation strategy. In short, lacking exit, the IPFs have the option of exercising voice – but it is a costly option that different IPFs pursue with different levels of enthusiasm.

Why Czech Privatization Differs from Russian

Perhaps the most interesting question about Czech privatization involves the sharp contrast between its experience and that of Russian privatization, where insider domination has been both the norm and a political necessity for privatization to achieve legislative acceptance. How did the architects of Czech privatization escape being forced to reach the same political compromises with insiders?

Ultimately, much of the answer lies in the power of ideology. As in Russia, insiders asserted that they deserved primacy, but from the outset the Czech privatization process was dominated by economists who were deeply committed to establishing free markets and unwilling to grant concessions to insiders. The issue was joined well before the start of large-scale privatization. In September, 1990, a unique joint session was held among the Czech, Slovak, and federal governments to finalize planning for small-scale privatization. The critical issue on the agenda was whether employees would receive a preference at this early stage. Although the majority of the legislators present (including Vaclav Havel) favored such a policy, critical administrative officials – most notably Vaclav Klaus and Dusan Triska – vehemently opposed such a policy on principled grounds and threatened to resign if they were overruled. The majority backed down, in part because these critical personalities were indispensable at this early stage.

Free market ideology may not, however, be the entire story. However determined the opposition of technocrats might have been, few believe that privatization could have proceeded in Russia without special concessions to insiders. Why then did the opposition of technocrats seem to make a difference in the Czech Republic? Two reasons suggest themselves.

First, within the Czech population at large, there had long been a pervasive sense that for an individual to advance to a senior level in industry or government, one had to be a party member. Disgusted at this pattern, many boards of directors saw the purging of "old Communists" in the executive hierarchy of their newly privatized firm to be the first order of business. Similarly, in the context of large-scale privatization, many Czechs realized that granting a preference for employees in the allocation of shares really translated into a preference for Communist party members. Far more than in Russia, this was politically unacceptable in the Czech Republic, particularly because of the bitter memories of Prague Spring in 1968 when Russian troops crushed the last previous effort to establish Czech independence.

Several of those interviewed made the point that, in response to the Prague Spring, both Russian and Czech Communist authorities had tightened ideological controls and made party membership a prerequisite to serious advancement in the administrative (and corporate) hierarchy. With the Velvet Revolution, this linkage in turn made the new reformers (and the public generally) less willing to tolerate favoritism for incumbent managers, whose prior advancement or position was seen as unjustly earned.

A second factor in the ability of the Czech planners to resist insider preferences was the strength and popularity of the central government (at least within the Czech Republic). Vaclav Havel was a national hero, and his administration had the ability to push through virtually any privatization program it chose to support. Thus, even though Havel himself apparently supported concessions for insiders, the more important fact was that he could successfully sell any program that his advisors convinced him was necessary for privatization to work.

Impacts and Consequences of Investment Privatization Funds (IPFs)

This section will focus on the impact of IPFs on both the structure of shareholdings and corporate governance generally within the newly privatized Czech economy. Three general areas need to be reviewed in more detail in this section before policy options can be sensibly considered: (1) the extent and significance of cross-ownership among Czech financial institutions; (2) the corporate governance activities of IPFs; and (3) IPF accountability and the problem of small "voiceless" funds that lack board representation.

Corporate Incest: Cross-Ownership in the Czech Financial Sector

At the outset, it must be remembered that two processes were occurring simultaneously in Czech privatization: first, IPFs were seeking to establish themselves as powerful financial intermediaries by acquiring and investing voucher books in privatized firms, and second, the indirect founders of the leading IPFs (namely, the major Czech financial institutions) were themselves being privatized. Predictably, these two processes did not occur independently of each other. Yet, when the dust ultimately settled, the extent of cross-ownership among the leading financial institutions came as a surprise to most observers.

To understand the level of cross-ownership that resulted, it is useful to start with the largest Czech financial institution, Ceska Sporitelna, the Czech savings bank, which is estimated to hold approximately 80 percent of the country's demand deposits. Ceska Sporitelna was also the founder of the largest IPF in the first wave. In the first wave, some 37 percent of its own shares were privatized (with another 40 percent being retained by the Fund of National Property or FNP and another 23 percent held by others). At the end of the first wave, the following firms owned the following equity percentages of Ceska Sporitelna's equity through their controlled IPFs:

Ownership of Ceska Sporitelna (after first wave, in percentage)

1. FNP	40.0
2. HC&C	12.9
3. Investicni Banka	8.8
4. Komercni Banka	3.9
5. Ceska Pojistovna	0.2
6. Vseobecna Uverova	1.6
7. Slovenska IB	0.8
8. Slovenska Poistovna	0.3
9. Agrobanka	0.6
Total	69.1

Even if one excludes the FNP's 40 percent, the fact remains that of the 37 percent of Ceska Sporitelna's stock privatized through vouchers in the first wave, roughly 80 percent (or 29.1 percent of its total outstanding stock) was acquired by a limited group of eight major financial institutions.

Nor is this example exceptional. In the case of Komercni Banka, the largest commercial bank in the Czech Republic, the level of concentration was even greater. Of Komercni's stock 53 percent was privatized through vouchers (while the NPF retained another 44 percent). At the end of the first wave, Komercni's six largest shareholders proved to be:

Ownership of Komercni Banka (after first wave, in percentage)

1. FNP	44.0
2. HC&C	17.6
3. Investicni Banka	10.8
4. Ceska Sporitelna	4.9
5. Vseobecna Uverova	4.3
6. Komercni Banka	3.4
Total	88.0

In the case of Investicni's bank (the third largest Czech bank after the two banks discussed above), a stranger pattern emerged: cross-ownership became coupled with self-ownership. The FNP retained 45 percent of Investicni's stock, but IPFs founded by Investicni's investment company acquired 17 percent of Investicni, their indirect parent. Another 6.9 percent of Investicni's stock was controlled by the Slovak Investicni bank, which is the parallel institution within Slovakia. Interestingly, IPFs founded by the Slovak Investicni bank acquired a total of 18.8 percent of their own indirect parent, Slovenska Investicni Banka. Although some IPFs controlled by some other banks also acquired shares in their parent banks (Komercni's IPFs, for example, acquired 3.4 percent of Komercni), IPFs founded by the Czech and Slovak Investicni banks invested in the stock of their grandparent banks to an unparalleled degree – perhaps to the extent that it is debatable whether these banks have truly been privatized.

This pattern of cross-ownership has a further dimension: not only do Investicni's funds own a large percentage of Investicni, but Investicni in turn holds more than 10 percent in each of the IPFs founded by its investment company (Prvni Investicni, a.s., or PIAS). This latter form of cross-ownership by which the grandparent owns blocks in the IPF founded by its subsidiary was the result of guarantees made by Investicni during the marketing stage of voucher privatization. Specifically, Investicni promised a CSK 15,000 loan to those who invested their entire voucher book with a PIAS founded IPF. As an alternative, PIAS also offered to buy back a voucher book investment in its sponsored funds at CSK 11,000. Ultimately, some 15 percent of PIAS's investors accepted one offer or the other.

A strong argument can be made that the high level of cross-ownership between Investicni and its funds has impacted adversely on its fund's shareholders. For example, a principal Investicni controlled IPF is Rentiersky Investment Fund (Rent IF). As of 31 March 1994, Wood Company Securities reported that over 50 percent of Rent IF's portfolio was invested in the banking sector (presumably with a substantial portion being invested in Investicni itself), but Rent IF was trading at a deep discount to net asset value of over 75 percent. The market price of a voucher book invested with Rent IF stood (as of mid-June 1994) at CSK 9,000 – less than half that of a voucher book invested at the same time with Zivno 1. Fund (then trading at CSK 18,300) or the YSE Fund (then trading at CSK 21,600). Possibly, this apparent discount could have been a response to other factors and not necessarily to poor portfolio selection. Second only to HC&C, PIAS has been the subject of repeated criticism and innuendo in the press, suggesting that it was involved in unfair self-dealing and insider trading transactions. Fear of future scandals may also be depressing its price.

That cross-ownership developed to the degree that Investicni and its sponsored IPFs illustrate must have surprised the original draftsmen of the

Czech privatization law. The Czech Investment Companies and Investment Funds Act (1992) provides simply: "An investment company or investment fund established by a bank or insurance bank may not purchase the shares of its founder, its depository, or other banks and insurance banks" (§24(11)). Yet, notwithstanding this provision, Investicni's IPFs own 17 percent of it and substantial blocks in Ceska Sporitelna and Komercni Banka as well. How could this happen? The answer involves, on one level, a legal technicality and, on another level, an issue of political motivation. Technically, Investicni (as with most other banks) founded an investment company (PIAS) as a wholly owned subsidiary, which in turn founded its various IPFs. From a hyper-technical perspective, because Investicni did not itself "establish" its grandchildren IPFs, they can purchase shares in it and in other banks.[33]

Such a narrow reading obviously frustrates the statute's apparent intent to prevent bank cross-ownership. One wonders then whether this narrow reading was unavoidable or was the product of political compromise and accommodation. To be sure, civil law has never been read or interpreted in the pragmatic, purposive way that U.S. courts traditionally have sought the legislature's intent in reading U.S. statutes. But, the political accommodation story also sounds promising. Czech privatization did seemingly depend (at least at its outset) on the active cooperation of the major banks in marketing and distributing voucher books. Once HC&C emerged as activist outsider with possible plans for acquiring control of a major bank, it would not be surprising if the major banks sought to protect themselves through collusion. The state may have tacitly cooperated (and quietly waived the statute's application by accepting a patent formalism), both as a political quid pro quo and because it too feared HC&C and the prospect that it might "loot" any bank that it controlled. This possibility cannot be presented as historical fact, but nor is it fanciful speculation.

In any event, the cross-ownership structure within the banking industry has not remained static. Rather, both Investicni and Komercni have begun by various means to dilute the ownership of the NPF. In 1994, Investicni announced a merger with the Czech postal bank. The strategic objective of the merger was to provide Investicni with a national retail network rivaling that of Ceska Sporitelna, but it also diluted NPF's ownership to under 40 percent. In contrast, Komercni engineered an equity subscription offering (in which the NPF by prearrangement did not subscribe), thus also diluting NPF's equity percentage. However, the NPF has announced that it will retain a minimum one-third interest in each of the major Czech banks to protect

[33] Presumably, PIAS cannot directly purchase shares in Investicni because it is a first-generation descendant.

against hostile takeovers and mergers (a two-thirds shareholder vote being necessary under Czech law for a merger). In consequence, the managements of both banks seem secure from any threat of a hostile raid. Finally, the Czech national bank has adopted and enforced regulations precluding any person or entity from acquiring more than a 10 percent interest in a bank without its approval. As a result of these regulations, HC&C is under an obligation to reduce its holdings in Ceska Sporitelna.

The fact that special rules were adopted to limit HC&C in its pursuit of major banks, while Investicni's IPFs have been allowed to invest both in it and other banks, suggests a political interpretation of the cross-ownership phenomenon. Much of the impetus for cross-ownership within the Czech banking sector may well have come as a response to HC&C, which was widely rumored to have intended a takeover of Ceska Sporitelna. Many of our interviewees treated it as common knowledge that HC&C had such a scheme but was stopped by the Czech National Bank and the Ministry of Finance. Arguably, the fear of HC&C acquiring a major Czech bank caused all Czech banks to make substantial cross-investments in each other through their IPFs as an anticipatory defensive reaction. In interviews with us, representatives of HC&C stressed that the major banks were a "club" or an "old boys' network" and would always protect each other.

Cross-ownership is not, however, a universal phenomenon (as, for example, it tends to be among trading partners in Japan). Only the two Investicni banks (Czech and Slovak) appear to have concentrated their portfolios in the financial sector of the economy (and with seemingly dismal economic results in consequence). Komercni, in contrast, appears not to hold any significant ownership in Investicni (while Investicni's IPFs hold 10.8 percent of Komercni). Thus, cross-ownership is not fully reciprocal, and seldom do others match Investicni's significant holdings in them.

Even a significant block of stock in a bank may not confer much influence. Surprisingly, the deputy general manager of PIAS (the investment company for Investicni) told us that he doubted that IPFs could be active investors in the banks, both because in his judgment no more than a 5 to 15 percent stake could be acquired in the market in most of them and because the NPF tended to favor the status quo and back the incumbent management. As evidence of this contention, he pointed to the fact that IPFs had been unable to secure representation on the managing boards of the banks (although they had secured representation on the managing boards of most other privatized companies). PIAS, he said, focused on bank investments largely because (1) restructuring would not be necessary (at least as compared with the industrial sector), (2) bank investments were safe, and (3) some liquidity was likely to be available in bank stocks.

Corporate Governance Activities

How active and successful have IPFs been as corporate monitors? This is a question that it is surely premature to answer definitively at this point, but which must unavoidably be addressed. To do so, it is useful to break the question down into several component parts.

Board Representation and Recruitment.

The major IPFs have successfully sought board representation on their portfolio companies, typically on the managing boards (with the exception of the banking sector where they have been forced to settle for seats on the supervisory board). By some accounts, there are already informal rules recognized by the larger IPFs as to their relative rights to board representation. According to one commentator, "The largest three to six fund-owners nominate up to three non-executive directors each to a company's management board – and usually hold the majority" (Meth-Cohn 1994). Others told us (not necessarily inconsistently) that any fund owning 10 percent or more would be entitled to at least one board seat. PIAS, which generally seeks to reach the 20 percent ceiling on its shareholdings in a company, indicated that it had "strong representation" in about 50-70 companies where it held such a stake, and that in such cases, it would have approximately five to seven representatives on such boards (only one or two of whom would be individuals from the executive management at PIAS with the others being "outside experts").

An initial concern in our interviews was how IPFs recruited directors. It quickly became apparent that this responsibility was basically handled by the investment company. PIAS, for example, told us that it had between 150 to 170 seats to fill on the managing boards of portfolio companies (which portfolio then consisted of about 300 companies). All of its representatives would have a contract with PIAS but would be obligated under it to represent the interests of the portfolio company (and not any special interests of PIAS). Usually one representative will serve on two to three boards, and to avoid conflicts of interest, the representative will be placed on boards of companies that are not in active competition or within the same industry.

How can an investment company recruit the necessary directors to fill the board seats that its IPFs are entitled to fill? We encountered quite different responses. PIAS illustrates the polar case of an investment company assembling a substantial cadre of director nominees. Although conceding that finding sufficient persons with business experience and expertise was a serious problem, PIAS' deputy general manager estimated that PIAS had assembled a cadre of 65 persons to serve as its directors, from the following sources:

1) 20 persons from the top management of PIAS;
2) 25 persons from the top management of Investicni Banka; and
3) 20 persons from the regional branches of Investicni Banka (usually to serve on the boards of local companies).

Alone among our interviewees, PIAS thus acknowledged that it used bank employees to staff board positions. Others acknowledged that fire walls between the bank and the investment company were often breached, but they went well out of their way to disclaim the use of bank personnel as directors.

In contrast HC&C, which assembled the smallest portfolio after the first wave (only 51 companies), estimated that it had a strong supervisory role in some 35 companies. To staff these seats, it employs five to seven outside persons as its board representatives, with each such person sitting on approximately five boards. In addition, HC&C uses its own local employees to serve on boards of regional companies.

At the opposite end of the numerical spectrum from HC&C is SIS, the investment company to Ceska Sporitelna. Having assembled a portfolio of 500 companies, SIS holds a total of 280 board seats (primarily at the managing board level). For the most part, it relies on its own employees to staff these positions but also uses some 10 to 12 "external collaborators." More importantly, it permits no individual to serve on more than two boards. In total, SIS has about 120 staff employees, and we were told that "almost everyone is engaged" in serving as a director. However, unlike PIAS, no employee of its parent, Ceska Sporitelna, is permitted to serve as a director. Obviously, the use to this extent of lower-echelon staff employees as directors raises questions about their competence and ability to perform. In defense of this approach, SIS personnel argued that the practical role of the director could simply be to vote with a coalition of IPF funds on the board, which coalition would independently decide on the policy to be pursued and would use the actual director merely as a nominee by which to implement that policy. Other interviewees have suggested that SIS's policy of conferring directorships on lower-echelon employees was more a compensation device by which to supplement their modest salaries with directors' fees and was regarded by SIS employees as an important fringe benefit of their employment.

Some investment companies recapture all or a portion of the directors' and consulting fees paid to their representatives on the boards of portfolio companies. Although no IPF that we interviewed disclosed or acknowledged this practice, knowledgeable observers at the Czech Management Center (which runs a training program in Prague for new directors) told us that this practice was becoming common (although it was far from standard). Obviously, to the extent this occurs, directors may be undermotivated to perform any true monitoring function and may understandably view such a practice as a signal that their intended role is less that of a monitoring director than an informational agent who is expected to bring valuable information learned at the board meetings to the investment company for trading purposes.

Board Governance

Common agreement existed regarding the frequency of meetings and the preference of the IPFs for seats on the managing board – but on little else. Boards of privatized companies are meeting continually, at least once a month and often twice a month, according to most interviewees. Unlike a U.S. or British board, there is generally little delegation of authority to a CEO or management team. Rather, as a representative of Creditanstalt Investment Bank recently told the press: "All the decisions that count have to be approved by the board" (Meth-Cohn 1994, quoting Wolfgang Lafite). But the logistical constraint this imposes on part-time directors serving on multiple boards was thought by a number of interviewees to result in informational overload on these directors and, in turn, a tendency to defer to the firm's managers.[34]

Most interviewees were highly skeptical of the supervisory board. It was characterized as a "declining institution," or "useless," or as a cosmetic institution where real issues could not be discussed because of the presence of employee-elected representatives. A few interviewees were equally critical of the managing board. Jan Suchanek, the chief executive of YSE, the investment company that is widely believed to have assembled (on a per share basis) the highest valued portfolio after the first wave, noted that his funds had representatives on 80 boards (out of a portfolio of some 126 companies) and used some 65 persons as directors. Nonetheless, he was highly critical of the performance of most directors (and particularly those appointed by the bank-affiliated funds), whose behavior he viewed as "trying simply to avoid risk." In particular, he saw the large bank funds as staffing boards with "old Communists" whose chief aim was to "avoid embarrassment." Even when the funds owned a majority of the stock, their representatives on the boards had little incentive to become involved in management affairs and saw their primary role as that of conduits for information (much of it presumably nonpublic) about the company back to the fund manager. Corporate

[34] Some also attribute this to the typical director's lack of industry experience. See comments of Wolfgang Lafite in Meth-Cohn (1994).

managers in his view were finding the typical IPF board representatives on their boards easy to manipulate.

No one else took this extreme or polar a position. But others, particularly managers, expressed the view that fund representatives lacked any strategy or business plans. Indeed, some felt that the board resisted giving strategic directions to avoid involvement in any failure. As the general director of Prago, a.s., who was newly appointed to that post on March 30, 1994, phrased it to us: "I was given the task of within three months to move the company from the red to the black. I explained that that's nonsense in that short term, and, in the end, they said . . . that the last quarter this year must be a profitable quarter." As he explained, because his company had lost 80 percent of its market with the insolvency of its major Eastern bloc customers in Russia and the Ukraine and the dissolution of Comecon, he did not expect to be able to overcome these reversals in the nine months that he had been given.

Some managerial interviewees maintained that IPF directors simply lacked the business acumen and experience to offer specific advice or alternatives. Others stressed that directors did not want to take responsibility, and still others (including the above quoted individual) felt that time constraints were the most important factor as IPF directors (and their investment companies) were simply attempting in most cases to supervise too large a portfolio of companies. A senior executive at PPF, a respected "private" investment company, remarked to us that he had seen some individuals (apparently connected with bank-affiliated IPFs) occupy as many as 10 to 13 board seats. An official at CKD, one of the largest Czech engineering firms, went this story one better, citing a case of one director (who was incompetent in his judgment) who was then serving on some 40 boards.

Most interviewees agreed that on those boards on which IPFs held a majority the board was prepared to fire senior management – and had frequently done so. In fact some noted that there was a general expectation that the incumbent managers in office at the time of privatization would be replaced because they were widely assumed to be "old Communists" whose status in the corporate hierarchy was presumed to result from political affiliations. But the tendency to replace successor managers has continued, and some view it more as an indication of the board's inability to take any alternative step in response to continued unprofitability.

IPF Cooperation

The first reports during early 1994 suggested that the major IPFs were cooperating easily on the boards where they shared representation. After all, they had obvious common interests in establishing internal controls, preventing managerial or employee diversions of assets, and securing competent management. As of June 1994, we did not hear reports of conflict among IPFs with regard to portfolio companies. This picture changed, however, later in 1994. Apparently in several instances, dissension had arisen among bank-affiliated IPFs as to which bank a portfolio company should use as its primary lender. In one instance, a board was reportedly split between a faction led by directors aligned with Komercni Banka and another faction associated with Investicni Banka, and the dispute essentially boiled down to which bank would serve as the lead lender.[35]

Such a conflict suggests that bank-affiliated IPFs at least sometimes may be serving more as agents of their bank sponsors than as agents of their own shareholders. In principal, if a bank controls a corporate board through its agents, it can extract rents from the company in the form of above-market interest rates. This fear has long been a concern raised about the German banking system and now appears to have arisen in the Czech context also. Where such board divisions arise and board paralysis thereby results, control appears to shift to the incumbent management. Although management may be able to avoid excessive interest charges by playing off one faction against another, it is equally possible that it may acquiesce to above-market financing rates in return for the guaranteed support of a powerful IPF. The outcomes are uncertain, but the common denominator is that once an IPF (and its sponsors) have a dual relationship (i.e. creditor plus equity shareholder) with a portfolio company, the relationship between the IPF and the company need not be a simple monitoring relationship, but can involve more complex trade-offs in which the IPF seeks an advantage for its sponsor at some cost in monitoring efficiency.

At present one cannot quantify the extent of this problem, but as discussed later, the Czech context raises it in a more problematic form than does the German banking system (where typically the bank itself holds a sizable equity stake).

Restructuring

Are IPF directors inducing privatized companies to undertake necessary restructuring? This is clearly a critical question, but answering it runs up against the enduring problem that chronology does not imply causation. *Post hoc* does not mean *propter hoc.* Some restructuring is clearly under way, but the role of IPFs in causing it is more ambiguous. Any visitor to the Czech Republic notices immediately that most enterprises (private or public) are characterized by overemployment. Even most public spaces (from museums

[35] Interview with Jana Matesova, Czech Management Center, December 1994.

to restrooms) are serviced by an inefficient surplus of attendants. But many Czech industries – particularly those in engineering, electronics, and agriculture – have, with the collapse of Comecon, lost their foreign markets in Eastern Europe and Russia that sustained such levels of employment.

In consequence, restructuring has been forced on many companies. During the last year, Prago, an engineering sector firm, reduced employment from 1,500 to 1,000 (or nearly 27 percent) and plans to cut another 400 to 500 workers, thus in total reducing employment by as much as 60 percent. ZPA Jinonice, an engineering and printing firm, told us that its mid-1994 employment stood at 350, down from approximately 1,000 in 1990. Similarly, it had lost 90 percent of its market with the disbanding of Comecon. Finally, CKD told us that they had reduced employment from 25,000 in 1990 to "just under 13,000" today. In these and other cases, the process has occurred without either significant trade union opposition or IPF instigation. Rather, the necessity for employment reductions was obvious to all involved in light of the basic fact that most Czech industrial firms had lost the Eastern markets that once supported them. Across the engineering and electronics sectors, plants have been closed and centralized without significant political unrest or opposition. To be sure, a factor making these layoffs politically acceptable to date has been the very low rate of unemployment (around 3.5 percent) in the Czech economy with virtually no unemployment in the Prague vicinity.

Still, it is not clear that managing boards have either driven or directed this process. The interviewed managers claimed that staff reductions were inevitable and were initiated by them well before voucher privatization took effect. Given the loss of 60 to 70 percent of their markets, they said they had no other way to meet their payrolls. Staff reductions had begun before the first wave of privatization, and IPFs in their view did not cause or hasten the process. Others believe that the existence of boards dominated by IPFs made it obvious to employees that staff reductions could not be delayed, but no interviewee pointed to direct action taken by IPF directors (or even ultimatums given) that had resulted in staff reductions, and several suggested that IPFs had had no role in this process.

Some have suggested to us that a principal reason why IPFs have had only limited impact on the restructuring process is that they lack the ability to provide financing (or, equally important, to withhold financing unless specific targets were met), technology, or the other forms of assistance that a strategic partner would provide. By definition, voucher funds lack capital, and although several investment companies have recently established cash funds, their resources are limited. In our interviews, no one phrased it this bluntly, but several management interviewees indicated an inability to make strategic plans until the firm's "true owner" was determined. Many Czech companies have had some 30 to 40 percent of their shares reserved for sale to a prospective single shareholder (presumably, a foreign corporation). With some consistency, the managers we interviewed acknowledged reluctance about making strategic plans, opening plants, or selling possibly peripheral assets without the consent of such a "true owner" (who they also viewed as the source of critical financing). In comparison to these possibly hypothetical future owners, IPF directors tended to be discounted as amateurs. At least implicitly, the NPF has shown a similar attitude, resisting efforts by companies to convert surplus or peripheral assets into cash through sales or dispositions on the ground that the future owner should decide these questions (even in cases where the board has a majority of IPF directors). The result is to leave these companies in a limbo-like transitional stage.

IPF Incentives

Participation in corporate governance is not costless. Thus, in evaluating the extent of IPF involvement in the governance of their portfolio companies, it is useful to compare the costs and benefits of "active ownership." Investment companies (and in some cases their banking parents) derive benefits from three sources: (1) from management and start-up fees charged their IPFs, (2) from share appreciation to the extent that they own or acquire IPF shares, and (3) from independent trading activities – possibly informed (or "tipped") by information gained from an IPF director. Investment companies are permitted to charge an annual management fee of an IPF of up to either 2 percent of the average net asset value of the fund or 20 percent of the IPF's annual profits (see Investment Companies and Investment Funds Act 1992, §27). Most investment companies have opted for the former option as the more profitable, and (possibly as a marketing matter) most seem to charge slightly less than 2 percent (i.e. 1.75 percent or 1.50 percent were common annual fees).[36] Given such a fee structure, investment companies have considerable reason to economize on their corporate governance activities. Few, if any, appear to have hired outside consultants, and most rely more on staff employees (whose primary responsibility has been marketing) for board positions than salaried outsiders. Milan Jurceka, the executive director of A-Invest (the investment company to Agrobanka) phrased the trade-off to us succinctly: "As to the profit of our company, our

[36] None seem to charge the greater of the two options. In addition to the annual fee, investment companies may also charge a one-time start-up or establishment fee, whose size is not regulated. Presumably, this one-time fee will not affect marginal decision-making about monitoring. HC&C appears uniquely to charge its IPFs for expenses incurred on their behalf. The amount of this fee (and what it covers) is not known.

profit last year of our Investment Company was like this: 4 percent came from dividends and profits from share companies, and 96 percent from the [trading] business on the Prague Stock Exchange and RM-S system. As to our expenditures, it was the opposite: 90 percent of our expenditures were to go to the share companies, and 10 percent from the wages of the specialist on the PSE and RM-S. This is a great difference. It is better to concentrate on the specialist in the PSE/RM-S because I expect a profit from them." A-Invest was a highly successful trading firm in 1993, earning a 20 percent return on its capital. Given this disparity between costly participation in corporate governance activities and cheap but lucrative trading profits, investment companies may become increasingly (and rationally) passive as shareholders.

Still, one important qualification to any such prediction emerges from the fact that many of the largest investment companies now tend to own between 10 percent to over 50 percent of the equity in their IPFs (as a result of guarantees made at the marketing stage). Thus, in these cases, their incentives may be much better aligned with those of the other IPF shareholders, and principal/agent conflicts should be mitigated.

But large equity stakes do not alone logically ensure activism. Investment companies must believe that the marginal benefits of shareholders' activism exceed the marginal costs. At present, many seem dubious about costly monitoring. Another possible explanation for apparent IPF passivity involves the set of investment opportunities that they confront. Some fund managers candidly told us that the most interesting investment opportunities in the Czech Republic today involved the shares of other IPFs. Given discounts of possibly up to 80 percent in IPF shares and (relatively) liquid financial assets if a small IPF could be acquired and liquidated, the expected return from this form of restructuring (in effect to eliminate the closed-end discount) at the IPF level is perceived by some within the Czech financial markets to exceed that from more traditional corporate restructurings. To be sure, Czech law precludes one IPF from acquiring shares in another (Investment Companies and Investment Funds Act 1992, §24(7)), and a merger between two IPFs would require Ministry of Finance approval. Still, investment companies can form investor groups to acquire controlling blocks in smaller IPFs and seek their liquidation. A Ministry of Finance official estimated for us that as little as a 10 percent block could control a smaller IPF (assuming it was formed as a joint stock company) and acknowledged that such control acquisitions had occurred and were in progress.

Bank/IPF Contacts: Does the German Banking Analogy Apply?

A common prediction about Czech privatization was that it would evolve in the direction of the German "universal" banking system rather than toward an Anglo-American market-oriented system of corporate governance. The conventional wisdom about the German system was that its major banks acted as careful monitors of managerial performance at client corporations because of their joint position as creditors in their own right and also agents for the shareholders for whom they typically serve as depository for most shares.[37] According to traditional argument, this dual relationship gives rise to economies of both scope and scale.

Although the evidence about the efficiency advantages of the German banking system is itself much in dispute (discussed later in the chapter), the Czech pattern must be recognized as different from the German in several important respects. First, German banks own substantial stock in their own right. Although they also typically hold substantially greater voting power through proxies granted them by individual shareholders, the significance of the large equity stakes that they do hold is that they tend to align their interests with those of the other shareholders. In contrast Czech banks hold virtually no equity in the portfolio companies held by their sponsored IPFs. This contrast means that the only benefit that a Czech bank receives from equity appreciation of a stock in an IPF's portfolio is an increase in the annual management fee that it receives (typically at or under 2 percent of the net asset value of the fund).

This distinction has particular importance because the latest research on the German banking system finds that "German banks improve the performance of German firms to the extent that they hold the firms' equity" (see Gorton and Schmid 1994, 35). Proxy voting power and other variables suggesting the bank's level of influence (i.e. supervisory board seats held) did not correlate closely with improved economic performance. Only when the bank was a substantial blockholder in its own right did a correlation between the bank's presence and the firm's economic performance become clear. Yet, in the Czech case, the bank is never a substantial blockholder (except in the unusual case where it holds a substantial interest in its own IPF).

Second, large blockholders are common in Germany; 85 percent of the largest quoted German companies have a shareholder owning 25 percent or

[37] For the conventional assessment that German banks do monitor corporate managements closely, see Carrington and Edwards (1979); Charkham (1989). See also Cable (1985). These reviews have recently been elaborately criticized in a full scale review of the German banking system, which finds that it devotes no more attention to monitoring than do banks in economies organized around stock markets. See Edwards and Fisher (1994).

more (see Gorton and Schmid 1994, 16). This suggests the likelihood of countervailing power, which could prevent a bank from extracting private benefits. Although Czech share ownership is highly concentrated, no single IPF can legally exceed 20 percent. To be sure, some have in fact done so, holding up to 30 percent, but such holdings have been tolerated only for a transitional period.

Third, most IPFs have only a weak incentive to maximize the value of their portfolio shares, because they do not expect (after the second wave) to have further opportunities (at least in the near future) to sell their shares. This is in sharp contrast to the typical open-end American mutual fund, which regularly offers its shares to the public. To be sure, the investment company sponsoring an IPF can expect a larger annual management fee if portfolio share value increases (basically 2 percent of the increase annually), but it cannot expect to double its asset value by selling additional shares. It knows that the privatization process is over and that there will be no third wave. Hence, its incentives to monitor to raise share value should logically be weaker.

Even among bank-affiliated IPFs, the pattern of interaction between the bank and its sponsor seems to be highly divergent. Some investment companies that are controlled by Czech banks (for example, SIS, the subsidiary of Ceska Sporitelna) protested that they could not (and did not) contact their banking parent for information about privatized companies in their portfolio, but rather maintained a strict fire wall between themselves and the bank.[38] In sharp contrast, another prominent investment company (A-Invest) indicated that it participated in regular, formalized discussions through quarterly meetings at which bank-appointed directors, regional managers of the investment company, and regional bank officials would meet to pool information about companies in the investment company's portfolio. A-Invest in particular stressed that what it desired most from these meetings was the financial data that any borrower would be required to provide and update periodically to its banking parent (Agrobanka). A-Invest did insist, however, that these collective conferences would use the information assembled to predict trends, discuss possible mergers and acquisitions, or evaluate management – but not to acquire information for use in securities trading. Still, A-Invest acknowledged that it had profited handsomely from its securities trading activities (it estimated a 20 percent return on

[38] Interviewees may, of course, have been inhibited by their knowledge of §28 of the Investment Companies and Investment Funds Act (1992), which provides that both employees of an investment company and an investment fund (among others) "are bound to treat as confidential all facts concerning the business interests of an investment company, investment fund or depository."

capital last year, primarily from trading activities). No other investment company was as candid about its disregard for fire walls between the bank and an investment company subsidiary, but PIAS did acknowledge relying heavily on employees of its banking parent (Investicni Bank) to serve as directors of its portfolio companies.

Most interviewees were familiar with the term "fire wall," and some understood it to be the Ministry of Finance's policy that there should be a fire wall between the investment company and its banking parent, at least with regard to IPF activities. No Czech statute seems to mandate such a fire wall, however, and others (most notably A-Invest) disputed the need for any such prophylactic rule, pointing out that the most valuable information was already in the hands of the bank in the form of credit data and that efforts to obtain such data could only benefit the IPFs.[39] In any event, a basic policy choice is framed here: should fire walls be encouraged? Or should banks and IPFs pool information to realize informational synergies from their multiple relationships with portfolio companies? The next part will return to this issue.

Policy Options: How Should the Regulatory System Be Changed?

Although the Czech experience is instructive and revealing in its own right, the preceding discussion ultimately sets the stage for a focus on the policy issues in voucher fund regulation – both within the Czech Republic and in other transitional economies. The Czech experience suggests that some recurring problems will need to be faced in any economy that is to be privatized through the use of voucher funds and also that some unexpected and unique problems – such as the high level of cross-ownership and the consequent consolidation of control within the Czech banking system – are predictably to surface in each individual context. Although this last issue of high cross-ownership may prove unique to the circumstances of Czech privatization, privatization achieves little if it only substitutes oligopoly for government ownership. Thus, this chapter will group the major regulatory issues under: (1) removing barriers to active ownership, (2) establishing effective IPF governance, and (3) ensuring competition: the antitrust issues.

[39] This argument may have been an effort to explain away §28 of the Investment Companies and Investment Funds Act, which imposes a duty of confidentiality on investment company employees but says nothing about their efforts to gather data from others.

Removing Barriers to Active Ownership

The most obvious barrier to IPFs behaving as "true" owners is the 20 percent ceiling on ownership by an IPF or related group of IPFs of a single firm's stock.[40] Clearly, such a rule is only tenuously related to any diversification objective (which goal is in any event more sensibly addressed by a narrower rule restricting IPFs to investing no more than 10 percent of their assets in securities of any one issuer) (see Investment Companies and Investment Funds Act 1992, §24(1)). The impact of this rule is to create a significant free rider problem in that a 20 percent owner will have less incentive to monitor and expend funds on corporate governance activities than will, for example, a 50 percent owner.

Other corporate governance issues, however, also deserve attention. Two-tiered boards are viewed by some as a means of confining the power of shareholder-elected directors. To date, the major Czech banks have restricted such directors (including those nominated by HC&C) to the supervisory board. Also, to encourage active monitoring, it may be desirable to authorize incentive fees in excess of the 2 percent ceiling now permitted an IPF management company under Czech law. Each of these topics is considered below.

The 20 Percent Ownership Ceiling

The case for eliminating the 20 percent ceiling is clear and straightforward: its abolition would facilitate corporate control transactions and permit an activist IPF shareholder to acquire control (or simply threaten to do so) in order to influence or oust a management that is resistant to shareholder pressure. Other shareholders (including even foreign owners) are not restricted by any similar ceiling and can today assemble a majority interest. Why then are IPFs specially singled out? Even when acquisition of control is

[40] The actual legal rule has three distinct provisions: Section 24(3) of the Investment Companies and Investment Funds Act (1992, as amended by Act No. 591/1992 Coll.) provides:

> "(3) Not more than 20 (twenty) percent of the total nominal value of securities issued by the same issuer may be owned by a unit trust or an investment fund."

To prevent evasion through the use of multiple funds controlled by the same investment company, §24(5)(a) of the same Act further provides:

> "(5) An investment company must ensure that:
> (a) the assets of all unit trust established and administered by that investment company do not represent more that 20 (twenty) percent of the shares of the same issuer;"

Finally, §24(6) provides:

> "The restrictions under subsection 5 also apply to investment funds established by the same founder."

not feasible (because, for example, of the above noted 10 percent diversification restraint), an IPF that acquires 30 percent will have a greater incentive to monitor managements. For the most part, the economic evidence tends to support the position that large shareholders create value for all shareholders, because they are a partial solution to the free rider problem.[41]

The case for retaining the 20 percent rests instead on political considerations and the fear that minority shareholders (and also other constituencies) will be exploited by a dominant IPF shareholder. Those favoring retention of the 20 percent ceiling fear that if a controlling block is assembled, the value of the minority shares will decline – either in anticipation of future exploitative conduct or because the public minority shares will be shorn of their control premium. The realism of this scenario is difficult to assess within the Czech context, but cannot be glibly dismissed.

In general, financial economics recognizes that those seeking to assemble a controlling block may seek to do so out of mixed motives: control seekers may believe either (1) that they can increase the future cash flows from the business or (2) that, once in control, they can divert resources to themselves in non pro-rata transactions that injure other shareholders.[42] In the latter case, financial economists would say that the acquisition of corporate control was motivated by a desire to obtain the "private benefits of control" – a polite euphemism for the gains that a controlling shareholder can reap at the expense of minority shareholders through unfair self-dealing, the payment of excessive salaries, the seizing of corporate opportunities, or similar forms of fiduciary abuse. Thus, the existence of private benefits from control implies that there can be both efficient and inefficient control transfers – that is, cases in which the control change increases shareholder value and cases in which it decreases it.

What is the respective balance between efficient and inefficient control changes? Although some universal theories have been formulated (Bebchuk), it is more likely that the answer will vary with the institutional context and that different legal and economic systems are more (or less) exposed to the problems of inefficient transfers of control. Within the United States, the limited available data suggest that efficient control transfers that enhance the value of the minority shares are significantly more common than inefficient transfers. However, on close inspection, these data raise as many questions as they answer. In the best-known such study, Professors Holderness and

[41] See, e.g. Shleifer and Vishny (1986), presenting data from a U.S. context that large, but noncontrolling, shareholders increase the value of a firm.

[42] See Bebchuk (forthcoming). Of course, it is possible for a control seeker to have both motives, in which case minority shareholders gain or lose depending on the relative balance of these two motives.

Sheehan identified a sample of 114 New York or American Stock Exchange companies in which an individual or entity owned between 51 percent and 95 percent of the outstanding common stock (Holderness and Sheehan 1988). From this sample, they culled out a further sample of 31 such companies in which a majority block of stock was transferred between 1978 and 1982. What happened to the public stock price when such a majority block was transferred? Measuring the cumulative abnormal returns, Holderness and Sheehan found that the stocks in their 31 firm sample earned statistically significant returns of 7.3 percent over the period from the day before the announcement of the transaction to the day after, and returns of 12.8 percent over the 30 day period beginning 20 days before the announcement and continuing until 10 days after. Obviously, such a finding suggests that majority control transfers tend to increase shareholder wealth.

But they also found a contrary undercurrent. In 35 percent of the 30 day observation periods for the 31 company sample, the abnormal returns were not positive. This is surprising because many transfers of a majority block are accompanied by a contemporaneous tender offer for the minority stock at a price substantially above the market price (in fact, such a contemporaneous tender offer was made in 10 of the 31 cases in their sample).[43] Even when a simultaneous tender offer is not made, the market may still expect (with good reason) that an above-market offer will later be made and so may respond positively to the control block transfer. Obviously, this expectation should bias upward the U.S. market's reaction toward controlling block transfers, even if a subsequent tender offer is made in only a minority of the cases. Given this tendency, the nonpositive market reaction to the transfer of a controlling block in 35 percent of the cases in the Holderness and Sheehan study suggests that the market was suspicious of the acquirer in these cases for some reason.

More importantly, because Professors Holderness and Sheehan studied only the market's reaction to a *majority* block transfer, their study provides no information about the market's response to the sale of a controlling block that consists of less than a majority of the shares. In the Czech context, however, if the 20 percent ceiling were lifted, the most common scenario would probably include smaller purchases (either in the open market, or more likely, in swaps between IPFs) whereby a large IPF acquired control without (at least initially) acquiring a majority block (indeed, it would be difficult to acquire majority control in a single transaction because the selling IPF would presumably own no more than 20 percent and probably less).

The possibility of a negative market reaction seems more likely in the case

[43] When these 10 cases were subtracted from their sample, the cumulative abnormal returns for the two time periods fell from 7.3% and 12.8%, respectively, to 5.5% and 9.4%, respectively.

of such a minority controlling block transfer. Why? Because the purchaser of a majority block is acquiring more shares than it needs to obtain effective control, the purchaser's behavior signals that it believes it can raise the value of all shares. In contrast, one seeking to obtain private benefits from control would rationally seek to buy as small a percentage of the stock as will enable it to obtain such benefits, because its future self-dealing behavior will predictably depress the market price once it is detected. In this light, if one can obtain the private benefits of control by buying 20 percent of the stock, it would seem a mistake to buy 40 percent, at least when the company is to be "plundered" in a manner that will drive down the public stock price.

Put differently, the higher the percentage of the stock that the control seeker buys, the greater the likelihood that it expects the value of the company to increase, and the less the likelihood that the control seeker is motivated by a desire to obtain private benefits. The logic of this position should be obvious: if one is buying control to loot the company (that is, in less pejorative language, to expropriate wealth from it through unfair self-dealing transactions, excessive salaries, nepotism, or the consumption of other prerequisites), then one wants to buy as little as possible, because the stock value should decline once the market anticipates such wealth expropriations. The anecdotal evidence about controversial American raiders (e.g. Victor Posner) is consistent with this hypothesis: they tend to remain minority (although controlling) shareholders and seldom buy all the stock – unless they have depressed its value and can purchase at a large discount. From this perspective, the more sensible policy prescription then would not be to impose an absolute 20 percent ceiling but might be to forbid stockholdings in the 30 to 50 percent range (where minority control is possible) and require that a control seeker who wishes to buy more than the level that would confer control must buy all or nearly all the remaining shares. As discussed below, several European states have adopted such a position (although clearly the United States has not).

Still, before advocating any policy proposal, we need to face more squarely a preliminary issue: can the private benefits of control really explain the control premiums often paid to acquire control? A study limited to the U.S. context suggests that the private benefits of control amount on average to between 3 percent and 4 percent of the equity value of a publicly held corporation.[44] Such a small benefit cannot explain tender offer premiums that in the United States often exceed 50 percent. This evidence might explain the

[44] Barclay and Holderness (1989). Control premiums are substantially higher in the case of privately held and thinly traded stocks in the United States, and it is possible that the private benefits of control are also higher in that context.

lack of enthusiasm within the United States for any prophylactic equal-sharing rule, because it suggests that large control premiums must primarily be paid by acquirers who anticipate synergistic and other efficiency-derived gains. However, studies conducted outside the United States imply that the private benefits of control tend to represent a much larger fraction of equity value in other countries (Levy 1982; Zingales 1992). Arguably, the lesser role accorded to private enforcement outside the United States and the absence of public agencies paralleling the Securities and Exchange Commission (SEC) may enable controlling shareholders outside the United States to appropriate more of a firm's value to themselves.

Where does all this leave us? Even if Czech law provides little protection for minority shareholders against exploitation by the majority shareholder, it still does not follow that minority shareholders will typically be injured if IPFs are permitted to assemble controlling blocks. What can be said (albeit cautiously because the empirical evidence is limited) is that there is a relatively greater risk of injury to the minority if a shareholder can assemble a minority controlling block (i.e. shareholdings in the 30 to 50 percent range) than if it can only make an any-and-all 100 percent offer. Still, it would go beyond the evidence to suggest that harm is likely to befall the public minority from the assembly of a minority controlling block.

Ultimately, the bottom line trade-off can be simply stated: do the likely efficiency gains from the emergence of a controlling shareholder able and motivated to monitor and replace management exceed the likely losses to the other shareholders from its ability to realize private benefits? In short even if a new controlling shareholder consumes more private benefits, this is not necessarily harmful to the minority if its greater ability and incentive to monitor management also increase efficiency within the firm.

Within the special context of the Czech economy and legal system, there is reason for skepticism about claims that either the likely efficiency gains or the likely private benefit losses would be significant from eliminating the 20 percent ceiling. First, on the efficiency gain side, the already highly concentrated character of shareholdings in the Czech economy means that two or more IPFs will often be able to hold *de facto* control of a corporate board. Even without raising the 20 percent ceiling, IPFs can form alliances to monitor, restrain, and replace incumbent managements. Clearly, this is happening today. Thus, the practical significance of eliminating the 20 percent ceiling may be chiefly confined to cases when either (1) there are numerous small funds and individual shareholders, but no more than one fund holding stock at or near the 20 percent level, or (2) there is a countervailing holder (such as a block held by the NPF or a management-held block) that disagrees with the IPFs as to the appropriate corporate policy.

Normally, in cases involving policy disputes, the easiest course would be for one side to buy out the other – but this cannot easily be done today in the Czech system where cash resources are limited and where the 20 percent ownership ceiling poses a legal obstacle. Thus, from a purely practical perspective, the greatest benefit from an elimination of the 20 percent ceiling may be that it authorizes an important alternative means of dispute resolution (the buyout) in circumstances where the parties are deadlocked. This is particularly useful in the Czech context where sales into a "thin" stock market may not be feasible.

On the opposite side of the ledger, the danger may also be exaggerated that controlling shareholders would exploit their position and consume increased private benefits if the 20 percent ceiling were relaxed or eliminated. First, even though Czech corporate law is relatively underdeveloped, the ability of IPFs to consume private benefits is constrained to a considerable extent by their special character and structure. Unlike private corporations or families, IPFs have no business of their own and thus cannot be lenders, suppliers, or customers to their portfolio corporations. This limits the opportunities for self-dealing. Confined to the status of equity holders, they are ill positioned to exploit the private benefits of control.

A possible response to this argument is that, even if IPFs are too remotely positioned to exploit control themselves, the investment companies that control them are in turn controlled by the largest financial institutions in the Czech Republic. Thus, these investment companies can arguably utilize their control over their IPFs to reap private benefits either for themselves or their banking parents. But if so, the appropriate policy response would be to condition the relaxation of the 20 percent ceiling on restrictions on transactions between investment companies (and their affiliates) and their IPFs' portfolio companies.

On balance, it is difficult to see any convincing reason for maintaining the 20 percent ownership ceiling. Not only are IPFs very different from the classic raider, who wishes to strip assets from the controlled company in self-dealing transactions, but Czech law requires a high supermajority vote (65 percent) to approve any follow-up squeeze out merger (in contrast to the prevailing 50 percent vote requirement in most U.S. states). Thus, the standard U.S. fear that, after control is secretly acquired, the minority will be squeezed out at an unfairly low price seems unrealistic.

The real question then is whether the 20 percent ceiling should be raised or simply abolished. Raising the limit to 30 or 35 percent (and then requiring that any additional purchases must be limited to an any-and-all 100 percent bid to all shareholders) has one possible advantage: it creates a system of cross-monitoring in which large block holders would monitor not only management but also the largest shareholder. At this 30 or 35 percent level, some support from other shareholders would still be necessary before the largest IPF could take action. In contrast, once the 50 percent threshold can be crossed, the rudimentary state of shareholder legal remedies under Czech law (and under civil law generally) suggests that minority shareholders would have little effective legal recourse if unfair self-dealing transactions were then implemented by the new controlling shareholder.

Two principal objections can be anticipated to such a system of reciprocal monitoring: first, a rule that purchases over 30 percent (or some similar level) could be made only by a tender offer would raise the costs to an IPF shareholder of effecting a synergistic merger between itself and the portfolio company, because it could not purchase a majority interest in the open market and then push through its merger proposal. As a practical matter, however, truly synergistic mergers between IPFs and their portfolio companies seem unlikely because the IPF has no business of its own to combine with the portfolio company. Hence, in the absence of related assets to combine, the likely synergistic gains would seem to be modest. Second, because the existing diversification rule prevents an IPF from investing more than 10 percent of its assets in a single company, there might be occasions in which an IPF could buy 51 percent but not 100 percent, and a mandatory bid requirement would block such a 51 percent acquisition.

Valid as this latter point may be, it would be at least partially addressed by moving up the ownership ceiling from 20 to 30 percent – and then requiring that additional shares be acquired only pursuant to a tender offer. This would still leave a shareholder who was blocked by diversification rules from acquiring 100 percent in a very influential position. Such a compromise would also closely resemble the British rules on takeovers, which have long required a shareholder seeking to acquire more than 30 percent to do so by a tender offer for all the remaining shares (see Demott 1987). In effect, partial acquisitions above 30 percent are impossible, unless the minority chooses not to tender its shares. Spain and Australia have also followed the British approach, and a proposed European Economic Community (EEC) directive on company law has recently advocated generalizing this approach (see Elhauge 1993; Luftmann 1992).

A European consensus appears then to be developing on the desirability of a mandatory bid (presumably at the highest price at which shares in the company have been recently purchased) once a specified threshold has been crossed. From a strictly economic perspective, this approach is vulnerable to the objection that if the bidder must pay all shareholders the same price, it cannot pay a control premium to the incumbent group holding control (who may prefer as a result not to sell in order to continue to enjoy the private benefits of control) (Bebchuk). Thus, some efficient transfer of control may be blocked by this equal-sharing rule. Still, this objection has less practical matter in the Czech context, where there are few preexisting control blocks to be bought out (given the short interval since privatization) and where management teams hold relatively small blocks. In short, few efficient transactions would likely be blocked if Czech law were to delete the existing 20 percent ceiling on IPFs and instead require that *any* shareholder seeking to purchase more than, say, 30 percent must do so by means of a mandatory bid for all shares at the highest price recently paid for shares in the company.

When an IPF acquires more than 20 percent of a company's stock, special rules would also be desirable barring its investment company (or any parent or affiliate thereof) from transacting business (in a material amount) with the portfolio company – at least unless the proposed self-dealing transaction were first approved by disinterested shareholders of the IPF. This rule would apply even if 100 percent of the portfolio company's stock were acquired, as its purpose is to protect the shareholders of the IPF as well as minority shareholders in the portfolio company.

Other Restrictions on Active Ownership

Both a number of Czech managers and some governmental officials expressed reservation in interviews about the propriety of IPFs seeking to behave as active owners. Some pointed to a policy expressed by the Organization for Economic Cooperation and Development (OECD) that mutual funds and unit trusts should not seek "acquisition of effective control." That policy statement, adopted by the OECD in 1972, in its "Standard Rules for the Operations of Institutions for Collective Investment in Securities," sets forth the following rule: "9th Rule: Acquisition of Effective Control. [An institution for collective investment] shall not acquire more than 5 to 15 percent of the voting securities of any one enterprise. When several [such institutions] are operated by the same management not more than 5 to 15 percent of the voting securities of any one enterprise shall be jointly held by [them]."[45] The stated rationale for this position was that institutions for collective investment (their term for mutual funds) were "ill-suited to exercise control over an enterprise, because the management of the [fund] is not governed by the wishes of the investors and can act as it pleases" (OECD 1972, 27). Interestingly, this rationale posits that because of their own internal corporate governance problems, investment funds should

[45] See OECD (1972). The 5 to 15% range specified in this rule was intended to give individual states some discretion in choosing a maximum level; it was not intended that any one jurisdiction would vaguely specify a 5 to 15% range (p. 27).

not seek to exercise control over portfolio companies. Although the governance of IPFs is indeed problematic (as discussed later in more detail), the immediate point is that those opposed to active participation by IPFs in the governance of their portfolio companies can use this claim that IPF fund managers are essentially unaccountable to the demand that they remain passive.

To date, this argument has had little impact at those portfolio companies in which IPFs hold in the aggregate a clear majority of the voting stock. But, at the major banks (where the NPF often holds a decisive swing block and where there is substantial cross-shareholding among banks), the IPFs have been largely confined to the supervisory board. The case for such a limited role seems weak, in part because the NPF holds (and will retain) sufficient shares to veto actions at the shareholder level that in its judgment threaten the public interest. Nonetheless, the continued use of a two-tiered board structure may under some circumstances interfere with the ability of IPFs to become active owners. To the extent that such a two-tier structure is retained, legislative clarification of the right of shareholders to elect nominees to both boards might be desirable.

Enhancing the Incentives for Active Ownership

IPFs are themselves legal fictions; they have little or no staff, and their own shareholders are typically highly dispersed. Thus, as a practical matter, they are likely to be dominated by the investment companies that manage them. Certainly, that has been the U.S. experience with mutual funds, even in a much more regulated market. In short, the investment company will predictably be the active decision-maker for the IPF, and it is thus important to align its self-interest with active participation in corporate governance if the original objectives of the architects of Czech privatization are to be realized.

At present, however, investment companies have considerable reason to be rationally apathetic about IPF involvement in corporate governance. The Investment Companies and Investment Funds Act requires that the "fee charged by an investment company for the administration of a unit trust, or for services it has rendered to an investment fund, may not exceed 2 (two) percent of the average annual value of the property held by a unit trust or of property of an investment fund, or 20 (twenty) percent of the financial result of a unit trust or investment fund."[46] Most investment companies prefer to use the 2 percent of assets standard, because few IPFs have received

[46] See Investment Companies and Investment Funds Act (1992, as amended by Act No. 591/1992 Coll., §27).

significant dividends from their portfolio companies. Indeed, in a highly competitive market, many investment companies charge less than 2 percent annually (1.5 percent is a common figure). As a result, however, an investment company managing perhaps several IPFs, each with a significant portfolio of a hundred or more companies, may have a strong incentive to avoid expenditures on costly corporate governance activities at any individual portfolio company – even if such activities are in the interests of the IPF's shareholders. As the chief executive of A-Invest, a large investment company, told us, corporate governance activities accounted for most of his firm's expenditures, but little of its profits (if indeed profits can ever be reliably so attributed).

The case for rational passivity by Czech IPFs is far stronger than in the case of U.S. mutual funds because IPFs do not expect to sell further shares in the future. Voucher privatization has essentially been completed, and even excellent performance by a fund manager will not translate into future receipt of vouchers in some eventual third or fourth privatization wave. Nor is there yet a practical way for an IPF to attract capital away from other underperforming IPFs. In contrast, most U.S. fund managers manage open-end funds, which are continually selling their shares to the public, and thus good investment performance as a fund manager translates into future fund share sales, which in turn will raise the base on which the annual management fee (also typically computed in the United States as a low percentage of fund asset value) is computed. Investors in poorly performing U.S. mutual funds will redeem their shares and reinvest in other funds. At present, Czech investors cannot easily move from one fund to another by withdrawing their funds and reinvesting. In the absence of such a procedure, there is less capital market discipline focused on Czech IPF managers. To be sure, Czech fund managers can expect additional compensation as the result of an increase in the value of the fund's assets, but closed-end funds cannot sell additional shares to raise the denominator on which their 2 percent annual fee is based. Hence, Czech funds have an even stronger incentive to pursue a cost minimization policy and avoid expending funds on corporate governance activities.

To illustrate, suppose intervention in a portfolio company's affairs to replace management (which intervention can only be undertaken by an investment company, as IPFs have no staff) would cost the investment company $20,000 in direct and indirect costs but would raise the value of the IPF's investment in the company by $100,000. This 5:1 ratio of benefits to costs sounds attractive, but it is still irrational for the investment company, as the $100,000 appreciation translates into only a $2,000 increased annual fee to it (or a net loss in the first year of $18,000). U.S. mutual fund managers might (occasionally and rarely) undertake such an intervention, but their aim is to market additional fund sales of an open-end fund based on their investment performance.

What is the answer to this problem? One possibility is the use of incentive fees (for example, the fund manager might receive 2 percent plus, say, 20 percent of all appreciation above some market index). Now, if the $100,000 gain were in excess of the relevant market index, the fund manager would receive $20,000 plus its $2,000 base fee. Activism would begin to pay. Unfortunately, §27 of the Investment Companies and Investment Funds Act focuses not on the equity appreciation the IPF has earned during the period but on "the financial result of a unit trust or investment fund." This seems the wrong focus, as equity appreciation, rather than dividends or cash flow, should be the test of a fund manager's performance.

Admittedly, incentive fees raise a moral hazard problem: because the fund manager profits on the upside and loses little on the downside, the fund manager thus has a strong incentive to increase the risk level of the fund's portfolio. It is not clear, however, that this abuse is a practical danger in the more limited Czech market (where risk levels are hard to assess and where fund leverage is restricted by a flat prohibition on the issuance of debt by an IPF). Moreover, even within the highly regulated U.S. markets, limited incentive fees are possible. Known as "fulcrum fees," they must be computed over a multiyear period (to preclude short-term risk-taking and the receipt of interim profits by the fund manager before the ultimate collapse of the overly risky portfolio) and must be based on the degree to which the fund outperforms some relevant market index.[47]

To sum up, investment companies cannot be expected to incur costs to enhance the portfolio value of their IPFs – unless they see a realistic payoff from such activity. The current 2 percent fee ceiling provides little incentive for expenditures on corporate governance activities. Ultimately, IPFs and their shareholders will get what they pay for – and no more. Unless the fee structure is changed, this implies that they will get very little on a continuing basis of boardroom activism.

Establishing Effective IPF Corporate Governance

Whatever the corporate governance problems at the level of the newly privatized Czech corporations, they may be dwarfed by those at the IPF level for three distinct reasons: first, with the appearance of unit trusts in the second

[47] In the United States, incentive compensation is restricted by §205 of the Investment Advisers Act of 1940, but its prohibition is partly relaxed by SEC Rule 205, which permits "fulcrum fees." See 17 C.F.R. §275.205-1 to 205-3 (1993).

wave of privatization, many funds are simply beyond shareholder control because their shareholders lack any voting rights. Second, even in the case of IPFs organized as joint stock companies (rather than as unit trusts), investment companies have caused their controlled IPFs to enter into noncancelable multiyear management contracts with them for periods typically equaling or exceeding six years. Third, of the 400-odd IPFs originally organized, many have become inactive shells, with limited assets and an investment company interested and able to do little more than collect its 2 percent annual fee until it effectively exhausts the IPF's assets. Other IPFs are trading at apparent discounts of up to 80 percent from their assumed net asset value. In an efficient capital market, such companies would likely be the target of hostile takeovers. But hostile takeovers of IPFs are substantially chilled under Czech law by the legal rule that provides that neither IPFs nor investment companies may "purchase participation certificates of other unit trusts or shares of other investment companies and investment funds, or shares of persons whose interest in such investment companies or funds exceeds 25 (twenty-five) percent" (see Investment Companies and Investment Funds Act 1992, §24(7)).

Voting Rights in Unit Trusts

Should unit trusts be permitted? Or, should their shareholders somehow be legislatively accorded voting rights? Clearly, the sudden popularity of the unit trust form seems more attributable to their character as tame investment vehicles immune from takeovers and control contests than to other considerations.[48] Yet, on a worldwide basis, unit trusts are a well known investment vehicle, and thus it may seem difficult to justify a prophylactic rule prohibiting an investment form widely used throughout the United Kingdom and Europe. Why then should they be restricted in the Czech Republic?

One response might be that there is a basic distinction between the unit trust, as known in most securities markets, and its counterpart in the Czech market. Typically, unit trusts are open-ended, meaning that there is an immediate right of redemption. Thus, unit trust holders may lack voting rights, but they have an equally (and possibly more effective) means of disciplining a substandard management: unit trust holders can withdraw their investment (usually on a daily basis) at a price determined by their proportionate interest in the unit trust's net asset value. In such a world, unit trust holders have effectively traded voice for exit.

[48] Proponents of the unit trust cited to us two cost savings from its use: it eliminates the need for a costly annual shareholders' meeting and for boards of directors. True as this may be, the costs involved seem modest.

Such an exchange may make sense elsewhere, but exit is lacking in the Czech market. Not only is there currently no right to immediate redemption (even in the case of funds that will eventually become open-ended), but the thinness of the Czech market makes secondary trading at best a sporadic phenomenon. Reliable financial data about the net asset value of an IPF also remain generally unavailable (with some exceptions). Given their limited ability to trade IPF shares (in the case of a closed-end fund) or to obtain redemption (in the case of an open-end fund), Czech shareholders in IPFs today lack both voice and exit.

Hence, legislative correction may be appropriate. In any event, the Czech experience might lead planners in other privatization programs to delay the use of the unit trust format until their equity market had matured. At least over the short run, there are strong arguments that the joint stock company form should be preferred.

Long-term Management Contracts

Even when there are voting rights (that is, when the joint stock company form is used), voting rights can still be trivialized by the use of long-term management contracts. As noted above, six year and longer management contracts between an IPF and its investment company have become common, and these can effectively divest the shareholders of an IPF of any meaningful right to vote.

The U.S. contrast here is instructive. Under U.S. securities law, the investment adviser to an "investment company" (which term includes all publicly offered mutual funds) must enter into a written contract that "precisely describes all compensation to be paid thereunder"[49] and which "shall continue in effect for a period more than two years from the date of its execution, *only* so long as such continuance is specifically approved at least annually by the board of directors or by vote of a majority of the outstanding voting securities of such company" (§15(a)(2) (emphasis added). Moreover, the contract must be terminable at any time (without penalty) by a vote of the mutual fund board of directors (§15(a)(3)), and it must terminate automatically "in the event of its assignment" of the management contract (§15(a)(4)).

In short, annual approval of the management contract (after the second year) is the norm. Intended to promote accountability, this requirement in theory allows an IPF to escape a weak investment company, which founded it. Should Czech law adopt this requirement? Because the institution of independent outside directors is not well developed to this point in the

[49] See Investment Company Act of 1940, §15(a)(1), 15 U.S.C. §80a-1 et. seg.

Czech environment, it might be more logical to require that both the board and the shareholders must annually approve the contract.

Still, this response leads to two further problems: first, some investment companies now own substantial percentages of their own IPFs as a result of share repurchases pursuant to guarantees made at the marketing stage. Thus, for shareholder approval to be meaningful, it would have to be defined in this context to mean independent shareholder approval (excluding the shares held by the interested party). Second, if shareholder approval is withheld, how is a replacement investment company to be chosen? Here the problem is that even independent shareholders might be threatened or coerced into approving the existing management contract if they feared that the consequence of a rejection of the contract would be that their IPF would be abandoned and left without any investment advisers (even for an interim period).

Of course, willing replacements would be at hand in any competitive market. But how are they to be chosen? Many mechanisms could work (a proxy contest, an auction, an obligation on the part of the board to find a replacement, judicial intervention, etc.), but some mechanism needs to be specified legislatively.

IPF Market for Control

Attempts to make shareholder democracy work at the IPF level are likely to prove futile. Candidly, even with the additional regulatory controls provided under U.S. law, mutual fund shareholders have remained passive, and the large mutual fund families (Vanguard, Fidelity, Putnam, etc.) have generally dominated the boards of their funds. In this light, the more important remedy for IPF shareholders may be the prospect of a corporate control contest.

In addition, the Czech IPF market structure seems plainly in need of efficient consolidation. Over 400 IPFs remain, and most are powerless, ineffectual, and small; some are mere inactive shells. Many will become insolvent in due course, as administration expenses and the annual management fee gradually consume their remaining assets. How then can their consolidation be encouraged?

The simplest answer is that, if legal obstacles are removed, consolidation is a natural process. Many firms today are interested in acquiring control of inactive IPFs. One incentive is the significant discount at which many IPFs trade in relation to the actual market value of their investment portfolios. Secondly, other investment companies may want to control an IPF founded by a now inactive investment company in order to outflank the 20 percent ownership ceiling (which applies to all IPFs "established and administered by that investment company") (see Investment Companies and Investment Funds Act 1992, §24(5)). If an investment company can form an alliance with other IPFs not established or administered by it, it can thus partially evade the 20 percent limitation.

At present some groups are attempting to obtain control of less active IPFs for both these reasons. A Ministry of Finance official estimated for us that the purchase of as little as 10 percent of the stock of an IPF (at least one organized as a joint stock company) could confer control.[50] But investment companies and IPFs are effectively excluded from this process by §24(7) of the Investment Companies and Investment Funds Act, which precludes both IPFs and investment companies from purchasing shares in other IPFs.[51]

The rational for such a sweeping prohibition is obscure. It might well be advisable to preclude an investment company from buying shares of its own IPFs, because of the asymmetric information it likely possesses. But precluding only IPFs and investment companies from investing in other IPFs makes little sense, particularly when individuals and other financial institutions are not similarly precluded. If the fear is that existing IPF shareholders will be overreached or coerced, this problem might be addressed by requiring any person who acquires some threshold level of an IPF (say 10 percent) to make disclosure to the market and to buy further shares only in a prescribed manner (possibly pursuant to a tender offer or possibly after simply stating the number of shares it intends to acquire within a specified period). Indeed, to the extent that individuals and others are currently purchasing control of smaller, inactive IPFs, permitting other IPFs to do so simply increases the demand for their shares and possibly creates a desirable auction market, thereby improving the price to the original IPF shareholder.

More generally, sensible policy planning should seek additional ways to encourage the consolidation of small IPFs. As a practical matter, only IPFs with sizable holdings obtain representation on the boards of their portfolio companies, and thus smaller IPFs are essentially voiceless. Although smaller IPFs can consolidate their portfolios, the 10 percent diversification requirement implies that a very small IPF will not be able to hold sufficient shares in any company to obtain board representation. Particularly when an IPF cannot obtain board representation, there is little for its investment company to do – except collect their 2 percent (or so) annual management fee. To be sure, a smaller IPF could contract out for expert management assistance, and a single investment company could efficiently manage a dozen or more small

[50] This assumes, of course, that there is not a long-term management contract between the IPF and its founding investment company that cannot be canceled.

[51] The text of this statute has been set forth in this chapter under the heading "Establishing Effective IPF Corporate Governance".

IPFs, thereby achieving economies of scale and aggregating sufficient stock to achieve board representation. But this is a largely illusory hope, because the original investment company has no incentive to surrender any of its annual management fee. Conceivably, management contracts could be assigned (in return for some premium paid to the original management company), but no such market appears to have developed. If it did, special safeguards might be needed.[52]

In short, smaller IPFs are likely to follow a cost minimization approach and expend less funds proportionately on corporate governance activities than their larger IPF colleagues, because they have little practical ability to influence their portfolio companies. Yet, notwithstanding the substantial discounts to net asset value at which they often trade, their investment companies will predictably resist liquidating them (because this would deprive them of their annuity-like annual management fee).[53]

What policy response is appropriate? Although it made good sense to open up the Czech privatization process broadly to all comers, the corollary of this policy of easy entry might be one of early exit. That is, an ideal privatization program might seek to liquidate and thus clean up those IPFs that have failed the market's test, rather than leave a small number of shareholders trapped in them. Inherently, given their small holdings, such funds are necessarily passive and voiceless and accomplish little of value to anyone. One route toward their consolidation might be a mandatory liquidation requirement applicable to very small IPFs (i.e., those attracting few voucher points) before the IPFs were initially permitted to invest their voucher points. Of course, this rule could be softened by an escape clause if a disinterested majority of the shareholders voted to exempt their fund (with shares held by the investment company itself being disqualified from voting on this issue).

A market remedy to this same end might be to allow any IPF to make a merger proposal for a small IPF (as defined) under which the small IPF would be merged into the larger, proposing IPF in return for shares of the latter if some level – say, two-thirds – of the smaller IPF's shareholders approved the merger. To be sure, such a process would risk conflicts of

[52] Serious legal questions exist as to whether a fiduciary should be able to sell its position to another at a profit. See *Rosenfeld v. Black*, 445 F.2d 1337 (2nd Cir. 1971) (mutual funds may recapture profit made by investment advisor on sale of its advisory contract to new investment advisers). Such transactions are today allowed under U.S. securities law, but are subject to special judicial scrutiny and procedural safeguards.

[53] One exception to this generalization may arise when the investment company owns shares in the IPF (possibly as a result of repurchases pursuant to guarantees). This pattern raises distinct, but also troubling, conflicts of interest.

interest. Sometimes, the larger IPF might make such a proposal believing that the smaller IPF's assets were undervalued. More often the investment company controlling the larger IPF might simply have an incentive to overpay for the smaller IPF, because its annual management fee would be based on gross assets in the new, merged IPF. Thus, an investment company could rationally pursue an inefficient policy of growth and size maximization that injured its own shareholders. As a result, both funds should be required to approve any such merger by an equivalent supermajority of disinterested shareholders.

Finally, a desirable congruence might be achieved between the legal rules applicable to corporations and those applicable to IPFs if any IPF were permitted to buy up to 30 percent of another – and then could proceed further only by making an any-and-all bid for 100 percent of the remaining shares at the highest price recently paid by it. Again, this would generalize the British takeover code, which seems on the whole to have worked smoothly.

Ensuring a Competitive Market: The Problem of Cross-Ownership

From a distance, the most surprising and striking fact about Czech privatization is the level of cross-ownership that resulted. Today, a limited group of financial institutions control through their wholly owned investment company subsidiaries the largest IPFs, which in turn hold (in the aggregate) controlling positions in much of Czech industry (including positions in these same financial institutions).

It was not supposed to work this way. The Investment Companies and Investment Funds Act seemed intent on preventing cross-ownership of this character when it provided: "An investment company or investment fund established by a bank or insurance bank may not purchase the shares of its founder, its depository, or other banks and insurance banks" (see Investment Companies and Investment Funds Act 1992, § 24 (11)). Unfortunately, although the intent of this language seems clear, it was easily sidestepped by the simple evasion of banks forming wholly owned subsidiaries, which in turn established IPFs. Thus, at least arguably, the bank was not the founder of the IPF, and the IPF could purchase the bank's shares. Moreover, such an IPF (because it was not in theory founded by a bank) could also buy the shares of other banks.

Whatever the intent of this statutory language, the first lesson from this experience is the need for literalistic precision in civil law legal regimes where neither the bar nor the judiciary is guided by any sense of legislative intent. Perhaps the result would have been different if the same provision had read:

"An investment company or investment fund organized, established, or controlled, directly or indirectly, by a bank or insurance bank may not purchase the shares of its founder or of any company holding direct or indirect control over it, or of other companies directly or indirectly controlled by, or under the common control with, such a company, or other banks and insurance banks." Such a definition would predictably work in a common law legal regime, but in a civil law country, an elaborate, detailed definition still seems necessary of "indirect control" (which definition would presumably look to whether any parent or grandparent possessed the power through stock ownership, contract, or otherwise "to direct or cause the direction of the management or policies" of the other company).[54]

Whatever the level of specificity needed, an adequate definition *could* presumably be drafted to prevent a repetition of the Czech experience. More debatable is whether the level of cross-ownership that actually emerged in Czech privatization was accidental and unplanned or rather the product of an implicit conspiracy or tacit acquiescence by governmental authorities who feared one or more of the following: radical change, loss of governmental influence, or the emergence of new charismatic economic actors whose future conduct could not be easily predicted or controlled. Some have suggested that the government originally believed its privatization program was dependent on the cooperation of the banks in marketing vouchers to the Czech population. Arguably, only the major banks could reach the citizenry in rural areas and hold their confidence. Although this premise seems overstated in hindsight, it could explain the willingness of Czech governmental officials to blink at the obvious evasion of banks using an intermediate tier subsidiary to escape the impact of §24(11) of the Investment Companies and Investment Funds Act. The government's fear might have been that unless major financial institutions sponsored IPFs, privatization would result in a vastly dispersed stock distribution without sufficient concentration for shareholders to pressure for necessary restructurings. Alternatively, the appearance of HC&C may have scared and threatened both the government and the financial establishment. Together, they agreed to blink at the law to protect banking institutions from a potential raider whose inclinations were unclear and integrity unproven.

All such scenarios are speculative. The issue for the future is what, if anything, should be done about the level of cross-ownership that emerged. Two distinct policy concerns should be acknowledged. First, the existing level of cross-ownership coupled with the government's residual ownership in the

[54] See SEC Rule 405, 17 C.F.R. 230. 405. A rebuttable presumption might also be established that 25% direct or indirect stock ownership was sufficient to confer control.

banks leaves too much decision-making power in the government's hands. As some see it, privatization has not yet fully occurred because the government has not truly cut the strings by which it can make its puppets dance. Second, cross-ownership raises the prospect of collusion among firms. If the same IPFs and investment companies control the major banks and also major firms in other sectors of the economy, it is possible that such control could be used to share information, restrain competition, and engineer a polite oligopoly. Indeed, to the extent that the major banks are also lenders to the major industrial firms, their self-interest is not for fierce, cost-cutting competitive battles to break out, but for stable, sustained growth and shared markets. In particular, because the banks (and their controlled investment companies) do not own much equity in the industrial sector, but rather simply advise IPFs for a fee, their economic center of gravity is that of a risk-averse creditor with a distaste for uncertainty and volatility.

In principle, what steps could be taken? Given the very limited liquidity in the Czech stock market, it seems infeasible to order bank-controlled IPFs to sell all (or most) of their investments in bank and insurance stocks. Indeed, the only companies that could purchase the investments (at a punitively large discount) are the private IPFs (such as HC&C), which would thereby also be placed in a position of controlling competing economic rivals. Moreover, the economic cost of such a radical divestiture policy might be borne by Czech shareholders generally – particularly if it produced a general decline in market price levels.

A simpler, but no less radical, reform might be to spin off the management companies from the banks. Banks and insurance companies could be required to dividend their shareholdings in their controlled investment companies to their own shareholders (possibly excluding the NPF). The result would leave the investment companies in control of many banks, but the banks would no longer be in control of investment companies. To soften this provision, banks could be exempted from this spin-off requirement if (within some period) their investment companies divested their bank holdings so as to fall below some minimal level.

Even these steps are incomplete. Investment companies, even once separated from their banking parents, are in a problematic position when they can hold seats on the boards of competitors. In the United States, such interlocking boards are severely restricted by the Clayton Antitrust Act, which (subject to some exceptions) prohibits any person from serving as a director of "any two or more corporations . . . if such corporations are or shall have been . . . competitors. . . ."[55] Some Czech IPFs seem to be

[55] See 15 U.S.C. §19. See, e.g. *Protectoseal Co. v. Baranick*, 484 F.2d 585, 589 (7th Cir. 1973).

complying with such a policy by not assigning directors to competing firms. What remains uncertain, however, is whether the investment company can still use its board positions to restrict competition between natural rivals.

Adoption of the U.S. procompetitive approach (either by requiring a divestiture by banks of their investment companies or by restricting an IPF from holding seats on the boards of competitors) would seemingly entail a fundamental rejection of the German model of corporate governance. Unlike the United States, German banks do have representatives on the boards of competitors, and German banks do have interlocking stock ownership. Any Czech divestiture proposal by which banks would be separated from their investment companies would seemingly sacrifice the informal synergies and arguably superior monitoring capacity that the German system of corporate governance in theory creates. Indeed, even the fire wall policy that the Ministry of Finance seemingly favors seems inconsistent with the conventional understanding of the German system under which a "universal bank" pools the information it acquires as a creditor and as an equity holder and employs this information to reward or discipline management from its position on the Supervisory Board.

Thus, a fundamental policy choice is posed here: should Czech IPFs be structured along the German model (in which case, the only reform needed might be to restrict one bank from controlling through its IPFs a substantial block in a competitor) or should fire walls and other informational barriers be placed between IPFs and their indirect banking parents? In short, is the close relationship between banks and IPFs a vice or a virtue?

In assessing this basic question, the latest data on the performance of German banks as corporate monitors provide little support for the academic view that an institution holding joint equity and debt stakes in a firm will be a superior monitor. Professors Jeremy Edwards and Klaus Fisher in a study published in 1994 by Cambridge University Press sharply attack the conventional wisdom about the involvement of German banks in German corporate governance (see Edwards and Fisher 1994). The standard assumptions about German universal banks, they acknowledge, have been that:

1. Because of their greater involvement and long term relationship with corporate clients, German banks tend to lend on a longer term basis and to enable their corporations to maintain higher debt to equity levels than corporations operating in economies characterized by market-based systems of corporate governance.
2. In times of financial distress, the close relationship between the universal bank and the corporate client tends to reduce the costs of bankruptcy because of the bank's ability to reorganize the company apart from

bankruptcy and provide new capital.

3. Through their control over equity voting rights (which they exercise through proxies given them by most shareholders), German banks exercise a major influence on the supervisory board of client corporations which reduces the agency costs incident to the shareholder/manager relationship.
4. By protecting the corporation from hostile takeovers, they also protect against an undesirable "short-termism" in corporate planning and managerial horizons.

If the German system had these effects, these are obvious justifications why Czech corporate governance should emulate the German banking system (even at the cost of high cross-ownership between banks). But Edwards and Fisher argue that the German system has none of these effects and support their case with the most detailed statistical evidence yet gathered about the German system.

Specifically, they find that:

1. The available evidence "casts considerable doubt on the claim that significant economies of scope exist between German banks' corporate governance role and their supply of external finance in the form of loans" (p. 230).
2. Very little equity finance was supplied by German banks to German corporations and little evidence indicates they played any significant role in screening equity issues (p. 231).
3. "There is no evidence that bank representation on supervisory boards provides German banks with information that is used to make loan decisions" (p. 231).
4. "Bank representation on company supervisory boards is not associated with greater use of bank loans by the companies concerned" (p. 232), and large German corporations financed less of their investments by bank borrowings than did comparable British companies (p. 232).
5. Evidence about interventions by German banks in times of financial distress is limited, but "does not give much support to the theoretical arguments which suggest that the costs of financial distress are lower in Germany" (p. 232). Rather, bank behavior in such periods "is no different from that of UK banks" (p. 234).
6. The claim that "German banks act as delegated exercisers of equity's control rights" has little evidence to support it (p. 236). Neither their incentives to act in such a capacity are clear, nor is their other evidence that they are in a position to subject German managers to a higher degree of monitoring and control (p. 236).

7. In short, "the argument that German banks perform a corporate control function . . . lacks both a solid theoretical foundation and convincing empirical support" (p. 237).

The problem with the academic theory, they find, is that it overlooks the institutional facts. German banks lend to corporations almost entirely on a secured basis, and under German bankruptcy law have little reason to monitor their debt investments.

Instead, the actual role played by German banks on supervisory boards, they speculate, may be very different and more questionable in its social value. By representation on boards across an industry, German banks may supply a "system of coordination by banker" to an industry.[56] This concept, however, should heighten the sensitivities of those who are concerned about the antitrust issue. Moreover, it suggests a system of partially centralized planning that, while preferable to pure state control, is still highly inconsistent with the ideal of free and competitive markets.

The debate over the relative attractions of the German versus alternative models of corporate governance will undoubtedly continue. However, those who remain proponents of the German universal banking system have recently stressed that it works when and precisely to the extent that German banks hold large equity positions in their debtor clients.[57] But this is the critical omission in the Czech system, which in truth has only a weak resemblance to the German model. The only (and weaker) incentive for the bank and its affiliates to monitor portfolio companies today in the Czech structure is the prospect of a management fee from the IPF to the bank's investment company, and often this income can be outweighed by the bank's interests as a creditor or its fear of displeasing incumbent management at the portfolio company.

In fairness, if the Czech system does not truly approximate the German universal banking system, it is even more removed from the U.S./U.K. system of stock market monitoring. Market transparency is almost totally absent in the Czech market environment, where most trading occurs off market and without any obligation for contemporaneous trade reporting. Nor are accounting or disclosure systems well developed. In addition, because closed-end fund investors cannot flee unsuccessful funds and unit trusts make shareholder voting irrelevant, there is little discipline over the market intermediaries. Given inefficient markets, techniques such as incentives fees

[56] Edwards and Fisher (1994), 239, citing A. Shonfield, *Modern Capitalism* (1965), 261.

[57] See Gorton and Schmid (1994), 35 ("Our evidence shows that German banks improve the performance of German firms to the extent that they hold the firms' equity").

and stock compensation, which work well in the United States, may only produce a stronger incentive for stock manipulation in the Czech market. The debate then between the German and U.S. models must also be framed in terms of which is more obtainable.

Summary

A long article deserves a short summary. The Czech experience provides an exemplary model of how to implement a system of voucher privatization and demonstrates that it can quickly create a shareholder culture where none has existed before. But the Czech system is not yet a model for corporate governance in transitional economies, because it is not yet clear how the Czech system will evolve. Whether investment privatization funds (IPFs) will develop into active institutional investors or passive agents of their indirect banking parents remains unresolved, but at present IPFs have the incentive structure neither of a universal bank in the German system nor of a British or American mutual fund in a stock market centered system. Truly, they are neither fish nor fowl.

On a different level, the contrast between the private IPFs and those affiliated with large domestic banks is also instructive. At the marketing stage, the private IPFs overcame their lack of recognition and basically outperformed the bank-affiliated IPFs in urban areas, while the bank-affiliated IPFs capitalized on their trusted reputations and retail networks in rural areas. But at the portfolio selection stage, the behavior of each deviated dramatically. Only the private IPFs (and not all these) focused on assembling a concentrated portfolio that would allow them to exercise leverage in the boardroom. The behavior of the bank-affiliated IPFs in seeking excessively diversified portfolios is at least consistent with the conflict of interest hypothesis that they will subordinate the interests of their IPF shareholders to those of their banking parents (who may prefer their IPFs to develop relationships with the maximum number of potential clients).

At present the relationship between banks and their IPFs is obscure. Some indications are that banks have relatively little interest in their investment companies, and certainly few economic incentives appear discernible that should interest them. If Western investors can be interested in IPF investments, this may change, but given the low transparency level of the Czech market, Western investors currently seem uninterested in such investments, desiring instead a joint venture or controlling stake, not a minority interest in an IPF.

All this points to a problem of incentives. Hedge funds and venture capital partnerships reward their managers with a share of equity appreciation. That this system creates adequate incentives has been abundantly clear in recent years. Czech and other regulators might learn from their success, but such a system of rewards requires an open, transparent marketplace in which gains can be measured and not manipulated.

The issue of fire walls presents a fundamental choice in terms of models of corporate governance. Much recent discussion of this issue has been blinded by an unthinking acceptance of the hypothesis that the German banking structure will produce superior monitoring and will reduce the agency costs of corporate governance. As this chapter has argued, the advantages of the German model are not self-evident and seem to result only under conditions not present in the Czech system. In turn the argument for fire walls rests on two different foundations: (1) the fear of insider trading, and (2) the fear of collusion among firms to restrain competition. Financial institutions with interlocking board seats on portfolio companies conceivably could be the marriage broker in the latter process, quietly inducing conscious parallelism of action among competitors. But these concerns must be balanced against the danger of more entrenched managements if IPFs were to be weakened because of their divestiture from their banking affiliates.

Today, it is premature to estimate how serious either danger is, or the trade-offs between them, but these questions should be a focus of the next study. The Czech experience has, after all, just begun.

References

Barclay, Michael, and Clifford Holderness. 1989. "Private Benefits from Control of Public Corporations." *Journal of Financial Economics* 25: 371.

BBC Summary of World Broadcasts. 1994. Czech Privatization Process Now Complete. 1 December (available on LEXIS/NEXIS library, curnws file).

Bebchuk, Lucian. Forthcoming. "Efficient and Inefficient Sales of Corporate Control." *Quarterly Journal of Economics.*

Black, Bernard. 1990. "Shareholder Passivity Reexamined." *Michigan Law Review* 89: 520.

Brom, Karla, and Mitchell Orenstein. 1993. "The 'Privatized' Sector in the Czech Republic: Government and Bank Control in a Transitional Economy." *Europe-Asia Studies* 46, no. 6: 21.

Cable, J. 1985. "Capital Market Information and Industrial Performance: The Role of West German Banks." *Economic Journal* 95: 118.

Carrington, J.C., and G.T. Edwards. 1979. *Financing Industrial Investment.* Macmillan.

Charkham, J. 1989. "Corporate Governance and the Market for Companies." Bank of England Panel Paper No. 25.

Claessens, Stijn. 1994. "Corporate Governance and Equity Prices: Evidence from the Czech and Slovak Republics." World Bank, Washington, D.C. Mimeographed.

Coffee, John. 1991. "Liquidity Versus Control: The Institutional Investor As Corporate Monitor." *Columbia Law Review* 91: 1277.

Cox, Jim. 1994. Czech Leader Sees Higher Unemployment. *USA Today*, 25 November, B-4 (interview with Vaclav Klaus).

Crawford, Phillip. 1994. As Privatization Phase Ends, Prague Market is Maturing. *International Herald Tribune*, 26 November.

Demott, D. 1987. "Comparative Dimensions of Takeover Regulation." *Washington University Law Quarterly* 65: 69, 93–99.

Edwards, Jeremy, and Klaus Fisher. 1994. *Banks, Finance and Investment in Germany*. Cambridge University Press.

Egerer, Roland. 1994. "Investment Funds and Corporate Governance in Emerging Markets: An Assessment of the Top Ten Voucher Funds in the Czech Republic." World Bank, Washington, D.C. Mimeographed.

Elhauge, E. 1993. "Toward a European Sale of Control Doctrine." *American Journal of Comparative Law*.

Fleming, Charles. 1994. Managed Investing: Retail Fund Investors Avoid Central Europe. *Wall Street Journal Europe*, 22 November, 13.

Gorton, Gary, and Frank Schmid. 1994. "Universal Banking and the Performance of German Firms." Wharton School Working Paper (October).

Grundfest, Joseph. 1990. "Subordination of American Capital." *Journal of Financial Economics* 27: 89.

Holderness, Clifford, and Sheehan. 1988. "The Role of Majority Shareholders in Publicly Held Corporations: An Exploratory Analysis." *Journal of Financial Economics* 20: 317.

Investment Companies and Investment Funds Act, 1992. Act No. 248 Coll. of 28 April.

Jaros, V., and M. Sanders. 1994. "Investment Privatization Funds." Wood Company Securities, Czech Equity Research Report (June): 4.

King, Neil, Jr. 1993. Czech Financier Scores Rich Success Even As Detractors Hope for His Fall. *Wall Street Journal*, 18 August, A7.

Kotrba, Josef. 1994. "Czech Privatization: Players and Winners." CERGE-E1 Working Paper No. 58: 5 (April).

Levy, H. 1982. "Economic Valuation of Voting Power of Common Stock." *Journal of Finance* 38: 79.

Luftmann, R. 1992. "Changes of Corporate Control and Mandatory Bids." *International Review of Law and Economics* 12: 497.

Mann, Bruce. 1993. "Privatization in the Czech Republic." *Business Lawyer* 48: 963, 964.

Mejstrik, Michal. 1994. "Czech Investment Funds as a Part of Financial Sector and Their Role in Privatization of the Economy." (April): 6.

Meth-Cohn, Delia. 1994. "Good Governance: Czech Investment Funds Are Learning About Corporate Governance Very Quickly." *Business Central Europe* (February): 30.

Mladek, Jan. 1994. "Mass Privatization: A First Assessment of the Results." Paper prepared for the OECD Group on Privatization, p. 3.

Organization for Economic Cooperation and Development (OECD), Committee on Financial Markets. 1972. "Standard Rules for the Operations of Institutions for Collective Investment in Securities." p. 28.

Pauly, Jan, and Dusan Triska. 1993. "Investment Funds in the Czech Republic." (October): 3. Mimeographed.

Rehak, Judith. 1994. Are "Emerging Europe" Debt Markets Just for Adventurous Investors? *International Herald Tribune*, 26 November.

Rock, Edward. 1991. "The Logic and (Uncertain) Significance of Shareholder Activism." *Georgetown Law Journal* 79: 445.

Rocks, David. 1994. Milestone for Privatization: Czechs Finish Share Selection on Bumpy Road to Capitalism. *Chicago Tribune*, 24 November, 3.

Roe, Mark. 1991. "A Political Theory of American Corporate Finance." *Columbia Law Review* 91: 10.

Shafik, Nemat. 1993. "Making a Market: Coupon Privatization in the Czech and Slovak Republics." World Bank, Washington, D.C. (April): 20.

Shleifer, Andrei, and Robert Vishny. 1986. "Large Shareholders and Corporate Control." *Journal of Political Economy* 94, no. 3: 461.

Zingales. 1992. "The Value of the Voting Right: A Study of the Milan Stock Exchange." CRSP Working Paper No. 369, University of Chicago.

5

INVESTING IN INSIDER-DOMINATED FIRMS
A Study of Russian Voucher Privatization Funds

ROMAN FRYDMAN, KATHARINA PISTOR, and ANDRZEJ RAPACZYNSKI

The authors would like to thank Alexei N. Makeshin and Olga Kisselova for their help in running the survey of voucher investment funds in Russia and Ying Zhu for dedicated computer assistance. Roman Frydman is grateful to the CV Starr Center for Applied Economics at New York University for providing support for his research.

The Environment

Design and Evolution in Mass Privatization

Mass privatization plans, of necessity, contain an important element of design. Their main goal, in addition to removing the state from direct control over enterprises, is to inject a critical mass of assets into the private sector and to change the configuration of the political and economic forces in the country. They are conceived as a result of a conviction that the more traditional ways of privatization are not only too slow, but also ineffective in dislodging the existing interest groups, opposed to an effective change in the way things are run. Unless a large number of firms undergo simultaneous transformation, the plans assume the old ways of doing things will persist, and even the new private sector might be corrupted by operating in an environment in which rent seeking and soft budget constraints predominate. As such, mass privatization plans, at least in their initial stages, do not rely on gradual, marginal changes in the status quo, but attempt to effect a global transformation of the economic and political environment, so as to alter fundamentally the incentive structure of the main actors and to weaken the relative position of the interest groups opposed to reforms.

But in doing this, the plans must take into consideration two extremely important factors. First, the difference between old style planning and the design of the reform programs is that the latter must always be mindful of the limitations of foresight – the uncertainties of the future make it certain that serious corrections in the original design will have to occur before the system stabilizes into a working economic order. Second, the plans do not operate in a vacuum. Although they attempt to change the balance of political and economic power, they must rely on some existing interests in order to push through the changes they propose. It may sound like a paradox – the plans must root themselves in the status quo in order to change it – but the proposition merely reflects a fundamental political reality. This means that compromises have to be made, and the challenge is to make it more likely that their cost will not be too great in the long run.

Both of these factors mean that the stage of design in the reform program must assume a process of evolutionary development in the next stage. The design stage may be compared to an activist constitutional period, in which new rules of the game are made and new incentive structures are created. But the design must not overdetermine the process. It must rather operate on the assumption that its main function is to make sure that the incentives created by the design will make it more likely that further evolution will proceed in the direction of greater openness, rather than ossify into a new suboptimal equilibrium. In other words, although the system created by the design cannot be perfect – and the necessity of initial compromises makes this even more obvious – it should be capable of *self-correction* in the future (Frydman and Rapaczynski 1994).

Specifics of Russian Design: Insider Domination

The dynamics and the uncertainties of the Russian voucher privatization program reflect this logic of the reform process. In order to be able to effect their far-reaching transformative objectives, the architects of the Russian program had to assure that the program had the support of some sufficiently powerful political and economic forces within the old system. The program had to have some losers and some winners, and the winners could not be all in the future. But the program also attempted to make it more likely that the structure it put in place would then evolve in such a way as to mitigate some of the dangers implicit in the initial compromises.

The main losers in the Russian privatization program were to be the old centralized industrial structures: branch ministries, industrial associations, trusts, and other lobbies for the status quo. The main winners, the forces with which the reformers allied themselves in the great push for quick privatization, were to be the managers and the workers of individual state enterprises, provided they broke away from the old structures. The oft-described privatization program thus essentially gave to enterprise insiders majority ownership of the overwhelming mass of former state enterprises, with the managers owning, on average, 9 percent of the shares and the workers owning some 56 percent.[1]

The reformers' assumption behind these moves was, presumably, that the overwhelming insider-domination of the privatized firms would not be desirable in the long run, but that the interests of the local insiders would be less monolithic than those of the old industrial lobby and that the resulting new ownership structure would be subject to gradual change. The main hopes for change were apparently placed in the workers, who were expected to sell their shares rather quickly to cash in on the huge premiums resulting from the mass giveaway, thus allowing for a gradual concentration of ownership in the hands of the managers and new outside owners. The ownership structure that would result from secondary-market transactions would, in turn, assure (1) that the managers, at least those whose enterprises were economically viable, could be weaned from reliance on state subsidies and that their incentive structure could be tied more closely to the economic success of their enterprises, and (2) that outside owners, including foreign investors, would provide the degree of monitoring and supervision necessary to prevent managerial shirking and opportunism and to open the enterprises to the influx of new capital and expertise. This direction of development of the viable enterprises would further weaken the insiders in charge of the white elephants, who would have less chance of succeeding in their demands for continuing subsidies and be forced to retrench and eventually close down their value-subtracting firms.

Is the System Evolving toward Openness?

Even at this early date, we may say with confidence that the Russian design was very successful in effecting a huge ownership transformation of the Russian industry. We can also state that the most successful of its elements was the gamble on the insiders, who helped to put the program through, despite the immense size of the country and the number of firms involved, with a speed that is quite unprecedented in the postcommunist world.

[1] Blasi and Shleifer (in vol. 2). Their evidence (as of December 1993) is based on data from 142 companies in 32 regions. For a detailed description of the Russian program, see Frydman, Rapaczynski, and Earle (1993).

Between January 1992 and the end of June 1994, approximately 14,000 companies were privatized through a combination of insider buyouts and voucher auctions, with an average of 18 percent of each company's shares offered to the public.[2]

As to whether the design of the Russian program will be anywhere near as successful in initiating an evolutionary process toward greater openness of the Russian ownership and governance structure, it is clearly too early to judge. The program did bring out a very high degree of popular participation: by July 1994, 132.7 million Russians made some use of their vouchers (even if only to sell them on the open market), and this number represents 87.8 percent of the 151 million voucher recipients. The program also included the participation of many institutional actors, prime among them privatization investment funds, new private and privatized companies that acquired shares directly or through intermediaries, and a number of so-called "social organizations."

But so far the evidence does not show any significant lessening of the insider domination of the Russian firms. Indeed, our survey indicates that, as of June 1994, insiders still held majority stakes in approximately 70 percent of the companies in which voucher funds were invested, and this number is not likely to have been significantly higher at any prior time. To begin with, 27 percent of companies going through voucher privatization chose the so-called Variant I or III, which did not give the insiders control over their firms.[3] Further, even in some Variant II firms, in which the insiders could buy 51 percent of their company's shares at bargain basement prices, if the firm was large enough, the insiders did not have sufficient funds to exercise all their rights. And finally, the universe of companies in which the voucher funds have invested is likely to be somewhat less insider-dominated than the whole population of Russian firms, since some (maybe even most) voucher funds may have a preference for noninsider-dominated firms, and there must be some fully (or nearly fully) insider-owned firms from which all outside owners (and *a fortiori* the voucher funds) are absent.[4]

Although it is too soon to judge how lasting the phenomenon of insider

[2] Boycko, Shleifer, and Vishny (1995) cite 15,779 as the number of voucher auctions at which shares of privatized companies were sold, and estimate the total number of privatized companies at ca. 14,000. As the authors point out, the number of voucher auctions is not a precise indication of how many companies were privatized, because the shares of many companies were offered at two or more separate voucher auctions.

[3] For figures concerning the choice among the three available variants, see Boycko, Shleifer, and Vishny (1995, ch. 5).

[4] On the basis of a different sample, Blasi and Shleifer (in vol. 2) report that insiders were majority owners in 65% of all Russian companies (median 60%) by the end of 1993. As compared with our (much larger) sample, their figures appear somewhat low.

domination will be, there can be no doubt that much of the future of Russian economic order depends on the answer to this question. Indeed, insider control is, for the time being, the feature that pervades the behavior of all actors on the Russian corporate governance scene and limits any influence that outside owners can have on the behavior of Russian firms. This in turn probably restricts the degree of restructuring that can take place in these firms and increases the severity of the agency problems endemic in the postcommunist environment (Frydman and Rapaczynski 1994, ch. 5). The purpose of this paper is to examine this issue by focusing on the behavior of the most important outsider owners of the Russian companies – the so-called Russian privatization funds – and the influence that insider domination might have on their behavior.

Who Are the Funds?

Any mass distribution of state-owned assets to a large number of recipients must consider some ways of mitigating the problems inherent in dispersed ownership. After all, privatization is supposed to be not just a transfer of title; its primary objective, besides removing the state from direct control over enterprises, is to reduce the agency problems generated by modern separation of ownership from managerial control. Too great a dispersion of ownership creates formidable collective action problems that prevent the new owners from monitoring the management, thus defeating one of the main purposes of the privatization program.

Moreover, to the extent that a mass giveaway of state assets does not assign to each recipient a specific security, but provides him with some form of artificial capital (vouchers), which the recipient can then choose to invest in any of the privatized companies, the program must reckon with the information costs and the nondiversification of risk facing the multitude of small investors. The voucher capital distributed to each recipient is too small to warrant a serious amount of investigation concerning available investment opportunities. It is also not big enough to allow for a proper level of diversification.

Mass privatization programs contain a number of devices designed to overcome these difficulties. The most important of them is the institution of privatization intermediaries, that is, legal entities the shares of which are owned by the beneficiaries of the giveaway scheme, but which in turn legally own the shares of the privatized companies. The intermediaries, insofar as they function as mutual funds, solve the informational problems of small investors, as well as allow them to acquire a share in a diversified portfolio of privatized companies (and perhaps some other assets). To the extent the intermediaries are not merely oriented toward trading, but also engage in active supervision of the companies in their portfolios, they help solve the collective action problems facing the millions of dispersed owners. How the intermediaries are able to fulfill these functions is among the main design issues in any mass privatization.

The Legal Framework

A distinctive feature of the Russian privatization funds has been the ease of entry and the relative laxity of prudential regulation of their activities.[5] Although certain state and state-controlled institutions could not be involved in their creation, any other party could be a founder, and the minimum charter capital was set at the entirely insignificant level of 500,000 rubles – even in October 1992 (when the law was passed), this amounted to a mere $1,200 (it was less than $500 in 1993). Even more significantly, there were no financial qualifications at all for persons holding management contracts with the funds; indeed, the fund managers frequently are individuals, rather than companies.[6] The extremely modest financial requirements may have encouraged the formation of truly private funds in an environment in which most established institutions had old links to the state, but together with the provisions allowing for incentive compensation, they may have also skewed the fund managers' incentives toward very risky investments.

The funds and the managers have to be licensed, but the licenses were apparently issued to any candidate who applied, provided a few statutory conditions were met. The funds must also operate as open joint stock companies, which means that their shareholders have all the voting rights necessary to make changes in the structure of the funds, and the law restricts the security of the manager's tenure by limiting any severance provisions to one-half of the yearly management fee.[7] So far, these provisions do not seem to have had any effect, but the open-joint-stock-company form leaves open the possibility of future takeovers and other struggles for control. The company form of the funds also means that they are essentially closed-end

[5] The voucher funds have been regulated by Presidential Decree No. 1186, 7 October 1992, On the Means for the Organization of a Securities Market in the Process of Privatizing State and Municipal Enterprises (Voucher Statute).

[6] Of 538 licensed managers, 346 were individuals, and 192 legal entities (data from the Voucher Fund Monitoring Group in Moscow).

[7] The fee itself may, according to the law, be very high: up to 10% of the fund's assets per year (Voucher Statute, Art. 34).

funds (and do not have to redeem their shares),[8] but the voucher statute also *prohibits* the funds from buying back their shares.[9]

Voucher funds could issue their shares in exchange for vouchers received by the citizens, but they were also authorized to issue them for cash. Given that voucher funds were likely to be cash poor and could not by law issue debt securities, the ability to sell shares for cash was potentially important, but at the same time it raised, especially under Russian conditions, the specter of a dilution of holdings of the widely dispersed and passive public shareholders. The funds were also permitted to trade in vouchers (as well as any other securities) and a large portion of their initial activities was, reportedly, in voucher trading. Indeed, vouchers became the first liquid security on the Russian market, and their prices fluctuated widely, both in nominal and real terms.

Given the Czech experience, voucher funds must have been originally seen as threatening to the insiders of Russian enterprises, who were eager to assert their control over the privatized firms and upon whom the architects of the privatization program relied as their main allies. The original regulations seem to have reflected these fears and a desire to promote the role of the funds as passive traders of securities rather than as active participants in corporate governance, since they limited the funds and their "affiliates"[10] to acquiring no more than 10 percent of the securities of any one issuer. This limitation was never enforced, and the funds often exceeded the allowed maximum. Some of these cases may have been unintentional, since the design of the voucher auctions made it impossible to know *ex ante* how many shares each bidder would ultimately receive, but the funds also acquired larger stakes intentionally, sometimes "parking" them with related entities that did not qualify as affiliates and sometimes making purchases through additional entities set up by the fund managers.[11]

[8] The closed-end nature of the funds, which is simply a necessity in the conditions of limited liquidity in the Russian securities markets, is confirmed explicitly by section 9 of the Voucher Statute.

[9] It is not clear whether that was meant as a precaution against selective payouts to favored shareholders or to discourage the funds from making promises of high returns similar to those made by the Czech funds. (Another provision of the statute, section 26, bars the Czech-style advertisement of promises of returns on investment.)

[10] Defined as entities owning more than 25% of the fund; the funds could not own other voucher or nonvoucher investment funds.

[11] Interviews with fund managers in an unpublished pilot study conducted in January 1994. Of the funds in the present survey, 76 own stakes between 20 and 25%; 27 between 25 and 50%, and four own some stakes of over 50%.

By the end of 1993, it became clear that the managers of Russian enterprises were firmly in control of their firms and that strengthening the power of outside owners was an important objective of postprivatization policies. Accordingly, the Privatization Program for 1994 raised the limit of any company's shares that may be owned by a single fund to 25 percent and included other regulations in support of outside shareholders.[12]

How Big Are They?

By the end of voucher privatization in 1994, there were over 650 licensed funds, but only 516 were at least minimally active – they responded to telephone calls by a group set up in Moscow to monitor their activities.[13] Voucher funds have been established throughout the Russian Federation, but particularly high concentrations are found in Moscow (62), Sverdlovsk (16), St. Petersburg (13), and Samara (13).

The voucher funds collected over 34 million vouchers, amounting to 23.2 percent of the total distributed to Russian citizens (see Table 5.1). While this proportion is not as large as that collected by their Czech counterparts (71.8 percent), it is nevertheless extremely impressive under Russian conditions. To begin with, many Russian citizens used their own vouchers (and probably some more purchased on the secondary market) – altogether 38.5 million vouchers or over 25 percent of the total – at closed subscriptions, during which the insiders could acquire the shares of their enterprises at enormous discounts. The same insiders also tried to solidify their control by purchasing their firms' shares during voucher auctions, often using enterprise funds for this purpose, and thus provided additional competition to the voucher funds. Indeed, the very tradeability of vouchers, which distinguished the Russian program from the Czech, imposed on the funds a situation in which they had to compete for vouchers with other groups of potential buyers. Furthermore, the Russian funds could not legally advertise promises of spectacular returns to the citizens whom they wanted to persuade to exchange their vouchers for the shares of the funds – something that was instrumental to the success rate of the Czech funds. Finally, the Russian funds, unlike the Czech ones, had no connections to huge state banks, with branches across the country, household names, and long-

[12] Section 9 of the 1994 Privatization Program. The other regulations included a limitation of insider membership on the board of directors to one-third of the total and a requirement that cumulative voting be used in electing company boards. GKI Regulation No. 44-r, 10 January 1994, On the Procedure for Approval or Reorganizing Voucher Investment Funds, also provides a legal basis for future mergers of voucher funds (subject to GKI's approval).

[13] Information obtained from the Voucher Fund Monitoring Group, Moscow.

Table 5.1. Accumulation and Investment of Vouchers by Voucher Funds (mid-May 1994)

	Number (in millions)	Percentage
Total distributed	151.00	100.0
Submitted at closed subscription	38.50	25.5
Submitted at voucher auctions	94.20	62.4
Collected by voucher funds	34.74	23.2
Invested by voucher funds	29.81	19.7

Source: *Kommersant*, 12 July 1994, and authors' calculations based on the data base of the Voucher Fund Monitoring Group, Moscow, corrected by more recent data from the survey.

Table 5.2. Concentration of Ownership among Voucher Investment Funds

Top no. of funds	No. of vouchers collected (in millions)	As % of vouchers collected by all funds[a]	As % of vouchers distributed[b]
5	9.23	26.57	6.11
10	11.49	33.06	7.61
20	14.56	41.92	9.64
30	16.37	47.11	10.84
40	17.49	50.34	11.58
50	18.25	52.55	12.09

Source: Survey data, authors' calculations based on the data base of the Voucher Fund Monitoring Group, Moscow, and data published in *Kommersant*, 12 July 1994.
Note: Since the data base of the Voucher Fund Monitoring Group of May 1994 contains many entries dating back to September 1993, we have used the data from the fifty largest funds in our survey, which include nearly all of the largest funds. The inclusion of any large funds missing from our survey would show an even greater concentration of ownership.
[a] Percentage of 34.74 million vouchers
[b] Percentage of 151 million vouchers

standing reputations. Thus, the payoff for preventing the old structures from, at least openly, creating and managing the voucher funds was a diminished role for the funds; a price that may well have been worth paying, but which has implications for the role of these financial intermediaries.

Where the Russian funds are truly small, compared with the Czech ones, is in the size of their share (rather than voucher) portfolio, since they purchased shares of the privatized companies primarily at voucher auctions organized by regional property funds, where prices, while generally low, were considerably higher than at the closed subscriptions for insiders (where the price equaled 1.7 of book value unadjusted for inflation).[14] As a result, the voucher funds, having invested nearly 20 percent of all the vouchers distributed to Russian citizens, managed to obtain only 5.7 percent of the shares of the privatized enterprises.[15] This makes them into relatively minor players on the Russian ownership scene, even though they are probably the most important private actors among the outside private owners of Russian firms.

Evidently to prevent the creation of very large individual funds, such as those that arose in Czechoslovakia during the first wave of mass privatization, an upper ceiling of 5 percent of the total number of vouchers was put on the size of any single fund. No Russian fund even approached this number; the largest, First Voucher Fund, collected 2.6 percent of all vouchers. Nevertheless, the concentration of ownership among the funds is quite high, with the five largest funds in our sample having collected 26.57 percent of the vouchers collected by all the funds and 6.11 percent of the total number of vouchers distributed to the population (Table 5.2). The largest of the funds are thus likely to be the major, perhaps dominant, players among the outside owners and may significantly influence the future dynamics of Russian corporate governance and financial intermediation.

The Sample

Of the population of 516 voucher funds, our survey, which was conducted in the summer of 1994, includes 148 funds, or over a quarter of all funds in operation.[16] In an attempt to reach a better understanding of the overall impact of the funds, the selection was weighted heavily in favor of the larger funds, with nearly all of the top funds included in the sample. Table 5.3 breaks down the population and the sample by fund size, showing the weight of the larger funds in both groups. As a result, in terms of the number of vouchers collected, our sample represents up to 69 percent of the total population.

Funds were interviewed in 28 different regions, with an overrepresentation of regions with a high concentration of large funds. As a result, 40 funds were interviewed in Moscow, 13 in Sverdlovsk, 7 in Krasnodar and Samara, 6 in Perm and Omsk, and less than 6 in each of the other regions. The funds surveyed are divided almost equally (50.7 vs. 49.3 percent) between those

[14] For a few examples of how low these prices were, see Frydman, Rapaczynski, and Earle (1993).

[15] This figure is obtained by multiplying the average proportion of the shares of the privatized companies sold at voucher auctions (18%) by the proportion of vouchers spent by the funds at these auctions (31.64%).

[16] Fund managers were interviewed in person on the basis of a standardized questionnaire.

Table 5.3. Population and Sample of Voucher Investment Funds
(by fund size)

	Number of funds	
Number of vouchers	Population no. (%)	Sample no. (%)
Over 1 million	2 (.04)	3 (2.02)[a]
500,000 to 1 million	3 (0.58)	4 (2.7)[a]
100,000 to 499,999	35 (6.78)	33 (22.3)
50,000 to 99,999	47 (9)	23 (15.54)
10,000 to 49,999	135 (26)	60 (40.54)
1 to 10,000	233 (45)	19 (12.84
0[b]	61 (11.82)	0
Missing data	0	6 (4.06)
Total	516	148

Source: The survey and authors' calculations based on the data base of the Voucher Fund Monitoring Group, Moscow.

[a] The number of funds of this size in our sample exceeds the number in the population, as reported in column 2. This is probably due to the fact that the sample data are from June/July 1994, while the population data are partly drawn from the May 1994 database of the Voucher Fund Monitoring Group (and a high portion of this data had been collected over the six months preceding that date). Generally, the same funds report somewhat higher numbers of vouchers in our survey than in the earlier monitoring group's study, possibly indicating significant acquisitions in the intervening period.

[b] Some registered funds did not make any voucher investments.

that invest nationwide and those that invest only regionally. On the whole, regional funds in the sample tend to be smaller, having invested an average of 82,500 vouchers, while the nationwide funds show an average of 183,000 vouchers invested.

The Portfolios

Because of potential overlaps, it is impossible to calculate the exact number of companies in the total portfolio of all the funds in our sample.[17] Ignoring the possibility of overlaps, the funds in the survey report that they are invested in 6,961 nonfinancial companies.[18] Given their average weighted stake (see Table 5.5) and the fact that the funds in the sample have invested approximately 70 percent of vouchers invested by all voucher privatization funds in Russia, we can say with a high degree of confidence that the funds in

[17] We asked each fund in how many companies it was invested, but we do not know how many companies have more than one fund among their owners.

[18] The funds in the sample also own stakes in 326 financial companies that, presumably, were not part of the universe of privatized companies.

Table 5.4. Companies in the Funds' Portfolios

Types of companies/ institutions	No. of funds that reported investing in types of companies	Number of companies in a portfolio(% of companies in a portfolio)		
		Average fund	Largest 10% of funds	Smallest 10% of funds
Non-financial companies	145	47.7 (89.6)	81.7 (93.8)	25.0 (72.9)
Production	144	40.1 (76.7)	68.5 (77.9)	21.4 (64.0)
Service	70	3.5 (5.3)	8.3 (8.1)	1.8 (4.1)
Trading	80	2.5 (4.2)	2.8 (4.2)	1.6 (4.4)
Other non-financial companies	36	1.7 (3.4)	2.1 (3.6)	0.2 (0.4)
Financial institutions	85	2.3 (10.4)	2.9 (6.2)	2.7 (27.1)
Banks	78	1.7 (7.2)	2.6 (5.7)	1.4 (14.3)
Other financial institutions	35	0.6 (3.2)	0.3 (0.5)	1.3 (12.9)

our sample own some stake in more than 4,000 (and perhaps even more than 5,000) companies (i.e. more that 27, perhaps more than 33, percent of the total which went through voucher privatization).[19] Thus, in addition to giving a detailed account of the behavior of the funds themselves, the responses to the questionnaire also allow us to form a broad picture of the postprivatization environment in Russia, including the behavior of company managers and other actors on the ownership scene.

Table 5.4 gives a picture of the funds' portfolios in terms of the number of companies they invest in and presents the types of companies in which the funds in the sample are represented. We see that all the funds are heavily invested in nonfinancial companies and particularly in production companies; this is an artifact of the supply available in voucher privatization and, to a lesser extent, in the Russian economy as a whole). Smaller funds are more heavily invested in financial companies, in part perhaps because some of

[19] We are also using Blasi and Shleifer's (in vol. 2) figure of 9% as the average combined stake of voucher funds in companies that have voucher funds among their owners (which, incidentally, shows that there is rarely more than one fund among the owners of an average company and that the funds in our sample, being weighted toward greater size, may also hold somewhat higher than average stakes).

Table 5.5. Size Distribution of Average Stakes Held by the Funds

Quartile	Average stake held by funds
First quartile	3.86
Median	6.38
Third quartile	9.09
Maximum	18.75
Mean	6.89
Mean for the largest 10% funds	9.08
Mean for the smallest 10% of funds	4.64
Weighted mean[a]	7.29

[a] Weighted by size in terms of the number of companies in the fund's portfolio

Table 5.6. Size Distribution of Stakes Held by the Funds[a]

Size of stakes(%)	No. of companies (% of companies)
Less than 5	3,941 (57.3)
5 to 9.99	1,370 (19.9)
10 to 19.99	989 (14.4)
20 to 25	457 (6.6)
25.01 to 49.99	118 (1.7)
50 to 74.99	7 (0.1)
75 to 99.99	0
100	0
Total	6,882 (100)

[a] Number of valid responses: 141

them specialize in such holdings and in part because they have greater liquidity needs (financial companies are considered more liquid).[20] Also, given the small supply of nonmanufacturing companies, larger funds may simply have no choice but to invest heavily in the nonfinancial sector.

We have noted already that, given the insider-domination of Russian enterprises, the stakes held by the funds are relatively small. The average sizes of these stakes for different categories of funds are shown in Table 5.5, which also shows that the larger funds tend to own larger stakes.[21]

Table 5.6, in turn, shows that not only are the average stakes low; but the funds also hold very few large stakes in any of the companies in their portfolios. They own blocks of shares of over 25 percent in only 125 companies (1.8

[20] Interviews with small voucher funds in a number of regions of Russia (unpublished pilot study of January 1994).

[21] See section on large funds for an analysis of the behavior of larger funds.

percent of the total).[22] Given the general concentration of ownership in Russia, especially in the hands of the insiders, this severely restricts the ability of the funds to exercise effective influence over the companies in which they are invested.

A peculiarity of the Russian voucher auctions needs to be mentioned here to keep the size of the average stakes in perspective. The size of the stakes might be taken as an indication of what kind of interest the funds had in the companies in their portfolio: the more active funds, for example, will naturally be interested in acquiring larger stakes. But the size of the stake may often be a matter of accident, since the funds did not know in advance how many shares they were bidding for during the voucher auctions. Bidders were simply told to submit the number of vouchers they were willing to bid for the shares of a given company, and the price of each share was determined by dividing the total number of vouchers by the number of available shares. Bidders then received the proportion of available shares corresponding to the number of vouchers they had each bid.[23] Given the imperfect information concerning the value of the companies sold at voucher auctions and the unpredictable number of people who might participate in the auctions,[24] a voucher fund could not confidently predict how many shares it would be able to purchase. Once purchased, the funds were often locked into their holdings, since the liquidity for most of the shares is very low (see Table 5.20). For this reason, the size of the stakes is a less reliable criterion of the funds' nature than one would otherwise expect.

Ownership Structure of the Funds

Voucher investment funds were designed as private institutions that would potentially play a key role as new outside owners actively promoting firm-level and economy-wide restructuring. To gauge how likely they were to acquit themselves of this task, we looked at who was among their founders (Table 5.7) and asked whether their starting point predisposed them in what could be seen as the "right" direction.

All funds, as we have seen, were founded as joint stock companies. Under Russian law, this means that a group of initial founders had to form the company, and then float it on the market (which, in this case, involved issuing the funds' shares primarily in exchange for vouchers received from

[22] As noted above, 25% is also the (unenforced) legal limit of fund ownership in any single company.

[23] Another type of bid allowed bidders to list a reservation price, but it was hardly ever used.

[24] The decentralization of the voucher auctions probably contributed to this uncertainty.

Table 5.7. Founding Parties of Voucher Investment Funds

Type of founding parties	No. of funds with one of the founders of a given type	Average percentage held by founders
Physical persons		
Managers of nonfinancial companies	32	38.91
Employees of the state administration	3	13.67
Managers or employees of domestic financial institutions	20	26.2
Other domestic individual investors	44	42.05
Foreign individual investors	0	0
Juridical persons		
Investment companies	27	44.15
Banks and other domestic financial institutions	32	37.09
State-owned enterprises	8	33.25
Privatized enterprises	36	53.58
(New) private enterprises	82	57.55
Foreign banks and financial institutions	0	0
Other[a]	28	36.3

[a] Includes social organizations, associations, small commercial organizations, and a Russian/foreign joint venture.

the population). Although the original ownership structure of the funds (prior to the first public emission of their shares) may be only an imperfect indication of the future behavior of the funds (since the public emission was bound to dilute the original owners), the founders are likely to have retained significant managerial control after the fund went public. Indeed, they were the parties choosing the management in the first place.[25] Also, it may be independently interesting to see who was among the funds' founders, since their identity might give an indication of the extent to which attempts might have been made to use the funds as a means for the old institutions to reproduce or perpetuate themselves. Finally, the relationship between voucher

[25] The funds' management is contracted out to other legal or physical persons, but since the majority of the funds are managed by individuals, rather than companies, data on the ownership structure of the management companies are less instructive than those on the initial ownership of the funds themselves, especially since the original fund owners were the ones who decided the identity of the management. The professional background of individual fund managers interviewed in the survey is similar to that of enterprise managers in Russia: 37.2% of all the interviewees were engineers, 37.8% economists, 30.4% were previously employed in state enterprises, but a large group (27.7%) comes from private companies, both financial and nonfinancial.

funds and other financial institutions may provide some indication of the degree of evolution undergone by both the new and the old financial sector.

The State

The architects of Russian privatization were very thorough, much more so than their Czech counterparts, in trying to prevent both direct and indirect state ownership of the privatized companies. Thus, not only were state-controlled entities prohibited from bidding for the companies themselves, but also the voucher fund regulations flatly prohibited any state structures or entities controlled by the state (i.e. ones in which the state holds at least a 25 percent stake) to act as founders or cofounders of voucher investment funds. This prohibition was generally observed, although eight funds in the sample report that "state enterprises" were among their cofounders, owning on average a 30 percent stake in the original fund.

The flat prohibition on state involvement was somewhat relaxed when the law was interpreted to allow so-called "social organizations" – an amorphous group ranging from labor unions to the association of the veterans of the war in Afghanistan – to act as founders of a fund.[26] Fourteen funds in the sample reported that social organizations were among their cofounders. But in general, the ownership role of the state, either direct or indirect, appears to be minimal.

Potential Circularity of Control

The primary investment objects for voucher investment funds were companies whose shares were offered in the privatization process and could be acquired for vouchers. The degree to which voucher funds were truly independent could be compromised if the same privatized companies or their management were directly involved in the creation of the voucher funds. Evidence from the sample suggests that potential targets of voucher investment funds were indeed quite active in establishing their future owners: 32 funds name managers of enterprises, and 36 name privatized companies as their cofounders. When they were present at the time of founding, managers held on average 38 percent in the original fund, and privatized companies held 54 percent.[27]

[26] The statute on voucher funds prohibited "entities owned by social organizations" to establish such funds. Based on this inconclusive wording of the regulation, the GKI (Russian Ministry of Privatization) decided to allow social organizations themselves to set up funds. See GKI Telegram, 10 February 1993, DV-22/951.

[27] As we shall see later in Table 5.19, the presence of privatized companies among a fund's owners has a highly significant dampening effect on the fund's involvement in fundamental restructuring.

Other Financial Institutions

The architects of the Russian program were also much more cautious than their Czech counterparts in allowing voucher funds to be linked to other types of financial institutions. The funds were prohibited from acting as banks or insurance companies, and the prohibition on the ownership by state-controlled entities naturally worked to restrict the role of old-style banks in the creation of the funds – perhaps the most important difference with respect to the Czech funds. But private banks, insurance companies, and other investment institutions were not prohibited from acting as cofounders, and the survey shows that numerous financial institutions did participate: 27 list investment companies, and 33 funds list banks and other financial institutions, including insurance companies, among their founders. Where these actors are present, moreover, they hold very substantial stakes: 44 and 37 percent, respectively. Furthermore, among the 42 voucher funds which are parts of a group of affiliated companies, 23 have a bank, 18 a pension fund, 15 an insurance company, and 31 an investment company among the other members of the same group.

In Table 5.7, we have listed investment companies as founders independently from banks and other financial institutions. The reason is that banks, even if they are often new, are likely to include a large number of entities "captured" by the old institutions, while investment companies are more likely to be the harbingers of a newly evolving financial order.

Foreign Financial Institutions

In contradistinction to the Czech Republic, foreign financial institutions have been entirely absent among the founders of voucher funds in Russia, and only two funds report that foreign financial institutions were a part of their management company. This is a rather unfortunate result, since these institutions have many skills lacking in Russia, where financial markets did not exist at all until a few years ago, and they have much greater access to the sorely lacking foreign capital.

New Private Founders

By far the largest role as founders of voucher funds is played by new private nonfinancial companies: 82 funds list them among their founders. Many among these founders are likely to be the most independent actors on the Russian corporate scene. But it should also be noted that a large number could be companies formed by managers of the privatized entities attempting to organize their own friendly funds in order to shield their companies from genuine outside influence.

The landscape of the founders of Russian voucher funds reflects a simple fundamental condition: that new institutions must be built with existing material. It is, therefore, hardly surprising to find many of the main actors in the old order among the founders of the voucher funds. In the absence of foreign inflow of human capital and expertise, the only truly new players with some track record of economic activity outside the state sector might be the investment companies created in the wake of the first Russian securities regulation in December 1991[28] and some of the new private actors with a background outside civil service or state enterprise management. But we see a significant diversity in the founders and no clear dominance of any one type committed to a particular policy or strategy of portfolio management.

The Investment Environment

Access to Information and Investment Criteria

The world in which the Russian voucher funds pick their portfolios and manage their investments is characterized by a remarkable absence of information – undoubtedly another effect of the insider domination of most Russian firms. As shown in Table 5.8, most companies do not disclose any financial information to nonshareholders, and when they do disclose it to shareholders, many funds (33.3 percent) view the information as poorly reflecting the actual financial situation and performance of the company. Perhaps most astoundingly, 12.5 percent of the funds report that *no* companies in their portfolios give them regular access to financial information, and 49.3 percent report that most companies do not provide such information. As a result, as seen in Table 5.9, the funds resort to spying on their own companies,[29] or rely on such deceptive indices of performance as the volume of output.[30]

Given the secretiveness of insider-dominated companies and the weakness

[28] Government Regulation No. 78 on Securities, 28 December 1991.

[29] This practice was also confirmed in a number of informal interviews.

[30] In addition to the effect of insider domination, there may also be another factor limiting the amount of information available to shareholders, namely, the fact that most Russian companies engage in widespread tax avoidance, and the disclosure of any financial data may get them into trouble with the state (which also happens to be a major shareholder). It may even be said that a rational shareholder in Russia would want the management not to disclose any information, since this may be a simple strategy of maximizing return on capital. We presume, however, that this factor, which was brought to our attention by Professor Bernard Black, is working concurrently with the effects of insider domination and does not invalidate the points made in the text.

Table 5.8. Access to Financial Information

	Percentage of funds
Funds with regular access to financial data in	
All	10.4
Most	40.3
Some	36.8
None	12.5
of the companies in their portfolios	
Additional information available upon request?	
Always	31.2
Sometimes	36.2
Rarely	14.9
Never	17.7
To whom is financial information disclosed?	
Any interested parties	3.3
Current shareholders only	96.7
Accuracy of disclosed information	
Good	0.8
Adequate	65.9
Poor	33.3

Table 5.9. Means by Which Funds Monitor Companies in Their Portfolios

	Percentage of funds
Review of financial data	75.4
Informal sources	71.6
Share prices	70.5
Volume of output	64.9

of other monitoring institutions (the capital market, above all), the question arises as to how the funds actually pick the companies for their portfolios. Table 5.10 lists the different criteria used by the funds to select companies for investment, and it reveals overall strategies that are understandable under the circumstances, but which differ significantly from what one would expect in a more stable market environment.

The most often used investment criterion is profitability. Although this is a rather standard gauge of success, its usefulness under Russian conditions

Table 5.10. Investment Criteria Used by the Funds

Investment criterion	Very important[a] (percentage)	Not important (percentage)
Profitability	64.6	6.2
Liquidity of companies' shares	60.0	13.1
Value of real estate	58.5	12.3
Quality of production equipment	46.9	9.2
Location of company	42.3	13.8
Personal contacts with company management	39.2	26.2
Business connections with other companies in the fund's portfolio	35.4	30.0
Expected cooperation with management to overcome employee resistance	32.3	29.2
Sales revenues	23.1	23.8
Quality of company management	20.0	32.3
Access to state credits	16.2	51.5
Large stake held by the state	14.6	59.2
Access to nonstate sources of finance	12.3	60.0

Note: We contrast only "very important" with "not important" investment factors. Since we eliminated the "moderately important" category, row percentages do not add up to 100.
[a] Percentage of funds listing each criterion as being in the "very important" category. Number of valid responses for every row of this table is 130.

seems very questionable. Profitability figures are notoriously unreliable in a world in which firms have a short history of operation under the market system, in which product markets (and prices) are still extremely imperfect, and in which accounting is utterly unreliable. The cost of fixed capital is accounted for in terms of unrealistic book values; receivables and payables are often paper entries, and inflation makes a mockery of most calculations. But profitability may be an indication of a short-term availability of cash, which may attract many cash-strapped funds hoping for quick dividends.

In addition to profitability, the funds seem most often to look to fundamentals that can be relatively easily determined without access to inside information: they look at the value of real estate, the quality of production equipment, and – most funds being small and regional – geographical location. By contrast, the funds tend to attach little importance to "business fundamentals," such as the quality of management, even though these might seem to be crucial in an environment in which the outside investor is usually powerless to effect any changes. The reason for this is probably that business fundamentals are very difficult to determine unless one has personal contacts with the management, in which case the funds are more ready to go in.

Finally, given the imperfection of the capital markets, the funds pay inordinate attention to the liquidity of their investments. The importance of liquidity is further strengthened by the fact that exit is often the only plausible strategy for an outside investor in an insider-dominated Russian environment.

The Other Players

To understand the dynamics of the Russian corporate scene, a few words must be said about the importance of other actors with whom the voucher funds interact in their attempts to influence the behavior of companies in their portfolios.

We have noted already that corporate insiders are the largest force among the owners of companies in which voucher funds are also among the shareholders. As shown by Table 5.11, insider ownership approaches 70 percent of the companies in the funds' portfolios. Even though the funds are the largest shareholders in some 7.7 percent of companies in their portfolios,[31] in most of even those companies the *combined* force of the insiders by far exceeds the voting power of the funds.

Next to the combined force of enterprise insiders and far ahead of the voucher funds, the most important single shareholder in Russian firms remains the state. In the early stages of the privatization process, before any shares were sold to outside owners, the state continued to own the largest block of shares in every enterprise, but there was a limitation on the extent of actual state power in corporate affairs: if the state block was larger than 40 percent, the excess shares were preferred and nonvoting. (Once sold to private parties, the preferred shares changed their status to ordinary common stock.) The state property funds (holding the state shares) then sold a large portion of their initial holdings at voucher auctions, bringing state ownership in most firms to between 10 and 31 percent (with all the state shares being voting common at this point).[32] Thus, even though voucher auctions amounted to significant divestment, they still left the state, when compared with any other individual shareholder, including managers and voucher funds, as the largest blockholder in nearly every Russian firm.

[31] All these companies are concentrated in 77 funds, each of which is, on the average, the largest shareholder in some 16% of the companies in its portfolio.

[32] The actual number of shares retained by the state depended on the privatization option chosen, the number of shares offered at voucher auctions, and the creation of employee shareholding trusts (FARP). Under privatization option 1, insiders could acquire initially 40% of total shares; adding 29% as the standard amount of shares that was offered at voucher auctions, this leaves 31% for the state. Under privatization option 2, after insider subscription (51%) and voucher auction, usually a block of 20% remained. FARP regulations allowed for an additional 5-10% of total shares to be allocated to an employee trust.

Table 5.11. **Relative Position of Funds, Insiders, and the State**

	Number (%)[a] of companies	No. valid responses
No. of companies in the funds' portfolios in which the fund is the largest shareholder (as % of total number of companies in the funds' portfolios)	505 (7.7)	136
No. of companies in the funds' portfolios in which the fund is represented on the board (as % of total number of companies in the funds' portfolios)	1,040 (15.1)	141
No. of companies in the funds' portfolios in which the insiders (workers and management together) hold more than 50% of outstanding shares (as % of the total no. of companies in the funds' portfolios)	3,844 (69.9)	116
Proportion (per fund portfolio) of companies in which the insiders (workers and management together) hold more than 50% of outstanding shares		
maximum	(100)	109
75th percentile	(93)	
median	(75)	
25th percentile	(0.2)	
No. of funds reporting that the state is a shareholder in any of the companies in their portfolios	124 funds; (no. of companies not available)	143
No. of companies in the funds' portfolios in which the state is represented on the board (as % of the total no. of companies in the funds' portfolios)	2,557 (46.9)	108
Proportion (per fund portfolio) of companies in which the state is represented on the board of directors		
maximum	(100)	
75th percentile	(98)	
median	(53)	
25th percentile	(9)	106

[a] The percentages are reported relative to the number of companies in the portfolios of funds giving a valid response to the relevant survey questions.

Table 5.12. The State as an Ally of Other Shareholders

Type of shareholder	% of funds reporting the state forms coalitions with this type shareholder[a]
Management	75.3
Outside investors (juridical persons)	24.7
Nonmanagerial employees	6.5
Individuals as outside investors	5.2

[a] The percentages are computed relative to the number of funds reporting that the state forms coalitions with other shareholders.

Our survey did not measure directly the extent of state ownership of the companies in funds' portfolios, but the survey data (see Table 5.11) concerning the frequency with which the state holds seats on the boards of directors confirm the importance of state power in Russian corporate life: while the voucher funds held board seats in only 15.1 percent of companies in their porftolios, the state held such seats in 46.9 percent of cases. Moreover, the state seems in most instances to be a manager-friendly shareholder. As shown in Table 5.12, of 77 funds reporting that the state forms coalitions with other shareholders, 81.8 percent report that the state forms such coalitions with the management or the workers.[33] Thus, the survey indicates that the presence of the state among the shareholders further strengthens the dominance of the insiders in most Russian firms. And since this presence is also likely to continue for the foreseeable future, so is the fact of insider domination.[34]

Although we lack systematic evidence on the behavior of other actors on the roster of shareholders in Russian firms, many of them are also likely to be allied with the management and solidify its control. Thus, for example, some firms are widely believed to have "parked" significant blocks of their shares with customers or suppliers, holding companies, friendly banks (many of which were owned by former state enterprises), or a variety of related establishments. Also, many Russian companies report having various other "commercial firms" among their largest shareholders. A portion of these firms is sure to consist of bona fide investors, genuinely unrelated to the companies they own, but it is also very likely that some of these commercial firms were in fact formed by managers of companies to be privatized or their

[33] A number of informal interviews with voucher investment funds and regional state property funds (which vote the state shares) in several regions conducted in preparation for this survey confirm this result.

[34] For a more detailed description and analysis of the role of the state in privatized companies, see Pistor and Turkewitz (in vol. 2).

friends and families in order to increase covertly the extent of managerial control. Such covert managerial purchases were often mentioned in interviews with various parties on the Russian corporate scene, and they are likely to diminish still further the extent of genuine outside ownership.

The remaining outside owners are most likely to be the dispersed, usually very small individual shareholders.[35] The voucher funds are thus probably the most important outside owners, and even though some of these funds may have also been "captured" by managerial interests, they are probably overall the most genuinely independent among the noninsider shareholders of Russian corporations.[36] In this sense, it may be said that their responses to the peculiar environment in which they must act are the most indicative of the predicament of an outsider investor in the insider-dominated Russian firms. In fact, how successful they are in breaking down the barriers posed by the insiders may be one of the most important questions concerning the future of corporate governance in Russia.

Role and Extent of Shareholder Activism in Postprivatization Environment

Along with the objective of depoliticization, *the* main purpose of privatization was to change the way companies had been run under the old Communist system. In part, the Russian privatization scheme was to change the incentives of management by giving managers partial ownership of their enterprises. But the improvement was also to come from better monitoring and supervision of management performance by the new private owners. The restructuring of privatized firms was thus to come significantly from the activism of new shareholders, with voucher funds playing a leading role. In this section we will inquire into how active the voucher funds in fact are in corporate affairs and what factors determine the nature and extent of their activism.

In a developed economy, shareholder activism is not a preferred strategy

[35] The level of foreign ownership in most Russian privatized firms is still so small as to be safely ignored.

[36] We made numerous efforts to identify in our sample the funds that might have been created or captured by managers of privatized enterprises in order to protect the insiders against genuine outside ownership. Although, as we shall see, some funds are clearly more friendly to managers than others, the presence of managerial interests is so pervasive among nearly all funds – which, given the extent of insider domination, simply must cooperate with management to achieve any of their objectives – that it is impossible to isolate any group of distinctly "managerialist" funds.

of most investors. Monitoring is costly and requires special skills, while returns from it must usually be shared with other, passive shareholders. A large number of investors in advanced markets prefer, therefore, to remain passive and rely on others to do the monitoring and supervision of management. When they are disappointed by corporate performance, they usually prefer "exit" (i.e. sale of their stakes) to "voice" (i.e. participation in corporate restructuring). Moreover, shareholder activism, even when it does occur in Western economies, is not, except in very special markets, an everyday occurrence – it is rather a strategy of last resort, with the investor interfering with management only in times of corporate difficulties that raise the possibility of managerial ineptitude or malfeasance.

In a transition economy, however, one might expect activism among investors to be much more prevalent. Liquidity and corporate governance institutions relied upon by Western minority investors for the protection of their interests are not present in most transition economies, so that exit is often difficult and costly, and the ability of an investor to "free ride" on the monitoring done by others is also limited. Indeed, the very need to protect one's investment from managerial overreaching or outright dishonesty often makes shareholder activism necessary. At the same time, returns from investor activism are also potentially greater in transition economies than in the more stable systems, at least with respect to those companies that do have a future in the new economic order, because companies are more mismanaged and more value can be created through some obvious forms of restructuring. Furthermore, in the absence of well developed markets, shareholder activism may be the only way to acquire valuable information affecting investment strategies and the management of one's portfolio.

Self-Proclaimed Activism

As expected, Russian voucher funds engage in a significant amount of shareholder activism, with only a relatively small minority (19.4 percent) adopting a purely passive stance. The remaining 80.6 percent (116 out of 144 funds in our sample) claim active involvement in important decisions in at least some of the companies in their portfolio (Table 5.13). Of these, 78.4 percent (87 funds) report that shareholder activism is their general strategy, and 85.6 percent (95 funds) believe that activism is necessary (important or very important) to protect their investment (Table 5.14).

Another expected reason cited by many funds to explain their activism (as seen in Table 5.14) is the lack of liquidity, which impedes exit when a company is underperforming. But what may come as a surprise, and throw significant light on the nature of the activism of Russian funds, is the near

Table 5.13. The Extent of the Funds' Activism

Companies in the fund's portfolio in which the fund is an active investor[a]	Percentage of funds[b]
None	19.4
Some	65.3
Majority	13.2
All	2.1

[a] A fund is considered to be an "active investor" if it spends significant resources and/or effort on monitoring and/or influencing major decisions, such as employment, investment, structure of production, sales, organization, etc.
[b] Out of 144 valid responses.

Table 5.14. Reasons for the Funds' Activism

Reason (in at least some of the companies in its portfolio)	Funds[a] reporting that a given reason is important (%)
The fund has been able to secure sufficient cooperation of the management to enable it to exercise effective influence over major decisions	90.1
The fund has to be active to protect the value of its investments because it cannot easily sell shares if the company's performance is considered unsatisfactory	85.6
The fund holds a sufficiently large stake in the company for the benefits of monitoring to exceed its costs	85.6
The fund has been able to secure the cooperation of other powerful outside shareholders to enable it to exercise effective influence over major decisions	81.1
The fund's investment strategy is to be an active investor in the companies in its portfolio	78.4
Although the fund holds a small stake in the company, the fund monitors the company in association with or on behalf of other shareholders	74.8
The fund has been able to secure the cooperation of nonmanagerial employees to enable it to exercise effective influence over major decisions	58.6

[a] Out of 111 valid responses.

universality with which the funds cite the ability to cooperate with management as a reason for their activism, at least in some of the companies in their portfolios. Cooperation with management may, of course, be quite common among activist shareholders in more advanced economies, where management is likely to be ultimately chosen by powerful investors. But in a transition economy, where low quality and opportunism of management are among the main causes of poor performance and where agency problems are likely to be rampant (Frydman and Rapaczynski 1994, ch. 5), this high degree of cooperation between management and the new shareholders is not likely to occur in the absence of special circumstances. Under Russian conditions, these special circumstances are, of course, the very high degree of insider ownership, which makes it extremely hard to exercise any influence over Russian firms, unless the cooperation of the management is secured. But this very fact also means that the nature of shareholder activism in Russia is likely to be severely restricted by the need to secure management cooperation, and that the measures that can be undertaken by the activist funds are likely to fall far short of any radical restructuring that would be apt to provoke managerial opposition.

Another surprising fact revealed in Table 5.14 is the frequency with which the funds claim that their stakes are large enough for the benefits of monitoring to exceed the costs, since we know that the average stakes held by the funds (shown in Table 5.5) are quite modest, and, generally, the number of companies in which the funds hold large stakes (shown in Table 5.6) is very small as well. There may be a number of explanations for this phenomenon. First, the survey question asked for reasons for activism in *at least some* (and not necessarily all) of the companies in the fund's portfolio, so that it might have been sufficient for a given fund to own significant stakes in no more than one company to cite the size of its stake as a reason for activism. The second, and more interesting, explanation may be related to the already mentioned conjecture that the returns from activism in transition economies may be significantly larger than in the more advanced economies, where simple restructuring measures are less likely to make a noticeable difference in performance. Consequently, although the funds hold a relatively small number of stakes that would be considered in more advanced economies sufficiently large for the benefits of monitoring to warrant the cost, smaller stakes may be sufficient to induce shareholder activism in transition economies, despite the well known free-rider problems.

Finally, Table 5.14 reveals the frequency with which shareholder activism in Russia involves coalition building, both among the outsiders and between the funds and some nonmanagerial insider interests, that may increase the power of the funds to influence corporate affairs. We shall return to this aspect of Russian corporate governance after reviewing some other facets of the funds' activism.

Board Representation and Shareholder Coalitions

Another clear sign of the shareholder activism of voucher funds is the frequency with which they participate in the governance bodies of Russian firms. Thus, 111 funds (78.7 percent of valid observations) report that they hold seats on the boards of directors in some of the companies in their portfolios.[37] Extrapolating from our sample, this would mean that approximately 15.1 percent of all privatized companies that have a voucher fund among their shareholders also have a voucher fund on their boards.[38]

How do voucher funds obtain their board seats? Nearly all funds report that the size of the stake is an important factor (see Table 5.15), and judging from the number of seats obtained, a stake in the range of 15 percent seems to be sufficient.[39] This threshold is not surprising, although it would probably be significantly lower if regulations concerning independent directors and mandatory cumulative voting were to be enforced.[40]

The funds also acquire board seats by forming coalitions with other shareholders – the most frequent partners in such alliances are shown in Table 5.16. Significantly, management is again the most common ally and, independently, 94.3 percent of the funds also report that cooperation with

[37] As seen in Table 5.15, the median number of seats held by a fund is much smaller than the mean. The reason for this skewed distribution is that larger funds with higher stakes hold disproportionately more board seats than the smaller funds.

[38] Also 26 funds report that they are represented on the management board. Six of these probably misunderstood the question, since they confused positions on the management board with those on the council of directors (which is not a managing body). But six funds report that the managing directors of some of the companies in their portfolios are "representatives" of the fund, and the same number of funds list chief financial officers as their representatives (two list the economic director). From other responses to the survey, it appears that 11 of the 26 funds reporting representation on the management board may in fact be "captured" and the representation of these funds among the management is likely either to reflect the dependence of the fund on the firm, rather than the other way around, or to result from a recreation of old inter-enterprise links on the ownership level. Still, the evidence does indicate that in a relatively small number of cases (amounting, on average, to 1.7% of companies in the funds' portfolios), the funds have a "hands on" involvement in management.

[39] See Table 5.6 for a distribution of the funds' stakes according to size. Although no exact calculations are possible from our data, there are probably fewer than 1,040 companies in the portfolios of our funds in which a fund holds a 15% (or larger) stake. The funds hold 1,040 board seats. But some board seats are obtained on the basis of coalitions, rather than the size of individual stakes (see below), and this makes the threshold of 15% roughly appropriate.

[40] These provisions were included in the Privatization Program for 1994, which was adopted by a presidential decree. See footnote 12 above.

Table 5.15. Funds and Boards of Directors

Number of funds represented on boards of directors	111
Total number of companies with a fund as a board member	1,040
Number of companies per fund portfolio in which the fund is represented on the board of directors[a]	
Maximum	50
75th percentile	10
Median	3
25th percentile	1
Average (mean)	7.4
Important factors in obtaining a seat on the board of directors (% of funds reporting that a given factor is important)[a]	
Size of stake held	99.3
Cooperation with management	94.3
Cooperation with other outside investors	88.6
Cooperation with the state	58.6
Cooperation with workers	47.9
Benefits of board representation as seen by the funds (% of funds reporting a given benefit)[b]	
Influence on management strategy	87.5
Access to information	84.7
Influence on dividend policy	76.4

[a] Out of 140 valid responses.
[b] Out of 144 valid responses.

management is an important factor in obtaining a board seat (Table 5.15). This probably means that most boards are "packed" with managerial members, and this fact limits the type of activism in which the funds may engage. Moreover, the presence of voucher funds on boards of directors should be viewed in light of the fact that the board is generally a weak body under Russian law, with no power to dismiss the general director.[41] But the funds also try to get board seats by forming coalitions with other outside investors, especially other funds and investment companies. These two types of shareholders represent a relatively small percentage of ownership, but they are among the most independent institutions, with fewer ties to the previous

[41] The right to dismiss the general director is vested exclusively in the shareholder meeting. Art. 124 of the Statute on Joint Stock Companies, Regulation No. 601 of the RSFSR Council of Ministers, 25 December 1990, and Art. 6.13 of the Model Statute for privatized companies adopted by Presidential Decree No. 721, 1 July 1992. Under the recently enacted Civil Code, this right may now be delegated to the council of directors, but only if the company's bylaws so provide (Art. 103).

Table 5.16. The Funds' Supporters for Board Representation

Type of shareholder	Funds listing a given shareholder as 1 of top 3 with which the fund cooperates to obtain a board seat[a] (%)
Management	82.7
Voucher funds	74.4
The state	30.8
Investment companies	24.8
Domestic commercial entities	21.8
Banks	12.0
Physical persons	12.0
Subgroups among nonmanagerial employees	10.5
Nonmanagerial employees	6.0
Foreign financial investors	3.0
Pension funds and insurance companies	4.0
Foreign trade investors	0

[a] Out of 133 valid responses.

regime, and they figure as primary allies of the funds much more often than their shareholder size would lead one to expect. This may be an indication that the funds' behavior on the boards is not always manager-friendly. Indeed, as we shall see, the funds do sometimes participate in the dismissal of managers and other forms of more "fundamental" restructuring.

A separate survey question inquired, more generally, who are the funds' main allies among shareholders and which shareholders are the least cooperative from the funds' point of view. The answers to these questions reveal a somewhat more complicated picture than the tactical alliances concerning support in board elections (see Table 5.17). Over 60 percent of the funds still list management among their three most important allies, which indicates not only that the funds must work with management if they want to be active at all, but also that the interests of these two groups may not be as diverse as one might suspect. Indeed, some managers may not be totally hostile to outside interests, and some funds might be "captured" by or linked to managerial interests so that they cannot be identified with "new" forces opposed to the old industrial nomenklatura. Equally significant, however, is the fact that nearly a third of the funds also list management among the three most uncooperative shareholders, which probably confirms our view of the funds as the most independent group of outside shareholders.

If the funds find ways to work with management, they are not nearly as successful in forming lasting coalitions with nonmanagerial employees: just over 11 percent list these groups as their allies and nearly half see them as

Table 5.17. Corporate Allies of the Funds (in percentages)

Type of shareholder	Funds listing a given shareholder among 3 most cooperative[a]	Funds listing a given shareholder among 3 most uncooperative
Management	67.2	32.8
Voucher funds	64.1	19.5
Investment companies	33.6	5.5
Banks	32.0	7.8
Domestic commercial entities	22.7	16.4
Physical persons	17.2	24.2
Subgroups among nonmanagerial employees	11.7	43.0
Nonmanagerial employees	11.7	46.9
Foreign financial investors	10.9	6.3
The state	10.2	50.0
Pension funds and insurance companies	9.4	14.1
Foreign trade investors	4.7	7.0

[a] Out of 128 valid responses.

among the most uncooperative. In light of what is known about alliances between workers and management in those Western countries in which employees are represented on the governing bodies of companies, this result is not surprising, but it does go against some of the hopes of the the architects of Russian privatization, who had anticipated that workers would not be hostile to outside owners.

Finally, the funds find the state to be the most uncooperative shareholder of all. The funds themselves view the state as, on the whole, more of a negative than positive factor: 31.5 percent believe that the presence of the state among the other shareholders has a negative impact on the value of their investment, while only 8.1 percent view it as having a positive impact. At the same time, 60.5 percent of the funds view the state's presence as "neutral." This large number of indifferent respondents is probably simply a result of the state's omnipresence among the shareholders of Russian corporations, but it may also be an indication that the funds, while clearly not in favor of state ownership, are not that hostile to it either.

Whatever the funds' own attitude, they clearly perceive the state as hostile to their interests: 50 percent view it as among the most uncooperative shareholders, and only 10.2 percent report that the state is among their allies. Overall, then, the interests of the funds and the state seem to be among the most divergent among the important actors on the Russian corporate scene, and to the extent that voucher funds become more influential over time, this may well serve the depoliticization of Russian companies, which the Russian reformers defined as one of the two major objectives of privatization. Until then, however, the state (as we have seen in Table 5.12) is in a firm coalition with management on the firm level, and it seems that management is able to cooperate with both the state and the voucher funds, even if those two have little sympathy for each other. This is probably another effect of the dominant position of management, which may be able to shift its alliances without serious risk that its two outside partners combine to challenge its position of control.

(It may be interesting to note that of the nine funds that view the presence of the state as enhancing the value of their investment, seven also list management among their top allies. These are likely to be managerially dominated funds, and as the numbers suggest, this tripartite unholy alliance is probably an exception rather than the rule.)

Services Provided by the Funds

Fund activism is not limited to board representation; according to their reports, the funds also provide a significant number of services to the companies in their portfolios. In fact, as may be observed from Table 5.18, they see themselves as providing quite an array of such services, from arranging all kinds of contacts to providing expertise in the areas of manage-

Table 5.18. Services Provided by Funds to Companies in Their Portfolios (in percentages)

Types of service provided	Funds providing service or arranging service provided by others[a]
Investment expertise	63.6
Expertise in restructuring or reorganizing the company	53.4
Management expertise	44.9
Technical know-how	20.3
Arranging access to domestic customers	63.6
Arranging access to domestic suppliers	44.9
Arranging access to foreign customers	23.9
Arranging access to foreign suppliers	19.7
Extending credit to the company	18.5
Arranging access to credits	
Domestic nonstate credits	42.4
Foreign credits	19.0
State credits	14.4

[a] These funds reported providing a given service to at least one company in their portfolio.

ment, restructuring, and investment. Some of these reports may be self-serving, especially since most funds are unlikely to have special "in house" expertise in many of these areas, and only relatively few report using outside help in this connection. Also, some of these "services" may be provided by the managerially captured funds and may have less to do with genuine restructuring than with reconstructing the old networks of connections among producers, customers, and suppliers who used to be tied together in the former branch ministries and nomenklatura associations. Provision of paid services may also be a way of siphoning some of the profits from a "friendly" company. But overall, the number of reported services is large and indicates an encouraging degree of constructive activism on the part of a significant number of funds. Of particular interest may be the fact that 19–24 percent of the funds report providing various kinds of access to foreign credits, customers, or suppliers. These numbers may not be huge, compared with the other forms of services, but given the isolation of the Russian economy and the extremely low levels of foreign ownership or management participation in the voucher funds, they are significant; indeed, one of the main functions of privatization investment funds, as originally proposed, was to facilitate precisely these kinds of business contacts and interactions (Frydman and Rapaczynski 1994, ch. 1).

Extent of Fundamental Restructuring and Limits of Shareholder Activism

We have seen that, as expected, voucher funds view shareholder activism as necessary to protect their investment during the period of economic transition. We have also conjectured that their returns from activism may be high enough to outweigh its cost even at relatively low levels of ownership. But what exactly is it that the funds are getting from their activism under the special Russian conditions?

According to their own perception, activism, and specifically obtaining a seat on the boards of directors, is useful for influencing management strategies, obtaining information, and influencing dividend policy (see Table 5.15). Our data independently confirm these reports, at least with respect to access to information, which is strongly correlated with having a seat on the board of directors. It is thus reasonable to believe that the other reported benefits are also real, and they provide a plausible indication that our conjecture about high returns from activism is indeed correct. Under Russian conditions, privileged access to information is key to a successful investment strategy, since publicly available information is scarce and the market for this kind of knowledge is extremely imperfect. Moreover, the ability to influence dividend strategy is also crucial for enhancing returns, given that the insiders have little incentive to distribute any excess cash to shareholders rather than consuming it in wages and other privileges or squandering it on inefficient investments.[42]

But returns from shareholder activism are also limited under Russian conditions by the extent of insider domination.[43] The funds may gain some voice in company matters, and management may sometimes be willing to compromise on its absolute control in exchange for services provided by the funds, or when the ownership share commanded by the management is in fact less than fully controlling, in exchange for the funds' support against other shareholders. The funds seem to wield even this limited influence in only a small minority of the companies in which they are invested.[44] Judging by such matters as the dismal access to financial data of most companies in the funds' portfolios (see Table 5.8), the funds seem to have hardly any impact on a great majority of their firms.

The funds' ability to act is particularly insignificant when it comes to more fundamental forms of restructuring, such as effecting the much needed changes in management personnel. The most drastic antimanagerialist measure – firing the general director – is still a rarity in Russia, despite the fact that most managers are former nomenklatura people, often chosen for their loyalty rather than their skills, and nearly always firmly rooted in the old ways of doing things. In our sample, only 69 funds report any dismissals of general directors in any companies in their portfolios, and the total number of cases reported, including possible overlaps, is 174. This number

[42] This is not to deny that Russian firms often are in dire need of additional investment, so that a dividend-maximizing policy may be harmful to their future prospects. But indiscriminate investment policy (as well as unwillingness and inability to retrench or cut costs) was an old disease of the Soviet system that still continues to shape the attitudes of many Russian managers. At the same time, contrary to widespread belief that the cash-poor voucher funds would demand dividends at all costs, there is no evidence of such an attitude in our survey – indeed, the funds rarely cite cash constraints as a reason for their actions. There is thus no particular reason to believe that the funds systematically prefer increased dividends in those cases in which the management can make a persuasive case for increased investment.

In addition to putting pressure on the management to pay dividends, and thus increasing its accountability for investment projects (as well as, perhaps, contributing to much needed economy-wide reallocation of capital), the voucher funds also attempt to enhance directly the efficiency of the management's investment policies; or at least they claim they attempt this, since 63.6% of them report providing investment expertise to companies in their portfolios – the type of service most often provided by the voucher funds (see Table 5.18).

[43] As we shall see in the next section, the activism of the funds may also be limited by the opportunities available in trading, despite the underdevelopment of the capital markets in Russia.

[44] We should remember that the funds are represented on the boards of only 1,040 companies, which amount to 7.4% of their portfolios (see Table 5.15). They may exert some influence in a few other companies, especially when they are allied with other shareholders who may represent them on the board, but the total number is still quite small.

amounts to 2.6 percent of companies in all of the funds' portfolios.[45] Furthermore, among the 69 funds reporting that a general director was fired in any company in their portfolios, only 51 claim to have actively participated in such dismissals.[46] Moreover, the relatively small stakes held by the funds mean that the funds participating in dismissals of managers must have had the cooperation of other owners, in many (perhaps most) cases including insiders. Dismissals may thus be occurring primarily in the most egregious cases of incompetence or dishonesty and, except for very few cases, not be a particularly strong indication of genuine restructuring. But even if only some of these cases indicate more fundamental restructuring on the company level, they may be quite significant for the future.

Consequently, to gain better insight into the nature of managerial personnel changes on the company level, we modeled the relation between the number of dismissals of general directors in the funds' portfolios and such explanatory variables as the size of the fund's portfolio, the degree of insider domination of the companies in which the fund is invested, the average size of the fund's' stakes, and the ownership structure of the fund. Estimates of the model, which measures the factors that determine on the margin the dismissal of top executive personnel, are presented in Table 5.19.

Unsurprisingly, the model reveals that on the margin the number of dismissals depends on the number of companies in the fund's portfolio, although given the overall small number of dismissals, the actual coefficient is quite small: by adding an additional company to a fund's portfolio, the chances of an additional firing increase by less than 2 percent.

Three other results are of more interest. First, the effect of the size of the stakes on the firing of general directors is nonlinear: there is no significant correlation between the two for funds with very small average stakes (under 4 percent), and the effects are quite different for average stakes in the range below 7.5 percent and those above it.[47] For funds with average stakes in the range of 4 to 7.5 percent, an increase in the size of the stake is by itself insignificant with respect to executive dismissals – not a surprising result, since firing a general director is a serious decision on which a small shareholder might not have a significant impact, regardless of owning 4 or 5

[45] This figure is much smaller than the one reported on the basis of more limited evidence by Shleifer and Vasiliev (in vol. 2).

[46] It is worth noting that even for this group of "activist" funds the number of dismissals per fund is quite small: 21 funds participated in the firing of 1 director; 23 funds in firing 2; 2 funds in firing 3; and 1 fund in firing 4, 5, 6, 10, and 20 directors respectively. Overall, these figures, including the obvious outlier, amount to 6.8% of the companies in an average fund's portfolio.

[47] The highest average stake in the sample was 18.75%.

Table 5.19. Turnover of Top Management

	Dependent variable	
	Probability that no. of dismissals of general directors in which the fund actively participated is greater than:	
Explanatory variables	0[a]	1[a]
No. of companies in the fund's portfolio	0.017 (0.06)	0.018 (0.04)
No. of privatized companies among the fund's founders	-0.045 (0.006)	-0.074 (0.05)
Proportion of companies in the fund's portfolio in which insiders (workers and management together) hold more than 50% of outstanding shares	-1.7 (0.02)	-2.1 (0.015)
Mean stake held by the fund for funds with average stakes between 4% and 7.5%, *and* reporting that other funds are among their top three allies	0.37 (0.007)	0.41 (0.004)
Mean stake held by the fund for funds with average stakes between 7.5% and 18.75%	0.11 (0.08)	0.12 (0.07)
Dummy variable: =1, if management is among top three allies of the fund[b]	-0.27 (0.65)	-1.41 (0.04)
Likelihood ratio statistic[c]	28.5 (0.0001)	39.5 (0.0001)
Association of predicted and observed probabilities	85%	89%
Number of observations	69	69

Note: For a discussion of methodological issues related to this and other statistical tables, see appendix.
[a] Maximum likelihood estimates of logistic equation; asymptotic *p*-values in parentheses.
[b] = 0, otherwise.
[c] Chi-squared with covariates.

percent of the shares. But when a fund in this ownership range reports that other voucher funds are among its top three allies, the size of the stake becomes very significant: for every 1 percent increase in the size of the fund's average stake, the probability of the fund's participating in the firing of a general director increases by some 40 percent. In other words, when funds enter into coalitions with each other, their power seems to increase very rapidly, and each percent of increase in ownership stakes begins to matter. The effect of coalitions seems to dissipate when the average size of a fund's stake reaches 7.5 percent, at which point the size of the stake also becomes significant on its own.

The second interesting result is the dampening effect of insider domination. This is visible on several levels. To begin with, insider domination of the companies in the fund's portfolio makes it less likely that the fund will participate in any executive dismissals: for each additional percent of companies that are more than 50 percent insider owned (which usually amounts to much less than one more insider dominated company), the dampening effect on the probability of an additional dismissal is about 2 (1.7 to 2.1) percent. Furthermore, the probability of a fund's involvement in any dismissals also decreases with the number of privatized companies among the fund's founders – a feature that, we conjectured, is a telltale of the "managerialist" nature of the fund itself[48] – and this effect is, in turn, much stronger for dismissals of more than one general director. Finally, if a fund lists management among its top three corporate allies, the dampening effect of this fact makes it in practice next to impossible for the fund to be involved in the dismissal of more than one general director in all the companies in its portfolio.[49]

The third interesting result is the already noted difference between the firing of one and more than one director. This difference can be seen from the fact that management friendliness is insignificant in the equation for a probability of dismissal of only one director (p-value, 0.65) and becomes (negatively) significant for the firing of two or more top executives. Similarly, as we have already noted, the dampening effect of the managerialist origins of a fund (having privatized companies among the founders) nearly doubles for the dismissals of more than one director. This probably means that, as we have conjectured, executive dismissals under Russian conditions often involve relatively uncontroversial cases of simple incompetence or dishonesty, rather than serious postprivatization restructuring. Having participated in a dismissal of a director in one company in one's portfolio, therefore, does not necessarily indicate anything special about the fund's involvement in fundamental changes at the company level. But the dismissal of a second or a third director is probably different: it might very well be an indication of an attempt at a more radical restructuring, which is likely to generate significant managerial opposition. Not surprisingly, therefore, manager friendly funds are not likely to engage in this kind of activity.

Given the overall very small number of executive dismissals in Russia, the model's estimates of marginal effects of various factors should be treated with appropriate caution. Firing of top managers is so rare that its effects are

[48] See the above section on the ownership structure of the funds.

[49] The dampening effect of manager friendliness (as measured by the listing of management among the fund's three top allies) on firing more than one director in all the companies in the fund's portfolio is -1.41. This is enough to outweigh the positive effect of a 3.5% increase in the size of the stake in the 4 to 7.5% bracket (3.5 x 0.41) and an 11.25% increase in the 7.5 to 18.75% bracket (11.25 x 0.12).

likely to be of no significance for the economy as a whole. But the model does reveal some tentative signs of restructuring in connection with the few cases of dismissals that do occur, and this may be a harbinger of some good news to come. If the pressure on the opening of Russian companies intensifies, the funds seem to represent outside forces interested in fundamental restructuring. Until that happens, however, voucher funds are unlikely to exercise sufficient influence to make a difference.

The funds play even less of a role in the process of downsizing employment (other than executive dismissals) in the notoriously overstaffed Russian firms. To be sure, an outside shareholder might not usually be actively involved in laying off nonmanagerial employees, but funds pursuing a consistent strategy of restructuring could be expected to insist on such changes. Only 11 percent (out of 136) of the funds in our survey, however, report dismissals of substantial numbers of employees in the companies in their portfolio, and the reports involve only 132 companies (including overlaps), that is 1.9 percent of the total in which the funds are invested. Although the funds may not be well informed about the overall instances of dismissals, it is certainly significant that in none of the cases in which dismissals occurred did a voucher fund play an active role.

Trading

Importance of Trading in Russia

We have explained already that compared with countries in which markets, especially capital markets, are more developed, one should expect more shareholder activism and less trading in the East European economies in transition. Despite this, trading is a surprisingly important activity of the Russian voucher funds, with 57 percent of the funds reporting that they are actively trading on the secondary market. One obvious reason is that, given insider domination of Russian firms, most forms of shareholder activism are blocked for outside investors. As a result, exit, even if liquidity is limited and the capital markets very imperfect, may often seem preferable to being locked into one's holdings without any realistic chance of exercising the option of voice. Indeed, we are faced with a somewhat paradoxical situation: by the funds' own admission, the shares they hold are largely illiquid, and yet liquidity was one of the main criteria of their acquisitions.[50]

Another factor contributing to high levels of trading among Russian funds

[50] Of all funds in the sample, 61.5% view liquidity as a very important investment criterion and a further 26.6% see it as moderately important.

Table 5.20. The Market for Shares (summer 1994)

	Funds (%)
Type of market on which the fund carries most of its trades	
Stock exchange	11.4
Private trades	88.6
Scope of market on which most of the fund's companies are traded	
National	39.5
Regional	36.0
Local	24.5
Average frequency with which the fund's companies are traded	
Irregular	59.4
Regular	40.6
(of which)	
Weekly	18.9
Monthly	9.9
Quarterly	11.8
Average percentage of the fund's companies traded	24.9

may be that, for reasons that need further investigation, the shares of many Russian companies were extremely undervalued in the early stages of the privatization process.[51] Large profits could thus be made from simply selling the stakes acquired at voucher auctions and from active trading on the secondary market.[52] This might have raised the opportunity cost of restructuring and additionally detracted from the incentives of Russian funds to become active shareholders.

While trading is an important activity of voucher funds, it is not one that comes without obstacles. Table 5.20 reflects the major features of the Russian capital market in the summer of 1994 as seen through the eyes of voucher funds.

The data confirm the obvious fact that capital markets are still very underdeveloped: most shares are traded off market, and the official stock markets play a rather minor role. Markets are also segmented, and the funds report that in a majority of cases shares of their companies are traded on either a

[51] Lack of confidence in the success of the program may have played a role, as well as no belief that the insiders of Russian companies would ever respect the rights of outside owners (Frydman and Rapaczynski 1994, ch. 6). Nontransparency of the decentralized auctions, often *de facto* excluding many potential bidders, may have also contributed to the low price levels.

[52] Of the 103 funds that decreased their stakes in some companies, 63% cited the opportunity of making large profits as their reason.

regional or a strictly local market. Indeed, most funds report no regular trade in their companies' shares: their trades are simply triggered by demand from a domestic or foreign investor attempting to gain control,[53] with most voucher funds merely free-riding on such events.

Effects of Insider Domination on Securities Trading

In addition to the weak development of capital markets, Russian traders also face other obstacles related to the insider domination of privatized firms. As evidenced in Table 5.21, the funds have been largely unable to tap the pool of shares held by insiders, and they trade mostly among themselves, with some shares also bought from other outsiders (domestic companies and banks). Managers do not seem to be selling at all, and workers are seen as largely inactive or only moderately active sellers.

The obstacles encountered by the funds are particularly serious when they attempt to increase stakes in companies in their portfolios (see Table 5.22). Interestingly enough, cash constraints to increasing stakes are cited by only 43.5 percent of the funds. Indeed, even this number is misleading because the cash-poor funds are smaller than the rest (measured by the number of vouchers collected, they amount to 20.1 percent of all the funds), while larger funds, perhaps as a result of ties to other financial institutions or because of gains made in voucher trading, seem to have much more cash than is often believed. But the funds cite other difficulties to increasing stakes, with 47 funds (43.5 percent of all who attempted to increase stakes) reporting that management's efforts to prevent workers from selling are among the most important barriers. In addition, 27.8 percent report that management (illegally) refuses to register transfers of shares to outsiders, and 22.2 percent claim that the market they trade in is controlled by the management.

The question of managerial coercion as a factor in preventing workers from selling their shares deserves a closer examination. As noted earlier, the architects of the Russian program hoped that most workers would quickly sell their shares in order to cash in on the large premiums resulting from the fact that they had acquired them almost without payment. This, in turn, was supposed to allow more outside investors to come in as shareholders and to mitigate the insider domination of privatized firms following the politically motivated concessions at the design stage.

[53] Fifty percent of all funds in the sample and 85.9% of those funds that say that shares in the companies they invest in are traded irregularly report that these are the main reasons for trades to occur.

Table 5.21. Share Acquisitions by Funds from Other Shareholders
(in percentages)

Type of shareholder	Very active in selling shares	Moderately active	Not active or generally unwilling to sell
Other voucher funds	50.8	31.1	18.1
Domestic commercial entities	22.1	33.6	44.3
Workers	21.3	32.8	45.9
Banks and other financial institutions	13.1	25.4	61.5
Domestic individual investors	12.3	40.2	47.5
Managers	2.5	3.3	94.3
Foreign investors	0.8	2.5	96.7

Table 5.22. Obstacles to the Funds' Increasing Their Stakes
(in percentages)

Obstacles	Percentage of those funds that tried to increase their stakes
Financial difficulties	
General lack of capital	43.5
Outside investors drive up share prices	32.4
Other difficulties	
Management prevents workers from selling	43.5
Employees are unwilling to sell	33.3
Outside investors are unwilling to sell	29.6
Management refuses to register share transfers in the shareholder register	27.8
Management or management controlled entities control market	22.2

As we have seen, the hoped for quick sell-off is clearly not happening (although there is some evidence of more modest selling activity). The usual explanation is the one that the funds give in their responses: workers are not selling because managers are making it impossible for them. Anecdotal and other evidence indicates that although formal voting-trust arrangements are rare, managers in fact use their power not only to persuade but also to coerce workers not to sell by threatening dismissals of those who defy them, as well as by controlling the shareholder register and illegally threatening not to record ownership changes resulting from insider sales.[54]

To the extent this story is correct, one could expect perhaps that better protection of minority rights, especially enforcement of basic rules concerning voting and share registration, might "emancipate" the workers, who are collectively the largest shareholders in nearly every Russian firm, and put them in a better position to sell their shares. To be sure, such enfranchisement might also bring greater worker participation in the governance of privatized enterprises – which most observers do not find an attractive prospect – but the level of worker organization required for an effective exercise of worker control might not be present.

It seems, however, that while the story of managerial coercion is certainly a part of the picture, it is most likely not the whole story. For in fact, managerial coercion, which might be hard to explain given the relatively low levels of managerial ownership, might simply function to organize the workers and help them overcome collective action problems that they face in achieving objectives they themselves desire. Assume that the workers are primarily interested in the security of their employment and that the managers are primarily interested in retaining their control, which they can do by preventing the workers from selling their shares and making sure that the shares are voted for the management. But in this case, the managers also have a clear interest in the security of their workers' employment, since once the workers leave the company, they are much more likely to sell their shares. By the same token, the employees also have an interest in not selling their shares, since that keeps the management interested in keeping them employed. But unless management fires those workers who sell their shares, the workers face a free-rider problem, since cash-strapped individuals may try to cash in on their premiums. If many do so, the interest (and to the extent outsiders come in as new buyers, the power) of the management in maintaining employment diminishes. Managerial coercion may thus simply enforce an implicit (or even explicit) agreement among the workers to refrain from selling.[55]

[54] A special presidential decree (Presidential Decree No. 1768, 27 October 1993, On Strengthening Shareholder Rights) was issued to curtail these kinds of abuses. Among other provisions, it required companies to release the control of their shareholder registers. But, as reported by *Kommersant Weekly* (No. 7, 28 February 1995, p. 42), a study, sponsored by the newly formed Russian Securities and Exchange Commission, of shareholder registration in the 3,400 largest open joint stock companies found that 44% of the companies have held on to their shareholder registers. Moreover, companies have proved quite inventive in requiring a number of documents with and without notarial certification as a prerequisite to registering a new shareholder.

[55] The fact that 33.3% of funds cite that "workers are unwilling to sell," in addition to all the reasons relating to managerial coercion (see Table 5.22), may be an indirect confirmation of the independent employee interest in maintaining a high level of insider ownership.

If this account of managerial coercion is accepted, then measures intended to protect minority rights, even if enforced, are not likely to be fully effective, and formal voting trusts may become more common.[56] A more likely engine of change may be a decisive hardening of budget constraints of privatized enterprises and an increasingly competitive environment that may come about as a result of firmer macroeconomic policy. If a tough macro policy were to be sustainable over a long enough time, even in the face of increasing pressure from enterprises for renewed support, it might force the privatized firms to lower their costs and increase their need for new capital. This, in turn, may lead management, despite its desire to maintain control, to issue new shares to outside investors and to lay off workers, who will then become outsiders (and probably be willing to sell their shares to more active investors). Until such changes occur, the insider domination of Russian firms is likely to persist.

There is, however, evidence in our survey that the funds *are* trying to increase their stakes on the secondary market and that they are quite successful in doing this. Thus, 75 percent of the funds in our sample attempted to increase their stakes in at least some companies in their portfolios: including overlaps, the number of the companies involved was 1,096, and the funds' success rate in increasing their stakes was 79.5 percent.

In order to sort out why voucher funds, despite the numerous difficulties they cite, can nevertheless report such high rates of success in expanding their stakes, we specified an equation modeling the impact of various factors on the success rate of the funds in increasing their original stakes on the secondary market (see Table 5.23).

The model shows quite clearly that overall the funds are able to increase their stakes because they trade with other funds. Indeed, the significance of the funds' trading activity for the ability to increase stakes is the only one that remains regardless of the impact of trading by any other groups listed in Table 5.21: even though our equation included dummy variables for the selling activity of these groups, their impact (which we did not report in Table 5.23) was insignificant. In particular, overall the impact of workers' selling their shares is insignificant as well – indeed, it is probably even less important than Table 5.23 might suggest, because the workers' trading is not clearly separated from trading by the funds. When dummy variable #2 is split into two complementary components – the first defined as taking the value of 1 whenever workers are active sellers and the funds are not, and the

[56] Forbidding such trusts, which would leave workers without legal means of enforcing their collective action decisions, might have some effect. But then it might also increase the pressure for extralegal enforcement mechanisms.

Table 5.23. Success in Increasing Stakes through Purchases on the Secondary Market

Explanatory variables	Dependent variable No. of companies in which the fund increased its stake by buying shares on the secondary market[a]
Number of companies in the fund's portfolio	0.04 (0.03)
Dummy variable #1: =1, If other funds are active sellers[b]	2.36 (0.09)
Dummy variable #2: =1, If workers are active sellers[b]	1.65 (0.17)
R-square	0.55
Number of observations	56

[a] OLS estimates; *p*-values in parentheses.
[b] = 0, otherwise.

second as taking the value of 1 whenever both the funds and workers are active sellers – the coefficient for the former becomes still smaller (.91) and the significance level drops even further (*p*-value, 0.49). The selling by the workers is significant (coefficient: 5.0; *p*-value, 0.08) only in those very few cases (5.7 percent) in which the funds are not active sellers – a negligible impact overall.

Once again, the picture that emerges from this model shows that the hoped for sell-off by insiders is not taking place. But independently of any flow of shares from insiders to outsiders, an important reallocation of holdings is taking place among the funds themselves, and this factor probably contributes to the strengthening of the funds' overall position. Indeed, the extent to which funds seem to be able to "trade upwards" into a position of being the largest shareholder is quite amazing: as shown in Table 5.24, which models the determinants of the funds' ability to become the largest shareholders of companies in their portfolios, every successful attempt by a fund to increase its stakes increases by over 40 percent the chances that the fund will also become the largest shareholder in one of the companies in its portfolio. (The success in increasing stakes also drives out all other potential explanatory variables in the equation reported in Table 5.24.) Given the concentration of ownership in Russian companies, in which management and the state always hold significant stakes, and the generally

Table 5.24. Changes in the Funds' Ownership Stakes through Purchases of Shares on the Secondary Market

Explanatory variables	Dependent variable: No. of companies in fund's portfolio in which fund is the largest shareholder[a]
Total no. of companies in the fund's portfolio	0.03 (0.02)
No. of companies in which fund increased its stake by buying shares on the secondary market	0.42
R-squared	0.54
Number of observations	57

[a] OLS estimates; *p*-values in parentheses.

low levels of liquidity, the reallocation of influence that is taking place through trading among the funds looks impressive. To be sure, we have seen (in the previous section) that this influence is far too modest to amount to control; nevertheless, the consolidation of holdings shows that trading does contribute to the strengthening of the voucher funds' position in corporate affairs.

The Determinants of the Funds' Trading Activity

We have already hypothesized that despite the low levels of liquidity among Russian companies, many funds trade because their attempts to become active shareholders in the companies in their portfolio are blocked by the insider domination of Russian companies, and that the incentive to trade has been additionally strengthened by the high profits that many traders realized by selling companies acquired at very low prices during the initial voucher auctions. The estimates of a logistic equation modeling the determinants of a fund's decision to engage in active trading, which are presented in Table 5.25, generally confirm our conjectures. The model shows that the decision to engage in active trading is essentially a function of four different factors: (1) the fund's alliance with management of companies in the fund's portfolio, (2) the ability of the fund to engage in shareholder activism (as measured by the number of board seats obtained by the fund), (3) the number of traded companies in the fund's portfolio,

Table 5.25. Determinants of a Fund's Decision to Engage in Active Trading

Explanatory variables	Dependent variable Probability that fund has been actively trading shares on the secondary market[a]
No. of companies in the fund's portfolio for those that report that the management is among their top three allies	–0.03 (0.02)
No. of companies in which the fund is represented on the board of directors	–0.07 (0.12)
No. of companies in the fund's portfolio that are traded.	15 (0.05)
For the funds that report they were able to make large profits from selling a block of shares	0.15 (0.03)
Likelihood ratio statistic[b]	23 (0.0004)
Association of predicted and observed probabilities	84%
Number of observations	59

[a] Maximum likelihood estimates of logistic equation; asymptotic p-values in parentheses.
[b] Chi-squared with covariates.

and (4) the fund's ability to make large profits by selling a block of shares of one or more companies in its portfolio. Of these explanatory variables, the first two have a negative impact on the probability that a fund will engage in active trading, and the last two have the opposite (positive) effect.

Although the *p*-value for the negative correlation between board seats and a decision to engage in active trading is borderline, the coefficient is quite high: for each company in which a fund has a board seat, the fund is 7 percent less likely to trade actively in any companies in its portfolio (and not just the company in which it is represented on the board). This seems to show that shareholder activism has a strong pull as an overall portfolio management strategy and that the strength of the obstacles to activism (voice) is indeed responsible for the funds' decision to trade (exit).

Another, to some extent related, portfolio management strategy that dampens the funds' propensity to trade is their widespread promanagerial attitude. Given that most Russian companies are both illiquid and insider-dominated (particularly management-dominated, with the two phenomena being obviously related), most funds (as we have seen in Table 5.17) try to ally themselves with the management of the companies in their portfolios. Some of the funds adopting this strategy, especially those that had privatized companies among their founders, may have started out as "managerialist"; others may have simply adopted this attitude because they came to be locked into very illiquid portfolios and learned that they had no other viable option. In any case, management friendliness, like shareholder activism,[57] seems to be an overall portfolio management strategy, so that the addition of a nontraded company to a fund's portfolio *lessens* the chance that the fund will engage in active trading in *any* of the companies in which it is invested.[58]

The most direct constraint on trading activity in Russia results, of course, from the limited liquidity of the securities market: on average, under 25 percent of the companies in the funds' portfolios are traded at all, and most of those are traded locally and irregularly (see Table 5.20). Since the funds had a limited ability to pick liquid companies to begin with (it was not even known at the time of most voucher actions which companies would trade on the secondary market), many ended up with portfolios that were sufficiently illiquid to discourage them from the initial investment necessary to develop a capacity to engage in active trading. But the model shows that a very small number of traded companies in one's portfolio are necessary for nonmanagement friendly funds to begin active trading: the addition of just four liquid companies increases the probability of becoming an active trader by 60 percent. (Even for management friendly funds, the addition of only five liquid companies has the same effect.) One thing this means is that engaging in any sort of trading leads very quickly to becoming an "active" trader: since by definition shares of companies acquired on the secondary market are traded, just a few such acquisitions are enough to move one up into this category.[59]

[57] Although our model indicates that the two are distinct factors, they may, of course, be closely related under the very special Russian conditions – it is enough to remember that most funds list cooperation with management among the most important factors in obtaining a board seat.

[58] This effect dissipates after a threshold of portfolio liquidity is reached: when the proportion of traded companies in a fund's portfolio reaches some 20% ([10]% for funds that also made large profits from trade), further addition of illiquid companies no longer decreases the fund's propensity to trade. For funds that do not list management among its allies, the addition of a nontraded company has no significant effect on trading activity.

[59] The concept of "active trading" was not defined in the questionnaire: the funds were simply asked whether they were "actively trading shares on the secondary market." It is possible, therefore, that the funds perceive themselves as "actively trading" at a lower level of activity than would be normal in another environment. It is also possible that the funds' responses were shaped by an environment of mid-1994, in which trading was much less common. At the initial voucher auctions, when the funds could not really predict which shares would become liquid, one needed to acquire, on average, 20 companies to increase by five the number of traded companies in one's portfolio – a very significant number, given that the median number of companies per fund in the sample is 35.

Finally, the initial undervaluation of shares at the voucher auctions seems to have given a tremendous boost to trading activity in Russia. As the model shows, the mere fact of having made significant profits from a sale of a block of shares of one or more companies in one's portfolio is enough to double the already high impact of the addition of one traded company to one's portfolio, bringing it to 30 percent. In practice, the large profits made from cashing in on the premiums resulting from the initial undervaluation of the Russian companies are themselves nearly enough to make a fund engage in "active trading."

Large Funds

The overall size distribution of Russian voucher funds, as measured by the number of vouchers invested (see Table 5.3, above), resembles a pyramid with a few very large funds at the top and many small and medium-size funds filling in the rest. Indeed, the largest fund (First Voucher Fund) is twice as large as the second and the third, respectively, and these two are each more than twice as large as the fourth largest fund. Only below the 500,000-voucher level does the field become somewhat more densely populated. (See Table 5.26.)

Beyond the top ten funds, the 36 largest funds, constituting the first quartile of our sample, invested 83.1 percent of all the vouchers in the sample. These funds also have on average significantly more companies in their portfolios: 69.9 for the funds in the first quartile; 42.3 for the remaining funds (p-value, 0.02).[60]

The large funds, including the few giants at the top, deserve special attention. Their very size makes them into a potentially very powerful force on the Russian economic scene. But in addition to their economic significance, they are also important politically. If, for example, the large funds were to turn out to be more management-friendly or more oriented toward rent seeking than the rest, they might be quite effective in organizing a powerful lobby to

[60] According to an estimate obtained from a regression on the number of companies and the number of vouchers, every time a fund invests an additional 100,000 vouchers, an additional two companies are added to its portfolio. But the differential in the number of companies held by the large and small funds is much smaller than that in the number of vouchers: the large funds hold 83% of the vouchers, and only 36% of the companies in the funds' portfolios. Even correcting for the fact that, on average, they also hold larger stakes (see below), the bigger funds seem to have invested in much more expensive companies. Whether their participation in voucher auctions bid up the share prices or whether they concentrated on more valuable companies (or both), we were unable to determine.

Table 5.26. Size of the Largest Funds

Top 10 funds in sample	No. of vouchers invested
Largest	4,000,000
Second largest	2,000,000
Third largest	1,880,000
Fourth largest	800,000
Fifth largest	551,185
Sixth largest	512,000
Seventh largest	500,000
Eighth largest	450,000
Ninth largest	397,000
Tenth largest	395,000
Total no. of vouchers invested by top 10 funds	11,485,185
As % of total collected by all funds in the sample	56%

protect the entrenchment of insiders or to keep the state in the business of dispensing its largess. Indeed, these funds might replace the old industrial associations (the elimination of which was among the main objectives of the voucher program) and help the companies they hold overcome the collective action problems they now face in lobbying the government for continued subsidies and other forms of support. Moreover, large funds, locked into their holdings in many nonviable production companies, might make it more difficult to close down the nonperforming industrial albatrosses, since any attempts at such retrenchment would mean not only laying off many thousands of workers, but also bankrupting the large funds with millions of shareholders. But, if the large funds are likely to bet on the economic success of their companies, they might become the leading agents of restructuring and supporters of further reform.[61]

To get an overview of the character of the large funds, we have compared them to the rest of the sample along most dimensions discussed in this chapter. The results of these comparisons are shown in Tables 5.27 through 5.29, which list all cases in which the differences were statistically significant.

The overall picture of the large funds that emerges from our comparisons is quite reassuring. The large funds, as investors, have significantly more cash (Table 5.29), better access to information (Table 5.27), and more sophisti-

[61] For a discussion of the political economy of privatization investment funds, see Frydman and Rapaczynski (1994), especially ch. 6.

Table 5.27. Investment Criteria and Access to Information of Large Funds

Investment criterion	Very important[a]		Not important		*p*-value
	Large funds	All others	Large funds	All others	
Quality of production equipment	47.06	47.31	0	12.9	0.07
Profitability	41.2	74.2	8.8	4.3	0.00
Business connections with other companies in the fund's portfolio	44.12	33.3	17.7	35.5	0.09
Expected cooperation with management to overcome employee resistance	17.7	38.7	32.4	29.0	0.06
Access to nonstate sources of finance	14.71	10.8	44.1	66.7	0.06

Access to financial information	Large funds	All others	*p*-value
Funds with regular access to financial data in all or most of companies in their portfolios	66.7	45.6	0.03
Additional information always available upon request (vs. rarely or never)	64.0	43.6	0.08
% of funds monitoring companies in their portfolios by means other than board participation	91.7	71.6	0.01
Means by which funds monitor companies in their portfolios			
Review of financial data	91.4	69.5	0.01
Informal sources	89.7	65.5	0.01
Share prices	88.0	65.5	0.03
Volume of output	85.7	58.6	0.02

[a] Percentage of funds listing each criterion as being in the "very important" category. Number of valid responses for each row is 127.

Table 5.28. Data Pertaining to the Activism of Large Funds

	Large funds	All others	*p*-value
Average % stake held	9.35	6.0	0.00
Average % of companies in a fund's portfolio in which fund is the largest shareholder	14.2	7.1	0.08
Average % of companies in a fund's portfolio in which fund is represented on the board	23.7	14.2	0.02
	Percentage of funds		
Companies in a fund's portfolio in which fund is an active investor[a]			
None	5.6	25.2	
Some	63.9	65.0	0.00[b]
Majority	27.8	7.8	
All	1.9	2.8	
% of funds that attempted to increase their initial stakes	86.1	70.1	0.07
Average % of companies in a fund's portfolio in which fund attempted to increase its stakes	28.6	15.4	0.02
Types of service provided by a fund			
Investment expertise	76.5	58.2	0.06
Expertise in restructuring or reorganizing the company	67.7	46.8	0.04
Arranging access to foreign customers	38.2	16.7	0.01
Arranging access to foreign suppliers	29.4	15.4	0.09
Arranging access to credits			
Access to domestic non-state credits	55.9	35.4	0.04
Extending credit to company	29.4	13.8	0.05
Access to state credits	23.5	11.4	0.1
Attitudes toward other shareholders as 1 of the 3 most cooperative shareholders			
Management	56.7	70.7	0.09
Voucher funds	53.1	68.5	0.08
Foreign financial investors	18.8	7.6	0.07
Foreign trade investors	9.4	2.1	0.08

[a] A fund is considered to be an "active investor" if it spends significant resources and/or effort on monitoring and/or influencing major decisions, such as employment, investment, structure of production, sales, organization, etc.

[b] *p*-value for the test of "none or some" versus "majority or all."

Table 5.29. Obstacles Experienced by Funds Attempting to Increase Their Stakes

Obstacles	% of funds among those that tried to increase stakes		*p*-value
	Large funds	All others	
Financial difficulties			
General lack of capital	22.2	49.5	0.00
Other difficulties			
Management refuses to register share transfers in the shareholder register	30.6	18.5	0.08

cated criteria for choosing the companies in their portfolios (Table 5.27). In picking their companies, they look much less at the notoriously unreliable profitability figures and concentrate instead on such fundamentals as the quality of equipment, access to nonstate sources of credit (indicating financial soundness), and business connections to other companies in their portfolios. (To be sure, this last criterion may also be a sign of recreating old vertical inter-enterprise connections, but such an interpretation is unlikely in light of the other characteristics of large funds. Instead, looking at business connections as a criterion for investment is more likely an effort to capitalize on the funds' expertise in certain areas or an attempt to exploit potential synergies among the companies in one's portfolio.)

Once large funds invest in a company, they are much more likely to keep well informed about it. They manage to obtain financial data of most companies in their portfolios[62] and uniformly use all available means to supplement the information provided by the management with that obtained from other sources. Perhaps most encouragingly, large funds are both more active as shareholders and less management friendly than the smaller funds.

The activism of large funds manifests itself in a variety of ways. Even correcting for their larger portfolios, they are represented on many more boards of directors, and they are more likely to provide a large array of services to their companies. What may be of particular importance in Russia is that they seem to be among the very few institutions with foreign connections, and they often report making those connections available to the companies in their portfolios.

[62] The 10 largest funds are even more successful than the rest: all of them report regular access in all or most of their companies.

The enhanced shareholder activism of large funds has several explanations. These funds are bigger and richer, and they are more likely to be able to afford the significant costs of monitoring. They also hold on average significantly larger stakes and are much more often the largest shareholders in their companies (Table 5.28), which gives them more power to make their influence felt. Perhaps most importantly, their very size is likely to have resulted in their acquiring rather large stakes in many illiquid companies. It must be remembered that the large funds often had a huge number of vouchers that they had to invest in a very short time,[63] and the nature of the supply simply did not allow them very much choice. Once such funds acquired their portfolios, they were probably largely locked in and had no other option but to try to maximize their value by becoming actively involved. This explanation is further confirmed by the fact that large funds are not particularly active traders, except for attempts to increase stakes in the companies in which they are already invested.

Interestingly, large funds are significantly less management friendly than the rest. They list management much more rarely among their top three corporate allies;[64] they cite much less often their connections to management as a reason for investment; and they report greater management hostility toward them, particularly the frequency with which management tries to prevent them from increasing their stakes by refusing to register share transfers in the shareholder register. Consequently, their shareholder activism may be of particular importance for the improvement of the performance of the companies in their portfolios.

Concluding Remarks

Filling the gap created by the withdrawal of the state from the commanding position of control over industry in Eastern Europe has constituted one of the most challenging problems of transition to an efficiently functioning market economy. Beyond many difficult conceptual and implementation problems, a massive transfer of assets in Russia and other East European countries has often required political support from enterprise insiders (managers and workers). While granting substantial benefits to the insiders

[63] Vouchers were originally to expire at the end of 1993 after only slightly more than 12 months. However, a presidential decree issued in October 1993 extended this deadline until 1 July 1994. See Presidential Decree No. 1591, 6 October 1993.

[64] It is perhaps worth noting that the large funds' attitude toward management seems to be quite bipolar. Thus, among the top 10 funds, five list management as their chief ally, while none of the rest lists it among their top *three* allies.

has softened their resistance to privatization and has very likely been crucial for a speedy transfer of assets from the state, Russia stands out as an example of how such *ex ante* political concessions may weaken the effectiveness of postprivatization corporate governance mechanisms and delay badly needed enterprise- and economy-wide restructuring. The future of the Russian economy depends largely on whether new outside owners, among whom voucher privatization funds studied in this chapter are potentially the most important, will be able to effect substantial improvement in the allocation of resources, now often opposed by the insider owners. Our results show that although there are many hopeful signs, Russia still has a long way to go before the privatization experiment accomplishes its ultimate objectives.

Appendix: Methodological Note

A number of tables in the chapter report the results of estimation of a series of relationships among a subset of variables measuring various aspects of funds' activities, particularly those related to trading and shareholder activism. We confine our multivariate statistical analysis to single-equation models. This may ignore simultaneity problems in some cases, but we believe that these problems are not serious. The models are estimated on the basis of a complete subsample of 59 to 69 respondents with nonmissing answers to survey questions concerning variables included in the estimated models. The use of this subsample in the estimation does not seem to introduce any apparent bias, since the relative frequency distributions of key characteristics, such as the size of funds or the number of insider-dominated companies in their portfolios, are very similar in the subsample to the distributions of the same characteristics in the whole sample of survey responses (148 funds).

We estimated two types of models: regression models and logistic equations. To avoid data mining, we tried to estimate the most parsimonious and simplest specifications motivated by clear prior theoretical considerations. Products of variables, including interactive dummies, were included only if they were thought to capture an important aspect of the estimated relationship. Such interactive variables and other products often turned out to be significant and provided some of the more interesting interpretations of the survey responses.

The reported equations include only variables that turned out to be significant. Whenever an interactive dummy was used, the complement was also tested, and if it is not presented, it turned out to be insignificant.

We also tested the overall fit of the estimated equations. For regression models this involved a conventional F-test and an examination of the stability of coefficients of retained variables when other variables were added to the equations. We examined studentized residuals to detect outliers and other specification problems. The reported equations seem free of any serious misspecifications.

For logistic equations, we were forced to rely on asymptotic likelihood ratio tests. These were supplemented by an examination of the Akaike Information Criterion and various measures of association between the predicted and observed probabilities. We also looked at the stability of estimated coefficients in the presence of additional variables. The selected models were superior to the rest according to a number of these criteria and seem to provide a good fit to the data.

References

Boycko, Maxim, Andrzej Shleifer, and Robert Vishny. 1995. *Privatizing Russia.* Cambridge, Mass.: Massachusetts Institute of Technology (MIT) Press.

Frydman, Roman, Andrzej Rapaczynski, and John Earle. 1993. *Privatization Process in Russia, Ukraine and the Baltic States.* Budapest: Central European University Press (in cooperation with Oxford University Press).

Frydman, Roman, and Andrzej Rapaczynski. 1994. *Privatization in Eastern Europe. Is the State Withering Away?* Budapest: Central European University Press (in cooperation with Oxford University Press).

6

THE POTENTIAL ROLE OF PENSION FUNDS
Lessons from OECD and Developing Countries

DIMITRI VITTAS and ROLAND MICHELITSCH

Our special thanks, with the usual disclaimer, are due to Dale Hanson and Cheryl Gray.

Introduction

Writers discussing the role of pension funds in corporate governance in Central European countries (the Czech Republic, Hungary, and Poland) and Russia are faced with two major difficulties. First, large funded pension plans are lacking in all these countries (as well as in all other East European countries and former Soviet republics). Second, even in countries that have long had funded pension plans and where pension funds have long become major institutional investors, the role of pension funds in corporate governance has been renowned for its passivity. Pension fund managers have traditionally been expected to vote with company management or sell their shares if they were unhappy with management's performance. Only in recent years have pension funds started to be forcefully involved in corporate affairs. But there is considerable uncertainty about the direction, form, and impact of their involvement, and there are also many unresolved policy and regulatory issues.

The most pressing and challenging task facing transitional economies today is enterprise restructuring. Clearly, or perhaps hopefully, the major part of the first phase of such restructuring will have been completed before pension funds can become large enough to deserve to play a part in the process. Thus, in the short to medium term the burden of enterprise restructuring and the leading role in corporate governance is likely to fall on the state, the banks, the investment funds, the managers, and the workers. All these and in some cases foreign companies and individual investors are likely to be the major owners of large corporations.

The social security and pension systems of all four countries are in deep trouble and in need of fundamental reform. This reform should include the restructuring and downsizing of public pension systems and the establishment of supplementary private pension funds. But even if pension reform were to be implemented immediately, pension funds commanding large financial resources and, therefore, able to become substantial company shareholders would take several years to develop. Large pension funds with a key role in enterprise restructuring and corporate governance would emerge in the immediate future only in the unlikely event of a massive transfer of equity stakes in privatized enterprises to newly created pension funds. Such a transfer would be inadvisable given the lack of financial expertise and the weakness of capital market institutions, but it is being discussed in some countries.

Although pension funds are unlikely to play a major part in enterprise restructuring soon, actions taken over the next few years will shape their future role in corporate governance and will also affect the financial health of both the corporate sector and the pension systems of each country. This chapter discusses the prospects for pension reform in these four countries and the factors that could influence the behavior of pension funds in the financial system and their role in corporate governance.

The Prospects of Pension Reform in Central Europe and Russia

Public Pension Systems

Common Features

The countries of Eastern Europe and the former Soviet Union have inherited social pension systems that have several features in common.[1] Perhaps the most common feature is that the social pension systems of all these countries are simultaneously faced with a growing financial crisis and a failure to provide adequate incomes to the vast majority of their pensioners. Other common features include: a largely monopillar "pay-as-you-go" structure (but with special regimes that benefit privileged workers); near universal coverage; high levels of expenditure as a percentage of gross domestic

[1] Fox (1994) discusses some of these common features. See also Holzmann (1994).

product (GDP); very high system dependency ratios (caused by low retirement ages and lax certification of disability pensions); high contribution rates; high targeted but unrealized replacement rates; deficient benefit formulas (including actuarially unfair provisions, short assessment periods, and falling accrual rates); imperfect inflation indexation; considerable scope for strategic manipulation; limited but growing evasion; and growing arrears.

Demographic Aging and Dependency Ratios.

Attention is frequently drawn to the demographic aging, not only of Central and Eastern European countries but also of advanced Organization for Economic Cooperation and Development (OECD) countries, and the problems that this will create for social security systems. The financial problem of aging will be upon us some 30 years from now if no action is taken to avert a financial crisis. But no country in the world can today be described as old since nowhere are those over 65 much more than 20 percent of the total population. And no country has a demographic old age dependency ratio (as distinct from a system dependency ratio) that is much higher than 35 percent.

Progressive demographic aging, caused by falling birth rates and longer life expectancy, will of course intensify the financial strains of pension systems. But demographic aging will affect funded schemes as much as pay-as-you-go (PAYG) ones, since the proportion of output that will be consumed by retired people is more important than how this will be financed (Barr 1992, Vittas 1993b).

The more pressing problems confronting the social pension systems of Central and East European countries stem from faulty design issues and structural factors that are independent of progressive demographic aging. All four countries have much higher system than demographic old age dependency ratios.[2] In 1992 the system dependency ratios were 46 percent in Russia, 49 percent in the Czech Republic and Poland, and 59 percent in Hungary. In contrast the respective demographic old age dependency ratios were 31 percent, 32 percent, 28 percent, and 36 percent. Thus, the gap between the two ratios was 15 percent in Russia, 17 percent in the Czech Republic, 21 percent in Poland, and 23 percent in Hungary.[3] See Table 6.1.

[2] For summary data on dependency ratios, contribution and replacement rates, future demographic structures, and other aspects of the public pension systems of the four countries reviewed in this chapter, see Table 6.4.

[3] The reported ratios are estimates and are not based on hard data because the pension systems of the four countries have weak records. There are also some conceptual and definitional problems with the data, such as the proper treatment of survivors' and disability

Table 6.1. System and Demographic Old Age Dependency Ratios, 1992

	SDR[a]	DDR[b]	Gap
Czech Republic	49	32	17
Hungary	59	36	23
Poland	49	28	21
Russia	46	31	15
United States	31	30	1
Switzerland	43	34	9

Source World Bank staff estimates.

[a] SDR: System Dependency Ratio (the number of pensioners, including widows, orphans, and disability pensioners, divided by the number of contributors).

[b] DDR: Demographic Old Age Dependency Ratio (the number of people 60 years and over divided by people between 20 and 59 years).

This high discrepancy between the two ratios is caused by the inclusion of surviving spouses and orphans among the beneficiaries, early retirement provisions for selected occupations or industries (miners, heavy industry, etc.), special provisions for working women, lax certification of disability pensions, unemployment, and evasion. Disability pensions accounted for 32 percent of the total in Poland and 27 percent in Hungary. Poland has a normal retirement age of 65 for men and 60 for women, yet the average retirement age is 57.5 years. For comparison, Argentina and other Latin American countries (e.g. Brazil) also suffer from large discrepancies between their system and demographic dependency ratios.

In some of the more advanced OECD countries, where social security systems are better designed and less exposed to strategic manipulation, the difference between system and demographic dependency ratios is much smaller. Thus, the difference between the two ratios is only 1 percent in the United States and 9 percent in Switzerland. However, the figures for the demographic dependency ratios for the United States and Switzerland are slightly misleading because the normal retirement age in these two countries is higher than 60. The high discrepancy in Switzerland is caused by the use of disability pensions as a way to tackle unemployment. Disability pensions represent 27 percent of total pensions, while in the United States they are less than 11 percent of the total. It should also be noted that Austria and Germany, two advanced OECD countries with quite large social pension

pensions. Including widows, orphans, and disability pensioners in the total number of beneficiaries inflates the system dependency ratio but lowers the average replacement rate. A rise in unemployment and evasion may also increase the system dependency ratio. System dependency ratios may vary significantly from year to year.

systems, have a discrepancy between system and demographic dependency ratios that is closer to that observed for Hungary and Poland, though exact figures cannot be easily calculated because of the number of programs.

Replacement and Contribution Rates

The four systems have very high targeted replacement rates. The statutory rate for workers who contribute for the minimum number of years[4] varied from 50 percent in the Czech Republic to 55 percent in Poland and Russia, to 63 percent in Hungary. In addition the maximum replacement rate for workers with longer contribution periods was 75 percent in Hungary, Poland, and Russia, and 78 percent in the Czech Republic. In practice, however, the average replacement rate (i.e. the average pension as a percentage of the average wage) was much lower, ranging from 34 percent in Russia to 49 percent in the Czech Republic and Hungary. Poland had a surprisingly high average replacement rate of 74 percent.[5]

The lower average replacement rate is caused by early retirement and dependent pensions as well as by the failure to fully index pensions to inflation. In Poland the high replacement rate is attributed to the large upward adjustment of pensions effected in 1991 and the subsequent indexation of pensions to average wages. The average replacement rate is also expected to increase in Hungary in the future, following the recent indexation of pensions to (net) wages. Switzerland and the United States report average replacement rates of 27 percent and 31 percent respectively.

Nominal contribution rates for pensions are also very high in all four countries. In 1992 they ranged from 27.2 percent of nominal wages in the Czech Republic to 30 percent in Poland, 30.5 percent in Hungary, and 32.6 percent in Russia. However, the effective contribution rates were much lower because the lion's share of contributions was paid by employers. Employers paid 20.4 percent of nominal wages in the Czech Republic, 24.5 percent in Hungary, 30 percent in Poland (i.e. 100 percent of pension contributions), and 31.6 percent in Russia. In the United States and Switzerland the nominal contribution rates, which are divided equally between employers and employees, are 12.4 and 9.6 percent respectively. In Switzerland the federal government and the cantons jointly contribute 3.3 percent of payroll for the

[4] The minimum contribution period is 25 years for men and women except for Poland and Russia where for women it is 20 years.

[5] These are nominal replacement rates (i.e. they relate the average pension to the average nominal wage). They can be misleading in the same way as nominal contribution rates. Expressing the average pension as a percentage of the average net wage (i.e. net of the pension contribution) shows that while the average net replacement rate remains at 74% in Poland and 34% in Russia, it rises to 52% in Hungary and 53% in the Czech Republic.

Table 6.2. Required and Nominal Contribution Rates, 1992

	SDR[a]	ARR[b]	RCR[c]	NCR[d]
Czech Republic	49	49	24	27.2
Hungary	59	49	29	30.5
Poland	49	74	36	30.0
Russia	46	34	16	32.6
United States	31	31	9.6	12.4
Switzerland	43	27	11.6	9.6

Source: World Bank staff estimates.
[a] SDR: System Dependency Ratio.
[b] ARR: Average Replacement Rate.
[c] RCR: Required Contribution Rate (for break even).
[d] NCR: Nominal Contribution Rate.

old age and disability pensions, while employers and employees share equally in contributing 8.4 percent of payroll for old age pensions and another 1.2 percent for disability pensions. As a matter of policy and system design, 20 percent of old age pensions and 50 percent of disability pensions are financed by the state.

Effective contribution rates, which are obtained by dividing total pension contributions by the nominal wage augmented by the employers' contributions, ranged from 23 percent in the Czech Republic and Poland to 24 percent in Hungary and 25 percent in Russia. These are very high by international standards. In the more advanced OECD countries, effective contribution rates are well below 20 percent.

Taking into account the system dependency ratios and average replacement rates, in 1992 the required nominal contribution rates to break even were 24 percent in the Czech Republic, 29 percent in Hungary,[6] 36 percent in Poland, and only 16 percent in Russia (see table 6.2). These compare with nominal contribution rates of 27.2 percent in the Czech Republic, 30.5 percent in Hungary, 30 percent in Poland and 32.6 percent in Russia. On the basis of these numbers, the pension systems of the Czech Republic and Hungary should break even (after allowing for administrative costs and some evasion), that of Poland should run a large deficit, and that of Russia should

[6] In Hungary further deterioration in the finances of the public pension system over the past few years has implied an increase in the required contribution rate for financial balance to 34%. This has been caused by an increase in the system dependency ratio to 66% and a rise in the average replacement rate to 52%. However, because of a fall in the share of covered wages in GDP (itself caused by the growing evasion that has contributed to the deteriorating dependency ratio), total pension spending has not risen as a proportion of GDP. Nevertheless, the public pension system is now suffering from a growing financial deficit.

accumulate a large surplus. The U.S. system is currently accumulating a surplus that will be used to finance the pensions of the baby boom generation. The Swiss system runs a small surplus, but this is wholly due to the state's contribution.

The financial position of different systems in transitional economies is affected by the growing problems of evasion and arrears. Evasion is increasing because of the high contribution rates and the growing role of the private sector, especially the emergence of small firms in the service sector. Arrears are caused by the financial difficulties confronting many large enterprises, especially in the state sector. Growing evasion and arrears imply that all four systems are probably suffering from large and growing deficits. In fact the Polish system runs a large deficit of over 6 percent of gross domestic product (GDP), a major drain on fiscal resources. The deficit of the Hungarian system is hidden by opaque accounting and reporting practices, while the Russian system suffers from a growing failure to collect contributions.

High Expenditures, Strategic Manipulation, and Dispersion

The financial burden of public pension systems is exacerbated by their largely monopillar structure and near universal coverage.[7] These translate into a high share of covered wages as a proportion of GDP and may explain why pension expenditures correspond to a much higher percentage of GDP in Central and Eastern Europe than is generally the case in Latin America and other low income countries. In 1992 the Czech Republic and Hungary had pension expenditure to GDP ratios of slightly over 10 percent, Poland reached almost 15 percent, while Russia had only 5 percent. In contrast most Latin American countries have pension expenditures that are well below the 5 percent level. In Poland total pension spending rose from 6.9 percent of GDP in 1988 to 14.8 percent in 1992. In the United States and Switzerland pension spending amounted, respectively, to 4.8 percent and 7.3 percent of GDP. But pension spending absorbs 14.8 percent of GDP in Austria and 10.8 percent in Germany.

Hungary and Argentina (before the recent Argentine reform) had broadly similar system dependency ratios and average replacement rates, thus implying similar required contribution rates for financial equilibrium of their respective systems (Vittas 1993c). The much higher pension expenditure to GDP ratio in Hungary implies that covered wages are a much higher percentage of GDP in Hungary than in Argentina. This results from the wider pension coverage and perhaps the smaller relative importance of

[7] The coverage of pension systems was historically high in former socialist economies. But growing evasion is causing a decline in coverage.

Table 6.3. Pension Expenditures, 1992

	RCR[a]	CWGDP[b]	PEGDP[c]
Czech Republic	24	42	10.2
Hungary	29	37	10.6
Poland	36	41	14.8
Russia	16	29	4.6
United States	9.6	50	4.8
Switzerland	11.6	63	7.3

Source: World Bank staff estimates.
[a] RCR: Required Contribution Rate.
[b] CWGDP: Share of Covered Wages in GDP.
[c] PEGDP: Share of Pension Expenditures in GDP.

profits and other nonlabor income in Hungary. Covered wages amounted to 42 percent of GDP in the Czech Republic, 37 percent in Hungary, 41 percent in Poland, and 29 percent in Russia. In Argentina the corresponding ratio was estimated at 20 percent in 1990. In Chile covered wages in the new reformed pension system were 34 percent of GDP in the same year. One consequence of this feature is the potentially high transition cost of pension reform in Hungary and other East European countries. See Table 6.3.

The pension systems of the four countries also suffer from strategic manipulation and growing dispersion of pensions. Strategic manipulation is encouraged by using shorter than lifetime career earnings for determining initial pensions. In the Czech Republic pensions are based on the best five years of the last 10 years of employment, in Poland on the best three of the last 12, and in Russia on the last two years of employment. In Hungary pensions were based on the best four of the last five years, but they are now based on all years since 1988.

A short assessment period weakens considerably the link between contributions and pensions and may give rise to capricious and even perverse redistributions. Use of the best few last years has also given rise to an increasing dispersion of pensions as a result of the growing decompression of earnings following the change of economic regime and transition to a market economy. This development unfairly benefits high income workers, who receive large pensions that bear little relationship to the contributions that were made when wages were more compressed.

Inflation Indexation

Failure to index properly to inflation also causes perverse effects, though such failure effectively acts as a safety valve for the financial viability of these systems. No country appears to have properly indexed the calculation of the reference or base salary for determining initial pensions, although Hungary is moving toward using indexed career earnings. In Hungary earnings since 1988 are taken into account and are indexed to wages up to two years before retirement. A current proposal considers indexing past earnings up to one year before retirement.

The Czech Republic is the only country of the four that does not use indexation for adjusting pensions in payment. Hungary used to adjust pensions in payment on an *ad hoc* basis; the adjustments favored lower pensions and partially offset the effect on the dispersion of initial pensions that resulted from the decompression of wages. More recently, Hungary introduced indexation of pensions to net wages. This move has put an end to the narrowing of pensions caused by the policy of differential under-indexation but has also exposed the pension system to high future costs.

In Russia pensions in payment are automatically indexed, but because the adjustment is effected on a quarterly basis and Russia has suffered from prolonged hyperinflation, the real value of pensions is substantially eroded before it is restored at the end of each quarter. Poland readjusted pensions in 1991 and indexed the readjusted pensions to average wages. This has boosted the real value of pensions and has kept them in line with rising real wages. Attempts to link pensions to average prices have met with political resistance and have been put off repeatedly. Public pension systems of the four countries are compared in Table 6.4.

Summary

The pension systems of the countries of Central Europe and Russia have many features in common. Perhaps the most important are both their growing financial crisis and their inability to provide adequate incomes to most of their pensioners.

The main factor behind these failures is their very high system dependency ratios, caused by low retirement ages and lax certification of disability pensions. Combined with near universal coverage, these have resulted in high levels of pension expenditures as a percentage of national income. Growing evasion and arrears are compounding the financial problems of public pension systems, which are saved from financial insolvency only by the partial indexation of pensions to inflation. However, in Poland pensions have been indexed to wages and the pension system is suffering from a large and growing deficit.

The pension systems are unable to maintain high targeted replacement rates, and they require high contribution rates. As a result, the scope for supplementary private pension funds is currently rather limited. As the

Table 6.4. Public Pension Systems

	Czech Rep.	Hungary	Poland	Russia
Minimum retirement age:				
Men	60	60	65	60
Women	53-57	55	60	55
Minimum contributory years:				
Men	25	25	25	25
Women	25	25	20	20
Base for pension calculation:	Best	All years	Best	Last
Years before retirement	5 of 10	since 1988	3 (10) of 12	2 (4 of 15)
Statutory replacement ratio (%):				
Net	54	67	55	56
Nominal	50	63	55	55
Adjustments for longer working periods (% per year):				
Net	1.1	1.1 (0.5)	1.3	1.0
Nominal	1.0	1.0 (0.5)	1.3	1.0
Maximum replacement ratio (%):				
Net	84	80	75	76
Nominal	78	75	75	75
Minimum pension (usually as % of minimum wage):	72	93	39[a]	100
Average pension (as % of average wage): (1991)	49	49	74	34
Nominal contribution rates for pensions (%): total	27.2	30.5	30	32.6
Employer	20.4	24.5	30	31.6
Employee	6.8	6.0	0	1.0
Effective contribution rates for pension (%): total	23	24	23	25
Employer	17	20	23	24
Employee	6	5	0	1
System dependency ratio (%):				
1992	49	59	49	46
2020		62(2016)	72	
Old age dependency ratio (%):				
1992	32	36	28	31
2020	44	54	44	50
2050	58	61	56	58
Pensions as % of GDP	10.2	10.6	14.8	4.6
Social security as % of GDP	21	27.6	19.9	5.2

[a] As % of average wage

public pension systems are run on a pay-as-you-go basis, they make no contribution to the accumulation of long-term financial assets.

The Case for Pension Reform

Although the public pension systems of Eastern European countries are in urgent need of reform, there does not seem be a strong political appetite for radical and fundamental reform. Even piecemeal reform, such as gradually raising the normal retirement age, increasing the assessment period for the calculation of initial pensions, and tightening eligibility conditions for early retirement and disability pensions, faces strong political resistance. A decision to increase the retirement age of women in Hungary had to be suspended in early 1994. In fact the only measures that have received support and have been implemented have included the automatic or *ad hoc* indexation of pensions to inflation and the use of early retirement to facilitate the restructuring process. Both of these measures have caused a sharp deterioration in the finances of the public systems.

A forceful argument can be made for deferring a fundamental reform of the systems until privatization and other more basic economic reforms are completed. Using the pension system to encourage workers to seek early retirement and thus ease the restructuring process may make more political sense than making people redundant and paying them unemployment benefits. Even though pensioners may continue to work in the informal sector, the same could be true of workers receiving unemployment benefits. The financial cost of early retirement and unemployment could be the same for the public budget, but the political cost of redundancy and unemployment could be much greater and could result in a substantial weakening of electoral support for continuing economic reform and restructuring.

There can be little doubt, however, that in the long run radical pension reform is unavoidable. Such reform should encompass a downsizing of the public system and the creation of fully funded private pension funds. The reformed public system should include raising the normal retirement age to 65 or higher so as to lower substantially the system dependency ratio and also prevent the progressive aging of the population from swamping the system. It should also include strong safeguards against strategic manipulation, such as:

- tightening the eligibility conditions for early and disability pensions;
- using indexed lifetime career earnings for determining initial pensions;
- applying linear accrual rates and providing for proportional pensions for

workers with shorter careers (and thus eliminating minimum contribution periods that tend to penalize workers with less than full careers);
- lowering target replacement rates to no more than 40 percent of average wages and even to no more than 40 percent of net average wages;
- lowering contribution rates.

The reformed public pension system could be based on flat pensions irrespective of career earnings. These could be subject to narrow or broad means tests. Under a narrow means test only retired workers with incomes and assets below a certain low level would be eligible for a state pension, while under a broad means test only retired workers with more than a certain high level of income and wealth would be excluded. The broad means test would be less expensive to administer, less stigmatizing to recipients of state pensions, and less apt to catch low income retirees in a poverty trap, but it would have a higher fiscal cost and would thus require higher contribution rates.

Alternatively, the reformed public pension systems could be based on a two-part structure: a flat minimum pension for every year of contribution and an earnings-related component based on indexed lifetime earnings, with the combined pension being subject to clearly stipulated limits. Such a system would be less progressive than a simple flat minimum pension, but it would have a lower fiscal cost (for a given total level of state pensions) and would entail fairer treatment of middle income workers.

Private Pension Funds

The structure for the reformed public pension systems will depend on local economic and political conditions. Whatever the chosen structure, the reformed public pension system should include substantially lower contribution rates to allow for the creation and expansion of private pension funds. In addition the successful promotion of private pension funds will require the enactment of enabling legislation, the development of a strong regulatory framework, and the modernization of financial markets. Considerable initiatives are under way in all four countries.

The Czech Republic

The Czech Republic introduced legislation permitting the establishment of supplementary pension funds (SPFs) in February 1994.[8] The act became effective in May 1994. These funds are set up as joint stock companies and are

[8] This section is based on an unofficial translation by Arthur Andersen, Prague, of the Czech Act on Supplementary Pension Insurance with State Contributions and Amendments Associated with its Introduction.

clearly separated from the powerful (voucher) investment funds (IFs) in the Czech Republic. Members of the boards of a SPF (i.e. management or supervisory board) may not at the same time be members of the boards of an IF. The same restriction applies to persons who are securities traders or members of the custodian institution that acts as depository for the securities owned by the funds. As in Germany, funds can grant a proxy to the custodian institution (normally a bank) to vote their shares, potentially making banks very powerful in corporate governance. The regulations are clearly aimed at restricting conflicts of interest. Employees of a SPF may not be members of its supervisory board to insure that it is independent even though supervisory boards in the Czech Republic are less powerful than in other countries such as Germany (which also has a two-tier board system). Unlike Germany, the supervisory boards in the Czech Republic do not elect and dismiss the management board. Other regulations (e.g. against self-dealing by SPF employees) are also intended to limit fraud and conflicts of interest.

The SPFs are required to disclose to participants their general investment strategy as well as their economic results by sending them annual statements and by publishing semi-annual results and the results of their last three business years. SPFs may invest in securities traded on a public stock exchange. They may invest up to 5 percent of their assets in shares of a single company and may buy up to 20 percent of an equity issue (the same limits apply for investment funds). SPFs could, therefore, potentially acquire sizable stakes in companies, if not individually, then collectively as institutional investors. However, SPFs are required to invest in a "prudent manner" and to ensure a "steady yield" on their investments. Whether or not these regulations will limit the equity investments of SPFs more than the limits mentioned above will depend on the interpretation of the law.

The voluntary pension schemes are set up as defined-contribution plans, that is, the contributions are defined, and the actual pension payments depend on the yield of the pension fund's portfolio, although defined benefit plans may also be established. SPFs also administer life insurance, survivor pensions ("inheritable pension"), and disability pensions. As their name implies, participation in the system is voluntary. The government subsidizes the system to some extent. Depending on the amount a participant contributes, the government adds up to 40 percent or CSK 120, on the basis of a specified declining schedule.[9] Participants can transfer their contributions (with their share of the investment income) to another SPF and also terminate the contract at any

[9] The maximum state contribution is CSK 120 . The following schedule applies:

Participant	State contribution	Participant	State contribution
100-199	40 + 32% of amount above 100	300-399	96 + 16% of amount above 300
200-299	72 + 24% of amount above 200	400-499	112 + 8% of amount above 400

time. These important regulations could increase competition among funds and allow participants to exert pressure on the funds to perform well. A potential drawback may be high administrative costs, although restricting switches between funds (e.g. to once a year) could mitigate this problem. The portability of pensions is much better in this private system; making labor mobility easier is an important advance in transitional economies with great need for restructuring.

The Czech law on private pension funds contains a number of interesting features. First, it is a voluntary system using tax credits (rather than tax exemptions) to encourage workers to participate. These amount to 24 percent for a monthly contribution of CSK 500. This amount is about 8 percent of an average monthly salary, the system clearly favors low income workers and thus avoids the regressive effect of tax exemptions. However, the tax credits are not dependent on workers contributing a minimum proportion (say 10%) of their monthly income. Thus, high income workers may subscribe for a contribution of no more than CSK 500. This will hold back the total size of the funds.

Second, the law allows workers to have one account with one pension fund. In this it follows the pattern established in Chile. The main motivation for this restriction in both countries is to increase the transparency of the scheme and facilitate compliance.

Third, the law allows workers not only to change funds but also to cancel their contracts and withdraw from the scheme. The law does not seem to prevent workers from cashing in the government tax credits together with their own contributions and the investment income credited to their accounts. Thus, the funds may help provide relief to unemployed workers. But again a large tax expenditure in the form of tax credits may fail to generate adequate funds for reasonably high supplementary pensions. At the end of 1995, 41 pension funds were operating, with 1.2 million members and only CSK 4 billion ($160 million) in accumulated balances. The average monthly contribution was CSK 300 ($12), while the average tax credit amounted to CSK 100 ($4).

Hungary

In Hungary an act on voluntary mutual benefit funds came into force in January 1994. The three types of funds to supplement the public social security system are mutual aid funds, health care funds, and pension funds. The mutual aid funds cover sickness, child raising, unemployment, and death and are organized on a pay-as-you-go (PAYG) basis. The health care funds also operate on a PAYG basis and provide health insurance, supplementing the public health care system. Pension funds are organized as fully funded defined-contribution plans based on individual capitalization accounts, although defined-benefit plans may also be established.

Funds are to be based on a common employer or on a profession, sector, or region. Membership fees have to be a uniform amount or a certain proportion of income for all fund members. Employers can also contribute (either in fixed amounts per employee or income-proportionate amounts), and thereby gain some control rights in the fund. They have a voice but no voting rights in the general meeting. If their contributions are 50 percent or more of total contributions, they have voting rights in the control committee. Contributions are tax deductible (subject to limits) as is the investment income of the fund. Contributions are also free from the high social security taxes. Benefits, both in the form of an annuity and as a lump sum payment, are subject to income tax. Contributions are collected in individual accounts. The minimum waiting period to withdraw the accumulated contributions and the investment yield is 10 years unless a member reaches the retirement age earlier.

Every fund member is an owner of the fund and has the right to inspect the books. The bodies of the fund are the general meeting, the board of directors, and the control committee. The general meeting is the supreme decision-making body of the fund and each fund member has one vote. It meets at least once a year[10] and elects both the board of directors and the control committee. No employees of the fund may be elected to the board of directors and neither employees nor members of the board of directors may be elected to the control committee. The board of directors is the managing body of the fund but may hire a manager for day-to-day activities. It meets at least once every three months. The control committee is chosen from among the members of the fund and supervises the activities of the board of directors. A further control institution is the Fund Supervision Agency, which is established by the Ministry of Finance and is responsible for licensing and supervision of funds.

The fund's property is to be invested in the sole interest of its members, and funds are only allowed to invest their own assets to avoid conflicts of interest. Investments have to be divided among different forms to reduce the risk for the fund and its members. Funds may not acquire more than 10 percent of an undertaking and may not invest more than 10 percent of their own assets in an enterprise that is affiliated with an employer member. At most 20 percent of fund assets may be invested with the same issuer (except government bonds) and at most 20 percent of fund deposits may be held in

[10] The control committee or 10% of the fund members also have a right to call the general meeting.

the same financial institution. At most 20 percent of fund assets may be invested in shares and bonds quoted on a stock exchange and at most 10 percent may be invested in unlisted shares and bonds, which are not quoted. Furthermore, at least 10 percent of fund assets must be in liquid instruments. The fund may delegate its asset management to investor organizations, but not more than 45 percent of its assets may be with one organization. Before funds reach a certain size,[11] they may not invest in securities (other than government bonds and state guaranteed securities).

What does not appear to be regulated in the law is the transfer of accounts from one pension fund to another, and transfer can apparently be restricted by the fund. The funds appear to have substantial freedom in establishing rules for the termination of membership.[12] The ability of fund members to move their account to another fund might help increase competition among funds, and lack of regulation could be seen as a serious shortcoming of the new law.

The tax deductibility of contributions and their exemption from high social security taxes provide a strong financial incentive for the creation and growth of private pension funds. However, because contributions are locked into long-term savings, the funds will be attractive only to workers above a certain level of income, who can more easily afford to save for the long term. The effect of private funds will be highly regressive and will also undermine further the financial position of the public pension system. At the end of 1995 there were over 120 pension funds in operation with a total membership of less than 200,000 workers and total accumulated assets of Ft 5 billion (about $50 million).

Poland

Poland has not introduced regulations for the private provision of pensions, although the need for a supplementary pension scheme has been the subject of extensive debate.[13] Such a scheme could be mandatory or optional, the former would support a faster development of supplementary pensions, the latter a market-economy approach. Another question is who should oversee the supplementary pension funds. Traditionally, any second tier in Poland has been provided by employers as company, sector, and occupation retirement pensions. Whether this should also be the form of the supplementary pension system in the future remains the subject of debate. It has not been

[11] For pension funds, mutual aid funds, and health care funds, respectively, the amounts are Ft 10, 15, and 20 million.

[12] § 15 (2): "The legal consequences of the cessation of membership as well as the procedures to be followed are to be regulated in the statutes."

[13] This section draws primarily from a draft paper by Jean de Fougerolles (1994).

decided whether tax incentives should support the development of an optional system, or whether the government should mandate the benefit and contribution levels of an optional system

Despite the lack of specific legislation, a private pension fund called the Polish Pension Fund (PFE) Kapital Rodzinny was created in 1993 under the law for cooperatives that has been in force for more than ten years. The operations of the PFE were challenged by the General Inspectorate of Banking Supervision of the National Bank of Poland (the central bank) and by the Insurance Department of the Ministry of Finance. The two regulatory agencies claimed that the PFE was engaged in banking and insurance activities without a license. In response to these challenges the PFE restricted its activities. The prosecution authorities were forced to drop their investigations because cooperatives are not subject to supervision by either agency. This underscores the need for enacting proper pension fund legislation and for clarifying which government agency should have responsibility for licensing and supervising the funds.

Russia

Following Presidential Decree No. 1077 of 16 September 1992, nonstate pension funds have been established in Russia.[14] There were 300 such funds in the middle of 1994, but their number rose to 800 by the end of 1995. They are generally small and operate more like savings banks than long-term pension funds. However, there may be some exceptions that intend to operate as proper pension funds.

A draft law has been prepared for the authorization and regulation of nonstate pension funds, but it is not clear how soon it will be enacted. In the meantime pension funds operate in a regulatory vacuum, which not only allows their founders to engage in misleading advertising campaigns, but also leaves considerable room for variations in practice. The situation is chaotic with little standardization in services and products, charges, or investment practices. Most funds are based on defined contribution plans with individual capitalization accounts for their members, but some offer additional benefits and are more akin to defined benefit plans. Some funds also have rules that allow withdrawals during unemployment spells. Most funds direct their selling efforts toward employers. Even though some funds engage in advertising oriented toward individual workers, the main emphasis is placed on signing up firms.

The small pension funds invest their assets in bank deposits and promise a

[14] This section draws on the findings of a World Bank mission to Russia in July 1994 and interviews with representatives of several pension funds.

guaranteed return to members that is no less than the rate offered on SBER savings deposits. Other pension funds diversify their investments into bonds and some equities and adopt internal rules based on international practice about investment diversification, information disclosure, and operating commissions.

Membership in most funds is small, rarely exceeding several thousand. However, some funds (e.g. the fund for electric power workers) have tremendous expansion potential. Assets are also quite small, mostly less than 1 billion rubles (half a million dollars in 1994), though one of the funds already had 17 billion rubles in mid-1994. Most pension funds invest their assets locally unless their management company has a foreign currency license in which case they may also invest in overseas assets.

There is considerable debate about the need and scope of regulation and supervision. Pension fund promoters urge enactment of a law to obtain tax benefits, especially removal of the triple taxation of pension saving (contributions are not deductible, investment income is taxed, and pensions are taxed). However, there is little agreement on other possible legal provisions. Some officials favor the separation of pension funds and managing companies, but others want to allow pension funds to have their own boards of directors and their own investment management capabilities. There is also little consensus on the nature of pension schemes, some favoring defined contribution and others defined benefit plans. The questions of vesting and portability are not being properly addressed, while information disclosure is supported if it is limited to an annual statement with the right for members to ask for more frequent statements.

On investment policies some officials favor diversified portfolios based on the prudent man concept, others prefer freedom to invest in the projects and securities of sponsoring companies. There is support for the enactment of legislation to clarify the status of pension funds but less for the creation of an inspectorate with supervisory responsibilities. There is concern that any investment regulations imposed by government will favor inefficient industries and social projects and will use the resources of pension funds as captive sources for financing the budget deficit. The concept of maximum limits (to ensure diversification) but no minimum requirements (to avoid direction of funds) is not yet fully grasped. However, some pension funds want restrictions on advertising to curb misleading claims.

The regulatory vacuum is likely to continue, even after the passing of a pension law. An inspectorate for pension funds has been created at the Ministry of Social Protection, but it will be a long time before it is properly staffed and develops an effective system of supervision. In the meantime there may be greater hope in encouraging a process of self-regulation with the association of pension funds acting as a sponsor of respectable institutions. This could develop a code of ethical conduct and business behavior that would encourage the adoption of sound and prudent practices and instill greater confidence in the pension fund industry.

Despite the problems, pension funds are likely to grow fast in the future, especially if fiscal incentives are offered, inflation is brought under control, the privatization program is successful, and the financial situation of industrial companies improves. They could play a big part in the development of capital markets and in corporate governance.

Summary

The Czech Republic and Hungary have enacted legislation that promotes the creation of supplementary private pension funds. These laws favor the creation of defined contribution schemes, although defined benefit plans are not precluded. In the Czech Republic a tax credit is paid by the state, up to a limit of CSK 120 for a CSK 500 contribution. This credit is used in lieu of tax deductibility of contributions and is, therefore, a less regressive tax incentive. In Hungary the law allows for the tax deductibility of both employer and employee contributions and also exempts such contributions from social security taxes. In both Hungary and the Czech Republic the law provides for prudential controls on investments to avoid overconcentration of risks and for adequate information disclosure to members. Some pension funds have been created in these two countries but they are very small.

No private pension laws have been enacted in Poland and Russia, although a draft act has been prepared in the latter. Very few pension funds have been created in Poland, but Russia has over 300 nonstate pension funds. The vast majority of these are little more than savings clubs. Russian pension funds operate in a regulatory vacuum, with little standardization in services and products or charges and investment practices, but some of these pension funds have the potential to acquire large memberships and become important institutional investors.

Large private pension funds are not likely to emerge and play a big part in the capital market unless the public pension systems of the four countries are restructured and downsized. Lower contribution rates will leave greater scope for the development of private pension funds.

The Role of Pension Funds in OECD and Developing Countries

Capital Markets and Pension Funds

If private pension funds are authorized in East European countries, should they be established as defined-benefit, employer-based schemes or as defined-contribution, nonemployer-based plans? What elements would determine their future growth and their role in the capital markets?

The experience of OECD countries and several developing countries suggests that defined-benefit, employer-based schemes are faced with growing problems of financial sustainability and fair treatment and require for their equitable operation strict and complex regulations that will lower their attractiveness for both employers and employees. Defined-contribution plans based on individual capitalization accounts also require robust regulation but are less affected by sustainability and equity problems.

In OECD and several developing countries a major determinant of the size and growth of private pension funds is the size of the public pension systems, their coverage, the nature of their liabilities, and their investment returns. Clearly, pension funds can accumulate substantial financial resources in a short time, but their impact on the capital markets will depend on both regulation and the investment attitudes to risk taking that emerge. In many European countries investment traditions have been more powerful than binding regulations in shaping the investment portfolios of pension funds. The investment policies of pension funds will also have important policy implications for investment returns, the rate of national saving, corporate governance, and the financing of small firms and new ventures.

Pension Funds as Pension Institutions

Historically, company pension schemes tended to be defined-benefit plans. This was because such schemes were initially conceived as personnel management tools with the triple objective of attracting skilled workers, rewarding loyalty, and facilitating the retirement of older workers (Hannah 1986, Williamson 1992). Defined benefit plans contained restrictions on vesting and portability that penalized early leavers and discouraged labor mobility. Moreover, by basing pensions on final salaries, they favored management workers (who receive larger salary increases late in their career) over rank and file workers. Defined-benefit company pension schemes absorbed the investment risk of accumulated assets, which also covered the inflation risk before retirement, thus providing insurance for achieving a targeted replacement rate at the time of retirement (Bodie 1990b). This insurance depended on a worker staying with the sponsoring company until retirement, but it failed to cover pensions in payment. The realization of the pension promises made by employers depended heavily on their integrity and solvency.

To discourage abuse of pension schemes by unscrupulous employers, various countries have enacted legislation that stipulates minimum standards for vesting and portability, more equitable treatment of all types of workers, including early leavers, and protection from the vagaries of inflation. These have increased the costs of pension schemes for sponsoring employers and have stimulated a trend away from defined-benefit and toward defined-contribution plans. The latter have traditionally been used by smaller firms in industries with more labor mobility and less stable employment patterns. Defined-contribution schemes can deal more effectively with the vesting and portability issues, but they transfer to workers the investment, replacement, and inflation risks. To overcome this problem, variable contribution rates may be used during the active life of workers, linking the rates to the investment performance of the funds and the targeted replacement rate, and indexed annuities may be used when workers retire.

Although defined-benefit occupational pension schemes have made a considerable contribution to the retirement income of a substantial minority of privileged workers, the growing instability of employment patterns, the increasing cost of pension regulations, and the increasing robustness of financial and insurance markets suggest that the relative attractiveness of defined-benefit schemes will decline further. The arguments for fully portable and nonemployer-based pensions are stronger in Eastern Europe. The need for substantial restructuring will lead to major changes and large mobility in the labor market, which in turn will create a need for fully portable pensions. Insolvencies will be quite common in Eastern Europe (rather than only at the margin as in mature market economies), and employer-based pensions would have potentially adverse financial effects on displaced workers. Reforming East European countries should turn their private pension funds toward defined-contribution plans based on individual capitalization accounts with variable contribution rates. At least they should allow workers to opt out of company schemes and join non-employment-linked personal pension plans, while any tax benefits should be made equally available to company and noncompany schemes.

Pension Funds and Asset Accumulation

The organization of the pension system has become a major determinant of differences in the institutional structure of national financial systems. In those countries where unfunded social security systems pay generous pensions to retired workers, funded pension schemes and to a lesser extent life insurance companies have been slow to develop. These countries include Germany, Austria, France, Italy and, to a lesser extent, Japan.

But countries where social security pensions have been more modest or where companies have been allowed to contract out of a major component of state pension systems (as in the United Kingdom), employer-sponsored funded pension schemes have accumulated large financial savings. Because the pension schemes of smaller companies are often insured and administered by insurance companies, both pension funds and life insurance companies have experienced considerable growth in these countries. This group comprises all Anglo-American countries (i.e. the United States, the United Kingdom, Canada, Australia, New Zealand and South Africa) and several continental European countries, such as the Netherlands, Switzerland, Sweden, Denmark, and Norway.

Unlike the traditional distinction between bank-based and market-based systems, the dividing line between countries with developed and underdeveloped pension funds (and insurance companies) is no longer a simple one between continental European and Anglo-American countries. In fact, pension funds in Switzerland and the Netherlands have wider coverage and larger assets, relative to gross national produce (GNP), than most Anglo-American countries.

Switzerland has long had an employer-based second system. This became mandatory in 1985, expanding coverage among employees of small firms and reaching over 90 percent of all workers. In the Netherlands occupational pension schemes are arranged by collective bargaining and are quasi-mandatory, achieving coverage of more than 80 percent. In contrast most Anglo-American countries have coverage of 45 to 60 percent. Switzerland and the Netherlands effectively offer inflation indexed pensions. Inflation indexing implies higher required funding levels; this may explain why pension fund assets in these two countries exceed 70 percent of GNP. Adding the assets of life insurance companies, which often manage the pension schemes of smaller firms, brings the total assets of contractual savings institutions to over 100 percent of GNP (Table 6.5).

Among Anglo-American countries, only the United Kingdom has pension fund and life insurance assets reaching similar levels. Although coverage is smaller in the United Kingdom and inflation-indexed pensions are less widespread, the total assets of pension funds are large because companies are allowed to contract out of the state earnings-related pension system. This imposes a greater liability on U.K. company pension schemes and thus a greater need for accumulating assets than, for instance, in the United States where company pensions are generally integrated with social security pensions.

Table 6.5. Pension Fund and Life Insurance Assets
(percentage of GNP)

	1970	1980	1990
Canada	31	31	46[a]
France	6	7	13[b]
Germany	10	14	22
Japan	8	13	41
Netherlands	45	63	107
Sweden	42	51	63
Switzerland	51	70	133[c]
United Kingdom	43	46	97
United States	43	49	75

Source: Davis (1993), Vittas and Skully (1991).
[a] 1989. [b] 1988. [c] 1987.

Among developing countries, large funded pension systems exist in a few countries, notably Singapore, Malaysia, and Chile, where they are based on defined-contribution plans with individual capitalization accounts. The systems of Singapore and Malaysia are centrally managed by national provident funds. In Chile the government mandated system is privately managed by decentralized, competitive firms subject to draconian regulations and supervision. South Africa, Cyprus, Zimbabwe, and to a lesser extent Brazil, India, and Indonesia, also have funded pension schemes that are mostly based on company plans. There are some developing countries with partially funded public systems, such as Egypt, Jordan, Tunisia, and the Philippines.[15] Most countries in Latin America (at least until the recent wave of pension reform), Eastern Europe, Francophone Africa, the Middle East, and East Asia have pay-as-you-go social pension systems that make little or no contribution to the accumulation of financial assets.

The size of pension funds depends on the coverage of the schemes, their length of existence and maturity, and the nature of their pension liability. Schemes that promise a pension based on final salary, indexed to subsequent inflation, in operation for a longer time and thus covering a more aged labor force will tend to have higher assets compared with younger schemes that operate defined-contribution plans and cover a younger labor force. High investment returns also increase the level of assets, although adjustments in contributions may offset the effect of high returns.

A major determinant of funding private pension plans and of the level of

[15] Some public pension systems in OECD countries are partially funded (e.g. Canada, Japan, Sweden, and the United States).

assets is also the tax treatment of pension saving. In most countries pension saving benefits from tax deferral, whereby annual contributions and investment income are exempt from tax, but pensions are subject to tax like any other income. If the total income in retirement is less than income during a worker's active life, then tax deferral will also result in lower lifetime taxes in a country with a progressive income tax system.

The vast accumulation of pension fund assets has led several countries to put limits on the tax privileges of pension funds.[16] These include limits on contributions and eligible pension benefits (United Kingdom), limits or nondeductibility of contributions in overfunded schemes (United States, United Kingdom, and Germany), taxes on assets in excess of specified overfunding levels (Netherlands), and taxes on investment income above a certain rate of return (Denmark). New Zealand has gone farther than any other country and has removed all tax benefits, subjecting pension saving to a full income tax. There has been a decline in pension fund assets in New Zealand following this measure, though the fall has been partly caused by the termination of overfunded and fully funded schemes and not just by a decline in the annual flow of saving and in worker participation in pension schemes.

The creation of funded pension schemes can generate substantial long-term financial savings in a relatively short time. In countries where labor incomes represent 50 percent of national income, pension schemes based on defined contribution plans covering 40 percent of the labor force with an average contribution rate of 10 percent would annually accumulate funds equal to 2 percent of national income. Since in the early years of pension funds outlays would be minimal, if the nominal rate of return on fund assets is equal to the nominal rate of growth of GNP, these pension schemes would accumulate resources equal to 10 percent of GNP over 5 years and 20 percent over 10 years. After the first 10 years the pace of accumulation will be affected by the growing volume of benefit payments. But expanded coverage, a higher contribution rate, higher investment returns, or an increase in the share of labor income in total income will all tend to accelerate the pace of accumulation. Defined benefit plans may accumulate even larger funds if the sponsors of the plans take account of projected pension benefits. The experience of Singapore, Malaysia, and Chile shows that once a credible and well-run system is in place, it can accumulate long-term resources at a fast pace (Vittas 1992; Vittas and Iglesias 1992; World Bank 1994).).

In the United States, and especially in the United Kingdom, contractual savings experienced a large expansion in the 1980s in relation to GDP as a

[16] For details, see Davis (1993).

result of the steep rise of stock market prices (Davis 1993, Vittas 1992, World Bank 1994). The much faster rise in the United Kingdom reflects the greater exposure of contractual savings to the equity market and the stronger performance of life insurance policies. Similar increases in the total assets of pension funds and life insurance companies were also observed in Switzerland and the Netherlands (see Table 6.5), although the increase reflected more an expansion of coverage and less an increase in the value of assets; pensions funds and insurance companies in these two countries invested a much smaller percentage of their assets in equities and real estate (see below).

Impact on Securities Markets

With the accumulation of large financial resources, pension funds can play a large part in countries' financial systems and, especially, in securities markets because pension funds have long-term liabilities they are able to invest in long-term assets. Not having the expertise to appraise individual projects and requests for finance by individual firms, they rely either on commercial banks for investing their funds (e.g. by placing them in bank deposits) or, seeking a higher return than is obtainable on bank deposits, on direct investments in marketable securities. These investments range from government and mortgage bonds to corporate bonds and equities. Pension funds may thus provide a large pool of investable resources that can stimulate the development of securities markets and encourage financial innovation. In the United States, many of the financial innovations of the 1970s and 1980s were in direct response to the needs of pension funds (Bodie 1990a).

Pension funds, in conjunction with other institutional investors, can act as catalysts for the modernization of securities markets, the development of efficient trading and settlement systems, the adoption of modern accounting and auditing standards, and the promotion of information disclosure. But the actual impact on capital markets depends on the behavior of institutions. It is a potential effect that is less likely to happen if institutions hold strategic holdings and trade less and if they are less interested in protecting minority shareholders.

A traditional argument against fully funded pension schemes was concern that in the absence of active securities markets, accumulated funds might be used as captive sources for funding government deficits, or if the funds were free to invest in nongovernment securities, they would invest in speculative or unsafe assets. For instance, funds could be channeled into overpriced real estate or into loans to related parties and equity stakes in related firms.

This argument was probably valid in the 1960s and 1970s when few developing countries had organized securities markets. But in the 1980s the large growth of the emerging securities markets shows that most countries have the potential to stimulate the development and modernization of their securities markets if they adopt sound macroeconomic policies, maintain financial stability, and remove obstacles that inhibit the development of markets. Even though most emerging markets suffer from structural and regulatory deficiencies, progress is being made in tackling these deficiencies and in creating more robust and transparent markets. In fact, the traditional argument against funded pension schemes overlooked the dynamic interaction that would evolve between growing pension funds and emerging financial markets and thus underestimated the contribution that pension funds and other institutional investors could make to the development of financial markets.

The allocation of pension fund assets varies considerably from country to country, reflecting both historical traditions and differences in regulation. In the United Kingdom, where fund managers have developed an equity cult since the 1960s in response to the high rates of inflation experienced by the U.K. economy, pension funds and life insurance companies in 1988 accounted for 55 percent of corporate equities. In the United States they held only 26 percent of corporate equities; U.S. long-term institutional investors held 56 percent of corporate bonds.

The equity cult of U.K. fund managers is also reflected in the composition of their portfolios. U.K. pension funds invested 72 percent of their assets in equities and other real assets against 46 percent for their U.S. counterparts (Table 6.6). The difference is much greater for life insurance companies: U.K. companies invested 51 percent of their assets in equities against less than 10 percent for U.S. companies.

In continental European countries, contractual savings institutions follow the pattern of American life insurance companies and place the largest part of their funds in government, corporate and mortgage bonds, and in long-term loans. This is true of insurance companies and pension funds in Switzerland, the Netherlands, and Germany. It is partly the result of investment regulations and partly the result of a traditional emphasis on conservative investment policies. Although pension funds and insurance companies are subject to upper limits on their holdings of equities (as well as on their holdings of overseas securities) and although their managers are seeking either increases in these limits or their complete abolition, their holdings of restricted investments are well below the specified limits.

The pattern in developing countries is similar to that of continental European countries. Except for South Africa where pension funds and life insurance companies have been free to invest in equities, most other countries' investment rules have favored bonds. In Singapore the Central

Table 6.6. Asset Allocations of Pension Funds
(percentage of assets)

	Real assets	Debt instruments
Canada		
1970	23	77
1980	23	77
1990	32	68
Germany		
1970	16	84
1980	18	82
1990	24	76
Japan		
1970	33	67
1980	15	85
1990	29	71
Netherlands		
1970	27	73
1980	19	81
1990	31	69
Switzerland		
1970	19	81
1980	27	73
1990	33	67
United Kingdom		
1970	59	41
1980	70	30
1990	72	28
United States		
1970	45	55
1980	41	59
1990	46	54

Source: Davis (1993).
Note: Real assets include equities and real estate; debt instruments include government, corporate and mortgage bonds, loans and short term assets.

Provident Fund (CPF) invests over 90 percent of its funds in government securities that earn a modest positive real rate of return. Despite the enforced captivity of its resources, the government of Singapore has refrained from investing all the funds in local development projects but has accumulated a substantial pool of foreign exchange reserves, which has grown to exceed the total balances of the CPF. Thus, the CPF effectively operates as a compulsory national mutual fund, investing indirectly in foreign assets through the government of the Singapore Investment Corporation and the Monetary

Authority of Singapore (including equities and direct investments in large mining and other projects) on behalf of Singaporean households.

In Malaysia the funds of the national provident fund have been used for development. However, the successful implementation of economic growth policies has ensured a modest real rate of return on the balances of the Employees Provident Fund. Other countries were not as efficient. In Egypt, a country where the social security system generates large surpluses (in 1988 accumulated reserves amounted to 40 percent of GNP), these resources have been placed with the National Investment Bank, the investments of which have suffered from highly negative returns. The provident funds in African countries (Ghana, Nigeria, Kenya, and Zambia) and nearly all the partially funded pension systems of developing countries have invested their resources almost exclusively in government bonds and low interest loans to members. Real returns on accumulated funds have been highly negative, and in some cases the real value of balances has been wiped out.

In Chile investments in corporate equities for the privately managed pension funds were less than 20 percent of total assets for most of the 1980s, mainly because of the imposition of tight restrictions on their investment portfolios. As a result, the pension funds were forced to invest heavily in government, mortgage, and corporate bonds as well as bank deposits. The gradual relaxation of investment rules has allowed Chilean pension funds to invest more in equities and, recently, they have been allowed to invest in foreign securities.

Investments in foreign assets have been affected by regulations, either foreign exchange controls or unnecessarily tight prudential controls. Following the removal of exchange controls and the relaxation of investment rules, pension funds in several countries have built up substantial holdings of foreign equities and bonds (see Wyatt (1993)). International diversification may increase portfolio returns, especially if pension fund assets become too big for the local markets, but the general result is a reduction in investment risk, stemming from the imperfect covariance of returns in different national markets.

Implications of Investment Policies

The investment policies pursued by pension funds and life insurance companies in different countries have important implications for (1) the profitability of their investments, (2) the required rate of contribution and thus the rate of national saving, (3) the financing of small firms and new ventures, (4) fund management practices, and (5) the role of pension funds in corporate governance.

As regards the profitability of their investments, a study (Davis 1993)

Table 6.7. Real Pension Fund Returns
(standard deviations in brackets)

	1966-70	1971-75	1976-80	1981-85	1986-90	1966-90
Canada	-3.3	-1.4	-1.2	6.1	7.9	1.6
	(1.4)	(11.7)	(4.0)	(15.1)	(6.7)	(9.8)
Denmark	-1.9	-1.3	0.8	17.7	-1.8	3.6
	(8.7)	(12.7)	(4.4)	(14.6)	(10.3)	(12.7)
Germany	5.0	3.3	3.3	7.7	6.3	5.1
	(3.3)	(2.7)	(4.4)	(4.9)	(5.9)	(4.4)
Japan	0.1	-0.5	-1.2	10.9	13.8	4.0
	(5.3)	(10.9)	(5.3)	(2.1)	(7.8)	(9.4)
Netherlands	1.7	-1.4	2.0	10.5	6.3	4.0
	(3.3)	(5.5)	(3.0)	(4.0)	(5.4)	(6.0)
Sweden	1.2	-3.5	-5.3	3.9	4.7	0.2
	(8.2)	(6.7)	(5.6)	(4.9)	(9.3)	(7.6)
Switzerland	0.8	-0.5	4.0	3.0	-0.2	1.5
	(0.0)	(6.3)	(8.0)	(5.4)	(7.2)	(6.4)
United Kingdom	4.2	-2.8	4.9	12.4	10.1	5.8
	(11.5)	(19.4)	(5.2)	(7.3)	(12.7)	(12.5)
United States	-5.4	-0.8	-1.9	8.1	11.2	2.2
	(6.5)	(13.8)	(6.9)	(13.0)	(12.2)	(11.9)

Source: Davis (1993).

simulating pension fund returns on the basis of asset allocations and annual asset returns for nine industrial countries over the period 1966-90 shows that average real returns varied from 5.8 percent in the United Kingdom to 0.2 percent in Sweden. Somewhat surprisingly, pension funds in Germany, the Netherlands, Japan, and Denmark showed higher returns than U.S. funds.[17] Among the nine countries, only Canada, Switzerland, and Sweden earned lower returns (Table 6.7).

U.K. pension funds invest a higher proportion of their assets in equities

[17] The reported returns are sensitive to the base and end year chosen. For instance, eliminating the 1967-70 period when U.S. pension funds earned negative returns would raise their average real return for the period 1971-90 to 4%.

and real property, resulting in higher overall returns and higher risk. U.K. funds also have one of the highest standard deviations of return. German and Dutch funds earn relatively high real returns despite focusing on bonds and loans because of high real interest rates pursued by their central banks. In contrast Swiss funds with a broadly similar allocation of assets earn much lower real returns. This seems to reflect the low real interest rate policy of the Swiss authorities, a policy that is motivated by concern about keeping both the nominal and real mortgage rate low and stable.

Among developing countries most pension funds (especially the provident funds in African countries and the partially funded public pension systems of the Middle East and Latin America) suffered from negative real rates of return. During the 1980s the average yearly real return for the Zambian provident fund was minus 25 percent, while in Egypt the extensively funded social security system suffered from a minus 12 percent real return (World Bank 1994). The main exceptions among developing countries were the provident funds of Malaysia and Singapore, where positive real returns between 3 percent and 5 percent were achieved (Vittas 1993a) and the decentralized private pension funds in Chile, which realized unusually high returns of over 13 percent on assets before operating expenses and 9.5 percent after deducting expenses.[18]

The extremely high performance of the Chilean pension funds stemmed less from their investments in equities, which as noted above were highly restricted, than from two unusual factors that prevailed during the 1980s in the Chilean economy. These were the high level of real interest rates following the severe financial crisis of the early 1980s and the subsequent large capital gains earned on bonds and other debt instruments that resulted from the large fall of real interest rates when the economy recovered and financial confidence was restored. In the 1990s the Chilean pension funds are likely to benefit from high returns in their equity investments, but it is doubtful that in the long run they will be able to continue to achieve real returns in excess of 10 percent.

The low real investment returns achieved by Swiss and Singaporean pension funds imply a high required rate of contribution and a high level of pension saving to achieve targeted replacement rates. Comparing the real returns and real wage growth in the United Kingdom and Switzerland shows that a 10 percent contribution rate over a 40-year working life in the United Kingdom would pay a 66 percent inflation-indexed pension over a 20-year

[18] Operating expenses were unusually high in the early years of the system. They have declined steadily and now amount to less than 2% of total assets (Vittas and Iglesias 1992; World Bank 1994).

retirement life, while a similar scheme in Switzerland would only pay a 22 percent pension (Davis 1993, Vittas 1993b). To achieve the same target pension rate, the Swiss contribution rate would have to be three times as high or 30 percent. The high rate of saving, which characterizes the Swiss economy in conjunction with the low real rate of return, may appear economically inefficient. Yet it may lie behind the high investment rate and the ability of the Swiss economy to operate with low inflation, low unemployment, and a steady rate of economic growth. Singapore is a high-growth economy, and this may explain the high rate of saving. Nevertheless, the low returns on provident fund balances and the high rate of forced saving may also contribute to the unusually and persistently high rate of national saving of over 45 percent of GNP..

The Swiss and Singaporean experience may explain an apparent paradox in the connection between funded pension schemes and saving rates. In principle, funding pensions ought to increase the rate of saving, but in practice (except Switzerland, Singapore, and Malaysia) most countries with funded pension schemes (from the United States, Canada, the United Kingdom, and the Scandinavian countries to Australia, New Zealand, and South Africa) are characterized by low saving rates. One explanation is the greater access to household debt available in all these countries, which allows consumers to offset some of the mandatory or nondiscretionary saving effected through pension funds. Another factor may be the higher rates of return achieved by pension funds compared with the rates earned by individual savers in these countries. Given a target pension rate, this would imply a lower required rate of saving. When pension fund returns are high and funds become overfunded, sponsoring companies lower their annual contributions or even take contribution holidays.

As regards their impact on sectoral finance, the growth of pension funds and other institutional investors may have undesirable implications for the financing of small firms and new ventures, because pension funds minimize their transaction costs by dealing in the more liquid securities of large companies. Moreover, pension funds have difficulty researching firms without track records, lack expertise in supplying venture capital, and also face prudential limits on the proportion of a company's equity they can hold. One solution for this problem is for pension funds to invest in venture capital companies and in mutual funds that specialize in small capitalization companies.

Regarding fund management practices, most studies for the United Kingdom and the United States show that active investment management consistently underperforms market indices. Lakonishok, Shleifer, and Vishny (1992) show that the equity component of U.S. pension funds underperformed the S&P 500 index by an average of 1.3 percent per annum in 1983-89, or by 2.6 percent if returns are value weighted. For the United Kingdom, Davis (1993) shows that while pension funds underperform their home market, they do so more severely in foreign markets. Such underperformance may justify a passive policy of investing in the market index, although passive indexation of investment portfolios might weaken the influence of markets on corporate performance and might require a greater and more direct involvement in corporate governance issues.

Finally, regarding corporate governance in those countries where pension funds invest mostly in bonds and other debt instruments, their role in corporate governance would be limited to creditor involvement when firms face financial difficulties and are unable to meet the repayment conditions and other covenants of bond issues. In several of these countries (especially Germany and Japan, and to a lesser extent the Netherlands and Switzerland) commercial banks play an important role in corporate governance through combinations of stock ownership, exercise of proxy votes, and board representation.[19] Insurance companies may also play an active part through limited stock ownership and board representation, but pension funds are passive observers. This status is reinforced in those countries (e.g. Germany, and to a lesser and declining extent Japan) where pension fund assets are reinvested in the sponsoring company as book reserves.

In Anglo-American countries where pension funds tend to invest more heavily in equities, they can play an influential part in corporate governance. However, except for South Africa, the role of pension funds has historically been passive, although recent trends indicate a changed attitude and a more activist approach. In South Africa pension funds and especially the insurance companies that manage most of these funds and other contractual savings are dominant in corporate governance and have controlling stakes in a large number of companies, including other financial institutions, such as commercial banks and even building societies (Gerson 1992; Vittas 1994).

Summary

The experience of OECD countries shows that large pension funds that play an important role as financial intermediaries and institutional investors have emerged over the years only in a small number of Anglo-American and Continental European countries, where social security pensions have been modest and social security contributions low.

Until the creation of nonemployer-based private pension funds in Chile in the early 1980s, most private pension funds were employer based. They were

[19] The role of banks in corporate governance and its relevance for East European countries is discussed in Gray and Hanson (1993).

originally created to further personnel management objectives, such as attracting skilled workers, rewarding loyalty, and facilitating the retirement of older, less productive workers. Their role as pension institutions providing retirement income insurance evolved over time in response to the rise of large corporations and the spread of collective bargaining.

In line with their retirement income insurance function, the majority of private pension funds were set up as defined benefit plans, but in recent years there has been a clear trend toward defined contribution plans. This change has been caused less by outright conversion of plans than by the underlying change in industrial structure, especially the decline of large manufacturing firms and the growth of smaller firms in the service sector. Tighter regulations on pension funds and the growing instability of employment patterns are likely to increase further the costs of defined benefit plans and reduce their attractiveness for both employers and employees.

Pension funds have accumulated large financial assets (in relation to GNP) in Switzerland and the Netherlands, where they have a wider coverage than pension funds in Anglo-American countries, and they also offer inflation indexed pensions. But their role as institutional investors in corporate equities has been limited by their preference for bonds and other debt instruments.

In contrast, pension funds in Anglo-American countries, and especially in South Africa, the United Kingdom and the United States, have invested heavily in corporate equities. But except for South Africa, pension funds in Anglo-American countries have tended to acquire small, diversified holdings that have limited their role in corporate governance.

Corporate Governance and Pension Funds

If pension funds were to become large institutional investors in Eastern European countries, what factors would determine their role in corporate governance? The experience of countries with large pension funds suggests that their investment policies would be a major factor. Investing in bonds and other debt instruments would clearly limit their role in corporate governance to that of passive creditors, who are involved in corporate control issues only when firms face financial difficulties. Investing in equities would offer greater potential, especially if strategic stakes were acquired. But if pension funds were to acquire small, diversified holdings, then their direct role in corporate governance would be limited by the free riding and collective choice problems associated with small holdings and dispersed ownership. The recent experience of the U.S. and U.K. markets suggests that pension funds could then rely on public criticism and collective bodies (to overcome the disincentives against active involvement of individual pension funds), initiatives to strengthen corporate governance structures, and development of specialized monitors.

Historical Evolution

The role of pension funds (and other institutional investors) in corporate governance differs considerably from country to country. Four types of experience can be identified. First are those countries where pension funds (and other institutional investors) are underdeveloped and thus play a limited role in their financial systems. In these countries, banks may be heavily involved in both corporate finance and corporate governance (as in Germany and Japan) or industrial and commercial companies may be owned and controlled by dominant family groups (as in Latin America and East Asia) or by the state (as in Africa, the Arab world, and the former socialist countries).

Second are those countries where pension funds have become large and control substantial financial resources but tend to invest in government and corporate bonds and other debt instruments. This group includes Switzerland, the Netherlands, and the Scandinavian countries in continental Europe as well as several developing countries with funded pension schemes, such as Singapore, Malaysia, and Chile.[20] In these countries pension funds act as passive creditors and are involved in corporate governance issues only when firms face financial difficulties. But even then, they play a passive role and follow the lead of the commercial and investment banks in organizing rescue and restructuring operations or in liquidating firms. When pension funds invest mostly in government bonds (as in Singapore and Malaysia), their role in corporate governance is obviously nonexistent.

Third are Anglo-American countries, except South Africa. In these countries pension funds have small, diversified equity holdings in a large number of companies, while banks and other financial institutions have been discouraged, either by regulation or tradition, from acquiring large controlling stakes in nonfinancial corporations. Ownership of corporations has become diffuse, and corporate control has rested with internal managers, often supported by external directors picked by chief executive officers. Institutional investors have traditionally operated as active portfolio investors, but passive shareholders. They have relied on the threat of takeover for disciplining corporate management.

[20] The role of the Chilean pension funds is likely to change as their holdings of corporate equities increase. Until now their equity holdings have been large only in the case of the privatized utilities, and their role in corporate governance has been confined to such companies.

Fourth is South Africa. It provides a paradox in that its financial system appears to fit the Anglo-American model (where securities markets play a greater role in corporate finance than banking institutions, and corporations are characterized by diffuse ownership and internal control by management), while its system of corporate governance seems to be closer to the Euro-Asian model (where banks have played a more central role in corporate finance than securities markets, and corporations are characterized by more concentrated ownership and stronger external control on management).[21] One of the features of South African finance is the large role played in corporate governance by contractual savings institutions. The four largest insurance companies, of which Old Mutual and Sanlam are mutual and Liberty and Southern are joint stock companies, own large stakes in numerous industrial and commercial companies as well as controlling stakes in the major South African banks (Vittas 1994).

As in the case of their portfolio investments, the different roles of pension funds in corporate governance reflect both historical traditions and regulatory differences. Except South Africa, the pattern of corporate governance in Anglo-American systems has its roots in the fear of excessive concentration of economic and financial power in the hands of a few institutions and groups. In the United States, pension funds have been discouraged from acquiring large equity holdings by the "prudent man" rule that has emphasized diversification and compliance with prevailing practice, while commercial banks, insurance companies, and mutual funds have been prevented from acquiring controlling stakes in nonfinancial corporations by government regulations (Roe 1990, 1991).

In the United Kingdom, tradition has exerted a more important influence than regulation. Although commercial banks have not been subject to prescriptive regulations, they have focused their lending operations on short-term, self-liquidating loans rather than on long-term loans and equity stakes (Kennedy 1987). This policy has enjoyed the tacit support of the authorities and has been reflected in the prudent man rule imposed on insurance companies, mutual funds, and pension funds. But U.K. institutional investors have been more openly critical of corporate policies than their U.S. counterparts, not only when corporations are underperforming, but also when they adopt low dividend payouts or award excessive remuneration to their senior managers.

The emphasis on small, diversified holdings has forced pension funds in

[21] This combination may have several advantages over the pure Anglo-American and Euro-Asian models, such as greater reliance on equity finance but with more effective monitoring of corporations than has been customary in the U.S. or U.K. markets (Gerson 1992).

the United States and the United Kingdom to play a passive role in corporate governance. Small holdings and dispersed ownership have created a collective choice problem since investors have little incentive to incur the high costs of monitoring and are prone to free ride on the monitoring efforts of others. In addition the fiduciary emphasis on compliance with prevailing practice has implied that no pension fund could deviate significantly unless such deviation was clearly beneficial to pension fund members and was not undermining the fiduciary standards of pension fund managers (Roe 1993).

Until the recent decline of the exit option, an important tradeoff between liquidity and control had emerged in the United States and the United Kingdom (Coffee 1991). Pension funds and other institutional investors valued liquidity and their ability to exit at low cost from an underperforming company. Control implied a decline in liquidity and incurring the large costs of monitoring and bail-outs, while the benefits from greater control were shared by all shareholders.[22] Whereas a combination of both liquidity and control seemed difficult to attain, a situation in which pension funds had neither liquidity nor control was gradually emerging. The recent initiatives discussed below are a response to this combination of lack of liquidity, lack of control, and lack of managerial accountability.

In contrast to the United States and the United Kingdom, regulation and tradition have encouraged the acquisition of strategic holdings in South Africa. Such stakes have implied greater control but at the expense of reduced liquidity for their holders. In the case of Sanlam (one of the two mutual insurance groups) the strategic holdings, which generally include investments of more than 20 percent of the capital of the investee company, have resulted from the traditional policy of encouraging the development of Afrikaner industry. In the mid-1980s, Sanlam set up a special holding company, Sankorp, to monitor actively the performance of its strategic holdings. Old Mutual has adopted a more passive stance but claims that its strategic holdings earn the same returns as its portfolio holdings. The joint stock insurance companies own fewer strategic holdings and their investment policies follow more closely the less active patterns prevailing in U.K. and other Anglo-American companies. Independent, self-administered pension funds, although collectively larger than the insurance companies, are individually smaller than the big insurance groups and follow their lead in investing in the equities of listed corporations.

[22] Black (1992a) points out, however, that large institutions do make investments in illiquid assets (e.g. in real estate and venture capital), while their liquidity needs may be met by the inflow of new money. Thus, if allowed by legal rules, large institutions could prefer control over liquidity. Black attributes the limited voice exercised by institutional investors in corporate affairs to legal obstacles and promanager conflicts (see below).

In South Africa the two mutual insurance groups are overshadowed by the corporate governance participation of nonfinancial conglomerates, such as the Anglo-American, De Beers, and Rembrandt groups. These conglomerates mainly originate from the mining sector and have acquired their extensive interests in industrial and commercial companies as they diversified and as a result of government policies of the last forty years. Together with the two insurance groups, four or five South African conglomerates are in effective control of 80 percent of corporate assets. This high concentration of corporate ownership has been bolstered by the imposition of tight exchange controls, which has prevented investment in overseas securities, and by the purchase of the stakes of departing foreign investors during the period of international economic sanctions.

It has been argued that private pension funds in the United States and the United Kingdom have been captured by corporate managers. Pension fund managers are appointed by senior corporate executives and therefore are not expected to monitor the performance of other corporations since that would invite monitoring of their own operations by the pension funds of other companies. Although there is validity in this argument, the basic premise that pension funds have been captured by corporate managers is misleading. It disregards the historical evolution of pension funds. Company pension schemes were created by corporations and were never independent of company management. If anything, their evolution suggests a gradual but steady decline in their dependence on corporate management priorities.

Company pension schemes were historically created as personnel management tools to attract skilled workers, reward loyalty, and facilitate the retirement of older workers. They imposed onerous vesting and portability restrictions on their members, and they were designed so that few workers would qualify for a pension. Their cost was intended to be small and easily absorbed from current revenues without any need to fund pension liabilities in advance. The rise of large companies in conjunction with the rise of trade unionism and collective bargaining led to a gradual but substantial increase in the coverage of pension schemes and to a relaxation of vesting and portability restrictions, although the schemes were still biased toward rewarding workers with long tenure (Hannah 1986).

This change gave rise to the need for funding and increased the cost of pension schemes. Tax incentives encouraged provisions against future pension liabilities, but early funding took the form of book reserves (i.e. reinvesting pension provisions in the assets of the sponsoring companies, a practice that is still prevalent in Germany and other countries). The widespread use of book reserves limited the role of pension funds as financial intermediaries and institutional investors. Their personnel management function and their role as pension institutions continued to predominate.

The big change in pension funds as institutional investors occurred in the 1950s when large U.S. corporations started to invest their growing pension reserves in other companies. To protect their sponsoring corporations from antitrust actions, pension fund managers acquired small, diversified holdings that precluded the exercise of corporate control and promoted the safety and soundness of accumulated reserves. Since their assets were small, pension funds acquired small stakes in liquid securities and adopted a hands-off approach in corporate management. If pension funds were unhappy with corporate performance, they could sell without suffering a big fall in market price.

Continuing growth in membership and growing pressures to protect the long-term interests of workers led to gradual relaxation of vesting and portability restrictions and to rapid accumulation of reserves to ensure adequate funding of pension liabilities. As pension funds (and other institutional investors) became collectively dominant shareholders of nonfinancial corporations,[23] they could no longer exercise the exit option without disrupting the market and suffering big falls in market prices. Recent attempts to develop effective means for exercising "voice" in corporate affairs are a response to the decline of the exit option.

In addition, pension fund managers have been adopting investment policies based on passive indexation as an effective strategy for achieving diversification with market returns and low transaction costs. However, passive indexation policies have limited their ability to divest from poorly performing companies and have increased pressures for more effective monitoring of corporate performance and for increasing the accountability of corporate managers. For instance, the California Public Employees Retirement System (CALPERS) – a largely passively indexed pension fund – analyzes companies in its indexed portfolio and targets poorly performing companies for action, including direct negotiations with management, withholding votes from directors, or mobilizing shareholder proposals to improve corporate accountability. A pension fund with a large portfolio (like CALPERS) has a special incentive to target the companies with the poorest management practices and performance. Even if the cost of activism exceeds the benefits from improving the performance of one targeted company, the threat of becoming the next target will generate an external discipline on managers of other companies in the portfolio to improve their performance.

[23] Among large U.S. corporations, institutional investors in 1988 owned 86% of the equity of Amoco, 82% of General Motors, 74% of Mobil Corp., 71% of Eli Lilly & Co., and 70% of Citicorp (Coffee 1991).

The growing involvement of U.S. and U.K. pension funds in corporate affairs has also been bolstered by the decline in hostile takeovers and tender offers, following the excesses of the 1980s and the defenses adopted by corporate managers. Hostile takeovers, based on tender offers and proxy contests, have been extensively used since the late 1950s to acquire poorly performing companies, replace managers, dispose surplus capacity, and make more efficient use of corporate assets. But hostile bids have also been used to acquire successful firms by large conglomerates engaging in empire building and searching for synergies and scope economies, often in unrelated markets. In the 1980s hostile takeovers through leveraged buyouts were used for breaking up large conglomerates and restructuring individual units, but they were also used for stripping valuable assets, for blackmailing corporate managements into paying huge ransoms to corporate raiders ("greenmailing"), and even for raiding the surplus assets of company pension schemes.

Evidence on systematic shortfalls in corporate performance in the United States and on the potential influence of monitoring by large shareholders is presented in Black (1992b),[24] who summarizes deficiencies in the functioning of corporate boards, corporate diversification strategies, value-reducing takeover decisions, management-entrenching governance structures, corporate cash retention and squandering, and excessive managerial compensation. He shows that

- independent directors do a better job than other directors in firing poorly performing managers and in discouraging bad acquisitions;
- conglomerates are less efficient than more focused companies;
- manager-controlled firms are more likely to diversify;
- many takeovers cause the bidder, or the bidder and target, to lose value;
- bidders with low efficiency and high cash flow are more likely to make bad acquisitions;
- combined bidder and target losses are greater when low efficiency bidders acquire high efficiency targets (in contrast, related takeovers, takeovers by well-run bidders, and takeovers of poorly performing targets are more likely to increase the combined value of bidder and target);
- pro-incumbent governance rules reduce stock prices;
- managers hoard cash and then spend it on poor projects;
- managerial compensation is excessive and unrelated to performance.

[24] Monks and Minow (1995), in a lucid and comprehensive overview of corporate governance issues, discuss case studies of corporations in crisis that include the recent travails of General Motors, American Express, Time Warner, Sears Roebuck & Co, Armand Hammer and Occidental Petroleum, Polaroid, Carter Hawley Hale, and Eastman Kodak.

Black suggests that institutional investors could add value by enhancing director independence, discouraging corporate diversification, pressing bidders to abandon suspect takeover bids, pressing targets to consent to value-increasing bids, insisting on more efficient governance rules, making it harder for managers to hoard unneeded cash, and linking managerial compensation to performance.

Anti-takeover legislation and more effective corporate defenses have made it more difficult for hostile bids to succeed, but they have also underscored the power vacuum and lack of accountability that have emerged in corporate governance (Monks and Minow 1991). Realization of this power vacuum has increased pressure on institutional investors to become more active shareholders. In the United States, the Department of Labor has urged pension funds to exercise their voting rights and to treat their proxy votes as plan assets subject to fiduciary standards. Also, regulations that discouraged institutional investors from talking to each other have been relaxed. In the United Kingdom, such restrictions did not exist, but there was, nevertheless, greater pressure on institutional investors to increase and improve their monitoring of corporate management.

Recent Initiatives

The past decade has witnessed a gradual transformation of pension funds (and other institutional investors) from active investors and passive shareholders into passive investors and active shareholders. Three types of initiatives have been taken: measures to exert greater public pressure on non-performing corporate management, measures to ensure better and more robust corporate governance structures, and measures to influence more directly corporate policy.

Greater public criticism of misbehaving and underperforming corporations includes criticism of overambitious expansion plans into unrelated areas that smack of empire-building, low dividend payouts, excessive managerial compensation, overgenerous compensation for retiring or redundant managers, and anti-takeover defenses that entrench the position of incumbent managers at the expense of shareholders. Open public criticism has been instrumental in mobilizing collective action by disgruntled shareholders and in raising the threat of regulation and legislation to prohibit alleged abuse and misbehavior.

But public criticism is not always effective. First, corporate managers may carry public opinion with them if they raise the prospect of job and tax revenue losses for the areas where their operations are located. Second, since the managers of private pension funds are effectively beholden to their chief executive officers, any such public criticism can only come from the managers of public pension funds, who are more independent of corporate managers (though they are under the control of politicians). Even professional fund managers, insurance companies, and mutual funds are often constrained in their public criticisms by the fear of loss of business from other corporations.

In the United States the leading role in criticizing the managements of underperforming corporations has been taken by the managers of public pension funds, such as the California Public Employees Retirement System (CALPERS), the New York State Common Retirement Fund, and other public pension funds in Wisconsin and other states (Bishop 1994). Public pension funds have been at the forefront of corporate governance issues, especially in states where they have not been subject to statutory limitations with regard to their equity investments.[25] Insurance companies and mutual fund management companies have been conspicuous by their silence. In the United Kingdom the lead in criticizing nonperforming companies has been taken by POSTEL (a large, previously public pension fund for postal and telecom workers), by Prudential (a large insurance company), and by M&G (a large fund management company).[26]

A more effective way of voicing public criticism has been the use of formal associations of pension funds (e.g. the Association of British Insurers and the National Association of Pension Funds in the United Kingdom) or *ad hoc* groupings of interested institutional investors (e.g. the Institutional Shareholders Committee in the United Kingdom or the Council of Institutional Investors in the United States). The last-named group was created 10 years ago and is a forum for big shareholders to discuss corporate problems. It regularly publishes a list of the 50 least performing companies and thus exerts pressure on the offending corporate managers without exposing any individual shareholder or pension fund manager to the threat of corporate retaliation.

Public criticism targeted at poor performers fosters corrective action but does little to prevent the mistakes and abuses of corporate managers who have treated their corporations as their personal fiefdoms and have behaved like the feudal lords of modern times. To forestall such abuses, action needs to be taken to strengthen corporate governance structures and, especially, to increase the accountability of managers. Well functioning corporate governance structures are also essential for protecting the interests of minority shareholders and for ensuring that incumbent managers or corporate

[25] Some concerns have been expressed about the incentives and constraints facing the managers of public pension funds. For a critical stance, see Romano (1993).

[26] The differences and similarities in the role of institutional investors in the United Kingdom and the United States are reviewed in Black and Coffee (1994).

raiders do not reap large gains at the expense of uncoordinated shareholders.

In the United States and the United Kingdom various groups published reports outlining the reforms that need to be implemented and underscoring the changes that company directors and institutional shareholders need to make in their behavior (NACD 1994; Conference Board 1994; Cadbury Committee 1992). In addition the Institute of Directors commissioned an extensive survey of directors from the Henley Management College. These reports argued that U.S. and U.K. corporate boards have only recently become concerned about improving their effectiveness and did not see a connection between board effectiveness and corporate performance.

The measures that are contemplated to strengthen corporate governance and improve the effectiveness of corporate boards include the following:

- separating the functions of chairman and chief executive officer;
- appointing nonexecutive chairmen in all companies above a certain size;
- electing independent external directors;
- cumulative voting for board elections;
- opening the proxy process to allow greater communication among shareholders;
- confidential voting at board meetings;
- expanding the role of board committees that are independent of executive directors;
- disclosing the amount and rationale of managerial compensation;
- opposing anti-takeover defenses that are designed to protect incumbent managers at the expense of shareholders.

Of these measures, the use of cumulative voting for board elections seems to be the most powerful tool for allowing institutional shareholders to elect directors who are truly independent of corporate managers and who actively protect the interests of shareholders.[27]

Extensive use of board committees to (1) select and appoint chief executive officers (to avert the perpetuation of the business policies of incumbent management), (2) vet managerial compensation (to prevent excessive packages that are unrelated to performance), (3) approve major expansion plans (to check managerial tendencies toward empire building), and (4) evaluate and respond to friendly and hostile bids (to ensure that shareholders receive maximum value from takeovers), creates a two-tier board

[27] In this context, Gilson and Kraakman (1991) have argued that institutional investors should recruit independent directors to monitor corporate behavior and performance on their behalf.

structure similar to the German practice but without the board representation of workers and the limited accountability of incumbent managers.

In addition, to protect minority shareholders, pension funds and other institutional investors have (1) advocated regulations that discourage the use of multi-class shares and pyramidal structures, (2) required adequate information disclosure, (3) ensured that transactions with related-parties are effected on market terms and conditions, and (4) stimulated the creation of liquid and transparent markets.

The efforts by various collective bodies (such as the Council of Institutional Investors, the National Association of Corporate Directors, and the Conference Board in the United States or the Institute of Directors, the National Association of Pension Funds and the Association of British Insurers in the United Kingdom) to spell out the duties and responsibilities of board directors and to emphasize the benefits of greater accountability of directors have increased awareness of these issues by large corporations.

In addition a small number of entities have emerged that specialize in monitoring corporate governance practices of large corporations in a number of countries.[28] Some of these entities rate the accountability of managers and their compliance with international standards of corporate governance. They play a crucial and influential role in advising institutional investors on how to exercise their voting rights.

Finally, initiatives to exert more direct influence on corporate policy and performance through significant equity stakes and board representation are considered. Because pension funds are constrained by their diversification policies and lack of in-house managerial expertise from acquiring large equity stakes in individual companies and seeking board representation, they have relied on companies specializing in leveraged buyouts (such as KKR in the United States) or on industrial conglomerates (such as the Hanson and BTR groups in the United Kingdom). These groups acquire control of targeted companies through tender offers and hostile takeovers. They finance their operations by issuing equity or debt and rely on their reputation as effective industrial managers for raising funds from pension funds and other institutional investors.

[28] These include the Investor Responsibility Research Center (IRRC) and the Institutional Shareholders Services (ISS) in the United States and Promotion of Nonexecutive Directors (PRO NED) and Pensions and Investments Research Consultants (PIRC) in the United Kingdom. As corporate governance rating agencies, these entities would be subject to the same constraints of cost and effectiveness that affect the operations of credit and bond rating agencies. Coffee (1990) highlights the dissatisfaction with the slow response to new information of bond rating agencies in the 1980s. Often, a rating change followed, rather than preceded, the market's adverse reaction to a deterioration in a corporation's financial condition.

A new technique has recently been developed in the United States that avoids outright control of companies and relies on an incremental approach (Gordon and Pound 1992). Under this approach, specialized companies raise funds from institutional investors to acquire substantial equity stakes in individual corporations and seek board representation to influence corporate policy. One form of this approach, exemplified by the Lens Fund operated by Robert Monks, includes non-negotiated purchases and aggressive tactics (such as public criticism and voting challenges) to induce change.[29] An alternative form relies on negotiated purchases that are welcome by incumbent managers and support them in their expansion or restructuring policies. (This is the approach used by Berkshire Hathaway, a fund operated by Warren Buffett.) The first form seeks to act as a catalyst in maximizing company value with a short- to medium-term horizon; the second form operates as patient capital with a long-term horizon.

Unresolved Issues

As a response to the mistakes and excesses of the 1980s, institutional investors and other disgruntled shareholders were forced to take action to remove incumbent managers of badly underperforming corporations. But except for leveraged buyouts and limited experience with the patient capital approach, the changes have not addressed the need to develop strategic investors with large holdings that could provide long-term support and commitment to corporate management. In Euro-Asian corporate governance, such long-term commitment and support have been provided by banks and other financial institutions, and by controlling industrial groups, which have large stakes in companies. But among countries with funded pension schemes and a large contractual savings industry, only South Africa has developed such an approach.

Strategic holdings avoid the problems of free riding and emphasis on short-term corporate performance that might result from the fragmentation of corporate ownership. They also limit the incidence of excessive managerial compensation, since executive remuneration is controlled by the strategic shareholders and can be more objectively linked to performance. The shortcomings of strategic holdings in the hands of a few institutions are the large concentration of economic power and the potential conflicts of interest between strategic investors and other groups of shareholders (the latter often suffer from reduced voting rights and limited access to information (Rock

[29] The difficulties of these new approaches are highlighted by the failure of the Lens Fund, which is organized as a closed-end mutual fund, to raise capital from CALPERS and other public or private pension funds (Coffee 1994).

1991)). Large strategic stakes may also lead to uncompetitive practices in industrial sectors dominated by companies controlled by the conglomerates, and the orientation of capital markets toward the financing of larger firms may inhibit access to external finance by new, dynamic companies. In South Africa where strategic holdings by institutional investors are widespread, Vittas (1994) recommends a triple burden of proof on proponents of conglomerates. This should show that strategic holdings earn risk-adjusted rates of return that are no lower than those obtained on portfolio holdings; that the industrial sectors remain sufficiently competitive, and that smaller firms are not denied reasonable access to external finance.

Effective monitoring takes time and requires specialists and experts who understand the law and are able to assess the performance of different corporations. Pension fund managers and trustees often lack the specialist knowledge that would be required to challenge the decisions and actions of corporate managers. Moreover, even if they did have such knowledge, it would be difficult to quantify the benefits from improved monitoring. For this reason most pension fund managers react more strongly to general points of principle than to company issues. Thus they might oppose any attempt to curtail voting rights, or they might support proposals to strengthen board structure and independence, rather than taking on disputes over business strategy or the competence of corporate managers. Working through a collective body could reduce the costs of monitoring, achieve economies of scale (especially for recurring issues), and more easily overcome free riding. For other initiatives, such as the use of specialized agencies, the cost of monitoring may be an inhibiting factor. Often, the threat of closer oversight may be more effective than reliance on specialized agencies. Collective bodies that review corporate performance may be the most effective form of monitoring from a cost/benefit viewpoint.

While separating the functions of chairman and chief executive officer will increase monitoring and oversight when it is first instituted to curtail the entrenched power and influence of executive managers, what will be the long-term effectiveness of such initiatives? There is no guarantee that a nonexecutive chairman may not become as identified with the fortunes of the corporation as its executive management. Independent nonexecutive directors might indulge in the same dispensation of perquisites as the unaccountable corporate managers did. Thus, institutional investors as large shareholders will have to monitor the performance of nonexecutive chairmen and other directors. Similar problems may also arise for independent collective bodies that may lose their independence if they are captured by executive managers of large corporations.

Finally, the perennial question of "who monitors the monitors?" will arise for specialized monitors, managers of pension funds, and other institutional investors. After all, the managers of these institutions act as agents for the large number of dispersed beneficiaries – the active and passive workers who are members of pension plans, the policyholders of insurance companies, and the small investors who place their savings with mutual funds and other financial institutions. To ensure that recent initiatives retain long-term effectiveness and that the managers of pension funds and other institutions serve the interests of their principals, further collective measures may be necessary, such as government regulation and oversight, adequate information disclosure and transparency, and greater involvement of public committees of informed, independent observers and experts (Pound 1992).

The role of pension funds and other institutional investors in corporate governance is still an issue of intense debate. As summarized in Coffee (1994), there are three different conceptions of the role of institutional investors. The first, which is popular within the business community and a large section of the academic community, sees institutional investors as short-term oriented and inclined toward fads and herd behavior. The second view sees institutional investors as prevented by legal rules and promanager conflicts from becoming more active in corporate affairs. This view argues that pension funds and other institutional investors have economic incentives to achieve gains from better monitoring but are regulated into passivity. The third view doubts that institutional investors have strong incentives to monitor and argues that they may have a preference for liquidity and passivity. It would seem that all three views have merit in explaining the current role of institutional investors in corporate governance. The increasing reliance on collective bodies, stronger corporate governance structures, and specialized monitors may represent an efficient and economical response to the challenge posed by the decline of exit and the need to exercise more effective voice.

Summary

Pension fund regulations and the incentives facing pension fund managers shaped their passive role in corporate governance. Traditionally, pension funds were expected to vote with management. They were constrained in their criticism of corporate governance by the threat of retaliation and loss of future business in the case of independent fund managers and by their accountability to senior corporate executives in the case of self-administered pension funds. If they were unhappy with corporate performance, they were supposed to exit by selling in the market.

Corporate discipline was exerted by the threat of hostile takeovers, which have been used extensively over the past 30 years to acquire poorly performing companies. But hostile takeovers have also been used to acquire successful firms, strip valuable assets, "greenmail" corporate managements, and "raid" the surplus assets of company pension schemes.

Anti-takeover legislation and more effective corporate defenses have weakened the threat of hostile takeovers and, therefore, created a need for other forms of corporate control. Exit by pension funds has also become more difficult. The cost of exit has also increased by the growing domination of equity markets by large institutional investors and the increasing inability of pension funds to sell without disrupting the market and suffering large price decreases. Use of the exit option has been further restricted by the growing trend toward passive indexation of equity portfolios, which hinders the disposal of underperforming equities. These developments have underscored the importance of exercising "voice" in corporate affairs.

Public pension funds, which are independent of corporate managers, have been less reticent in their criticisms of underperforming companies. Although they are accountable to politicians and government bureaucrats and are often subject to political pressures, they have been able to attract public attention to the power vacuum that has emerged in corporate affairs. In contrast, private pension funds have continued to be dependent on corporate managers and to be heavily constrained in their ability to take individual action against underperforming companies.

New solutions have emerged to fill the power vacuum in corporate affairs and to increase the accountability of corporate managers:

1. Existing collective bodies have been encouraged and new ones have been created to voice public criticism of underperforming corporations, free from the fear of retaliation that has inhibited individual pension fund managers.
2. Various initiatives have been promoted to strengthen corporate governance and increase the effectiveness of corporate boards in supervising executive managers.
3. Specialized agencies have emerged that scrutinize the governance structures and practices of different corporations and advise pension funds on how to exercise their voting rights.
4. Various specialized monitors of corporate performance have appeared. Some of these take non-negotiated stakes in underperforming companies and adopt aggressive tactics to change corporate policy, improve performance and enhance value. Others adopt a more patient approach and acquire friendly stakes that provide support and commitment to incumbent managers to achieve long-term growth.

All these initiatives are of recent origin. Although they were instrumental in changing the top management of some heavily and persistently underperforming corporations, their long-term impact remains to be seen. The risks of excessive concentration and abuse of economic power and of the potential conflicts of interest between pension funds, including their collective agents, and other shareholders have yet to be properly addressed. Moreover, the new approaches may be captured by corporate managers, and their long-term effectiveness has yet to be fully tested. Finally, the questions who monitors the monitors and how appropriate checks and balances are created remain to be answered.

Lessons and Policy Implications for Transitional Economies

The following lessons and policy implications emerged from this discussion of the prospects for private pension funds in Central Europe and Russia and their potential long-term role in corporate governance. The countries reviewed, like all transitional economies, have public pension systems that face severe financial pressures and fail to provide adequate pension benefits to the majority of their pensioners. Although radical pension reform may not be politically feasible soon and may even be inadvisable in the interest of sustaining political support for privatization and enterprise restructuring, fundamental pension reform will be unavoidable in the future.

The experience of the more advanced OECD countries (and some innovating developing countries) suggests that the public pension system should be downsized and its benefits rationalized to offer adequate, affordable, and sustainable benefits and to encourage the creation and growth of private pension funds.

Private pension funds could be organized as voluntary or mandatory, based on company schemes or nonemployer-related funds, and arranged as defined benefit or defined contribution plans. The shortcomings of company-based defined benefit plans suggest that transitional countries should opt in the longer run in favor of nonemployer, defined contribution plans based on individual capitalization accounts with full and immediate vesting, full portability, and full funding. To cope with the need for a targeted replacement rate, such schemes could operate with variable contribution rates, reset periodically in accordance with the salary growth of each worker, the cumulative investment return on the worker's account, and the targeted pension benefit.

Once established, private pension funds will accumulate long-term financial resources at a rapid pace. The speed will depend on the coverage of the schemes, the rate of contribution, the investment returns, and the rate of growth of real wages. Pension funds are also likely to have a major impact on the modernization of securities markets, stimulating innovation, fostering better accounting and auditing standards, and promoting greater information disclosure.

Their role in different securities markets will be shaped by future regulations on their investments and by the traditions that are likely to emerge. In general, given their long-term obligations, pension funds could become major investors in corporate equities. Marketable debt instruments, such as government bonds, corporate bonds, and mortgage bonds or securitized mortgage-backed instruments, could also benefit from their development. The experience of the more advanced OECD countries suggests that investments should be governed by prudential concerns, should favor sensible diversification, and should emphasize investment returns commensurate with the risks involved. Rigorous accounting and auditing standards and information disclosure to the regulatory authorities and their members would be essential.

The role of pension funds in corporate governance will also depend on regulation and tradition. They will face conflicting incentives, pressures, and constraints. To diversify their risks and protect the value of funds under management, they will be pressured to acquire small equity holdings. But if pension funds dominate the equity market, the liquidity of their holdings may become more illusory than real. They will also be pressured to adopt a policy of passive portfolio indexation to keep costs down and improve their investment performance. As a result, a vacuum in corporate governance may emerge, with limited corporate accountability, unless pension funds actively exercise voice in corporate affairs and intensively monitor the performance of individual corporations.

The experience of the more advanced OECD countries suggests that pension funds will be more effective in exercising voice in corporate affairs through collective bodies, specialized monitors, and robust structures of corporate governance. In this way they could achieve greater coordination, keep monitoring costs down, and avoid the problems of free riding. However, experience with these initiatives is relatively limited and their long-term effectiveness remains to be seen.

References

Barr, Nicholas. 1992. "Economic Theory and the Welfare State: A Survey and Interpretation." *Journal of Economic Literature* (June).

Bishop, Matthew. 1994. "Survey on Corporate Governance." *The Economist* (January 29).

Black, Bernard S. 1992a. "Agents Watching Agents: The Promise of Institutional Voice." *UCLA Law Review.*

——. 1992b. "The Value of Institutional Investor Monitoring: The Empirical Evidence." *UCLA Law Review.*

Black, Bernard S., and John C. Coffee, Jr. 1994. "Hail Britannia: Institutional Investor Behavior under Limited Regulation." *Michigan Law Review* 92: 1997.

Bodie, Zvi. 1990a. "Pension Funds and Financial Innovation." *Financial Management* (autumn).

——. 1990b. "Pensions as Retirement Income Insurance." *Journal of Economic Literature* (March).

Cadbury Committee. 1992. *The Financial Aspects of Corporate Governance.* London: Gee and Co. Ltd.

Coffee, John C., Jr. 1990. "Unstable Coalitions: Corporate Governance as a Multi-Player Game." *Georgetown Law Journal.*

——. 1991. "Liquidity versus Control: The Institutional Investor as Corporate Monitor." *Columbia Law Review* 91: 1277.

——. 1994. "The SEC and the Institutional Investor: Half-Time Report." *Cardozo Law Review.*

Conference Board. 1994. *Corporate Boards: Improving and Evaluating Performance.* New York.

Davis, E. Philip. 1993. "The Structure, Regulation and Performance of Pension Funds in Nine Industrial Countries." Policy Research Working Paper 1229. World Bank.

de Fougerolles, Jean. 1994. "Pension Reform in Poland." Institute for East-West Studies. Mimeographed.

Fox, Louise. 1994. "Old Age Security in Transition Economies." Policy Research Working Paper 1257, World Bank.

Gerson, Jos. 1992. *The Determinants of Corporate Ownership and Control in South Africa.* Los Angeles: University of California.

Gilson, Ronald J., and Reinier Kraakman. 1991. "Reinventing the Outside Director: An Agenda for Institutional Investors." *Stanford Law Review.*

Gordon, Lilli A., and John Pound. 1992. *Active Investing in the U.S. Equity Market: Past Performance and Future Prospects.* Newton, Mass.: Gordon Group Inc.

Gray, Cheryl W., and Rebecca J. Hanson. 1993. "Corporate Governance in Central and Eastern Europe: Lessons from Advanced Market Economies." Policy Research Working Paper 1182, World Bank.

Hannah, Leslie. 1986. *Inventing Retirement: The Development of Occupational Pensions in Britain.* Cambridge: Cambridge University Press.

Holzmann, Robert. 1994. "Funded and Private Pensions for Eastern European Countries in Transition?" Unversity of Saarland, Research Paper 9404.

Kennedy, William P. 1987. *Industrial Structure, Capital Markets and the Origins of British Economic Decline.* Cambridge: Cambridge University Press.

Lakonishok, Josef, Andrei Shleifer, and Robert W. Vishny. 1992. "The Structure and

Performance of the Money Management Industry." Brookings Papers on Economic Activity: Microeconomics.
Monks, Robert A.G., and Nell Minow. 1991. *Power and Accountability*. New York: HarperBusiness.
——. 1995. *Corporate Governance*. Cambridge, MA: Basil Blackwell Inc.
National Association of Corporate Directors (NACD). 1994. *Performance Evaluation of Chief Executive Officers, Boards, and Directors*. Washington, D.C.
Pound, John. 1992. "Beyond Takeovers: Politics Comes to Corporate Control.", *Harvard Business Review* (March-April).
Rock, Edward B. 1991. "The Logic and (Uncertain) Significance of Institutional Shareholding Activism." *Georgetown Law Journal* (February).
Roe, Mark J. 1990. "Political and Legal Restraints on Ownership and Control of Public Companies." *Journal of Financial Economics* 27.
——. 1991. "A Political Theory of American Corporate Finance." *Columbia Law Review* 91: 10.
——. 1993. "The Modern Corporation and Private Pensions." *UCLA Law Review*.
Romano, Roberta. 1993. "Public Pension Fund Activism in Corporate Governance Reconsidered." *Columbia Law Review*.
Vittas, Dimitri. 1992. "Contractual Savings and Emerging Securities Markets." Policy Research Working Paper 858, World Bank.
——. 1993a. "Swiss Chilanpore: The Way Forward for Pension Reform?" Policy Research Working Paper 1093, World Bank.
——. 1993b. "The Simple(r) Algebra of Pension Plans." Policy Research Working Paper 1145, World Bank.
——. 1993c. "Options for Pension Reform in Tunisia." Policy Research Working Paper 1154, World Bank.
——. 1994. "Policy Issues in Contractual Savings in South Africa." Financial Sector Development Department, World Bank (June). Mimeographed.
Vittas, Dimitri, and Augusto Iglesias. 1992. "The Rationale and Performance of Personal Pension Plans in Chile." Policy Research Working Paper 867, World Bank.
Vittas, Dimitri, and Michael Skully. 1991. "Overview of Contractual Savings Institutions." Policy Research Working Paper 605, World Bank.
Williamson, Sam H. 1992. "U.S. and Canada Pensions Before 1930: A Historical Perspective", in *Trends in Pensions 1992*, edited by J. A. Turner and D. J. Beller. Washington, D.C.: U.S. Department of Labor,
World Bank. 1994. *Averting the Old Age Crisis: Policies to Protect the Old and Promote Growth*. New York: Oxford University Press.
Wyatt Company (H.K.) Limited, The. 1993. *Global Perspective: A Summary of Wyatt's Surveys on the 1992 Investment Performance of Retirement Fund Assets in Major World Markets*. Hong Kong.

7

DIRECT INVESTMENT, EXPERIMENTATION, AND CORPORATE GOVERNANCE IN TRANSITION ECONOMIES

BRUCE KOGUT

I would like to thank Saul Estrin, Brian Pinto, Chuck Sabel, Lazlo Urban, and especially Cheryl Gray for helpful comments on an earlier draft, as well as Andy Spicer, Farahnaz Ali, and Jared Minsk for research assistance. Financial assistance was provided by the Stockholm School of Economics through a grant from the Sasakawa Foundation.

Introduction

The transition of socialist to market economies has demonstrated the old lesson that social transformation is driven by both economics and politics. That the design of privatization schemes varies by political conditions across countries is not especially surprising in light of history. The persistence of the state and its administration, of cultural values, and of social and political institutions influences the set of feasible evolutions of even transitional states.

Of course, if there were a known best way to organize an economy, the influence of politics and social values might be seen as a constraint. But capitalism is not limited to any single type, nor can it be ruled out that a superior form of capitalist organization is yet untried. A desirable feature of any reform package is the allowance for an evolutionary path of trial, error, and adaptation.[1] Given the ambiguity in knowing the best elements to adopt

[1] See Frydman and Rapacynzski (1994) and Murrell (1992) for two alternative applications of evolutionary ideas to economic transition.

or create, politics and social institutions play an important role in guiding the process of evolution and transformation.

Foreign direct investment represents one of the most important ways by which knowledge of the relationship among organizational components is gathered and disseminated. One of the unique benefits of foreign direct investment is the experimentation of the core set of complementary practices that influence performance, and yet are transferable across borders. This role of experimentation is all the more valuable in environments where the rebuilding of institutions is still early.

It is not surprising that countries in transition from state socialism to capitalism are periodically ambivalent about direct investment. Foreign control is sometimes linked to the transfer of more productive methods that appear to violate social contracts or to displace other companies. If the perceived or real value is the transfer of wealth or control from a group of national citizens to foreign owners, the legitimacy of foreign direct investment is in question. Since multinational ownership concerns trade-offs among components in a transnational system, conflict potentially exists between national developmental objectives and the package of foreign control and better methods offered by direct investment.

In this chapter, I highlight the role that foreign direct investment plays in influencing the economic evolution of the East and Central European countries. The perspective I employ is evolutionary in the sense that social relationships inside and between firms are viewed as embodying economic knowledge and as governed by rules and institutions. Foreign direct investment contributes to the generation of new knowledge, partly through the provision of capital and technology and partly through its effect on the transformation of the rules and institutions that govern the organization of work. The entry of foreign firms sometimes results in the destruction of knowledge within and among existing domestic enterprises. This destruction can be positive when relationships among existing enterprises are depoliticized and when competition is increased. It can also be costly, such as when core firms in a supplier network disappear.

The chapter is divided into parts. The first section presents an overview of the firm as governed by rules and embedded in a social context. In the next two sections, I review the theory of foreign direct investment, the data on investment in Eastern Europe, and examine statistically the relationship between economic growth and direct investment in general. In the next section, I analyze the influence of direct investment on the governance, organization, and institutions of transition economies. The analysis in this section draws upon field research in Russia, Poland, East Germany, and

Latvia.[2] The next section suggests a set of policies regarding competition and ownership policies toward foreign entry.

The conclusions of this chapter endorse a liberal policy toward encouraging direct investment flows. In part, the positive contribution of direct investment is achieved through the transfer of control to motivated foreign investors. But in the larger perspective of the overall economy, the benefits of direct investment are generated through the participation of foreign firms in the process of entry of new firms, the creation of competitive incentives in the product market, and the provision of organizational solutions that serve as templates to be imitated by domestic firms.

Overview

In the few years since the turning toward capitalism, a number of important policy decisions have been introduced in the economies in transformation. Prices have been radically decontrolled in most countries, currencies have been made convertible, and the monopoly of international trade has been eliminated. The first policy target of getting the prices right by eliminating distortions has been achieved relatively early.

The subsequent stage of transformation involves a more complicated process. The issue is no longer creating prices that signal the relative scarcity of factors and goods. The challenge instead is the evolution of economic systems that encourage the acquisition and creation of new knowledge about organizing economic activities. In contrast to the ease by which the quality of information can be improved through decontrolling prices, the knowledge of *how* to organize and manage cannot be centrally mandated. The micro-economics of transformation are different from the macro-economics of price determination.

Because knowledge of how to organize cannot be created through liberalization, the policy considerations are variables that can be only indirectly manipulated through reform policies regarding the decentralization of decision-making to firms. For a number of reasons, private ownership is a

[2] As part of a research project organized by the Stockholm School of Economics, I participated in round table discussions with multinational corporations held in Stockholm, Latvia, and Poland. In addition, structured interviews were held with managers of five American multinational corporations in Moscow and Warsaw in September 1994, as well as interviews with Russian entrepreneurs. A research associate, Andy Spicer, conducted 34 background interviews with foreign and Russian managers, as well as with officials and researchers at Russian government and research institutions.

policy objective that has been widely embraced as a way to depoliticize economic decision-making and to match ownership incentives with management.

In most Central and East European countries, privatization programs have returned small enterprises to private hands. Varying but still generally large proportions of the large industrial concerns have been sold off or transferred to private hands through vouchers. By the end of 1994, the Czech Republic, Poland, Hungary, and Russia had succeeded in privatizing from 60 to 80 percent of their economies (CS First Boston 1994; "Czech Republic: The New Bohemians," *The Economist*, 22 October 1994, 23–7.

Given the abundance of well-educated workers, an obvious question is why privatized firms are not performing better in transitional economies. A candidate answer is that there is an absence of governance mechanisms to provide incentives to managers and workers to change their practices. The data and studies on transition economies point overwhelmingly to the persistence of the past, as well as to political impasses to change.[3]

Privatization does not, in any obvious way, generate knowledge about how to organize and manage economic activities. It does create the potential for what Oliver Williamson (1985) calls "high-powered incentives" to operate inside the firm. Oversight of top management by corporate governance is one, and likely important, element in the overall creation of incentives.

But the limits to change are not only political; they are also cognitive. The inherent difficulty in designing economic systems is that history has run only a small number of experiments. The past persists because change is, to use David Stark's expression, based on the recombination of what is already known. The strong tendency toward the status quo reflects the salience of social and cultural values, but also the limitations to identifying alternatives and working through their complex permutations. The incremental nature of change in economic development, as Nelson and Winter (1982) have eloquently argued, is a product of cognitive limitations in identifying and understanding alternatives. Because these limitations are constraining, an economy evolves partly through imitation, but also through a process of the birth and death of firms.

The difficulty of knowing what new practices to adopt and how to implement them is even more complicated at the system level. The casual observation of the impressive wealth and capitalist variety of countries such as the United States, Germany, and Japan suggests that a frontier of best governance practices hardly presents the conventional smooth and marginal trade-offs

[3] See the studies by Coffee, Earle and Estrin, Pistor and Turkewitz, and Stark (in this volume and its companion).

that allow for a bit more of one feature at the expense of another. The complexity of the problem of finding the right elements in a governance system is characterized by trying to discover the existence of true versus fictional complements.

It is this linkage among elements that defeats the serial testing of individual institutional elements, as if they were components on a printed circuit board. Assume that an economic system consists of N possible elements, such as equity or debt financing, quality circles, work councils, firm unions, and so on. An attempt to figure out the optimal complements requires then a search among $N!$ permutations. As Romer (1992) notes, a deck of cards presents 52!, or 10^{68}, permutations. Working out a best combination, given the cost of experiments, is likely to drive the search toward incremental and evolutionary improvement.

A governance system should not only provide monitoring and incentives for performance. It should also encourage experimentation, adoption, and diffusion of better practices. Incentives are not only monitoring devices, they are also signals of what is important inside an organization. In part, the problem of experimentation can be reduced to trying to match assets to owners with the appropriate knowledge of how to organize work. The issue is not only the provision of control, but also the establishment of a market for experimentation.

One of the important ways by which the complexity of search and experimentation is reduced is the role played by imitation. In this context, direct investment is more than the extension of ownership and governance across borders. It presents a template of the feasibility of alternative modes of organization adapted to the domestic environment. It has a quasi-public good characteristic insofar as other firms may observe the successful outcome of organizational experiments from proven companies.

Of course, observations are incomplete and prone to error. Because organizational knowledge is embedded in social relationships, it is difficult to replicate. Moreover, the knowledge of the firm spills over its boundaries to include its relations with suppliers and customers. A firm cannot easily imitate new ways because its existing economic knowledge is not separable from the social context. Direct investment, as a demonstration of an alternative model, is a powerful force for change because it acts as an "existence proof" of viable paths of development and as agent in the competitive process by which inefficient firms are eliminated. But the adoption and adaptation of new practices, because of the complexity of reorganizing social relationships, cannot be rapid, no matter what the competitive and governance incentives are.

Foreign Direct Investment

Direct investment is a complex phenomenon that represents the transfer of organizational knowledge, as well as foreign competition across borders. Because balance of payments statistics are the main source of data on international capital transactions, direct investment is often identified as a financial flow. Given the large demand for capital in transition economies, the typing of direct investment as a capital flow is particularly common.

This classification is unfortunate, for direct investment may occur without any financial flows. The value of a license granted to a subsidiary to use a parent's technology is frequently capitalized and treated as an equity stake. No money crosses borders, there is no balance of payments entry (except for future royalties and fees), and yet an equity transaction with a claim to some ownership control has occurred.

Because the distinguishing feature of direct, as opposed to portfolio, investment is *control* over economic assets across borders, the standard treatment of explaining direct investment is to focus on the interaction among three sets of variables: location, ownership, and internalization (Dunning 1979). Location refers to the costs of producing in one country versus another. These costs consist of the payments to factors of input, of transportation and commercial policy (e.g. tariffs), and of the creation (or loss) of economies of scale.

Ownership captures the idea that a firm usually must possess knowledge that generates a competitive advantage. The Hymer (1960) condition states that since foreign firms are at a disadvantage relative to domestic firms, the profitability of a foreign investment must be based on the possession of an advantage that earns compensating economic rents. This advantage may represent a one-off discovery of a particular process or product. But more likely, it represents a firm's capability to innovate and adapt, to manufacture or service, or to advertise and distribute.

In any transaction unconstrained by law or national regulation, a firm faces the choice between exploiting its advantage by ownership or by contract. Internalization is the decision of a firm to extend its advantage through an extension of ownership control. When this extension of a firm's boundaries crosses national borders, direct investment is the outcome.

A complementary, but more dynamic, way to categorize direct investment explanations is to consider the interaction among firms and locational advantages by looking at strategic motives. Explanations tend to emphasize one of three motives: push of competition, pull of the foreign market, or the benefits of coordination and combination of international assets. Each of these motives holds particular implications for transition economies.

"Push" and the Transfer of Advantage

Direct investment frequently consists of the transfer of intangible knowledge or assets to a foreign market. Due to the importance of owning intangible competitive advantages, the multinational corporation prevails in industries tending toward oligopoly. The advantages that lead to faster domestic growth are those that promote expansion over borders and an extension of home rivalry to overseas markets. As a result, the push of home-created advantages toward new foreign markets results in the recreation of these oligopolies in overseas markets. At the international level, the expansion of oligopolies overseas can reduce competition, but most studies find that internationalization also has competitive effects in disturbing national oligopolies (Caves 1982, ch. 4).

The importance of oligopolistic rivalry is clear in the list of major investors in Central Europe. In Table 7.1, the top investors are listed for Poland, the Czech Republic, and Hungary. The striking pattern is the prominent role played by a few industries (e.g. autos, consumer products, telecommunications) and a few firms (e.g. Asea Brown Boveri, Coca-Cola, and Proctor & Gamble). This pattern appears to replicate the distribution of flows in direct investment to Western countries; the sectoral distribution is highly correlated across countries (Anand and Kogut 1995).

"Pull" and Agglomeration Economies

Another motive for direct investment concerns the attraction exercised by particular locations. At the simplest level, this attraction exists through the importance of proximity to the market for selling and marketing of goods, or the attractiveness of a country as an export platform. Market access is an important motivation, particularly to avoid transportation and commercial barriers, such as tariffs.

Direct investment is also pulled toward certain countries in order to tap into localized pools of knowledge, much like the sourcing of raw materials. The difference is that access to knowledge in foreign markets usually requires the co-location of other knowledge resources, such as research and development or production. In this sense, agglomeration economies extend across borders, attracting foreign investment in local technological poles.

The evidence for this pulling effect is thin. Cantwell (1989) found mixed evidence that production was pulled toward countries leading in the creation of patented knowledge. Analyzing Japanese investments in the United States, Kogut and Chang (1991) noted that the primary driver of Japanese direct investment was the push effect of technological rivalry in the home market;

Table 7.1. Top Ten Foreign Investments in the Czech Republic, Hungary, and Poland, 1990-94

Investor	Local Partner	% Share	Investment (million $)	Sector
Czech Republic				
Volkswagen (Germany)	Skoda Automotive Works	70	700	Automotive
Linde (Germany)	Technoplyn	51	117	Industrial gases
Coca-Cola Amatil (Australia)	Nealko Kyje	52	82	Beverages
Asea Brown Boveri (Sweden/Switzerland)	Prvni brnenska strojirna	67	N.A.	Food and energy
Nestlé/BSN (Switzerland)	Cokoladovny	53	95.5	Food/confectionery
Kmart (USA)	Various	100	120[a]	Retail
Philip Morris (USA)	Tabak Kutna Hora	70	187	Tobacco
Glaverbel (Belgium)	Sklounion	67	100	Plate glass
Air France (France)	Ceskoslovenske Aerolinie (CSA)	19	150	Aviation
Proctor & Gamble (USA)	Rakona	100	24	Consumer goods
Hungary				
Ameritech (USA), Deutsche Bundespost Telecom (Germany)	Matav	30	875	Telecommunications
General Electric (USA)	Tungsram	100	550	Lighting
Volkswagen-Audi (Germany)	Audi Hungaria Motor (greenfield)	100	420	Automotive
US West International (USA)	Westel, Westel 900 (JV-greenfield)	49	330	Telecommunications
General Motors (USA, Germany)	GM Hungary (greenfield)	67	300	Automotive
Suzuki, C. Itoh, International Finance Corp. (Japan, International)	Magyar Suzuki (JV-greenfield)	60	250	Automotive
PTT Netherlands, Telecom Denmark & other Scandinavian operations (various)	Pannon GSM (JV-greenfield)	100	250	Telecommunications

Allianz (Germany)	Hungaria Biztositoi (JV)	67	220	Insurance
Transroute International, Banque Nationale de Paris, Caisse des Depots, Strabag (France, Austria)	Hungaria Euro-Expressway	N.A.	200	Motorway construction & operation
Alco (USA)	Kofem-Hungalu subsidiary (JV)	51	165	Aluminum
Poland				
Fiat (Italy)	FSM	90	2000	Automotive
Coca-Cola (USA)	Greenfields; JV with Rignes (Norway)	100	230	Beverages
Polish-American Enterprise Fund (USA)	Various	[b]	227	Multisector
International Paper Company (USA)	Zaklady Celulozowo-Papiernicze	80	315	Paper
European Bank for Reconstruction and Development	Various	[b]	138	Multisector
Asea Brown Boveri (Sweden/Switzerland)	Zamech; Dolmel; Elta; Polish State Railways; Elektrim	76;76;51; 30;10	120	Power & energy, railways
Curtis International (USA)	Electronics plant; business center	100;20	100	Electronics, construction
Unilever (Netherlands)	Pollena Bydogoszcz; Olmex; Roma	80;70[c]	96	Food & consumer goods
Epstein (USA)	Animex (JV); Golub/USA & National Bank (JV)	51;49; (with Golub)	200	Construction, food
Proctor & Gamble (USA)	Greenfield	100	190	Consumer goods

Source: Financial Times Statistics; Polish Foreign Investment Agency, January 1994; *Business Europe*, 28 February 1994

[a] Includes Slovak investment

[b] Not applicable

[c] Investments include equity and loans granted

however, joint ventures tended to be pulled into sectors where U.S. firms relatively outspent their Japanese competitors on research and development. In a recent paper, Almeida and Kogut (1994) found that for certain regions (e.g. Silicon Valley), knowledge spillovers are localized, and that spillovers flow to foreign and domestic firms located in these regions with no discernible differences. Krugman (1992) points out that locational advantages may be created if the investments in one area of an economy generate economies of scale in related industries.

Because of these externalities, the social benefits may well diverge from the private returns. Not surprisingly, most East and Central European countries engage in various degrees of incentives to attract investment. However, there appears to be a fundamental difference between fiscal revenue and industrial policy concerns (Török, 1994). The Czech Republic has been most aggressive in eradicating all tax incentives for foreign direct investment (FDI). Poland has also eliminated tax holidays as of January 1994, while providing tax breaks for both domestic and foreign investors. Hungary and Bulgaria offer moderate tax incentives. Romania is unusual in offering rather attractive tax incentives with little restrictions, though it continues to require government approval and restricts the types of positions foreigners can hold.[4] Russia's policy on the registration and requirement of approval of foreign direct investment is unclear. According to the Vice Prime Minister Alexander Shokhin, tax holidays and free economic zones have been proposed (Shokhin, 1994). Free economic zones have been created in the Czech Republic, Hungary, Poland, Romania, and Bulgaria, as well as in other countries in transition.

The low emphasis on incentives of the Czech Republic and, to a lesser extent, Poland may be an outcome of their proximity to Germany, which is the leading trade partner of the region. About one-third of Czech exports are destined for Germany. In a calculation of geographic accessibility, Sachs (1993: 99) notes that Poland is closer than Spain to the high density location of West European industry. The Czech Republic is even more favored as a location if similar calculations are made. In Poland and the Czech Republic, Germany is responsible for 30 to 40 percent of the direct investment flow. To compensate for locational disadvantages, Romania, Bulgaria, and Hungary employ incentives, perhaps partly out of competition with countries closer to West European industry. The dominant Greek investment in Bulgaria highlights the fortuitous nature of proximity to strong economies.

The fiscal consequences of the tax incentives are suggested by the large

[4] See Gray and Jarosz (1993: 10,16). Frydman, Rapaczynski, and Earle (1993) have a useful review of the policies regarding direct investment up to 1992.

number of ventures registered as foreign. Siotis (1994) reports that these tax shelters in Romania have caused the number of projects with direct investment to soar from 1,600 in 1991 to 26,000 in 1993, though committed funds fell on a per project basis from $168,000 to $27,000. Meyer (1994) estimates that foreign joint ventures accounted for 41 percent of new enterprises in 1989 in Hungary; over 17,000 enterprises reported foreign equity participation by 1992. As noted in the literature on tax incentives, policies to attract foreign investment have ambiguous effects due to the distortionary and fiscal effects.[5]

The impetus to competitive bidding for investment arises partly out of the similarity in wages among Central European countries. Török (1994) notes that hourly wages vary from $1.14 in the Czech Republic to $1.82 in Hungary, with Poland as an intermediate case, but that social taxes increase labor costs by about 50 percent. Given the low costs of wages in East Asia and the expectation that labor costs will rise, polled investors cite low labor costs as a minor consideration for investment (Gatling 1993).

"Hybridization" and the Multinational Network

The multinational corporation is a particularly important mechanism of change because it bridges the knowledge of how to do things that prevails in different countries. Direct investment is tied to the organizing principles of work that prevail in the source country at a particular time. The United States was a source of knowledge in the standardization of work and in mass production. Its expansion overseas was the transfer of this knowledge to other countries through the organizational extension across borders. Mass production systems were location-specific in origin, but firm-embodied in knowledge.[6]

An instructive case for understanding the effect of direct investment on transition economies is the Fawley Refinery in the United Kingdom, where Esso tried with success to implement a productivity incentive plan in its acquired operations (Flanders 1964). The object of contention was not only the wage bill (which was improved under the new plan), but also the changed job and status classifications. In particular, the reclassification of the foreman from a union representative to a member of the managerial staff conflicted with the prevailing industrial relations norm.

This hybridization of different national organizing principles represents

[5] For a thorough review, see Guisinger *et al.* (1985).

[6] See Hounshell (1984) for a history of the slow evolution of mass production in the United States, and Chandler (1990) and Kogut (1992) for an examination of the expansion of U.S. firms on the basis of this knowledge.

the advantage of a multinational firm over strictly domestic firms. For a company with established foreign subsidiaries, incremental direct investment need not be motivated strictly by the push of home-created advantages or the pull to innovative locations, but potentially by the advantages of operating a multinational network.[7] Statically, coordination of this network generates an operating value through the shifting of production in response to exchange rates, or the transfer of technology from one site to another. More dynamically, the network creates the possibility of generating innovations in work practices through the hybridization of knowledge gained by operating in multiple sites.

For example, General Motors through its German Opel operations is transferring Japanese quality circles to its Eisenach plant in the former East Germany. The use of teams is curtailed in the institutional environment of West Germany due to the refusal of unions and work councils to agree to the innovation. The more fluid environment of eastern Germany permits greater experimentation with forms of work drawn from multiple national experiences. Similarly, Volkswagen has experimented more extensively with group work in its Chinese and Hungarian facilities than it has been able to attempt at its West German plants.

Data on Aggregate Trends

One of the weakest links in former socialist economies was the paucity of institutions to support international trade and investment.[8] Whereas the majority of goods traded in the Western world are between affiliated firms located in different countries, the Soviet bloc developed few multinational corporations. Yet, despite the need for foreign capital and technology, the levels of direct investment have not been high in the transition economies. In Table 7.2, the small proportion of Central and East European countries in overall direct investment flows is shown.

Table 7.3 indicates the minor role played by direct investment in most countries. The balance of payment data show that Hungary, Poland, and the Czech Republic (Czechoslovakia) are responsible for over three-fourths of the flows into the transition countries. Since FDI is a stock, we can only get a rough measure of its importance by looking at its proportion of gross national product (GNP). The numbers are instructive, with Hungary standing out as having attracted the most direct investment in the early

[7] See Kogut and Kulatilaka (1994) for an explicit treatment.

[8] See Kraft (1977) for a conventional discussion of international economic cooperation among the Soviet bloc countries and its silence on the question of multinational enterprise activity.

Table 7.2. Stock of Foreign Direct Investment: Country and Region, 1988-93
(billions of U.S. $)

Outward	1988	1989	1990	1991	1992	1993*
France	51	75	110	130	161	186
Germany	104	121	152	171	187	201
Japan	112	156	204	235	252	266
United Kingdom	184	204	229	237	252	277
United States	346	390	432	467	489	529
World	1,179	1,393	1,628	1,817	1,988	2,165

Inward	1988	1989	1990	1991	1992
Developed countries	909	1,093	1,291	1,432	1,545
Western Europe	412	509	634	729	821
North America	401	478	538	574	586
Other developed countries	96	106	119	128	138
Developing countries	245	275	311	357	410
Africa	25	30	33	36	39
Latin America and the Caribbean	98	105	115	132	149
East, South, and Southeast Asia	123	140	163	187	219
Central and Eastern Europe	—	—	1	2	3
World	1,154	1,368	1,603	1,792	1,963

Source: United Nations Economic and Social Council. 1994. *Transnational Corporations in the Word Economy and Trends in Foreign Direct Investment to Developing Countries*, including in particular the "Interrelationship of Investment, Trade, Technology, and Development."

* 1993 figures are estimates.

period of transition. Of course, given the fall in gross domestic product (GDP) of some of these countries, this percentage has risen slightly in subsequent years.

Russia is reported to have attracted as much investment as Estonia, with an estimated stock of $2.7 billion. (See Table 7.4 for a breakdown.) The machine building and metal working industry has attracted almost a quarter of the investment. Importantly, about 85 percent of total private capital flows to Russia has been in the form of direct investment.[9]

Despite the importance of large firms in accounting for the vast proportion of reported direct investment flows, the average investment size is not especially large. The distribution of size shows a dramatic drop-off after

[9] *Moscow Business Monitor*, "Foreign investment in Russia described in report: machine-building in lead," 5 July 1994.

Table 7.3. Foreign Direct Investment Inflows in Selected Countries

	Inflows million U.S. $		Four year stock		
			Million U.S. $[a]	Million U.S. $[b]	As % GDP
	1992	1993	1993	1993 per capita	1993
Bulgaria	42	62	164	18	1.7
Czechoslovakia (Cz Rep.1993)	1,073	568	2,414[c]	234[c]	7.9[c]
Hungary	1,479	2,339	6,009	583	16.4
Poland	678	1,697	2,749	72	3.2
Romania	77	48	178	8	0.7
Russian Fed.	700	1,100	1,800[d]	12[d]	1.0[d]
China	7,156	23,115	36,381	32	6.6

Source: International Financial Statistics, International Monetary Fund, February 1995; some FDI values for 1993 from Meyer (1994).
[a] Estimated as cumulative inflows.
[b] Estimate based on *Economist 1993 Yearbook* statistics.
[c] Includes Slovakia for 1990 to 1992.
[d] Missing data for 1990, 1991.

taking into account the largest investments (Meyer 1994). For example, Russia reported over $2.9 billion in direct investment for 1993 (though balance of payment data show $1.7 billion). At the same time, over 5,400 joint ventures were registered (Aslund 1994). Smaller investments are especially prevalent in service industries, where initial capital contributions can be low compared with the manufacturing sector.

To get a sense of the relative magnitude of direct investment in Central and East European countries, consider China, which is frequently cited as a far greater magnet for direct investment. In 1992 China attracted an estimated $7.1 billion in direct investment; in 1993, actual flows rose to $23.1 billion.[10] About 74 percent of these investments were in the industrial sectors. However, unlike other transition economies, the size of state-owned Chinese enterprises still dwarfs foreign affiliates. In 1992 it was estimated that 30 of the top 500 manufacturers were foreign affiliated. While foreign direct investment made up about 8 percent of total investment in 1992, the percentage surely rose dramatically in 1993. Yet, on a per capita basis, China has not fared better in attracting direct investment than Eastern Europe.

What is striking is the prominence of Hungary. To a large extent, its attractiveness lies in its longer history of openness; Hungary accepted a larger share of direct investment before 1989 (especially after the 1986 revision of

[10] The information in this paragraph is taken from Zhan (1993). Figures cited are balance of payment numbers from the IMF.

Table 7.4. Foreign Investment in Russia by Sector, by year-end 1993

	Accumulated (thousands of U.S. $)	No. of enterprises
Machine building and metal working	600,172	326
Fuel	396,980	55
Trade and food services	365,153	742
Construction	153,277	153
Other industrial	134,315	53
Woodworking, wood pulp, and paper	132,107	174
Construction materials	111,222	24
Health care and social security	97,081	64
Finance, credit, insurance, and pensions	82,735	35
Food	70,666	81
Science and research	63,868	171
Culture and art	61,906	32
Transport and communications	53,680	81
Foreign trade	48,210	20
Dwellings	46,466	31
Nonferrous metallurgy	45,773	21
Fish breeding	38,408	61
Marketing	32,492	3
Light industry	32,169	97
Chemical and petrochemical	29,882	37
Medical	16,978	36
Information and computing services	14,180	41
Other material production	12,713	87
Agriculture	8,059	34
Forestry	7,117	25
Ferrous metallurgy	6,846	20
Logistics and distribution	4,939	67
Management	3,982	22
Printing	3,875	24
Public education	3,035	25
Services	1,990	8
Public societies	1,783	7
Electricity	1,171	3
Glass and china	582	6
Purchases	133	5
Flour milling and mixed fodder	42	1
Total	2,683,987	2,672

Source: Moscow Business Monitor, 5 July 1994

the law governing joint ventures) than any other Central European country, but primarily in its consumer goods sector. The lower amounts to the Czech Republic and Poland are also reflections of their privatization process, which has restricted foreign investment more than Hungary. In 1992 about 80 percent of the privatization revenues in Hungary came from abroad, although the share fell to 50 percent in 1993 (UNCTAD, 1994).

Direct Investment and Growth

Does foreign direct investment matter for growth? There is considerable evidence that the growth of countries is not strongly related to direct investment flows. A striking aspect is the wide variation in the role that direct investment has played in Asian countries. Overall, direct investment in the region has grown quickly, from 10 percent of the world total in the early 1980s to 17 percent in the 1992 (UNCTAD 1994). Japan, Korea, and Taiwan have engaged in fairly restrictive policies; Singapore, Thailand, and Malaysia have actively pursued direct investment. In the period from 1980 to 1985, direct investment as a percentage of gross domestic capital formation was only 0.5 percent for Korea and 1 percent for Taiwan; the 1985 to 1987 period showed an increase to 1.4 percent and 3.3 percent, respectively. In countries such as Indonesia and Malaysia, the percentages for the same periods run at 11.1 percent and 14.4 percent for the former, and 8.2 percent and 8.7 percent for the latter. Yet, despite variation in policies toward direct investment, all these countries have grown at high rates.

To place these observations on a stronger footing, we re-estimated the model of Mankiw, Romer, and Weil (1992) in their study of growth rates of countries. They found that the Solow model augmented for human capital formation provides a rather good fit to cross-sectional data on the per capita income of 98 countries for the time period from 1960 to 1985. Using this estimated model, we calculated the residuals for these countries. These residuals were then correlated with the average direct investment flow (from the balance of payments) per capita.

The estimated model of Mankiw, Romer, and Weil is a cross-country regression of GDP divided by the working force in 1985 on the investment rate, working force growth (adjusted by income growth and the depreciation rate), and human capital investment proxied by the percentage of the working age population in secondary school.[11] Our estimates to this

[11] Working force growth rate is adjusted by the growth in per capita income and a capital depreciation rate; the sum of these two factors is set to 0.05. See Mankiw, Romer, and Weil (1992) for a discussion.

Table 7.5. Augmented Solow Model
(dependent variable: log GDP per working age person in 1985)

	Full sample (78 countries)		Non-OECD countries		OECD countries	
	(1)	(2)	(3)	(4)	(5)	(6)
Constant	4.78	5.72	4.92	5.77	7.74	6.68
	(0.59)	(0.42)	(0.65)	(0.48)	(1.39)	(1.28)
Log (investment over GDP)	1.33	0.60	1.01	0.49	0.52	0.32
	(0.19)	(0.157)	(0.23)	(0.18)	(0.43)	(0.38)
Log (workforce)	-0.57	-0.47	0.11	-0.14	-0.12	-0.19
	(0.14)	(0.09)	(0.31)	(0.22)	(0.15)	(0.13)
Log (school)	-	0.71	-	0.64	-	0.78
		(0.08)		(0.09)		(0.29)
No. of observations	78	78	56	56	22	22
R^2	0.57	0.79	0.28	0.63	0.10	0.35

equation are given in columns one and two in Table 7.5 for the full sample of 78 countries. (The sample of countries is different from Mankiw *et al.*, since we were unable to collect additional investment data for all countries.) The results, not surprisingly, correspond closely to Table 1 in Mankiw, Romer, and Weil (1992).[12] Investment in human capital has a significant impact on GDP per capita, and its inclusion in the model improves the fit significantly.

The importance of including a measure of human capital in the estimates is particularly evident in the sample of non-Organization for Economic Cooperation and Development (OECD) countries. The fit improves dramatically, and the coefficient to the work force variable switches signs to the expected direction. (We would expect that an increase in the work force, holding capital constant, should lower per capita income.) Even in the small sample of OECD countries, the coefficient to investment in human capital (column 6) is significant.

As a speculative exercise, we apply the above estimated model to predicting the GDP per capita for East European countries based on 1991 data. Of the many caveats in this extrapolation, two are particularly important. The Mankiw *et al.* specification is derived from a steady-state model; clearly, the macroeconomic conditions in 1991 were in considerable fluctuation. Second, their estimates were calculated for the time period 1960 to

[12] Following the procedure and coding of Mankiw *et al.*, we took out oil producing countries. Both Venezuela and Indonesia remain part of their non-oil producing sample. Removing them from the sample changes the magnitudes of the coefficients, but the significance levels are scarcely affected.

Table 7.6. Estimated GDP Per Capita of Eastern Europe in 1991
(in U.S. $)

	Actual GDP (per capita) (1)	Predicted GDP (per capita) (2)	Predicted with fixed human capital (estimate) (3)
Bulgaria	1,840	4,033	6,783
Ukraine	2,340	3,189	4,100
Romania	1,390	5,413	7,473
Poland	1,790	4,653	6,364
Czechoslovakia*	2,460	5,858	7,840
Russian Federation	3,220	5,263	7,006
Hungary	2,720	5,357	7,173

*Czech data for work force and human capital are average of Hungarian and Polish measures.

1985. We are essentially applying the estimated coefficients for predicting 1985 income to 1991 data.

With these caveats in mind, the exercise is useful in providing a heuristic comparison. We collected data on schooling from UNESCO's yearbook, using the same procedure used by Mankiw *et al.* in calculating the measure of human capital as the fraction of the population of working age adults between the ages (approximately) of 14 to 19 in secondary school. Domestic investment shares and labor force growth are taken from the World Bank's handbook on economic data for developing countries for 1993.

In Table 7.6, we give the reported GDP per capita and the predicted value from the estimated model for the OECD countries. Of course, the monetary values are strongly affected by currency rates; high investment rates are a consequence of the fall in income (Romanian investment of GNP is estimated to have been 33.5 percent in 1991.) To provide some sensitivity to these estimates, the predicted values were re-estimated assuming a higher level of human capital investment; we used the value of 10, compared to a maximum of 12.1 in the overall sample and to the modal range in the actual data of 6 to 7. These results, which are given in column 3, serve the heuristic value of indicating the shortfall of the current performance of East European countries in transition to their predicted potential.

An examination of the residuals from the regression given in column 2 of Table 7.5 provides insight into other countries that underperform the predicted GDP per capita. The country outliers that are shown to be much poorer than predicted include several African countries (e.g. Ghana, Togo, and Zambia) and south and east Asian countries (e.g. India and Philippines);

Table 7.7. Correlation of Average FDI
(per capita and residual from Table 7.5)

	Full sample (78 countries)		Non-OECD countries		OECD countries	
Regression col. no.	(1)	(2)	(3)	(4)	(5)	(6)
	0.115	0.11	0.33	0.34	-0.27	-0.34

of all countries, Jamaica is estimated to have most underperformed its prediction. Countries that performed better than the prediction include South Africa and Rwanda, Canada, and Guatemala.

To see if this variation reflects more than measurement error, we correlated the residuals from Table 7.5 with a balance of payments measure of average foreign direct investment per capita for the period from 1965 to 1985 – the International Monetary Fund (IMF) did not collect such data systematically for earlier years. The correlations between FDI per capita and the residuals corresponding to the columns in Table 7.7 are given in Table 7.5. An important result is that the correlations are quite different for non-OECD and OECD countries, positive for the former group and negative for the latter.

It should be kept in mind that the effect of foreign investment *as capital investment* is already captured in the estimation through the investment rate. Foreign ownership, arguably, brings something extra to the table in the form of technological and managerial knowledge. These externalities appear as particularly important for less developed countries.

Of course, there are several other possible explanations for these results. The residual can be interpreted as an estimate of total factor productivity. Direct investment is likely to be pulled toward countries where there are location-specific externalities.[13] The causality between direct investment and growth is, as a result, ambiguous.

To sort out some of the causality, a regression of the residual on both per capita GDP in 1960 and FDI was performed; initial GDP per capita was found to be significantly and positively related to the residual; FDI per capita is insignificant and its coefficient is of minor magnitude. Another specification was estimated by replacing GDP per capita in 1980 in the regressions reported in Table 7.5 by the log difference in GDP between 1985 and 1960 for GDP per capita; the same independent variables were used, along with

[13] As in other studies, Kogut and Chang (1991) find that industry growth rate has a significant influence in attracting foreign investment. This result should be robust to an economy overall.

average FDI per capita. Average FDI per capita, once again, did not appear as significant.[14]

Since there is such variation in policies toward FDI, the speculative finding that direct investment does not appear to explain further growth when the effect of investment in physical and human capital is parceled out is not surprising. As noted earlier, such countries as Korea and Taiwan have been circumspect regarding direct investment. Convergence to a world production frontier does not seem to require direct investment.

Yet, the convergence of a large group of poorer (largely Asian) nations points to the spilling of knowledge across borders. Pack and Page (1994) analyzed largely the same data as Mankiw *et al.* but tested the influence of export propensity on growth rates. They found that, in addition to human and physical capital investments, exports and a measure of openness (as captured through the equivalent of law of one price calculations) were significantly related to growth. Since multinational corporations are important agents in world trade, their findings do not imply a ranking of exports over direct investment as a preferred instrument to tap into a pool of world technology. But, rather, their results indicate that integration in the world economic community provides the opportunity for learning.

Direct investment dominates other alternatives for the absorption of technology when the acquisition of new knowledge is costly by other mechanisms. Teece (1976) estimated that the costs of technology transfer varied from 2 to 56 percent of total project cost. Transfer costs declined with the age of the technology and the number of users, that is, to the extent to which the technology was known and codified. Kogut and Zander (1994) found that knowledge that was difficult to codify would tend to be transferred within the firm rather than through licensing and would also transfer more slowly (see also Zander and Kogut (1995)).

These findings suggest that the borders of firms are the least permeable when knowledge is of a tacit or proprietary nature. The public good characterization of technology, as Romer (1992) and others have noted, confuses the traits of nonrivalry and excludability. The use of a chemical process by an American firm does not influence the costs of its use by a Korean firm. But nonrivalry does not mean that use of the formula cannot be excluded through patent protection or tacitness.

Direct investment occurs when a firm exploits its knowledge in a foreign

[14] These results conflict with the study by Blomstrom, Lipsey, and Zejan (1994) that indicates a significant and positive effect on growth for a particular sample of countries. Though using similar data and sample, I could not replicate the result using the Mankiw *et al.* specification with FDI added. We leave open the question of the relationship of growth and direct investment.

country within its boundaries rather than through a market. Failure of the market for technology is one reason why direct investment is preferred. But a more prosaic reason is simply that a firm specializes in the creation and transfer of particular kinds of knowledge that are better replicated inside the firm than between firms.

Governance and Direct Investment

The transfer of uncodified knowledge by direct investment is likely to be critical for transition economies. Though rich in scientific and technical training, these countries have inherited a stock of organizational knowledge that is poorly suited for competition in world markets. Knowledge of quality production, marketing, and customer response is lacking, since domestic competitive markets did not exist. Experience in exporting was usually isolated in foreign trade organizations that had little influence over the production and management of the production units. Marketing to developed countries was frequently conducted by Western firms, who sometimes acted as brokers in barter or compensation deals. Unlike the Asian economies whose firms evolved in competitive markets, the enterprises in the Soviet bloc did not, by and large, develop the expertise to compete in capitalist settings.

There are three ways in which the extension of equity-based control across borders influences the evolution of corporate capabilities in the foreign country:

1. Organizational capabilities: The investing firm has superior methods in the form of the knowledge of operations and in their control through supervision, authority, and incentives.
2. Organizational form and institutional governance: The foreign firm implements a superior method of organizing and external control, either indirectly through the form of financing (e.g. debt and equity structure) or directly through the re-creation of oversight institutions.
3. Competitive externalities: By increasing competition in the host country, the foreign firm generates information on the x-inefficiency of competitors in the local country and generates incentives for imitation.

The following analysis is informed by interviews held with managers of foreign multinational companies and with government officials (see footnote 2.) A structured interview format was conducted with managers of five American multinationals operating in Poland and Russia, and background interviews were held with other managers and officials. Questions were oriented toward identifying the role of work councils and unions, local and foreign representation on boards, and competitive effects on suppliers, customers, and competitors.

Organizational Capabilities

The considerable documentation of the difficulties of imposing new methods tends to obscure the fact that internal governance is easier to transfer than external governance for obvious reasons. Case studies and the managerial literature are replete with the conflicts between headquarters and subsidiaries regarding the reporting and control requirements. In certain cases, due to prohibitions on the transfer of data across borders, control systems conflict with local law. The legal or contractual right to implement certain bonus plans have not infrequently been opposed by labor unions and law. Control rights clearly are limited in cases of dismissal and of liquidation. The United States is, in this regard, far more the outlier than comparable European countries.

By and large, firms are given a relatively wide range of latitude in their control over their foreign managerial staffs. Whereas certain countries, such as Sweden, have both union and legal protection of managerial staffs, the restrictions on the task assignments, promotions, and employment of management are generally far weaker. (Gray and Jarosz (1993) report that only Romania restricts the types of positions that foreigners can hold.) Direct investment carries very strong implications for managerial control, especially for acquisitions.

An issue of some importance is the representation of workers and work councils in internal governance, and legal restrictions on severance and dismissal.[15] Poland has, surprisingly, moved toward a regime that has progressively weakened the power of work councils in corporatized companies (Weinstein 1995). The Russian privatization program has allocated a certain number of shares to workers, but the dispersion of these shares and the incentives for workers and managers to dispose of poorly diversified holdings appear to lead to an increasingly weakened voice of labor in enterprise decisions.

Interviews with foreign firms in Poland and Russia strikingly confirm the weakness of labor unions in their new (or "greenfield") operations. All the managers interviewed using a structured format at the five companies reported a condition almost of passivity on the part of workers. In the case of

[15] Both the Czech Republic and Poland have moved to ease these restrictions, especially easing the financial burden of restructuring by layoffs. See *Business Eastern Europe*, 4 April 1994 and 2 May 1994.

one company in Russia, employee relations were not up to par at one joint venture, but their wholly owned operations were without unions and work councils. For blue-collar workers, pay tends to be set near market conditions. Though 50 million of the 70 million workers in Russia are reputedly union members, the workers were described as poorly organized. Even in Poland, where the heritage of Solidarity has created a more active labor force, workers in the newly created ventures were viewed as unrepresented by unions or by work councils. Published reports of labor conditions in the Czech Republic and Slovakia also suggest labor conditions that are fairly docile.[16]

However, pay for white-collar workers in foreign firms in Poland and Russia is substantially above the market. At a large pharmaceutical company, most of the sales force hold medical degrees and earn three times the market norm. The age is young; in general, firms reported a preference for hiring younger workers. Sales incentives in kind, such as vacations, were initially resisted but were eventually accepted. Due to the high technical qualifications and requirements of the sales force, this company represents a polar extreme but is not unique. An American telecommunications company in Russia also paid a wage plus bonus for operators for their pager service business. Yet, again, qualifications matched the wage, as all operators were university graduates. In fact, within the first weeks of operation, several of the operators were moved into more advanced positions. The impression given by these trends is a widening gap between blue- and white-collar wages.

The transfer of technology and new methods of organizing were also extended to some suppliers. At a minimum, companies, such as a large food company, seek to establish a set of operating principles among their Polish and Russian bottle suppliers. The pharmaceutical company signed on the Institute of Biotechnology in Warsaw to package their drugs. To bring their supplier up to standard, Western technology was imported, along with quality circles. Clearly, the company is able to pursue a policy of skimming the cream, both in terms of hiring qualified doctors as sales agents and of contracting to one of the more sophisticated companies in its sector. However, all interviewed managers stated a clear preference for working with a foreign rather than a local bank as soon as it was permitted, partly due to the required expertise in handling foreign exchange, but also due to the excessive inefficiency of the local banking system.

[16] An example is the successful negotiation by Kmart with its Czech union that resulted in an agreement setting up performance bonuses. The union in the Slovakian stores turned down the offer, insisting on a standardized wage package unrelated to performance. Kmart, which is the largest foreign investor in Slovakia, refused, and implemented the Czech plan successfully without union interference. See "Management issues: wrestling with the trade unions," *Business Eastern Europe* 28 February 1994, 1–2.

Corporate Form and Governance

Direct investment is channeled through two organizational forms: joint ventures or single firm dominated investments. (In some cases, a firm may have less than a 100 percent equity position, but the outstanding shares are dispersed among many shareholders who do not exercise control.) A joint venture can be defined to include the creation of a legally independent concern, or as a minority stake in an existing enterprise. An acquisition can be used as a means to establish a joint venture position or single control position. Alternatively, an investment may be in new operations. Each of these investment kinds, which are obviously not mutually exclusive, raises particular implications for governance and for political sensitivity regarding foreign ownership.

Through acquisition, direct investment has played a major role in the privatization programs of many transition economies. In the process of evaluating these companies, foreign suitors have required stronger regulations and laws regarding accounting standards, protection of intellectual property, and the repatriation of profits. In this sense, they have been an active force in institution building (McMillan 1993).

There is, again, wide variation among countries regarding the treatment of foreign participation in privatization. Of the 52 large privatizations in Poland by 1992, 25 had large shares of foreign ownership, with 12 cases of shares greater than 80 percent and 10 more greater than 50 percent; however, foreign participation in the privatization of small firms was restricted. The Czech Republic also excluded foreign firms from participating in the first wave of privatization. Hungary, by contrast, has sought active foreign involvement in its privatization program.

Russia, which has allowed 100 percent foreign ownership since 1991 but has heavily restricted until this year participation in privatized companies, has established a liberal policy allowing foreign companies to purchase shares of privatized companies. Recent estimates indicate that 10 percent of such shares are held by foreign companies (GKI Press Release, #298-4678, 1994).[17] Again, Romania represents the other end of the spectrum with only three privatizations including foreign investors in the years just after transition (Odle 1993); however, as noted earlier, foreign investments in joint

[17] Of course, fact has surpassed fiction, for Russian law lags behind actual practice. In an unpublished EEC report, the consultants Arés Associés (1994) note in reference to a particular law that "because of the fact that the Law was adopted rather long ago, this article isn't designed for the specifics of portfolio investment in the shares of joint-stock companies. Most of the clauses of the chapter wasn't [sic] developed in sub-laws and regulations and hardly are ever applied in business practice."

ventures with state-owned and privatized companies have been frequent. All in all, UNCTAD estimates that 67 percent of direct investment flows were related to privatization activities between 1988 and 1992 (UNCTAD 1994).

The participation of foreign firms in the privatization process has merits and a few demerits. On the plus side, the foreign firm brings managerial and technological expertise to the firm. On the minus side, during a period of transition when domestic savings have largely eroded due to inflation, values of enterprises can be depressed because of wealth constraints or market imperfections, especially the difficulty of selling the securities. Frydman and Rapaczynski (1994) argue that an advantage of a mutual fund scheme (which permits foreign capital) is that it prevents a "fire sale" of assets. The role of foreign capital in resolving problems of capital shortage is, of course, not unambiguous, as liquidity is gained at the cost of the transfer of shares, and potentially, ownership to foreign buyers at depressed prices.

The data regarding depressed prices are startling. Boycko, Shleifer, and Vishny (1993) make some rough calculations indicating that the Russian manufacturing industry has a dollar value between 5 to 10 billion, roughly the size of smaller firms in the Fortune 500. The ZIL company, with 100,000 employees, has a valuation of $16 million. In an unpublished study, CS First Boston generated similar numbers, estimating Russian equity to be valued at $8.5 billion. To provide some comparability, they calculate that the productive capacity of a ton of Russian cement is worth two-thirds of a percent of a ton of a Western company; a megawatt of electricity capacity has a worth of 4 percent; and even a barrel of proven oil reserve is valued at less than 1 percent of a Western operation (CS First Boston 1994).

There are, of course, some situations that suggest that direct investment into privatizing companies is not taking advantage of a "fire sale" as suspected. First, given adequate foreign suitors, the price of the assets should be bid up to reflect their value in a world market unconstrained by illiquidity. The only commodity production valued close to Western valuations, according to First Boston, is tobacco-related activities, reflecting the large Western equity position in the Russian tobacco industry. Second, the value of the enterprise, because it will benefit from foreign technical assistance that might necessitate that property rights be guaranteed by ownership, will often be worth more to foreign buyers.

It is not surprising that the value of newly privatized stocks rises dramatically given their lower initial valuations and the influx of Western capital. The recent valuations of Russian companies that have floated shares in Western markets show remarkable capital gains. The price of acquired companies in the more open markets of Central Europe is close to Western valuations (CS First Boston 1994).

Table 7.8. Number of FDI Projects in Selected Central and Eastern European Countries, 1 October 1991 to 31 March 1993 (by type of transaction)

	Number of projects and percentage							
	Acquisitions		Joint ventures		Greenfield investments		Total investments	
Country	No.	%	No.	%	No.	%	No.	%
Czech Republic	62	34	60	33	59	33	181	100
Hungary	121	36	121	36	92	28	334	100
Poland	48	30	46	28	68	42	162	100
Russian Fed.	113	3	285	71	106	26	402	100

Millions of U.S $ and percentage

	$	%	$	%	$	%	$	%
Czech Republic	880	63	444	32	66	5	1,390	100
Hungary	1,093	35	1,141	36	929	29	3,163	100
Poland	3,135	56	1,706	31	722	13	5,560	100
Russian Fed.	1,167	11	9,239	88	152	1	10,559	100

Source: Anthony Robinson, "Ex-Soviet bloc attracts $42bn," *Financial Times*, 28 September 1993; *World Investments Report*, 1994.

The low asset valuations are clearly fueling speculations in the Russian market. In an interview, the president of one of the mutual fund associations noted that 10 to 20 percent equity share is frequently sufficient to provide a swing vote for many privatized concerns. Even minority shares held by foreign firms can play a major role.[18] But he also observed that local capital preferred to keep foreign investors out during a period of low asset values. Not surprisingly, an interview with an investment entrepreneur who acted to find foreign buyers for companies in the second wave of privatization took the opposite position. If the notion of liquidity trading is a distant concept to the highly imperfect Russian capital markets, the importance of information trading between a foreign investment sector and domestic sellers was well understood.

The problem of insufficient information also hampers the foreign buyer in efforts to avoid overpaying. One reported solution has been issuing convertible bonds with a low par value and no interest. If certain performance targets are not meant, the debt is converted into equity (Gatling 1993: 107). Still, this financial structure only provides a floor to the foreign investor if the equity is worth something.

An alternative to acquisition through privatization programs or other means is the prevalent use of joint ventures. Before 1989 a few countries, particularly Hungary, allowed and encouraged foreign joint ventures. Since then, joint ventures have become common to all the transition economies. In Table 7.8, estimates of the frequency of joint ventures for the largest countries are provided. (The data are to be taken as indicative.) Russia, due largely to its initial legal restrictions on foreign ownership, has favored joint ventures the most. Poland, on the other hand, has a large number of greenfield (i.e. new plant) investments, though the value is only 13 percent of the total.

A joint venture accomplishes four important tasks. First, it provides a foreign party with a legal governance structure by which to enforce *organizationally* its claim to technology and its use. Second, because a joint venture is an enterprise as opposed to a sale of technology license, it serves as a vehicle to transfer tacit knowledge for which markets are inadequate. Third, a joint venture allows a foreign party to isolate the more attractive assets and to avoid potentially acquiring a large labor force that would have to be restructured. Lastly, joint ventures invariably have exit clauses that define rights and priority of acquisition among the parties. Western experience shows that joint ventures are very often acquired, especially when the market turns out

[18] By an appeal to a Shapley-value argument, the foreign firm places a high value on its purchase of shares exactly because of its swing role in determining the winning coalition in a given dispute. A more placid observation is that a 25% share provides, as in Germany, the legal position of minority veto rights.

to be good and the legal right to acquire is exercised by the dominant party (Kogut 1992). It is at the time when new capital investments are required that partners to a joint venture are forced to reconsider their commitments and the relative value of the venture to each side. A common outcome is that one party sells out to the other and walks away with capital gains; the other party gains full control.

This option-like feature is often present as well in minority equity stakes. In Russia many direct investments, partly due to the lock on shares by entrenched management and employees, in corporations take a minority share. For example, Siemens bought 10 percent of the Kaluga Turbine Plant; BAT bought a minority position in the Saratov Tobacco Factory through a tender offer, with $40 million committed to be invested; Procter and Gamble bought 14 percent in the Novomoskovskbythim joint stock company, with a promise to invest $50 million in capital equipment; and Zellstoff und Papier purchased 30 percent of Zhukovsky Cold Storage in 1993, with a realized increase in production of 32 percent over the following year. In all of these cases, capital and technology were transferred to struggling concerns and serve to establish a foothold for future expansion. It can be expected that some of these ventures, in their role of providing a future option to expand, will be converted to full ownership as capital markets develop.

An area of conflict, however, between foreign owners and a country concerns the use of external control over a subsidiary's operations. There is surprisingly little known about the local governance of foreign subsidiaries, except that they tend to adopt local practice while subject to control of the foreign parent. Generally, national laws have held the parent responsible for the debt and financial claims owed by the subsidiary. As a result, high debt of a subsidiary does not carry the disciplinary incentive assumed in the general literature on governance.

The companies interviewed all reported that supervisory oversight was carried out by regional headquarters outside the country of location. Only one joint venture with two state-owned enterprises associated with a ministry in Russia reported a local board of significance; yet, the composition of the board was dominated by the foreign company. (Board positions were unpaid.)

In summary, the impact of direct investment on wider governance institutions is mixed. Joint ventures and acquisitions, in particular, have required changes in law and have increased pressure to create more perfect and efficient capital markets. However, since foreign-owned subsidiaries largely act independently of governance oversight in the local economy, they cannot serve as models for legal reform regarding boards of directors or banks invested with powers of oversight. Where they do influence institutions is through their efforts to influence regulatory and standard-making policy, as well as laws to improve the efficiency of capital markets, especially regarding such issues as the registration and transfer of equity-share ownership.

Competitive Externalities

One of the most important influences of direct investment is on the incentives for competing domestic companies to improve their performance. Blomstrom and Wolff (1994) found that direct investment in Mexico increased the productivity in the sectors in which foreign firms compete. But they could not sort out whether these effects were due to the elimination of weak firms, spillovers in the form of learning by domestic companies, or the creaming of a higher quality labor force in the foreign sectors. In a case-oriented study, Dunning (1986) found some evidence that the adoption of Japanese methods in England was promoted more by competition than by British suppliers learning from Japanese assemblers. Blomstrom and Wang (1989) show, moreover, that competition engenders increased incentives to learn by competing firms.

As stated earlier, there is little empirical evidence to show that direct investment is required for economic growth. The Asian experience, which has large national differences, shows that reliance on export markets for competitive discipline, along with human and physical capital accumulation, has served as a successful strategy for a number of countries that have restricted inward investment. Yet, an important difference in the Asian and transition economies experiences is that the latter are far more bereft of the accumulation of managerial knowledge in their enterprises. Direct investment brings an immediate transfer of Western practice to companies with adequate technical levels, but poor managerial expertise.

The negative side is that direct investment has been largely oriented, when measured in value, toward the acquisition of large companies. Whereas many of these companies show the fastest growth rates, they also appear in the more oligopolistic sectors of these economies. To a certain extent, the acquisitions of the larger concerns reflect the extension of oligopolistic competition to Eastern Europe. The purchase of one auto company in Czechoslovakia leads to a rival purchase or joint venture in Poland. Similar patterns, as seen in Table 7.1, can be discerned in the food and telecommunication industries.

These acquisitions are potentially troublesome due to long-standing policies in the socialist countries to concentrate production in highly specialized groupings of companies. There are, consequently, some indications that these purchases are partly motivated by defensive and monopolistic considerations. General Electric acquired the Hungarian company Tungsram in one of the first acquisitions. Since selling its shares in Osram, General Electric had seen rapid entry through acquisition by European competitors into its home American market. The acquisition of Tungsram achieved an offsetting position in the European market, while at the same time eliminating a potential low-cost entrant in the lucrative light bulb market. GE has invested an additional $400 million in Tungsram.

The acquisition of Lehel in Hungary by Electrolux is a natural outcome of a long contracting relationship between the two parties. However, Lehel is the only other producer in Europe of a small refrigerator that does not rely upon a compressor. Though the work force fell by 40 percent following the acquisition, productivity and exports have increased. Only one product line has been added to replace the divested products, and the factory remains highly specialized. The distribution channels are being used to support the introduction of the Electrolux-branded lines. Currently, the company is very profitable, with about a 90 percent market share in Hungary.[19]

One of the most impressive investment strategies has been carried out by the Swedish-Swiss concern, Asea Brown Boverie. By May 1994 it controlled 58 companies in 16 countries. In Poland it owns four out of the five makers of power-generating equipment. In Russia, it controls eight companies, plus is a partner in four joint ventures.[20] These operations have been integrated into a world production system, while providing ABB with important and unique access to these markets.

The acquisition of potentially monopolistic positions is especially troubling in the service sector of the smaller or regional economies. The telecommunications company in Estonia, for example, reached a joint venture agreement with a Swedish company to help manage the network. An attractive feature of a telecommunication contract is that due to international pricing and tariff regulations, East European countries earn foreign currency in the transmission of foreign calls. Consequently, a deal with a local telephone company generates foreign earnings, plus monopolistic control in a highly regulated local market. The incentive for investment by the Swedish partner in local service in Estonia is not very large and has been modest.

However, even in the case of the purchase of monopolistic positions, there is an important contribution played by foreign companies in lessening the historic holdups between suppliers and buyers. Frydman and Rapaczynski

[19] See "Electrolux AB Enters Hungary," Kjell Nordstrom and Jan Erik Vahlne, Stockholm School of Economics, 1994.

[20] See "ABB'S Big Bet in Eastern Europe," *Fortune*, 2 May 1994.

(1994) note that the transition to capitalism poses the danger of exposing firms, which stood in an administrated relationship to each other before, to potential exploitation of one by the other due to the dependence of one party on the other. Partially by bringing in the knowledge of the sources of supply in a world integrated economy, foreign investment acts as an effective curb on the hazards of small numbers haggling. The bridging role of the multinational corporation across borders opens the narrowly specialized relationships among firms to wider competition.

But the cost of world integration is the erosion of dense national networks among firms. Since the capital of any enterprise is partly its position in a network and knowledge of other firms, this process of change can eliminate otherwise viable enterprises in a period of transition.[21] To believe that transporting a firm from one setting to another does not diminish its economic value underestimates the value of knowing the environment. In the process of transition, the competitive process destroys valuable knowledge between firms and institutions.

This knowledge is, in many ways, valued and preserved through the acquisitions and joint ventures that are targeted by foreign concerns. Motorola, for example, has entered into multiple contracts with the telecommunications university in Moscow, both as a way to fund research and to develop useful contacts for recruiting and sales. Its joint venture with two groups attached to the Ministry of Telecommunications has also established important inroads into the licensing and regulatory process. Because it recognizes the value of existing relationships, direct investment provides the resources to maintain otherwise bankrupt institutions.

The implications of the competitive role played by direct investment, when duly qualified for the potential of monopolistic abuse, are best appreciated in speculating for the long term. Direct investment plays two roles through new firm startups and through acquiring the more promising enterprises in the traditional sectors of an economy. The self-reported growth rates of the interviewed firms are impressive. One firm in Russia reported growth at a rate of 200 to 300 percent per year. Another company in Poland expected market penetration rates to approach West European levels in a few years.

To give an appreciation of the implications, consider a recent study by Kennedy (1994), who looked at two sectoral clusters in the Polish economy. The first cluster consisted of private firms that grew from 29 to 80 percent of output between 1989 and 1994 and its share of GNP rose from 49 to 53 percent between 1989 and 1993; a second cluster showed a growth of only 9

[21] See Pistor and Turkewitz in vol. 2, as well as Grabher (1990) and Kogut *et al.* (1992).

percent to 23 percent of the private enterprise share. The more dynamic cluster was characterized by a tripling of the number of firms due to new entry, with privatization playing a small role in new firm formation. In the stagnant sector, the total number of firms fell. An important difference is the pattern of direct investment, which was roughly in equal proportions in both clusters, but was twice the size in the more stagnant sector. Direct investment is about equal in the dynamic and stagnant sectors. However, given the declining output in the stagnant sector, direct investment plays the major role of acting as a powerful force for restructuring older enterprises.

The implied projections of this process of transformation point to a growing share for new firm entries; a shrinking traditional sector will give way to faster growing enterprises, many with substantial foreign involvement. A rather small percentage of the existing industrial base can generate a substantial transformation of the existing economy by the force of its own growth, as well as its spillover effect on the rest of the economy.

It would be fanciful to suggest at this juncture that foreign investment in these countries has caused new hybridization of work practices. By and large, the investment process is driven by the push of existing advantages into these new markets. The largest investor in Poland is Coca-Cola, which is pursuing a standard strategy of securing bottle suppliers while investing in bottling plants, a strategy recently extended to Russia. Given the productivity advantage of Western practices, the transfer of the advantage to local markets is bound to be the principal objective.

There are modest signs that in the process of solving problems unique to the transition economies, organizational innovations are created. For example, the Italian metal company Lucchini has acquired a 51 percent stake in the steel works Huta Warszawa. The work force has been reduced from 12,000 to 3,000. Yet, many of the workers were severed by spinning off divisions into cooperatives that were then contracted by Huta Warszawa. As a result, Huta Warszawa has built up satellite cooperatives operating under worker–owner incentive structures (see the description in "Reducing the work force: Lucchini restructures Huta Warszawa," *Business Eastern Europe*, 15 November 1993).

Policy Implications

In considering policy objectives for Eastern Europe about direct investment, this potential for innovation and hybridization – even if dimly recognizable amid the gigantic task of restructuring the economy – should be an important guiding light. Frydman and Rapaczynski's (1994) observation that design should be evolutionary in principle is fundamental. Policy creation should not lock into a narrow set of objectives during this period of rapid transformation, and objectives should be influenced by the political and social values of a country. An important consideration remains choosing the policies that move reform forward.

There are four types of recommendations that respect the principle of permitting the process to organize itself while establishing boundaries of tolerance:

1. *Competition policy.* A primary objective of transformation is to establish competition. In Hungary, 48 of the 114 cases examined by the monopoly office involved abuses of dominant power – though most cases were dismissed (Langenfeld and Yao 1994). One of the most important elements in the Polish transformation was reducing tariffs to allow for international competition to hold down monopolistic pricing during a period of extreme industrial concentration (Sachs 1993).

Direct investment should be subjected to a well articulated competition policy that is applied to domestic and foreign enterprises. A screening of investment applications traditionally results in conflict among ministries, much as the Exon-Florio amendment in the United States that establishes the right of the U.S. government to reject acquisitions threatening national security tends to pit the departments of defense and commerce against one another. It is fairly well established that the assignment of which ministry should regulate direct investment has tangible effects on the degree to which a government opens its borders to foreign firms (Vernon 1985).

Establishing an appropriate regulatory framework is a priority for foreign companies. Standards in the local markets are required to conform to international norms and to permit easy exporting to other countries. Moreover, because of their visibility, foreign companies usually apply high environmental and quality standards. Regulation forces these costs onto local firms as well, and thus removes them as factors in competition. The demand for regulation may, contrary to expectation, be greatest in the sectors in which multinational corporations are active.

Langenfeld and Yao (1994) argue that regulatory and competition policy-making functions should be assigned to different agencies. There is an inherent conflict in the task to regulate competition and to assure competition. The tendency of ministries to assume a regulatory role over enterprises with state shares, as observed in Russia by Pistor and Turkewitz (in vol. 2 of this book), is an example of such conflict.

2. *Privatization and ownership.* An important question is whether a nation should preserve ownership over a few key enterprises. In this regard, the privatization of other countries provides a wide range of models, with the

strategy of France to preserve a strategic share for domestic investors (the so-called *noyaux durs*) being of particular interest. Except for restricting particular sectors (e.g. the Russian defense industry), none of the transition economies has articulated a clear vision of the limits to foreign penetration.

There are complex economic arguments as to why ownership should matter, but there are also important political considerations, especially in light of the public scrutiny that caused the collapse of well-publicized sell-offs in the Czech Republic and Hungary.[22] The tolerance of direct investment is also embedded in historical considerations, especially about German investment in Polish and Czech real estate.

The economic arguments boil down to a few. One is the question whether innovative resources are reinforced or depleted in the host country if foreign firms take over research-intensive enterprises. (See Tyson (1992) for one statement.) Another argument concerns the creation of industrial concentration to tip a region or nation toward agglomeration. (See Krugman (1992) for a cautious evaluation.) Finally, imperfections in capital markets, which surely plague transition economies, raise important issues regarding valuations.

The danger of policy restrictions on foreign direct investment is especially great in countries with highly politicized firms and weak governments. In the initial period of transition, a primary role of direct investment is not only to provide the capital and managerial knowhow, but also to secure the process of reform. A restrictive policy can threaten reform during a period of vulnerability, especially in Russia where foreign capital is providing one of the few spearheads to break up the equity coalition of workers and managers.

However, as the process matures, a policy on ownership may be politically required to maintain public confidence. The Czech experience provides one implicit model, whereby a liberal policy encourages foreign portfolio investment in mutual funds but a more guarded policy is applied to foreign acquisitions. A more forceful policy is to adopt the French model by finding domestic firms to take strategic positions in newly privatized enterprises. But this model is likely to be sorely deficient in application if both the capital resources and managerial skills are lacking among these strategic investors (see Coffee in this volume.)

If there is a choice about how much foreign investment should be allowed, then the implicit issue is what the criterion of choice should be. A rule consis-

[22] In the Czech Republic, prolonged negotiations subsequent to an agreement for the partial acquisition br Air France of the national air carrier led to the collapse of the deal. Recently, a sale of a majority share of the last large state-owned hotel in Hungary to an American investor collapsed under political pressure to hand the chain over to the state-run social security fund, which is backed by trade unions supporting the governing party. See *The Economist*, 28 January 1995.

tent with the studies on growth and the absorption of technologies is to let foreign capital enter in those industries where domestic knowledge is most lacking and where the purchase of the relevant technologies on world markets is the most difficult. Pharmaceuticals is a good case: where research is costly, heavily patented, and the knowledge of discovery often tacit, direct investment provides an important conduit to the world technological frontier. Steel, while potentially benefiting from direct investment, consists of technologies that can often be purchased and that the local country has the expertise to absorb.

A policy less open to distortionary effects and corruption is for the state to hold shares in a privatized company. As Pistor and Turkewitz (in vol. 2 of this book) note, after the first wave of privatization in the Czech Republic, the government still held 28 percent of equity on average; in Hungary the government share in large privatized compares is estimated at 34.2 percent; and in Russia the government share ranges from 10 to 31 percent. But this pattern is not unusual and corresponds to privatization experiences elsewhere (Perotti and Guney 1993). To sell a privatized company, as noted by Earle and Estrin (in vol. 2 of this book), gives away the option to sell later at a higher price. But also, by holding a stake in the firm, the government retains a credible interest in refraining from engaging in policy acts that damage the economic value of its shares.

3. *The rate of transition.* A subtle problem in transformation is that restructuring requires unemployment in the process of change. Poland is vastly ahead of Russia in its transformation, but it suffers a 16 percent rate of unemployment compared with 2 percent in Russia. A survey conducted by *The Economist* of 87 Western companies found that overstaffing is estimated to range from 20 to 50 percent (Gatling 1993: 25). It is a good maxim that long-term unemployed workers are more likely to challenge reform than employed workers in secure jobs. In this environment, foreign firms are critical actors in the reform process.

What are the policies for direct investment that maintain the political acceptability of transition at a maximum speed? A simple answer is to encourage direct investment while restricting the layoff of employees. It is obvious that such restrictions, insofar as they incur operating expenses for the investing firm, deter investment and transformation. The critical watershed is to generate expectations that transformation will succeed rapidly and that unemployment is an investment in a better future. The dilemma is that the rate of change is predicated on moving workers out from losing enterprises, while expectations are negatively influenced by the amount of unemployment (Aghion and Blanchard 1994).

An example of using direct investment to preserve the privatization process is the policy of avoiding decisions to shut down firms due to imperfect capital markets or perverse incentives. Perotti (forthcoming) has argued that a flaw in transition arises from the funding of unprofitable enterprises that are heavily in debt to banks. The attractiveness of lending to failing firms arises due to the probability-weighted value of providing incremental funding in the hope that a turnaround will result in a repayment of the outstanding loan. Banks, or the state, end up investing in losing firms in preference to profitable ones.

Trying to sell politically sensitive cases to foreign investors to relieve the problem is, obviously, one of the most important elements in a privatization strategy. The wisdom of requiring restructuring before privatization, gathered from the U.K. experience, has the unwanted result of reserving the worse prospects for last or of creating a state-owned portfolio of companies that represent especially thorny political problems (Sachs 1993). However, selling unstructured firms at large discounts transfers potentially large capital gains to private, and sometimes foreign, investors.

Stiglitz (1992: 171) has noted that it is senseless to pay the private sector for bearing the political risk of restructuring if the state controls the policy variables. Particular policies may be difficult for the state to enact, such as the closure of large mines. But some restructuring policy decisions bear lower political consequences.

A good candidate policy for achieving restructuring prior to privatization is the elimination of bank debt. A program of equity for debt swaps that securitizes the value of these failing firms and sells the instruments to foreign investors succeeds even in the absence of restructuring, but at the same time, opens the door to the formation of investors to acquire strategic positions. Removing the debts of failing firms from banks' balance sheets should be a primary objective.

4. *Experimentation.* Because multinational investment transports practices from foreign sites, it represents a quasi-experiment in which the experiences of subsidiaries from different countries serve as templates of successful practices in the local environment. To benefit from this process of adaptive learning, hasty adoption of restrictive laws should be viewed with suspicion. A good example is the potential adoption of labor laws based on the German model, which would mandate work councils. While group or team work is increasingly being adopted in Europe, work councils in Germany often object to their loss of control. Agnosticism is not a bad policy when there is superstition regarding what practices belong together.

There is another aspect to experimentation that cautions policies that are too proactive in championing new markets. Experimentation demands that results of the experiment be observed. A policy that too quickly subsidizes investment in particular areas has the unwanted outcome of discouraging entrants with better ideas. In Poland, for example, the growing market for mortgage loans has received international subsidization that has placed new private (and foreign) entrants at a disadvantage. In a time of efficient capital flows across borders, public sector subsidies to new growth markets have the negative impact of driving out variation and entry.

Conclusions

Investment is attracted to growth. There is, consequently, a self-reinforcing process by which investment and economic development are coupled in a joint causality. Direct investment, not surprisingly, also flows to those sectors that are growing rapidly.

The issue facing transition economies is how to start this growth process. Direct investment is believed to be more important than domestic investment, because it brings with it technology and management. By serving as a successful template in the local economy and through large-scale training programs, the foreign company acts to loosen the cognitive constraints to change.

A volatile issue is the effect of multinational corporations on the political objectives of interested groups. By establishing efficient productive units in the local economy, multinational corporations place competitive pressure on competing firms to adopt similar practices. Economic pressure will alter the political balance between labor and management, as well as between entrenched managers and strategic investors. Economic change is a difficult process because it requires shifts in power among political groups.

A way to attenuate these conflicts is to increase the potential gains as a way of detracting from zero-sum conflict between more efficient and failing firms, or between qualified and redundant labor. A strategy of exports is attractive from a strictly economic view as one of the mechanisms that attracts investment through growth. And it is through export growth that benefits to cooperation and change can be realized with lower redistributional costs.

For this reason, it is useful to consider direct investment in the context of the overall evolution of the economy and the agglomeration of new industries. The dynamic potential of new and foreign firm entry provides the greatest long-term hope for transformation. It is as an agent in social experimentation, as well as a conduit of capital and technology, that multinational corporations play an important role in the transformation of the formerly socialist countries.

References

Aghion, Philippe, and Olivier Jean Blanchard. 1994. "On the Speed of Transition in Central Europe," National Bureau of Economic Research, No. 4736.

Almeida, Paul, and Bruce Kogut. 1994. "Geography and Technology: Localization of Knowledge and the Mobility of Patentholders." Working Paper, Reginald H. Jones Center, Wharton School, University of Pennsylvania.

Anand, Jaideep, and Bruce Kogut. 1995. "Technological Capabilities of Countries and Foreign Direct Investment in the United States." Working Paper, Reginald H. Jones Center, Wharton School, University of Pennsylvania.

Arés Associés. 1994. "Emerging Markets Investment Funds in Russia." Intermediary unpublished report to the European Commission, June 6.

Aslund, Anders. 1994. "Russia: Muddling On." Department of Economics, Wharton School, University of Pennsylvania. Mimeographed.

Blomstrom, Magnus, and Edward Wolff. 1994. "Multinational Corporations and Productivity Convergence in Mexico," in *Convergence of Productivity: Cross-National Studies and Historical Evidence,* edited by William Baumol, Richard Nelson, and Edward Wolff. New York: Oxford University Press.

Blomstrom, Magnus, and Jian-Ye Wang. 1989. "Foreign Investment and Technology Transfer: A Simple Model." National Bureau of Economic Research, No. 2958.

Blomstrom, Magnus, Robert Lipsey, and Mario Zejan. 1994. "What Explains the Growth of Developing Countries?" In *Convergence of Productivity: Cross-National Studies and Historical Evidence,* edited by William Baumol, Richard Nelson, and Edward Wolff. New York: Oxford University Press.

Boycko, Maxim, Andrei Shleifer, and Robert Vishny. 1993. "Privatizing Russia." Brookings Papers on Economic Activity. The Brookings Institution, Washington, D.C.

Cantwell, John. 1989. *Technological Innovation and Multinational Corporations.* Oxford: Basil Blackwell.

Caves, Richard. 1982. *Economic Analysis and the Multinational Enterprise.* Cambridge, Eng.: Cambridge University Press.

Chandler, Alfred. 1990. *Scale and Scope. The Dynamics of Industrial Capitalism.* Cambridge, Mass.: Harvard University.

CS First Boston. 1994. "Russian Capital Markets" (private distribution).

Dunning, John,. 1979. "Explaining Changing Patterns of International Production: In Defence of the Eclectic Theory." *Oxford Bulletin of Economics and Statistics* 41: 269–95.

Dunning, John. 1986. *Japanese Participation in British Industry: Trojan Horse or Catalyst for Growth.* Dover, New Hampshire: Croom Helm.

Flanders, Allan. 1964. *The Fawley Productivity Agreements: A Case Study of Management and Collective Bargaining.* London: Faber and Faber Ltd.

Frydman, Roman, and Andrzej Rapaczynski. 1994. *Privatization in Eastern Europe: Is the State Withering Away?* Budapest: Central European University Press.

Frydman, Roman, Andrzej Rapaczynski, and John Earle. 1993. *The Privatization Process in Central Europe.* Budapest: Central European Press.

Gatling, Rene. 1993. *Foreign Investment in Eastern Europe.* London: *The Economist* (in association with Creditanstalt Bankverein).

Grabher, Gernot. 1990. "Citadels in the Desert." Wissenschaftszentrum, Berlin. Mimeographed.

Gray, Cheryl, and William Jarosz. 1993. "Foreign Investment Law in Central and Eastern

Europe." Policy Research Department Working Paper No. 1111, World Bank, Washington, D.C.

Guisinger, Stephen, *et al.* 1985. *Investment Incentives and Performance Requirements: Patterns of International Trade, Production, and Investment.* New York: Praeger.

Hounshell, David. 1984. *From the American System to Mass Production 1850–90.* Baltimore: Johns Hopkins University Press.

Hymer, Stephen. 1960. *The International Operations of National Firms: A Study of Direct Foreign Investment.* Ph.D. dissertation, Massachusetts Institute of Technology. Cambridge, Mass.: MIT Press, 1976.

Kennedy, Robert. 1994. "A Tale of Two Economies: Economic Restructuring in Post-Socialist Poland." Harvard University. Mimeographed.

Kogut, Bruce. 1992. "National Organizing Principles of Work and the Erstwhile Dominance of the American Multinational Corporation." *Industrial and Corporate Change* 1: 285–325.

Kogut, Bruce, and Nalin Kulatilaka. 1994. "Operating Flexibility, Global Manufacturing, and the Option Value of a Multinational Network." *Management Science* 123–39.

Kogut, Bruce, and Sea Jin Chang. 1991. "Technological Rivalry and Japanese Direct Investment in the United States." *Review of Economics and Statistics* 73: 401–13.

Kogut, Bruce, and Udo Zander. 1994. "Knowledge of the Firm and the Evolutionary Theory of the Multinational Corporation." *Journal of International Business Studies* 23: 625–45.

Kogut, Bruce, Gordon Walker, Weijian Shan, and Dong-Jae Kim. 1992. "Knowledge of the Network and the Network as Knowledge." In *The Embedded Firm,* edited by G. Grabher. London: Routledge.

Kraft, Gerhard. 1977. *Die Zussammenarbeit der Mitgliedslaender des RGW auf dem Gebiet der Investitionen.* Berlin: Akademie-Verlag.

Krugman, Paul. 1992. "Toward a Counterrevolution in Development Theory." *Annual Conference on Development Economics,* supplement to the *World Bank Economic Review,* 15-38.

Langenfeld, James, and Dennis Yao. 1994. "Competition Policy and Privatization during the Transition of Central and Eastern Europe to a Market Economy: An Organizational Perspective." In *Government and Markets,* edited by H.J. Blommestein and B. Steunenberg. Boston: Kluwer Academic Publishers.

Mankiw, N. Gregory, David Romer, and David Weil. 1992. "A Contribution to the Empirics of Economic Growth,." *Quarterly Journal of Economics* 107: 407–37.

McMillan, Carl. 1993. "The Role of Foreign Direct Investment in the Transition from Planned to Market Economies." *Transnational Corporations* 2: 97–119.

Meyer, Klaus. 1994. "Direct Foreign Investment in Central and Eastern Europe: Understanding the Statistical Evidence." Discussion Paper Series No. 12, Center for International Studies (CIS) Middle Europe Centre, London Business School.

Murrell, Peter. 1992. "Evolution in Economics and in the Economic Reform of Centrally Planned Economies." In *The Emergence of Market Economies in Eastern Europe,* edited by Christopher Clague and Gordon Rausser. Cambridge, Mass.: Blackwell Press.

Nelson, Richard, and Sidney Winter. 1982. *An Evolutionary Theory of Economic Change.* Boston: Harvard University Press.

Odle, Maurice. 1993. "Foreign Direct Investment as Part of the Privatization Process." *Transnational Corporations* 2: 7–34.

Pack, Howard, and John Page. 1994. "Accumulation, Exports, and Growth in the High Performing Asian Countries." *Carnegie-Rochester Papers on Public Policy*, 199–236.
Perotti, Enrico. 1993. "Bank Lending in Transition Economies." *Journal of Banking and Finance* 17: 1021–32.
Perotti, Enrico, and Serhat Guney. 1993. "The Structure of Privatization Plans." *Financial Management* 84–98.
Romer, Paul. 1992. "Two Strategies for Economic Development: Using Ideas and Producing Ideas." *Annual Conference on Development Economics,* supplement to the *World Bank Economic Review* 63–92.
Sachs, Jeffrey. 1993. *Poland's Jump to the Market Economy.* Cambridge, Mass.: Massachusetts Institute of Technology (MIT) Press.
Shohkin, Alexander. 1994. "Foreign Investments and Russia." Russian government press release.
Siotis, George. 1994. "Foreign Direct Investment in Central and Eastern Europe," Study prepared for the Director General II of the European Commission, Brussels.
Stiglitz, Joseph. 1992. "The Design of Financial Systems in the Newly Emerging Democracies of Central Europe." In *The Emergence of Market Economies in Eastern Europe,* edited by Christopher Clague and Gordon Rausser. Cambridge, Mass.: Blackwell Press.
Teece, David. 1976. *The Multinational Corporation and the Resource Cost of International Technology Transfer.* Cambridge, Mass.: Ballinger.
Török, Adám. 1994. "Industrial Policy and Foreign Direct Investment." *Review of Industrial Economics* (Hungarian; article in English) special issue: 7–37.
Tyson, Laura. 1992. *Who's Bashing Whom?* Washington, D.C.: Institute of International Economics.
United Nations Conference on Trade and Development (UNCTAD). 1994. *World Investment Report.* New York: United Nations.
Vernon, Raymon. 1985. *Exploring the Global Economy. Emerging Issues in Trade and Investment.* Cambridge, Mass.: Harvard University.
Weinstein, Mark. 1995. The Transformation of Post-Socialist Poland: Economic, Institutional, and Ideational Determinants of Macro-Institutions and Firm-level Practices, thesis in progress, MIT.
Williamson, Oliver. 1985. *The Economic Institutions of Capitalism: Firms, Markets, Relational Contracting.* New York: Free Press.
Zander, Udo, and Bruce Kogut. 1995. "Knowledge and the Speed of the Transfer and Imitation of Organizational Capabilities: An Empirical Test." *Organizational Science* 3: 383–97.
Zhan, Xiaoning James. 1993. "The Role of Foreign Direct Investment in Market-Oriented Reforms and Economic Development: The Case of China." *Transnational Corporations.* 2: 121–48.

INDEX